Research Methods for Cyber Security

Research Methods for Cyber Security

Thomas W. Edgar

David O. Manz

ELSEVIER | SYNGRESS®

Syngress is an imprint of Elsevier
50 Hampshire Street, 5th Floor, Cambridge, MA 02139, United States

British Library Cataloguing-in-Publication Data
A catalogue record for this book is available from the British Library

Library of Congress Cataloging-in-Publication Data
A catalog record for this book is available from the Library of Congress

ISBN: 978-0-12-805349-2

For Information on all Syngress publications
visit our website at https://www.elsevier.com/books-and-journals

Working together
to grow libraries in
developing countries

www.elsevier.com • www.bookaid.org

Publisher: Todd Green
Acquisition Editor: Brian Romer
Editorial Project Manager: Anna Valutkevich
Production Project Manager: Punithavathy Govindaradjane
Cover Designer: Mark Rogers

Typeset by MPS Limited, Chennai, India

Contents

Part I   Introduction

Part II Observational Research Methods

Part III   Mathematical Research Methods

Part IV   Experimental Research Methods

Part V Applied Research Methods

Part VI   Additional Materials

About the Authors

Thomas W. Edgar is a Senior Cyber Security Research Scientist at the Pacific Northwest National Laboratory. He has completed research in the areas of secure communication protocols, cryptographic trust management, critical infrastructure protection, and developing a scientific approach to cyber security. Edgar's research interests include the scientific underpinnings of cyber security and applying scientific-based cyber security solutions to enterprise and critical infrastructure environments. His expertise lies in scientific process, critical infrastructure security, protocol development, cyber forensics, network security, and testbed and experiment construction. Edgar has a B.S. and M.S. in Computer Science from the University of Tulsa with a specialization in information assurance.

David O. Manz is currently a Senior Cyber Security Scientist in the National Security Directorate at the Pacific Northwest National Laboratory. He holds a B.S. in Computer and Information Science from the Robert D. Clark Honors College at the University of Oregon and a Ph.D. in Computer Science from the University of Idaho. Manz's work at PNNL includes enterprise resilience and cyber security, secure control system communication, and critical infrastructure security. Enabling his research is an application of relevant research methods for cyber security (Cyber Security Science). Prior to his work at PNNL, Manz spent 5 years as a researcher on Group Key Management Protocols for the Center for Secure and Dependable Systems at the University of Idaho (U of I). Manz also has experience in teaching undergraduate and graduate computer science courses at U of I, and as an adjunct faculty at Washington State University. Manz has co-authored numerous papers and presentations on cyber security, control system security, and cryptographic key management.

Foreword

The security field—whether one calls it security, cybersecurity, information assurance, information security, or something else—is delightfully frustrating, being an field that both moves at a glacial pace, and literally transforms itself overnight. There are so many challenges! Connect two previously disparate systems, and very often, system security properties (and vulnerabilities) will be entirely different. Change the user community from, say, a highly regulated government agency to a family home, and the methodologies we accept in the name of security become unacceptable. One does not fire the family 5-year old because she writes down a password! As scientists, how do we measure these differences?

There is also the question about what security actually means. We might start informally, and say that security means making sure that systems do "what we want." Our next step might be to see whether the system in fact does what we want, and take steps toward designing security in. But—consider categories such as confidentiality, integrity, and availability. These are often used to bin "what we want" into manageable chunks, so as to whether these properties are preserved. If one steps away from pure mathematical rigor, it is easy to spot a problem with designing in security. Security properties are not inherently good or bad. That value judgment is situational. If we are attempting to shut down a spam botnet, many of us hope the "availability" property can be defeated. The owners (or renters) of the botnet might disagree. Is there a way that we can conduct a general experiment to see when availability holds?

As well, new possible security concerns emerging all the time. Two current debates: is privacy a subset of security? What about cyber physical systems— is there a line between fault tolerant approaches that prevent mechanical failures, and security features intended to preserve availability? Does it make a difference if we are talking about a nuclear power plant or an autonomous vehicle? Here is a newer one. Machine learning is ubiquitous—is it a security issue if machine learning algorithms used in job applicant selection (say) might lead to discrimination against certain parts of the population? What is adversarial machine learning—and can it be detected? There is no shortage of questions, and the field seems more likely to expand than to shrink. As researchers and scientists, we need to decide how to approach these questions in a useful manner.

Fortunately, although the security field does not lend itself to easy answers, progress has been made in how we approach such questions about security, and this has been one of the more important contributions of the emerging Science of Security community. And, as a practical matter, it is in helping the reader discover how to pose and answer such questions using a scientific methodology that this book by Dr. Manz and Mr. Edgar shines. They have included a wealth of ideas that should be helpful to researchers, from how to get started with research in security, to thinking through the kinds of scientific investigation that would be most applicable. They also have more complex considerations involving experimentation, operating in a real-world environment (especially when you cannot afford to break the system under scrutiny!), and how to produce results that will serve as a foundation for other researchers, through replication and other methods. The authors do an excellent job of making it easy to understand how to apply traditional scientific concepts; and this will help both new researchers and more advanced practitioners achieve results that will stand the test of time.

One last thought. Science, like security, is complex. We cannot always control every variable, nor do we always know exactly what to measure. It is important to remember that security itself is a new field, and we have not yet achieved the remarkable precision of measurement that one finds in long-standing disciplines, such as physics, and even in the most upscale physics laboratories, we still today see measurement tools and sensors enhanced with duct tape and foil. Science, like security, is constantly under refinement. Those of us who practice this still-new field of a rigorous approach to security questions are often learning as much about how to conduct that science as we are about security. Many thanks to the authors, who have articulated the scientific approach of today, in hopes that it will support good work in the present, and enable others to do an even better in the future.

Deborah A. Frincke

Preface

PURPOSE

Working as professional researchers at a U.S. national research laboratory has provided us with a couple of unique perspectives. First, we have been uniquely involved in a nexus of academic, government, and industry research, privy to the perceptions and processes of each. Second, we work in an environment where we are often able to work with researchers and rub shoulders across a spectrum of fields: biology, chemistry, ecology, physics, and so on. Through these perspectives we have, over the years, noticed how little the cyber security field understands and leverages scientific methods.

Cyber security is a young field of science. As it naturally grew out of the computer science field, it has a strong grounding in mathematical science. Owing to its relative youth, cyber security academic programs have not matured and do not teach scientific methods to students. We posit this is core to the field's inability to generate general and impactful theories. There is a need for a reference book that presents a scientific approach to cyber security and the importance of rigor in research.

Currently, the cyber security field is in a red queen's race, defensive researchers are expending great amounts of resources to maintain status quo with attackers. However, ground is being lost. Tremendous effort is spent on trying to come up with the next killer app or an exploit for the last years app. There is an insufficient amount of effort to discover the fundamental science of cyber security. In our journey to discover how to define and measure cyber security, we have come to the belief that our field needs to progress through the use of research methods. The purpose of this book is to provide an introduction to research methods that we, or our colleagues, have found useful in performing cyber security research.

AUDIENCE

This book is intended for undergraduate students, graduate students, and faculty who seek to understand how to execute cyber security research. Additionally, the information in this text can both be used by researchers as an introductory text for scientific research in the context of cyber security, or as a guide and reference for those seeking to execute specific research. By reading straight through the book, a perspective on cyber security science and an understanding of the various issues and methods of executing research can be gained. However, if a reader has a specific research question they would like to investigate and answer, then the book provides a path to help drive straight to the most appropriate chapter that is of relevance and help.

While designed for university coursework, the information in this book can also be useful and beneficial for professional cyber security practitioners. Obviously, this book can be used as a reference and refresher for cyber security researchers and developers. Cyber forensics investigations require rigorous, procedural methodology. Applying scientific methodology and concepts can provide the necessary rigor of developing supporting evidence as well as bringing a skeptical eye to the challenge. Cyber incident response and analysis is largely a process of asking questions and answering hypotheses of what occurred. Observational and experimental research methods are helpful techniques in these endeavors. Our hope is that this book can bring a new perspective and thought process to the entire field of cyber security for researchers and practitioners.

ORGANIZATION AND STYLE

This book is organized around two pathways of use. The first is the common straight read-through to learn all of the concepts and techniques. Reading each chapter in sequence will provide an overview of all research methods as well as approaches to answering research questions. Information in earlier chapters are leveraged and built upon in later chapters. Additionally, a second style of use is for readers who have a specific research question or project they would like to execute. Chapter 3 provides logic and reasoning for selecting a research approach and method and then provides directions to the appropriate chapter covering those topics. This enables users who are after guidance and reference to quickly get to the information they need.

This book is separated into six different parts. Each part covers a grouping of information: an introduction to science and cyber security, observational research, formal research, experimental research, applied research, and useful ancillary materials. Within each part, there are multiple chapters. Each chapter covers a specific topic. The research method chapters leverage example research to help show the process in and reasoning behind using specific methods. The examples are loosely based on real research, we or colleagues, we know have performed in the past. All data and results are fictional and were designed to highlight aspects and issues of the research process.

We purposely used a more informal style in this book. Our goal is to teach the concepts and practice of research in an approachable, everyday manner. Our hope is that readers find this style readable and unintimidating. As professional researchers, we are aware of and have to deal with the realities of performing research and, while some philosophy of science is discussed, we try to address limitations in the text.

To provide extra insights and fun discussions we have provided breakout boxes throughout the text. There are two types of breakout boxes: *Did You Know?* and *Dig Deeper*. The *Did You Know?* boxes provide fun and interesting facts surrounding information that is covered in the text. *Dig Deeper* boxes discuss topics in more depth and direct readers to where further information on a topic can be found. The intent of these boxes are to provide a fun pedagogical aid for students and readers.

Acknowledgments

We appreciate the expertise and hard work provided by our colleagues in assisting with topics needed to fill the full spectrum of research methods:

Chapter 1   Mark Tardiff

Chapter 6   Satish Chikkagoudar, Samrat Chatterjee, Dennis G. Thomas, Thomas E. Carroll, George Muller

Chapter 7   Thomas E. Carroll

Special thanks goes to our publisher team at Elsevier; Brian Romer for supporting the idea for this book and Anna Valutkevich for her extreme patience and guidance in helping us reach the finish line.

Finally, our most heartfelt thanks goes out to our spouses and children: Sharon Edgar, Alexis Edgar, Caitlin Manz, Matthew Manz, and Henry Manz. Our wives' support and patience with this process allowed this book to come to fruition and our children were always helpful in keeping a smile on our faces through this long process. Additional thanks goes to Caitlin Manz for providing her editorial eye and review skills to turn our professorial babbling into clear and concise text.

Introduction

To raise new questions, new possibilities, to regard old problems from a new angle, requires creative imagination and marks real advance in science.

Albert Einstein

## CHAPTER 1

Introduction to Science

Science is a powerful tool through which humans have made amazing societal and technological advancement. Science has enabled us to understand our place in the universe, prevent and treat diseases, and even create the Internet. Why then with such a powerful resource at our disposal do we not apply more science practices to cyber security research? If we want cyber security to grow and evolve as a science then it is necessary to start focusing our research on more scientific methods.

In this book, we aim to provide you with and introduction into what it means to execute science in the context of cyber security research by following rigorous and established methods. This book seeks to borrow from the thousands of years of development of the scientific method in other disciplines, and to enhance the conduct of cyber security research as a science in its own right. The intended outcome from using this book is research that is relevant, repeatable, and documented such that colleagues can understand and critique the results and conclusions. The focus of this book is on the practical side of science, the research methods that can be used to perform your research. However, as this may be your first foray into the world of science, it is important to first explain what science is and provide an example of how, over time, it has had a major impact on our knowledge and understanding.

In this chapter we will introduce you to science, defining the various meanings of science, and how science has been cultivated within different fields of research. The continuum of science will be presented to explain where different methods fit in the spectrum. Finally, the concepts of science will be presented through an example. The example will explore the historical progression and improvement of knowledge through science for our, now, well-known solar system.

Research Methods for Cyber Security. DOI: http://dx.doi.org/10.1016/B978-0-12-805349-2.00001-7

CHAPTER OBJECTIVES

- Introduce science
- Overview of forms of research and their types of methods
- Describe the continuum of discovery and the hierarchy of evidence
- Explore historical scientific advances in astronomy to contextualize concepts

WHAT IS SCIENCE

Science is an overloaded term that is used under many different contexts. It is important to understand that science represents three things: a philosophy, a body of knowledge, and a process to discover knowledge. The philosophy of science explores what it means to be an observer of the universe from within it. The body of knowledge of science encapsulates that which we have learned about the universe. Finally, the method of science is a rigorous process to generate evidence for knowledge assimilation from observing the world. While all aspects of science are interesting topics worth in-depth exploration, this book is focused on the practical aspects of science and the methods of collecting knowledge about cyber space and security.

What science is not is engineering. Engineering turns the knowledge gained through science into usable applications and solutions to address challenges or problems. While technically applying science is not science, it is a critical part of cyber security and similar to science, which requires a rigorous process if done right. Therefore, applied research methods are covered in this book.

The process of science has evolved into current forms with the goal of instilling confidence in what we learn from observation. In order to achieve this there are multiple important characteristics of research methods. First, research methods provide a rigorous and methodical approach to study. This ensures that the execution of research is thoroughly conceived and disciplined. Second, research methods provide a process to empirically ground theories and conceptual models. Third, research methods ensure that evidence is driven by logical and reasoned thinking. Finally, research culture is imbued with a healthy level of skepticism to always challenge the approach and results found to instill confidence in accepted knowledge.

Through the process of research science strives for knowledge with two valuable attributes. First, knowledge explains phenomena and what processes affect behavior in systems. Second, it provides an ability to predict future events by projecting from current state and possible stimuli. Armed with this type of knowledge, we are able to effectively engineer technologies that solve societal problems or make some process more efficient. In the case of cyber security, the goal of scientific exploration is to gain the knowledge to make it possible to quantify security and predict what tools and practices will enable us to thwart or stymie cyber attackers.

TYPES OF SCIENCE

Science can take many forms. In our quest for knowledge we have explored many different fields of study. Each field represents a core set of questions that to answer them pose unique challenges. Owing to these challenges, each field has developed an approach to scientific research to best generate empirical evidence to validate theories. Out of these approaches have fallen a set of research methods that are used by their research communities to continue to build their knowledge base. The following table provides a brief overview of the different types of researches with example fields of study.

As you can see in Table 1.1, each category of research relies upon different forms of research methods. However, each field uses all forms of research methods at some level. The majority of this book covers these forms of research and specific useful methods for cyber security research. These forms of research include observational, mathematical, experimental methods.

Observational—The phenomenon of interest is embedded in a larger system that is dynamic. The investigator can seek instances where the dynamics are less noisy, but it's not possible to conduct an experiment free of influences from uncontrolled or uncontrollable variables. Very often, a test bed or microcosm is developed, which is a simplification of the natural environment in order to gain an understanding of basic relationships among variables associated with the phenomenon of interest.

The vast majority of science research engages in some form of observational experiments, using simplifications to gain understanding. One example is biological research using genetically controlled strains of experimental

Table 1.1 Description and Examples of Branches of Science

Branch of Science	Driving Scientific Approach	Example Fields of Study
Physical Sciences	The physical sciences are driven by controlled experiment validation of theories.	Physics, Chemistry
Life Sciences	The life sciences have a cross between observational methods to learn about life systems and experimental investigation of how living beings chemistry works.	Biology, Ecology
Social Sciences	Involves qualitative or descriptive research. Uses best fit models and observation to define operational models.	Psychology, Sociology, Criminology
Mathematical Sciences	Uses formalisms, logic, and mathematical constructs to define and explore abstract space and conceptual models.	Logic, Mathematics,
Data Science	Computational field that uses algorithms to generate models and hypotheses from empirical data.	Machine Learning, Artificial Intelligence

animals to clarify dose responses to chemicals or pharmaceuticals, and tissue cultures to study the basics of cell biology without the complexities of those tissues functioning within a live organism. Another example is physics experiments conducted with accelerators to control the energy and location of subatomic particle collisions in order to be able to collect data on the outcomes of those collisions.

In all of these cases, one can argue that the experimental setup is artificial and that the results may not reflect what actually occurs in the wild. However, collecting data on fortuitous subatomic particle collisions in wild is not practical, and testing chemicals and pharmaceuticals on humans as initial experiments is unethical. Test beds are necessary in order to advance our knowledge.

Mathematical—Unlike experimental and observational research, mathematical research is based upon logic and formal proofs. There is a persistent debate on whether mathematics is actually a science because science relies on evidence, not logic. We will leave that debate to others. What is true is that advances in mathematics are very often the precursors to advances in experimental and observational sciences. Mathematics is necessary for data collection, analysis, and interpretation.

Experimental—The investigator has full control of the phenomenon being observed and the mechanisms for data collection. All of the variables are known and can be either held constant or made to change in order to assess the consequences of those changes on the phenomenon of interest. An example is conducting experiments on a pure substance to determine its state (gas, liquid, solid) at various temperatures and pressures.

The boundary between experimental and observational research is at best a blurry line. Research requires controlled experiments to generate basic understanding and observational experiments to test the relevance of basic understanding to phenomena in the wild. In both cases the conclusions are based on evidence.

One additional form of research we cover is applied research. Applied research leverages concepts and techniques from the other forms of research to study and assess our ability to apply knowledge to solving or addressing a societal problem. Applied research is a core topic in cyber security research because the overall objective of securing a system is applied.

SCIENCE IS MESSY

Short definitions of science typically include the concepts of gaining systematic knowledge of the physical and natural world through data collection and experimentation. Refining the definition becomes problematic because the practice of science is much messier than the conceptual description. Fundamental to science is conducting experiments to investigate relationships and causality for phenomena of interest. An oft-repeated premise in the debate of applying the scientific method to cyber security is that the cyber environment is ever changing and in unpredictable ways. The notion of a repeatable experiment in a cyber environment is sometimes represented as unattainable. Fundamentally, research in cyber security is an observational science in that we can observe what occurs in many ways and at many scales. We are unable to conduct fully controlled experiments at the scales that are meaningful for operational relevance. There is a rich history of operational sciences with exactly this dilemma.

We rely on many observational sciences for understanding the world around us and for anticipating what is about to occur. Examples include atmospheric sciences, ecology, hydrology, agronomy, and cosmology. To further complicate the endeavor, domains such as economics are not only observational but are also profoundly influenced by human judgments, perceptions, and cultural values. In the practice of these fields, it is very often the case that progress occurs through a combination of experiments and observations that span multiple scales. As an example, fundamental to atmospheric science is the understanding of relationships among temperature and pressure to establish a triple-point diagram for the phases of water under different conditions. These diagrams can be developed by conducting controlled experiments in a laboratory. The insights from the experiments and resulting diagrams inform models of atmospheric processes that simply can't be investigated with controlled experiments. We are unable to generate homogeneous clouds at multikilometer scales to investigate their behavior. Similarly, we can conduct experiments on laboratory animals to gain insight into the efficacy and side effects of new pharmaceuticals, but there is no substitute for human trials to determine the impacts to humans. Variations in genetics, culture, lifestyle choices, and nutrition make it extremely difficult to separate the influence of the pharmaceutical on the response of the individuals from variations in the population.

Fig. 1.1 is a schematic diagram of the progression of observational science and the trade-off between simple experiments that generate results that can be interpreted and repeated versus the realism embodied in those experiments relative to the processes in nature that we want to understand. The path to operational relevance is unknown, but experience indicates that failing to start with simple experiments very often leads to distractions and biases that impede progress to the goal of insight. What makes this difficult is that very often our best efforts result in firmly held beliefs that are simply not true. In the absence of experiments to challenge our assumptions, the apparent progress we're making is an illusion.

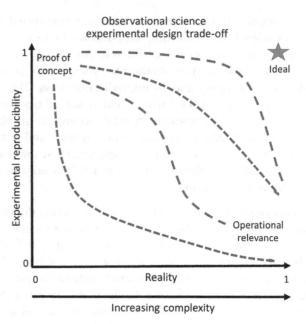

FIGURE 1.1

Experimental repeatability versus operational relevance.

The science of cyber security shares many attributes with the observational sciences ones listed above. The trade-offs between simple experiments and operational relevance are part of the ongoing discussion in the community on how to increase the scientific rigor of research to better understand cybersystems. The following discussion uses the development of the heliocentric model of the solar system as an example of the evolution of knowledge and fundamental principles in the domain of astronomy where the scale at which we can conduct experiments is vastly different from the scale of the phenomena that we want to understand. The intent is to provide an example that can inform the evolution of the investigations and insights into cybersystems. The path of discovery necessarily starts with empirical descriptions of how the system works. The goal should always be to move toward physical and mathematical models that illuminate physical and systems principles and that generalize across various realizations of cyber systems. The solar system example also emphasizes the impact of the perspective of the observer on what is observed. There are key advances in the progression from a geocentric universe to a heliocentric solar system within a vast universe that occurred only because the investigator was able to analyze the same data from a different perspective.

Hierarchy of Evidence

Not all empirical evidence provided by research methods is equal. Some research methods generate stronger evidence than others, while some develop relative rankings of evidence, called the *hierarchy of evidence*. This discussion on the "Hierarchy of Evidence" is not meant to forever cast in stone, "better" or "worse" methods of cyber security research. Much discussion was had about even including this topic. However, for a curious reader, it is useful to point out the relative merits and detractions from the various methods of research presented throughout this book, specifically observational methods. The following discussion should hopefully encourage readers to question what sort of research is being conducted or leveraged to build a case for or against any position. The simple question of what sort of study, or experiment, you will use, will help draw out the utility and applicability regardless of the ranking.

One of the commonly cited rankings, at least from the medical community comes from Trisha Greenhalgh who proposes that the research community rank types of research follow this hierarchy:

1. Systematic reviews and meta-analyses of "Randomized Control Trials (RCTs) with definitive results."
2. RCTs with definitive results (confidence intervals that do not overlap the threshold clinically significant effect).
3. RCTs with nondefinitive results (a point estimate that suggests a clinically significant effect but with confidence intervals overlapping the threshold for this effect).
4. Cohort studies.
5. Case-control studies.
6. Cross-sectional surveys.
7. Case reports.[1]

The hierarchy here places appropriate emphasis on randomized, controlled experimentation. But more "valuable" than a single experiment is a bevy, a preponderance of multiple rigorous experiments that share similar finds, so-called definitive results. This is the reason that reproducing research is so important in any field, but the lack of reproducible research continues to handicap the field of cyber security. These large analyses of several experiments will lead to foundational understandings in our field.

Of lower rank in the hierarchy are the various types of observational studies. Special emphasis should be made that these forms of research are very much worth doing. They are worth doing in and of themselves, but especially worth doing when other types of research are not able to be conducted (for financial, technical, or ethical reasons). The value is not at all in the decision of what sort of research to conduct, rather, it is in helping the researcher, and the audience better understand how to interpret, build upon, and leverage the results. For example, a case study that concludes with a connection between a behavior and a response would be very different from a large randomized controlled hypothetico-deductive experiment that concludes the same thing. Again it is less about the input and conduct of research and more about how the results are used.

Another hierarchy worth mentioning comes from an article on observational research still from the medical community,[2] "Observational Studies: Cohort and Case-Control Studies," by Song et al. looks at exploration-discussed, evidence-based research (medicine) and describes the levels of evidence.

Levels of Evidence-based Medicine	
Level of Evidence	**Qualifying Studies**
I	High-quality, multicenter or single-center, randomized controlled trial with adequate power; or systematic review of these studies
II	Lesser quality, randomized controlled trial; prospective cohort study; or systematic review of these studies
III	Retrospective comparative study; case-control study; or systematic review of these studies
IV	Case-series
V	Expert opinion; case report or clinical example; or evidence-based on physiology, bench research, or "first principles"

FROM PTOLEMY TO EINSTEIN—SCIENCE AND THE DISCOVERY OF THE NATURE OF THE SKY

From the dawn of civilization, the night sky has pulled at the human imagination and stimulated the curiosity and creativity of those attempting to navigate land and sea. Along the way, the night sky also became elemental to various belief systems from prosaic forms such as astrology to the tenants of early Christianity that held the Earth as the center of God's creation based on the Old Testament. The boundaries between the physical and metaphysical pursuits were often blurred or nonexistent.

Early in the development of civilizations the cycles of the Earth (day), Moon (month), and Sun (year) became the basis of timekeeping and calendars. Evidence of the earliest calendars date back to 8000 BC. All of the civilizations in Europe, Asia, and the Americas developed their versions. Calendars continue to be important to the annual repetitions of civil and religious events as well as keeping track of significant cultural histories.

Early calendars were based upon lunar cycles. The average lunar cycle is 29.5 days and 12 lunar cycles generate a year that is 354 days, or 11.25 days short of a solar year. Early civilizations accommodated the offset with intercalary periods to realign the calendar with celestial events, such as the vernal equinox. The adjustments tended to be arbitrary and the accuracy of those calendars was poor. The Egyptians developed the first known solar calendar. The challenge with a solar calendar is having a discrete celestial event to mark the start of the year. Sirius is the brightest star in the sky and is occluded by the Sun for part of the year. The reemergence of Sirius in the eastern sky just before sunrise coincided with the flooding of the Nile River. The heliacal rising of Sirius was used as the starting point of the Egyptian solar year.

Much has been written of astronomic investigations of the solar system and the universe over the course of the 2500 years from the Classical Period to the present. There are contemporary treatises that have survived to the modern day and historical analyses of the trajectory of astronomic discoveries in civilizations located in Asia, Europe, Africa, and the Americas.

The following barely scratches the surface of the richness and complexity of the evolution of our current understanding of the motions of the celestial bodies. Our primary purpose is to learn about the practice of science and the influence of culture through the works of Ptolemy, Copernicus, Galileo, Kepler, Newton, and Einstein.

A Science Continuum of Discovery

As we investigate the development of our knowledge of the solar system, it will be useful to consider the information in the context of a continuum of understanding that helps to recognize the maturation of our insights into how the natural systems function. The paradox is that our ability to assess where we are in the continuum is often thwarted by strongly held beliefs. It is exactly for this reason that the scientific method is essential for advancing our knowledge of the world around us. The scientific method requires that beliefs and preferences are subordinated to data and information.

Fig. 1.2 is a representation of a science continuum of discovery. Many endeavors to understand a particular phenomenon start with a very poor understanding of what actually occurs and what stimulates or causes changes that are interesting to the investigator. This is the left side of the diagram. As individual observations are made, patterns typically emerge. These patterns underpin a conceptual model for how things work. This is an inductive process of taking specific observations to develop a general model.

Once a conceptual model is developed, it can be challenged for its veracity. The center of the diagram represents the domain of classical experiments

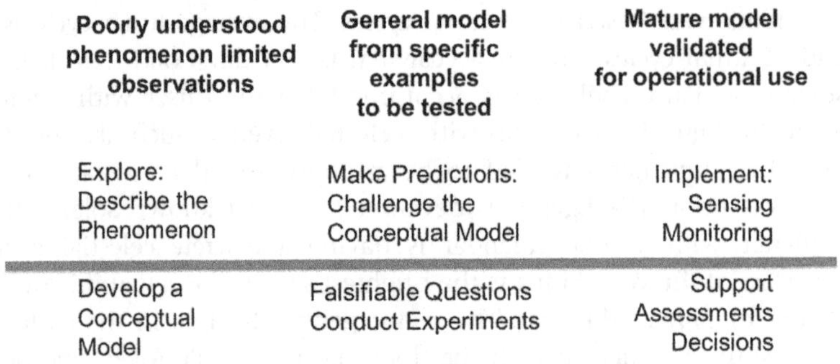

Poorly understood phenomenon limited observations	General model from specific examples to be tested	Mature model validated for operational use
Explore: Describe the Phenomenon	Make Predictions: Challenge the Conceptual Model	Implement: Sensing Monitoring
Develop a Conceptual Model	Falsifiable Questions Conduct Experiments	Support Assessments Decisions

FIGURE 1.2
A science continuum of discovery.

conducted within the constraints of the scientific method. This is a deductive process where a general understanding or model is challenged and refined with specific observations and experiments.

Finally, the right side of the diagram is where science becomes useful. As will be demonstrated by the evolution of our knowledge of the solar system and the universe, understanding does not have to be perfect in order to be useful and to have impact.

While the continuum in Fig. 1.2 appears orderly, it is important to recognize that science is a very messy proposition. It is challenging to accurately assess the maturity of understanding of a system and often a single observation can reveal fatal flaws in well-accepted models.

It takes courage and humility to start over at the left end of the continuum. There are also social pressures within scientific domains that impede the very thing everyone wants, which is a more complete understanding of how the world works. The scientific method challenges our desire to be right with evidence of what actually occurs. Cultural belief systems are often so strongly entrenched that challenging them with evidence can put the investigator in peril. Nonetheless, eventually the pursuit of knowledge embodies a recurrence of evidence that cannot be denied.

DID YOU KNOW?

The commonly used business lingo "paradigm shift" actually has its roots in the philosophy of science. In the 1962 book "The Structure of Scientific Revolutions" physicist and philosopher Thomas Kuhn coined the phrase paradigm shift to attempt to explain the societal influence on science. The premise is that certain conceptual models and theories become entrenched in cultures of research and that there is great social inertia to move away from them. It takes a significant result or amount of evidence to change of perspective, or shift the paradigm, of fields of study from long-held beliefs.

The Ptolemaic Model and Supporting Assumptions

The Earth as the center of the universe, or the geocentric model, emerged early in the Classical Period (roughly 8th-century BC to 6th-century AD) as part of Greek astronomy and philosophy that strongly influenced perceptions of science and philosophy throughout the Mediterranean, southwest Asia, northeast Africa, and Europe. The casual observations available today of the Sun, planets, and stars rotating around the Earth and the apparent stillness of Earth relative to those rotations were the basis of the development of a mathematics that describes and predicts the locations of celestial bodies. Alternative models not centered on Earth were posited but the geocentric model prevailed until it was challenged by Copernicus in the 16th century and eventually gave way to the heliocentric model in the 17th century.

DIG DEEPER: FORWARD AND INVERSE PROBLEMS

A forward problem starts with knowledge of causal factors and calculates the results.

An inverse problem is solved by collecting observations and estimating the causal factors.

The vast majority of questions in science, including the arrangements and motions of planets in the solar system are inverse problems.

The geocentric model of celestial motion is interesting to our understanding of science from several perspectives. The first is that the model is grounded in empirical evidence, or knowledge gained by means of our senses. The ancient astronomers were remarkable in their ability to make measurements of locations of the Sun and planets with the naked eye and to develop mathematical representations of those measurements and movements. Arguably, the most famous and enduring author was Claudius Ptolemy who standardized the geocentric model in a work called *Almagest* in the 2nd-century AD.

The Ptolemaic model requires several assumptions beyond the Earth being stationary and the center of the universe. Observations of a planet from Earth over time scribes a path that reverses direction. Ptolemy's resolution of this phenomenon consisted of a larger orbit around the Earth (deferent) and a smaller epicycle, which is a circular path that rotates on the deferent, as shown in Fig. 1.3.

Representing the Ptolemaic conceptual model in equation form provided the means to develop the diagram in Fig. 1.4 that shows the application of the astronomic equations for deferents, epicycles, and equants to the locations of the Sun, Mercury, and Venus relative to the Earth, as printed in the Encyclopedia Britannica in 1771. The dominant features in this diagram are the epicyclic loops. It's also interesting that the Sun and planets each have their own frequencies of epicycles.

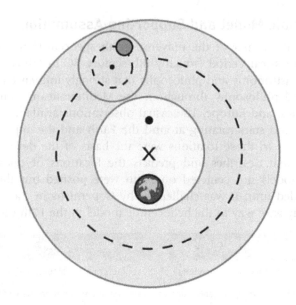

FIGURE 1.3
Ptolemaic astronomy—large donut shape with a dashed line is the deferent, the small dashed circle is the epicycle. The center is at X. The black dot is the equant point to adjust for being slightly off center and Earth is opposite the equant.

Fig. 1.4 highlights the assumption that planetary masses change direction within their complex orbits around the Earth. Galileo's law of inertia was unknown until 1612. What's also interesting about this assumption is that there isn't a proposed mechanism that would cause the Sun or the planets to change direction. The empirical evidence of planets changing direction was sufficient validation.

Another assumption was related to the distances from the Earth to the stars. One line of reasoning in defense of the geocentric model was that if the Earth was in motion then the relative positions of stars in constellations should change due to parallax depending upon the relative location of the Earth. The constellations appear to be constant in the relationships among their stars. The error in this line of evidence was that the Greek astronomers and their descendants assumed the stars to be much closer to Earth than they actually are.

Another assumption in the Ptolemaic model is that the large orbits (deferents) of the planets are circular. This assumption was rooted in a philosophical notion that a circle is in some sense a thing of perfection. It was a matter of belief that God's creation would necessarily be perfect and therefore the orbits of the planets circular. An additional assumption of the model was that the celestial bodies moved at a constant speed.

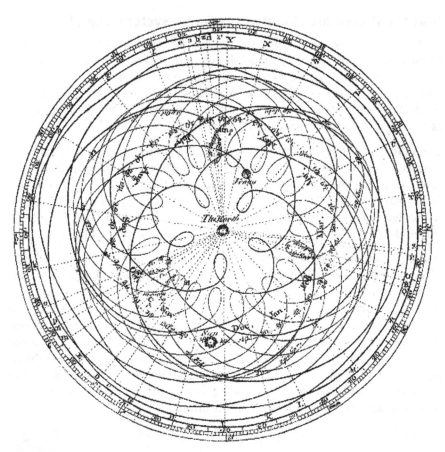

FIGURE 1.4

Orbits of the Sun, Mercury, and Venus around the Earth, from Encyclopedia Britannica 1771.

DIG DEEPER: CONFIRMATION BIAS

The tendency to recall or emphasize evidence that supports your point of view or preexisting beliefs, sometimes going so far as rejecting as erroneous any observations that challenge those beliefs.

The Ptolemaic model was built on preexisting beliefs about the God's plan, the shape of orbits, and distances from the stars.

The correct implementation of the scientific method is a mechanism for requiring that assumptions be documented and that all data be considered. Data are rejected only when a reason can be defended for doing so. Even with the best of intentions, confirmation bias can be a pernicious problem in the face of evidence that challenges long-held assumptions.

Was the Ptolemaic Model of the Solar System Useful?

With hindsight, we can see that the ancient astronomers fully implemented the science continuum. They made observations and developed a conceptual model. That model was coherent with their observations and also aligned with the dominant belief system regarding God's creation. Finally, they implemented calculations for predicting annual events. The model required a fair amount of tinkering to realign it to their observations.

From the perspective of tracking or anticipating annual events, the model was not very accurate but it did function. A completely different question is the extent to which the Ptolemaic model represented the motions of the planets in the solar system. As a representation of the solar system the Ptolemaic model was seriously flawed. The prevailing belief at the time also considered the model to represent the whole universe, also an unsupportable conclusion.

It's important to recognize that most of science is directed at solving problems and that there is an urgency in making science useful. Complex problems typically have many iterations through the science discovery continuum, often finding that the most basic assumptions are flawed causing a restart with initial observations that are interpreted from new perspectives. We never actually know whether we've gotten it right. There are always more observations that can be considered in novel ways that stimulate new thinking. This is the dilemma for scientists interacting with policy makers. The desire by policy makers is to base their decisions on certainty. A scientist can only represent the data and their interpretations.

DIG DEEPER: EMPIRICAL AND PHYSICAL MODELS

Empirical models are based upon observations and data relationships to characterize and predict the states of a system.

Physical models spring from known properties of the system and use measurements to apply those properties to specific systems.

The Ptolemaic model of the universe is an empirical model, estimating the arrangements of the planets and the universe purely on assumptions and observations. Through the work of Kepler and Newton, a physical model of the solar system was possible that is based upon fundamental properties of mass, inertia, and momentum.

Emergence of the Heliocentric Model

The geocentric model dominated astronomy for about 15 centuries. As noted earlier, the Catholic Church considered the geocentric model to be consistent with the teachings of the Bible. Example scriptural quotes from the King James Bible are: First Chronicles 16:30 states that "the world also shall be stable, that it be not moved." Psalm 104:5 says, "[the Lord] Who laid the foundations of the Earth, that it should not be removed for ever." Ecclesiastes 1:5 states that "The sun also ariseth, and the sun goeth down, and hasteth to his place where he arose."

In much the same way that Greek astronomers were "natural philosophers," the scientists of the Middle Ages and the early Renaissance were also often clerics of the Catholic Church. Popes, Cardinals, and priests were actively engaged in the discussions of the mechanics of astronomy and its relation to scripture. Consequently, exploring the possibility of an alternative to the geocentric model carried the weight of challenging both scientific and religious orthodoxy. The cultural context was also important in that the Church conducted inquisitions in the 13th and 16th centuries to root out and punish heretics. Proposing an alternative to the geocentric model ran the risk of being judged as heretical by the inquisition with consequences including torture and death.

Nicolaus Copernicus

There are occasional accounts of astronomers proposing models that challenge the geocentric perspective in the written record from the Classical period to the Renaissance, especially by non-Christian astronomers, but none of them gained influence in Europe until the work of Nicolaus Copernicus. Two aspects of the Ptolemaic model motivated Copernicus. There was disagreement among astronomers regarding the order of the planets from Earth, and calendars based upon the Ptolemaic model were inaccurate and biased.

Copernicus was able to resolve the order of the planets by allowing the center of the planetary system to move to the Sun, (Fig. 1.5). His model also had the Moon revolving around the Earth. His system continued to assume that the planetary orbits are circular and that planets moved at a constant speed which substantially increased the error of his predictions with the heliocentric model. In fact, his predictions were no better than the Ptolemaic model.

The extraordinary achievement of the Copernican model is that he shifted his frame of reference for analyzing the night sky to standing away from the system and observing the motions of the Sun and the planets. His model extended beyond the empirical experience of standing on a still Earth. In doing this, he was able to have the Earth rotate on its axis and attribute the apparent motion of the Sun and stars to that rotation. Apparent planetary movements were a combination of their orbits and the Earth's rotation. Another consequence of his model is that all planets rotate around the Sun in the same direction with planets closer to the Sun completing their orbits

FIGURE 1.5
Heliocentric model by Copernicus. Constant ordering of the planets with the Moon revolving around the Earth. Circular orbits and constant speeds.

more quickly. Finally, the Copernican model did not require retrograde motion to resolve the empirical locations of the planets over time. A controversial assumption of the Copernican model was that the stars are sufficiently far from Earth that changes in location due to parallax from the Earth's rotation were not observed.

Copernicus was cautious with his results, initially sharing them only with his close associates in 1514. He delayed the publication of his work, *"De revolutionibus orbium coelestium, (On the Revolutions of the Heavenly Spheres)"* until 1543 and is reported to have died on the day it became available from the printer. The Church initially showed intellectual curiosity about his findings and eventually banned it as a heretical text. A redacted version of the work was allowed for use in calculating calendars.

Was the Copernican Model an Improvement?

The irony of the Copernican model of the solar system is that the critical false assumptions of circular orbits and planets moving at constant speeds made it no more accurate than the Ptolemaic model. The key contributions were in ordering the planets correctly and simplifying the conceptual and mathematical relationships of the solar system. He also restricted or bounded the problem to the Sun and the five known planets. This is an important departure from the earlier models that attempted to represent the whole universe. Another key outcome of his work was that he solved the problem of the Earth moving around the Sun without observing changes in the relationships of the stars due to parallax. His proposition was that the distances to the stars was sufficiently vast that the parallax could not be observed.

DIG DEEPER: OCCAM'S RAZOR

Named for William of Ockham, (1287–1347), who developed the heuristic that among many competing hypotheses the one with the fewest assumptions should be favored over more complex models. This not a formal or logical requirement of the scientific method, but has been valuable in the conduct of science to prefer simpler conceptual models that rely on fewer assumptions to make correct predictions.

Although Copernicus predates William of Ockham, his influence upon understanding the motion of the planets is to reduce the number of assumptions is an application of the concept of Occam's razor.

It's important to realize that Copernicus used the same observations as all the astronomers before him. He didn't have better measurements or new phenomena to influence the model and his results were still an empirical understanding of how celestial bodies moved over time. This is truly a remarkable achievement, given that he was educated in the centuries of dogma that preceded his work.

Johannes Kepler

Kepler worked with Tycho Brahe whose contribution to astronomy was to collect empirical measurements with much greater accuracy than had been achieved previously. Brahe produced his own model that combined elements of the geocentric and heliocentric models. He correctly had the planets revolving around the Sun and the Moon revolving around the Earth. He erroneously had the Sun revolve around the Earth.

Kepler acquired a time series of Brahe's measurements for the location of Mars and his focus was to improve the accuracy of the heliocentric model. His data analyses eventually challenged the assumptions that the orbits of planets are circular and that the speed of planets are constant. His investigations looked at different geometries for the Martian orbit and he discovered that the data fit the formula for an ellipse when the Sun was located at one of the foci. He published this work in 1609. He continued this work for the five known planets and determined that each of them could be modeled as an ellipse with the Sun at one of the foci. That work was published in 1617 and 1620.

The profound contribution that Kepler made beyond elliptical orbits and varying speed is that he generalized his results into three laws of planetary motion. The first two laws (Fig. 1.6) were published in 1609, (*Astronomia Nova*), and the third published in 1619, (*Harmonice mundi*). Kepler's laws were largely ignored for about 80 years.[3] Kepler's laws are:

- The path of the planets about the Sun is elliptical in shape, with the center of the Sun being located at one focus. (The Law of Ellipses)
- An imaginary line drawn from the center of the Sun to the center of the planet will sweep out equal areas in equal intervals of time. (The Law of Equal Areas)
- The ratio of the squares of the periods of any two planets is equal to the ratio of the cubes of their average distances from the Sun. (The Law of Harmonies)

Kepler's third law compares the period of the orbit of a planet to the average radius of that orbit from the Sun. The law states that the ratio of the square of the period divided by the cube of the average radius is a constant.

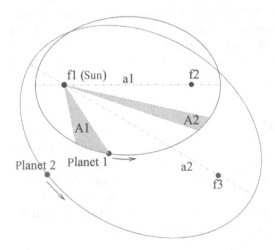

FIGURE 1.6

Kepler's first and second laws. The Sun is located at focus f1. Areas A1 and A2 are equal in area and time interval. The velocity of the planet at A1 is greater than at A2.

The constant is the same across all the planets. This relationship holds for other orbiting bodies, such as the moons of Jupiter or man-made satellites orbiting the Earth.

Kepler's contributions are a generalized physical model that represents the motion of the planets with much greater accuracy than the previous models based on circular orbits. An important subtlety of the second law is that the velocity of the planet must change over the course of the orbit for the equal intervals to have equal areas. The planet accelerates as it gets closer to the Sun and decelerates as it moves farther away from the Sun.

Kepler's Contributions in the Context of the Science Continuum of Discovery

Kepler had an advantage over the previous investigators in that his data were more accurate than the previous observations. With the increased accuracy he was able to investigate the orbit of Mars and develop the elliptical model. It is still inspiring that he was able to suspend the current assumptions and dogmas in order to represent planetary motion in a more accurate way. Furthermore, we were able to generalize the model with his third law and find a unifying constant for the solar system. His third law has relevance to this day for space travel and satellites.

From the perspective of science discovery, Kepler's results demonstrate the transition from purely empirical models to a rudimentary physical model that can be used to make predictions. The physical model is rudimentary in the sense that he didn't have the insights of fundamental properties of mass in motion that soon followed through the work of Galileo and Newton but his third law allows for the prediction of the average radius or the period of a satellite or hypothetical planet, given the system constant. In the case of the solar system, the constant is associated with celestial bodies orbiting the Sun. Constants can also be estimated for Earth, using the Moon and Jupiter, using its four moons.

Galileo Galilei

Galileo contributed to the refinement of the heliocentric model for planetary motion in two significant ways. His first contribution was the development of a telescope that enabled him to observe celestial bodies with far greater resolution than the naked eye. The geocentric model required all celestial bodies to rotate around the Earth as part of God's design of the universe. Galileo discovered the four moons of Jupiter that rotated around that planet. This observation was incoherent with the geocentric model. It was also a fatal flaw of the geocentric model as a religious philosophy. He also observed phases of Venus, much like the phases of the Earth's Moon. Venus having phases was additional evidence that Earth could not be the center of the system.

Galileo's second contribution to the development and defense of the heliocentric model was his work leading to the principle of inertia. His statement of the principle, at least as it is translated in the modern day, was, "A body moving on a level surface will continue in the same direction at a constant speed unless disturbed." As elaborated by Feynman in a Caltech lecture[4]: I, "...if an object is left alone, is not disturbed, it continues to move with a constant velocity in a straight line if it was originally moving, or it continues to stand still if it was just standing still. Of course this never appears to be the case in nature, for if we slide a block across a table it stops, but that is because it is *not* left to itself—it is rubbing against the table. It required a certain imagination to find the right rule, and that imagination was supplied by Galileo."

The retrograde motion of planets in the Ptolemaic model could not be justified without forces to "disturb" their progress. In contrast, the Copernican model allowed the planets to progress in simple orbits. Galileo also conducted experiments to demonstrate that the acceleration of gravity on a projectile was independent of the force of propulsion on the projectile. Essentially, two projectiles, one dropped from a height and another shot horizontally from the same height would hit the ground at the same time. The independence of these forces eventually becomes the basis for a planet being acted upon by the gravitational attraction of the Sun and its speed through space resulting in an orbit.

The contributions by Galileo are interesting from several perspectives. The first is that he based his conclusions on observations and experiments. Much of the history of science to that point was an amalgamation of observation with philosophy. It's also noteworthy that Galileo and Kepler were contemporaries. The widely held belief is that Galileo knew of Kepler's laws, but Galileo ignored them in his own work. Galileo continued to discuss the planetary orbits as circular. The third perspective is cultural context. Galileo's observations and conclusions were at odds with Church doctrine. He was brought before the inquisition in 1633. The sentence of the inquisition[5] was:

- Galileo was found "vehemently suspect of heresy," namely of having held the opinions that the Sun lies motionless at the center of the universe, that the Earth is not at its centre and moves, and that one may hold and defend an opinion as probable after it has been declared contrary to Holy Scripture. He was required to "abjure, curse and detest" those opinions.

- He was sentenced to formal imprisonment at the pleasure of the inquisition. On the following day this was commuted to house arrest, which he remained under for the rest of his life.
- His offending *Dialogue* was banned; and in an action not announced at the trial, publication of any of his works was forbidden, including any he might write in the future.

Galileo's Contributions in the Context of the Science Continuum of Discovery

Galileo made fundamental contributions to the understanding of motion of celestial bodies in several ways. The first is that he developed a telescope that allowed him to make observations that falsified prevailing dogma that had been in place for 15 centuries. His second substantial contribution was to apply experimental results to system scales that are vast and beyond the realm of experiments. He applied his law of inertia to the motion of planets. In the beginning of this chapter we claimed that there are many scientific domains where the scale of experiments in controlled environments is different from the scale of the system that we seek to understand. Astronomy is an observational science and Galileo has the insight to apply his experimental results from dropping and projecting small weights to the motions of planets.

This chapter started with a discussion of Fig. 1.1 and the value of simple experiments to support the understanding of complex phenomena. It is impossible to know what impact Galileo's experiments could have had in modifying the perspectives of the astronomers from the Classical period and whether the geocentric model would have persisted for 15 centuries, given the incoherence between that model and the experimental outcomes. Nonetheless, the evolution of our knowledge of planetary motion provides evidence that experiments at controllable scales can have profound relevance to understanding much larger systems.

The work of Galileo combined with the Kepler's laws makes it possible to generate a physical model of planetary motion that has fidelity to the observations and is generalizable to systems at scales different from the solar system.

Isaac Newton

Isaac Newton is reported to have been born on Christmas Day, 1642, the day that Galileo died. He had a profound influence on the practice of evidence-based science and his seminal work, "Philosophiæ Naturalis Principia Mathematica ("Mathematical Principles of Natural Philosophy"), first published in 1687, is the basis for classical mechanics. In it he proposed laws of motion and developed the concept of universal gravitation.

Newton's laws of motion, restated in modern English on the NASA web page, are:

> The first law states that every object will remain at rest or in uniform motion in a straight line unless compelled to change its state by the action of an external force. This is normally taken as the definition of inertia. The key point here is that if there is no net force acting on an object (if all the external forces cancel each other out), then the object will maintain a constant velocity. If that velocity is zero, then the object remains at rest. If an external force is applied, the velocity will change because of the force.
>
> The second law explains how the velocity of an object changes when it is subjected to an external force. The law defines a force to be equal to change in momentum (mass times velocity) per change in time. Newton also developed the calculus of mathematics, and the "changes" expressed in the second law are most accurately defined in differential forms. (Calculus can also be used to determine the velocity and location variations experienced by an object subjected to an external force.) For an object with a constant mass m, the second law states that the force F is the product of an object's mass and its acceleration.
>
> For an external applied force, the change in velocity depends on the mass of the object. A force will cause a change in velocity; and likewise, a change in velocity will generate a force. The equation works both ways.
>
> The third law states that for every action (force) in nature there is an equal and opposite reaction. In other words, if object A exerts a force on object B, then object B also exerts an equal force on object A. Notice that the forces are exerted on different objects. The third law can be used to explain the generation of lift by a wing and the production of thrust by a jet engine.

Newton made two simplifying assumptions. The first is that all masses are points in space. A point in space has no volume. His second assumption is often called an inertial frame of reference. This assumption places the observer relative to the motion of interest, such that the motion can be represented by a simple vector consisting of speed and direction (velocity). The idea of positioning where the observations are made was initiated by Copernicus, carried forward by Galileo and became integral to Newton's laws of motion.

For our purposes, the comparison of Kepler's laws and Galileo's inertia to Newton's laws and universal gravitation illustrates a maturation in the context of the science continuum in Fig. 1.2. Kepler's laws and Newton's laws would appear to be addressing the same phenomena. The difference in the dynamical systems that they describe is that Kepler was able to model and predict the position of planets based upon sets of observations that characterized their previous path. Newton used Kepler's work and went further by investigating the forces necessary for the planets to deviate from a simple straight path. Kepler laws describe what happens, Newton's laws address why it happens. Newton also developed the idea of universal gravitation, which provides for a centripetal force between masses as one orbits the other. The forces associated with Newton's laws are the influences on the path of an object that "disturb" that path in Galileo's parlance.

DIG DEEPER: DYNAMICS AND KINEMATICS

Dynamics, also called kinetics in older sources, is a part of classical mechanics that studies the motion of objects with mass and the forces that influence their path.

Kinematics is a branch of classical mechanics that investigates the path of objects with no regard to forces acting on the object to define the path.

Kepler established the kinematics of planetary motion, opening the way for Newton to develop the dynamics of planetary motion.

The additional development by Newton was to generalize the understanding of objects in motion. Galileo was able to extrapolate his experiments on motion and inertia to the Copernican heliocentric planetary system. Newton's laws are applicable to objects in motion, almost independent of mass. Newton's development of classical mechanics is constrained by what could be observed at the time. For the vast majority of what we can observe with our senses, the classical laws are adequate to describe the phenomena.

Newton's Contributions in the Context of the Science Continuum of Discovery

Newton's contributions to the understanding of the motion of planets was to make the transition from a phenomenological description of planetary orbits based upon measurements of their positions over time to the development of three fundamental laws of motion that apply to masses, spanning many orders of magnitude. The simplifying assumption of point masses introduces a certain amount of inaccuracy, but in most cases of masses where the distance between the masses is much greater than their radii and their motions are at speeds below the speed of light, the inaccuracies tend to be minor.

The other contribution that Newton made to planetary motion and prediction was the development of the Calculus in order to address masses being acted upon by changing forces and rates of acceleration. Calculus was also developed contemporaneously and independently by Gottfried Leibniz. Having a calculus for changing rates provided the basis for developing formal proofs of Newton's laws.

Albert Einstein

Owing to Newton's success at extending experiment-based concepts of mechanics to the scale of planets, it's natural to ask, to what extent it is possible to extend Newton's concepts of inertia to the very small scale of atoms and to the very large scale beyond planets. Are the fundamental relationships of mass, inertia, and gravitation, as described by Newton, coherent for scales beyond the perceptual frame of the human senses? It turns out, not always. The framework of classical mechanics must be extended.

Albert Einstein was a champion of consistency among frameworks. He was also a student of the work of those who came before him. Newton's laws were the basis of physics research for two centuries and likely defined much of what Einstein would be exposed to as a student. Investigations on the boundaries of the scale beyond those considered by Newton, such as electromagnetic fields by Maxwell and Faraday surfaced difficulties in the generalizability of the laws. These difficulties were identified decades before Einstein was born and would also inform his curiosity.

From the classical period of the ancient Greeks through the time of Newton, much of the evolution of our understanding of the world and heavens around us depended upon observations with the human senses. Galileo's telescope is a poignant demonstration of the influence of an emerging technology on how we perceive the world around us. The challenges to Newton's laws and classical physics emerged as investigators developed new ways of sensing phenomena in the natural world, which are beyond direct human perception. As instruments augment human senses, new phenomena, and questions arise that challenge the dominant understandings of how things work. The idea of observations being relative to the point of view of the observer emerged with the Copernican heliocentric model, was essential to Kepler's ellipses, was discussed by Galileo and captured Einstein's imagination.

An essential element of Einstein's contribution to how we understand the physics of moving bodies today is that the speed of light is a constant. He further proposed that even though all measurements and observations are dependent upon a frame of reference, or observation point relative to the thing being observed, the speed of light is still a constant. This simple statement has profound consequences. If two observers measure the speed of light and one of them is stationary and the other is moving rapidly toward the light source, the only way that they both get the same value for the speed of light is if time slows down for the observer in motion. The phenomena is called time dilation. Time as an absolute in the Newtonian construct is no longer valid. Time is relative. Similarly, absolute space in Newton's laws is also plastic and indeed time and space are a four-dimensional continuum. The presence of large masses in the space–time continuum cause distortions such that the orbits of planets and satellites that we witness as human observers are actually the shortest distance between two points in a curved space–time fabric. In the context of space–time, gravitation is not a force but rather an artifact of masses following that shortest path.

Another result of Einstein's work was to relate mass to energy and, in a relative sense, determine that they are realizations of the same thing. The famous equation $E = mc^2$ simply states that the energy equivalence of a mass is that mass times the speed of light squared. We discussed earlier that the speed of light is a constant, which means that if the energy of a mass is increased, its mass must increase. Boil water to make coffee and the mass of that water will increase proportional to the amount of energy added to the water to make it boil divided by the speed of light squared. While this has no practical impact upon making coffee, it has significant consequences for subatomic particles and is seminal to modern chemistry and materials science.

Are Einstein's Contributions an Improvement to Understanding Planetary Motion?

Einstein's relativity influences our daily lives in a variety of practical ways. One example is that the satellites associated with GPS travel at speeds around the Earth sufficient to require time adjustments associated with time dilation. Failing to do so would result in positioning errors of over a kilometer within a 24-hour period. But, does relativity add to our understanding and prediction of the location of planets?

Newton's development of the foundations of classical physics provided the means for making accurate predictions of the motions of celestial bodies using causal forces and relationships to construct physical models. From that perspective, Newton's classical laws of motion are adequate and if planetary motion were the only objective, the problem could be considered solved. However, the nature of all experimental science is that there are always errors. Whether the error comes from the measurement system or intrinsic wobbling of the system being observed, things go awry. The relativistic equations actually account for error in planetary orbits that the Newtonian system does not capture.

The universe that Einstein perceived is vast, possibly beyond what most of us can imagine today. His work is important to and does not trivialize the

FIGURE 1.7
LIGO Laboratory, Hanford, Washington.

question of where the planets in the solar system will be. The solar system is actually a simple proof of principle for his theories. Einstein published two theories of relativity. The first called the *Theory of Special Relativity* addressed masses at a constant velocity. Ten years later, he published a *Theory of General Relativity* that accommodated acceleration of a mass in motion. Only in the last couple of years has it been confirmed that *General Relativity* is relevant to very large energy densities associated with the collision of black holes. The recent observation by the Laser Interferometer Gravitational-Wave Observatory (LIGO) (Fig. 1.7) of gravitational waves, ripples in the fabric of space–time, that are theorized to result from the collision of two black holes were quantified. In order for such an observation to be possible, it required understanding noise that occurs on scales smaller than atoms. The theory that Einstein published in 1915 was validated by the LIGO experiments in 2016.

Einstein's Contributions in the Context of the Science Continuum of Discovery

Einstein's theory of relativity and discussions of the limitations of classical mechanics expanded the frame of reference for understanding mass and energy across scales from subatomic particles and waves to black holes. The profound influence of Einstein is that one hundred years after his theories were published, we continue to explore methods to confirm or refute them.

There is a paradox in the emergence of Einstein's theories. Early in this chapter, we considered a science continuum where poorly understood phenomena require observations to come up with a general notion or conceptual model of how the phenomenon works. The conceptual model provides a basis for specific experiments or observations leading to modifications and improvements. The maturation of the model leads to theories and laws, much like Kepler's and Newton's laws. Einstein learned from the work of those who preceded him, specifically Copernicus, Kepler, Galileo, and Newton, and many others. From that work he developed theories at expanded scales, which required decades to develop methods to test them. The paradox is that for most of this evolution of understanding, laws and theories are derived from observations and experiments. Einstein was able to use the previous work to postulate theories for scales of observations and experiments that were not achievable in his time.

An interesting question is to what extent Einstein informed our understanding of planetary motion and the solar system. The work of Copernicus, Kepler, Galileo, and Newton served to challenge the geocentric model of the universe and provided evidence of the existence of a solar system that could be defined and modeled as part of the cosmos but not the center of the universe. From the perspective of the solar system and planetary motion, Einstein's work was not necessary to update our planet-scale understanding of solar system. Einstein's work does improve predictive calculations and models. Einstein's work and his theories are essential in placing planetary motion in the context of all matter and energy. From that perspective, Einstein's work substantially enhances our understanding of the solar system in the context of the universe.

SUMMARY AND CONCLUSIONS

This chapter provides an overview of science and how it is conducted, followed by a brief historical review of the investigations to understand the planetary motions of the solar system. Several key concepts emerge that are necessary to consider in the conduct of science for cyber security research.

The science continuum provides a context to science investigations relative to the maturity of understanding for the phenomena of interest. This matters because implementing scientific results to operational environments often fails due to poorly formed conceptual models based on inadequate information and interpretations. The geocentric model of planetary motions around the Earth and the belief that the Earth is the center of the universe is a prime example.

We can also see in the progression of understanding of the solar system that operational models don't have to be perfect to be useful. The geocentric model was used for recording historical events and predicting the onset of seasons. It was seriously flawed and required periodic tinkering to realign it with known events, but it was used nonetheless. As a description of planetary motion, the geocentric model was completely wrong. What's interesting is that misrepresenting planetary motion did not prevent the development of rudimentary calendars.

The development of the heliocentric model of planetary motion required a change in the point of reference or perspective by Copernicus. The concept of changing perspective was the seminal idea that followed from Copernicus to Einstein and is fundamental to the theory of general relativity.

The validation of the heliocentric model and the rejection of the geocentric model required two contributions. The first was Galileo's telescope that had sufficient resolution to discover the moons of Jupiter. Evidence of these moons was the fatal flaw in the belief that all heavenly bodies orbited the Earth. The second contribution was Galileo's experiments leading to the concept of inertia and his application of experimental results to planetary motion. The key points are improvements in measurement capabilities and the emergence of a rudimentary physical law that challenged retrograde planetary motion in the absence of a force to cause it.

The impact of cultural belief systems on the development of the geocentric and heliocentric models of planetary motion demonstrates how challenging it is to separate discovery from beliefs. This is a fundamental reason for conforming to the scientific method in conducting science investigations. The heliocentric model also changed the scale of the model from the whole universe to the Sun and the five visible planets.

The work of Galileo and Kepler established the groundwork for Newton to develop the classical laws of motion. This is a critical transition from empirical models of planetary motion to a model based upon physical laws. The model also generalizes beyond the Sun and planets to any mass in motion.

The impact of Einstein upon our understanding of planetary motion was to further expand the context of the solar system and place it in a frame of reference that spans subatomic particles to black holes.

Discovery in the Realm of Right and Wrong

After 2500 years of investigation and discovery, it's fair to ask whether our knowledge of the solar system and the motion of masses is complete. Also, there is a continuing debate in the philosophy of science on whether

Newton was wrong and Einstein was right. It's important to consider that Newton was correct in developing a physical explanation of the motion of masses on Earth that could be extended to celestial bodies. As others attempted to expand the reach of that explanation to other spatial and temporal scales, they found deficiencies. Einstein's theories of relativity were able to address those deficiencies with remarkable changes in how the physical world is perceived. Importantly, Einstein's perceptual frame of reference is not observable directly by human senses.

Science is fundamental to assembling evidence in support of discovery. What science can't do is provide absolute answers. To ask whether Newton was wrong and Einstein was right misses the point. Newton developed a set of laws that are adequate to describe and predict the motion of masses in many contexts. Those laws fail at very small and very large scales and at velocities approaching the speed of light. Einstein's theories are consistent with Newton's laws and expand the spatial and temporal scales. In the context of science, adequacy and effectiveness are more meaningful considerations than right and wrong because science does not operate on absolutes.

As you can see from our example, scientific discovery can improve our understanding of the universe. This knowledge has led to technological advancements that enable the many commonplace activities we take for granted in society. Now that you are aware of what science is and how impactful its practice can be, we have one more introductory chapter before getting into the research methods discussion. The next chapter is an introduction to cyber security and perspectives on the science of cyber security. If you do not have a general knowledge of cyber security, the next chapter will provide a crash course. If you already have a strong foundation of cyber security knowledge, it will still benefit you to at least read the sections on defining cyberspace and the science of cyber security to gain an understanding on our perspective that underlies the rest of this book.

Endnotes

1. Greenhalgh, T. "How to Read a Paper. Getting Your Bearings (deciding What the Paper Is About)." *BMJ: British Medical Journal* 315.7102 (1997): 243−246. Print.
2. Song, Jae W., and Kevin C. Chung. "Observational Studies: Cohort and Case-Control Studies." *Plastic and reconstructive surgery* 126.6 (2010): 2234−2242. PMC. Web. April 10, 2016.
3. O'Connor, J. J., & Robertson, E. F. (1996, Feb. & march). History topic: Orbits and gravitation. Retrieved from http://www-groups.dcs.st-and.ac.uk/~history/HistTopics/Orbits.html.
4. Feynman, R. (n.d.). The Feynman Lectures on Physics Vol. I Ch. 9: Newton's Laws of Dynamics, from http://www.feynmanlectures.caltech.edu/I_09.htm.
5. Linder, D. (n.d.). Papal Condemnation (Sentence) of Galileo in 1633. Retrieved February 25, 2017, from http://law2.umkc.edu/faculty/projects/ftrials/galileo/condemnation.html.

## CHAPTER 2

Science and Cyber Security

Cyber security is a young field of research. Digital computational systems have been in existence for less than 100 years. Networked computing has only existed for around 50 years. The full weight of cyber security issues were not observed until the 1980s and 1990s when the Internet became a consumer grade resource. Over these time periods, the advancement and complexity of cyber space has increased exponentially. Cyber security concerns have increased as the technical domain has expanded. As such, the cyber security field is still trying to catch up with the rapid growth and capabilities of cyber space.

Before jumping into discussions and examples of how to perform cyber security research, it is important to first define and describe cyber security concepts. In this chapter, we will introduce you to the field of cyber security. We will cover what constitutes cyber space and what it means to secure that space. In addition, we will provide a brief overview of core concepts of cyber security. Finally, we will provide an introduction to some of the research subfields within cyber security.

As cyber security is a young field, there isn't complete agreement across all of these topics. Through this chapter we want to provide you with a broad perspective. As the goal of this book is to enable you to engage in the research field, it is important for you to understand the different perspectives. As such, we will provide competing ideas and perspectives throughout this section. As part of these discussions, we will also explain our own current understanding and beliefs.

In this chapter, we will use analogies to other fields of science to help clarify concepts and increase understanding. While analogies are good for explaining the high-level concepts, they can be a dangerous tool. Often the analogies work well at an abstract, highly conceptual level, but completely fall apart at a detailed level. We have seen researchers execute large research programs on the basis that analogies work because they appear as such at the conceptual level. Much effort is spent trying to make the concepts from the other field fit, when in

33

Research Methods for Cyber Security. DOI: http://dx.doi.org/10.1016/B978-0-12-805349-2.00002-9

reality they may very well not. Therefore we caution readers that while we use analogies for explanatory reasons, we do not suggest that these analogies be used for areas of research unless you have strong reasons to trust the analogies.

CHAPTER OBJECTIVES

- Define cyber space and cyber security
- Introduce foundational concepts of cyber security
- Discuss the philosophy of a cyber security science
- Provide an introductory overview of the cyber security research field

DEFINING CYBER SPACE

As cyber security can be considered simply the act of making cyber space safe from damage or threat, it is important to define cyber space before discussing cyber security. This task isn't as easy as one would think. There are different perspectives of cyber space and these definitions have evolved over time.

DIG DEEPER: CYBER SPACE OR CYBERSPACE?

There are varying perspectives on how to write out cyber space. The etymology of the word comes from joining the words cybernetics and space. As you see throughout this book we chose to use the two-word version. Cyber has become a commonly used adjective that relates things to metaphysical, virtual, or digital representations. It has become a modifier similar to physical. More awkwardly, sometimes the word cyber is used as shorthand for cyber security, which while semantically untrue, has been gaining traction. "Oh you work in cyber" means cyber security and not cyber space or cyber space—related fields. Finally, real-world examples of security can be used to help explain one word or two. For example, National Security, Social Security, physical security, home security, network security, computer security, are all two words. The lack of understanding of the word cyber seems to force some to merge it into one, misleading concept, cyber security. For all of these reasons, we prefer, and will continue to use cyber security, as two words.

While there are a lot of definitions of cyber space from national and technical bodies, they all agree in the metaphysical or virtual aspect of cyber space. However, they all essentially organize or cluster around what is and isn't included within their definition. The set of concepts upon which definitions all agree or disagree are: data, technology, and people.

Data Perspective

The first perspective view of cyber space centers around the data or information that resides in cyber space. The methods of transmittal and storage are irrelevant, and the focus is on how to encode and construct information into transferable data. This perspective came from the information theory space, which is directed toward the digitization and encoding of information. Hence, the focus is largely on the constructs of how to generate information in cyber space and provide protective measures for it or access control, which we will discuss more later. The information theory work that is the underpinning of our current systems happened before networks and the Internet occurred so there aren't really any cyber space definitions per se. However, this data and information centric perspective is still used and followed by subsets of the cyber security field. Later, the broad topic of Information Assurance (IA) came about, to address, in part, some of the limitations of computer and network only security. Instead of protecting the systems and communications media, the information itself, in transit and at rest should be identified, valued, and protected.

DIG DEEPER: EARLY COMPUTERS

Some of the world's first computers were developed as part of the effort in World War II for decoding enciphered messages by the German military. The efforts at Bletchley Park in the United Kingdom during World War II had large historical impact on the development and direction of computational system design.

Technology Perspective

The next perspective was formed in the 1990s, around the time cyber space transitioned from a fictional concept into an academic term to define an ontological concept. The technological perspective is that cyber space encapsulates data or information and the technology that is necessary to transmit it. This includes the hardware, silicon, and wires, as well as software, operating systems (OSs), and network protocols. The majority of the definitions with this perspective basically use cyber space and the Internet interchangeably.[1] However, some of these definitions extend well beyond current technology and include any form of information transmission, such as the postal service.[2]

Cybernetic Perspective

The most recent perspective, and the perspective we agree with, is that cyber space includes the human in addition to the data and the technology. We agree with this perspective because, **cyber space** is the metaphysical construct created from the confluence of digital hardware, the data it creates and manages, and the humans that interact with the hardware and produce and consume the information contained in the data. This perspective acknowledges that the human is as much responsible for the dynamics of the system as is the data and the technology. Cyber systems would not have a

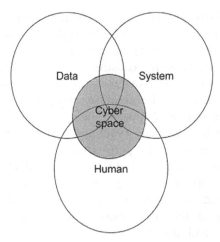

FIGURE 2.1

Cyber space at the overlap of data, system, and human

function without human intervention. A common cyber security statement is that users are the weakest security link. This is because users are often targeted directly with attacks against their psychological behavior, such as clicking on bad links or executing malware. Their thoughts and interaction with cyber systems are part of cyber space because they represent the physical manifestations of the activity within cyber space (Fig. 2.1).

DID YOU KNOW?

The term cyber space was first coined in the context of networked computational systems and popularized by William Gibson, a science fiction writer. He first used it in his short story "Burning Chrome" and then explored the concept more in his novel *Neuromancer*. He has been quoted stated that he used the word because it was "evocative and essentially meaningless."[3]

DEFINING CYBER SECURITY

Cyber space is integrated into every facet of our daily lives, and cyber security is a part of every interaction. Whether it is the security mechanisms on our computer, the passwords to our online services, or the microchips in our credit cards, cyber security is a part of all of or interaction with our cyber-enabled world. When cyber security works as it should, nobody notices it. When it fails it can turn into major news.

With an understanding of cyber space, we can now define cyber security. In its most simplistic definition, it is the security of some relevant portion of cyber space. A key concept of security, which holds true in cyber security as well, is that there is no such thing as perfect, or absolute security. Claiming something is "secure" or "protected" is a sure sign of a sales pitch, or a lack of understanding of security. Security is always conditional, and limited. That is to say, a system may be protected against remote theft, of files, for the authorized owner, over the local area network. This sort of limitation carries two key points of information. First, secure from what (network-based threat), secure for what (data theft for the legitimate user). These bits of information are often implicit in security, but become crucial and explicit in cyber security. Yet, a more comprehensive definition of **cyber security** is measures and actions taken to prevent unauthorized access to, manipulation of, or destruction of cyber resources and data. Cyber security includes the technologies, policies, and procedures to secure something within cyber space. You may have heard other terms such as computer security, which is the securing of computational systems and network security, which is the securing of communication media or others. Cyber security is an inclusive term that covers all of the various perspectives of securing parts of cyber space. Additionally, there is the broad topic of Information Assurance (IA). Instead of protecting the systems and communications media, the information itself, in transit and at rest should be identified, valued, and protected. In some cases, this is a subset of cyber security (the data portion of cyber space), but this is also broader, as IA includes risk management for all information, be it hard copy, solely memorized, or in other forms in the real physical world. Additionally, IA has business and mission management and continuity emphases, that again can make it a subset or superset of cyber security. However, like physical security is the securing of physical spaces, cyber security is the securing of cyber spaces. Note, as we will discuss later in the chapter, it is easy to fall into the trap of thinking that cyber security is analogous to physical security. There are distinct differences that make cyber security more challenging at this time.

Attributes of Cyber Security

Over time, a set of fundamental attributes of cyber security have been defined. These attributes are desirable characteristics of a secure system. The original set of attributes, which are still frequently discussed as a core set, were the confidentiality, integrity, and availability (CIA) triad. However, the CIA triad is too coarse to differentiate the finer aspects of cyber security, so additional attributes have been added.

Confidentiality

Confidentiality is the attribute that has to do with preventing unauthorized users from accessing data. The key feature of this property of cyber security is to keep information within cyber space private to only those parties who should be privy to it. Confidentiality is provided through mechanisms that prevent users from getting to the information they are not allowed to access. Or, in open communication areas of cyber space, logical obfuscation techniques are used such that only appropriate users can discover the meaning of the message.

Integrity

As an attribute, **integrity** relates to only allowing authorized users to modify data in cyber space. When data is exchanged between actors in cyber space, it often passes through shared areas where other actors have the ability to modify data before it reaches its recipient. Therefore, a critical concept of cyber security is that some data is critical and must remain unchanged between sender and receiver.

Availability

Availability is the characteristic of cyber security, which states that resources and information within cyber space are accessible in a timely and reliable manner. If you only view cyber security as the end goal, the optimal conclusion is that you should turn off all computers, encase them in concrete, and shoot them into space, and then everything would be secure. However, computers have utility and must operate at some level to be useful. Therefore, availability is a critical attribute of cyber security that helps balance the restrictions of the system against the utility of the system.

Authenticity

Authenticity, the first-added attribute beyond the original three, is assurance that the identities of parties involved in an exchange of resources within cyber space are who they claim they are. Actors within cyber space are projections of physical objects, either people or systems. To enable decisions on who and what is allowed access to resources, it is critical to have the ability to authenticate actors within cyber space to their physical reality with some level of assurance. Authenticity applies to actions and data within cyber space; that is, you authenticate actions and data as having come from a user.

Nonrepudiation

Nonrepudiation is the facet of cyber security that relates to attribution of actions within cyber space to the actors who actually performed them. This goes beyond authenticity and integrity to include auditable logging of actions, such that it is difficult for an actor in cyber space to refute their activities. Auditing and logging are crucial aspects of cyber security that often are given insufficient attention during design, development, and even operations of cyber systems. You can only ensure confidentiality, integrity, and so on, if you have present evidence to attest to the fact. Often cyber security systems rely on partial or missing information, which will compromise the end results.

These above attributes establish the dimensions around which a system can define security requirements. However, as a field, we still lack sound methods to quantifiably measure these attributes in a system. Therefore we are still left with largely qualitative measures of security. When it is possible to accurately measure the security of a system, the field of cyber security will graduate to a well-established scientific field.

CYBER SECURITY FUNDAMENTALS

To fully understand what securing cyber space means, it is necessary to define the foundational concepts. An underlying concept that is the basis for cyber security, and security in general, is the concept of having privileges or rights and authorization to access or perform actions. Cyber security in general articulates that the authorized are allowed to access things or perform actions and also prevents the unauthorized from doing the same. The rest of the section will focus on providing an overview and discussion on the fundamental concepts of cyber security. We will first introduce the concepts of attackers, and then explore security by design.

While the previous section listed attributes that define the security of a system, they do not discuss the other side of the coin: the attacker of the secure system. Security can be viewed from both a defensive and offensive perspective. There are some core concepts around the offensive perspective that define the who, what, and how of defeating cyber security.

Vulnerability

A **vulnerability** is weakness in a system, either by design, configuration, or process, that renders it open to exploitation by a given threat or susceptible to a given hazard. A system is said to be vulnerable when it provides the opportunity for a threat to break a security attribute it is meant to maintain. Vulnerabilities are caused by mistakes and our fallible ability to design secure systems. System is also used in the broadest sense of the word, a user is part of the system and therefore introduces vulnerabilities. Policies, data artifacts, and humans can all have vulnerabilities that adversaries can take advantage of, do not fixate on just software, network, or hardware vulnerabilities.

Exploit

An instance of a technique designed to take advantage of a vulnerability in a system to breach its security is an **exploit**. An exploit is the realization of a vulnerability. While there can be many vulnerabilities in a system, there isn't an exploit until a threat actor develops a tool or method to take advantage of the vulnerability to subvert a system's security.

Threat

A **threat** is any deliberate source of potential damage or danger. In cyber space, damage from threats is adverse impacts to the operation of a system or the resources, including data, of a system. A threat is someone or a group with intent and capability for doing harm. For a more in-depth discussion of threats see Chapter 14, Research with an Adversary.

Threat Actor

An individual, group, organization, or government that conducts or has the intent to conduct or execute attacks against cyber space systems is a **threat actor**. A key differentiator between hazards and threat actor is intent. Threat actors have intent and means to inflict damage on systems, whereas hazards happen by chance.

Threat Vector

A **threat vector** is the method or means by which a threat attacks a target. Some lexicon incorrectly define malware, such as viruses, worms, and bots, as threats. However, these are more accurately defined as threat vectors. Malware is simply one method by which a threat can execute attacks against a target and exploit their vulnerabilities.

Attack

An attempt by a threat to gain unauthorized access to a system's services, resources, or information, or to compromise integrity of the system or its data is an **attack**. An attack is a single-contained attempt to exploit a specific vulnerability. A series of attacks over a longer period is generally referred to as a **campaign**.

Malware

Malware is software that exploits vulnerabilities in a system by performing an unauthorized function or process. Viruses, worms, bots, adware, and tro-jans are all forms of malware. Malware is a common threat vector in cyber space.

Secure System Design Principles

Saltzer and Schroeder[4] described a set of design principles that provide good rules of thumb for producing systems that can meet high levels of security containing the attributes we discussed in the previous section. All of the following are theoretical principles, but note that we still lack strong empirical evidence on how to quantify these principles in real systems. However, they are a good ideal to strive for in achieving and have been generally accepted in the field.

Economy of Mechanism

The **economy of mechanism** principle states that systems should have a simple and small design. General system designers have expressed a similar philosophy: keep it simple, stupid (KISS). Both principles are based on the premise that the more complex a system, the higher probability of errors or mistakes are present. In cyber security these errors are what lead to vulnerabilities and ultimately compromise. Therefore, a system should be designed as simply as possible to meet the security requirements to reduce likelihood of errors.

Fail-safe Defaults

Fail-safe defaults is a principle where access should be denied by default and only granted based on explicit permission. This principle has led to a mechanism of operation called whitelisting. Whitelisting is the process of explicitly declaring what permissions should be granted and anything not granted is prevented. Whitelisting is common in firewalls, OS permissions, and policy-based intrusion-detection systems. This is the inverse of blacklisting, which is specifying and preventing actions that are known to be bad, which is commonly used by antivirus technologies. Whitelisting is a good practice, as it forces one to note everything that should be allowed, which reduces the probability of mistakenly allowing something that shouldn't be. However, in practice, our systems have become quite complex, which makes operating everything with a whitelisting philosophy very difficult.

Complete Mediation

Complete mediation is a principle where every access to every object or resource should be checked against permissions. In order to verify if an actor in cyber space should be doing an activity, those activities must be mediated by some process to first decide if they should occur. This principle is easier said than done as it is often unexpected or unplanned actions that subvert protection mechanisms.

Open Design

A common trope in cyber security is security through obscurity. **Security through obscurity** means that the security of a system is based mainly on its nonpublic processes and protocols. This is seen as a terrible basis for security, as someone always discovers how a system operates. Instead, as the **open design** principle states, security mechanisms should be open to scrutiny and their security properties should be based on sound mathematical and scientific properties. That is to say, the security of a system should not rely on the confidentiality of its operation or processes. Open design has been a key principle in cryptography as no expert in the field trusts cryptographic algorithms that haven't been open to and able to withstand scrutiny for years.

Separation of Privilege

Separation of Privilege is a principle that states that realms of authority within cyber space should be reduced to as minimal a space as possible. A mechanism that requires more than one person, resource, or asset (like a key) will be more secure. This principle covers both authority of actors, what authoritative permissions users should have, and security mechanisms, what processes or resources are required to authorize actions in cyber space. For actors, this includes reducing global authority and in some cases forcing multiple actors to perform some highly critical actions. A well-known example is a **separation of duty** for nuclear weapons launch. The so-called "two-person rule" requires that two separate, qualified, and authorized individuals are required for highly critical duties, such as nuclear weapons launch. Limiting universal powers like this is critical to addressing such large-scale actions.

Least Privilege

Closely related to the separation of privilege principle is the least privilege principle. **Least privilege** is a concept that only minimal privileges should be provided to actors and process within cyber space to perform their necessary duties. By reducing to minimal privileges reduces the possible set of actions that can be taken within, and thus the scale of bad actions that can be taken.

Least Common Mechanism

Least common mechanism is the principle that a secure system should limit the amount of shared mechanisms. This applies to both security (protection functions) as well as general mechanisms. This is because the failure of a shared function means the security of all sharers is compromised by one action. Limiting defense-in-depth and defense-in-breadth are two common concepts in cyber security that have grown out of the least common mechanism principle. The concept of least common mechanism is to limit the impact of any security failure. **Defense-in-depth** does this by layering security controls such that if one security mechanism fails one of the other layers of security will hopefully detect or prevent the failure. **Defense-in-breadth** leverages different instances of one type of control with the promise that a vulnerability in one will not be replicated in another. This is a direct implementation of least common mechanism. This is also called system diversity, where the same functionality (OS, web server) is implemented differently for each instance. This clearly limited the ability of a common shared vulnerability, as the software level at least.

DIG DEEPER: ANTI-DIVERSITY

Note, as with most concepts in cyber security, there is a counter argument against system diversity (and therefore least common mechanism). The claim is that if one has an important function, lets say hospital database, and it is implemented once, the best possible solution will be chosen given the real-world constraints that exist. If however, because of least common mechanism, several different approaches are implemented, most, by definition will be inferior, and less secure than the "best of breed." This argument then concludes, that it is better to strive for one secure implementation, and not several (perhaps less secure) options. This is an interesting research question open for investigation to determine if in fact diversity or antidiversity produce a more secure system.

Psychological Acceptability

Psychological acceptability is the principle that security must be as intuitive and easy to use as possible. The premise for this is that if security is a barrier to using systems, users will try to find ways to go around security controls. Additionally, the more complex, and alien, a system (both protection, and function) the more likely mistakes will be made, which can lead to the overall degradation of security.

CYBER SECURITY CONTROLS OVERVIEW

The concepts of cyber security discussed so far are all ephemeral concepts. Implementations of these concepts are necessary to realize security into a real system. Cyber security controls are the tools and techniques by which levels of security attributes can be applied to a system. A significant amount of applied research has focused on building security controls. These are the common tools that we see and use within our computers. It is important to understand the currently available and used security controls to understand how cyber security research has been applied.

All security controls must reflect a policy. A control without a policy is meaningless and policy without a control is useless. For example, a small business might declare that all passwords should be changed every 6 months. This defines the risks (forgetting passwords, compromise of password), the mechanism (domain policy controls), and applicability (all users). Often technologists will jump right to a control or mechanism without consideration for a policy. If there is no reasonable policy that would use the control then it is worthless at best and deceptive at worst. Policy is the formal definition of what it means for a business to be cyber secure, under what conditions, constraints, adversaries, and circumstances. This will vary from business to business even in identical circumstances.

Over time, quite a few different control mechanisms have been developed. While there are different methods and instantiations of the controls we will discuss, for this overview we will only provide a high-level description of each category of control. In most cases, these categories of control are applicable across the different physical media of cyber space, computer systems, and communication networks.

Access Control

Access control is a mechanism by which actors' identities within cyber space are authenticated and then authorized to perform actions or access resources. The first critical step in access control is the authentication of a cyber space actor's identity. **Authentication** within cyber space requires some form of mapping physical identity to cyber identity. **Credential factors** are a set of data that represents some form of evidence that provides assurance of an actor's identity. Table 2.1 defines the three categories of credentials and examples of technologies and techniques for using them. Authentication processes validate user-supplied credentials against stored and protected copies or artifacts, like hashes, of the credentials.

After authentication comes authorization. **Authorization** is the process of allowing or preventing an action or access to data based on a set of privileges associated with a cyber actor. **Privileges** are possible actions that are granted or

Table 2.1 Authentication Credential Factors

Factor Category	Examples
What you have	Certificate, key, RSA (Rivest, Shamir, and Adleman) token, smart card
What you are	Biometrics, (i.e., fingerprint, retina, facial and voice recognition), typing characteristics, physically unclonable function
What you know	Password, PIN
Where you are[a]	GPS coordinates, cellular triangulation, geotagging, country codes, and so on

[a]While not always considered a 4th factor, location is sometimes used as well.

Table 2.2 Access Control Models

Access Control Model	Description
Mandatory (MAC)	Privileges are maintained by a centralized authority. Users do not have authority to alter or grant privileges even for data they generate. Active directory group policy is an example of MAC.
Discretionary (DAC)	Privileges are defined in relation to identities or groups and those with a privilege have the discretion to pass that privilege on to others. The Unix file system is an example of DAC.
Role-based (RBAC)	Privileges are assigned to a role with defined responsibilities. Individuals are assigned to roles to be granted privileges. RBAC is used throughout cyber systems. A common example is administrator accounts that provide users with superuser privileges.
Attribute- or Rule-based (ABAC)	Privileges are granted based on rules of approved attributes and their relation to the user, the requested resource and contextual environment information. ABAC enables restricting access based on dynamic information like, for example, what IP address range a user is coming from or the time of day for the access.

restricted based on what is defined as allowed for a cyber actor. Multiple models of access control exist. Table 2.2 provides a description of access control models.

DIG DEEPER: INFORMATION SECURITY MODELS

There are multiple information security models that define sets of privileges and how users may interact with them. All of these models are based on theoretical logic axioms to prove that they maintain security. The Bell-LaPudula,[5] Biba,[6] and Clark-Wilson[7] models are famous and generally taught in the introduction to cyber security courses. However, there are other models developed for different operational paradigms such as databases and preventing conflict of interest. Other models for research are Take-Grant,[8] Graham-Denning,[9] Brewer and Nash,[10] and Harrison, Ruzzo, and Ullman.[11]

Situation Awareness

Situation awareness is the process of monitoring a cyber system to understand its current state and status. A core concept of situational awareness is being able to distill important information from streams of data from cyber space to generate knowledge that enables one to take action. There are increasing levels of situation awareness that one can achieve.[12] Table 2.3 describes the levels of situation awareness and provides examples in the context of cyber security.

Situational awareness is a field that includes many different aspects. There are the sensors that collect the first level of data. This includes the science of

Table 2.3 Levels of Situation Awareness

Level	Description	Example
1	Perception of the elements in the environment	Firewall logs, system event logs, packet capture
2	Comprehension of the current situation	Determination of current threat or risk level, determination of an attack
3	Projection of future status	Prediction of attack types, prediction of threats, prediction of vulnerabilities

how to collect data, where to collect data, how much data to collect, and how to normalize data streams. Commonly, host- and network-based tools generate logs that are used for cyber security situation awareness. Firewalls, system event logs, antivirus, packet captures, netflow collectors, and intrusion detection systems are all examples of common cyber space sensors.

Level-two situation awareness (SA) is when you start to generate information from the data to determine a current situation. Generally, level-two SA requires the bringing together of data and performing some level of analytics. The simplest form is signature-based tools such as antivirus and intrusion detection systems. These systems have encapsulated previous knowledge of detected attacks into signatures that detect and alert you when they are detected in operational systems. More advanced systems such as security information and event managers (SIEMs) provide infrastructure to bring together datasets from multiple sensors for performing correlations. Also, vulnerability analysis to determine how many unpatched vulnerabilities exist in a system is also a form of level-two SA.

The third and final level is hard to achieve and, as such, there are few examples of effective tools. Things such as cyber threat intelligence, which provide information on active threat actor methods, techniques, and targets, provide some level of predictive information to enable taking preemptive security measures.

Cryptography

Cryptography is the study and application of mathematical constructs and protocols to provide logical mechanisms for securing data and communication from eavesdroppers. Two forms of modern cryptography exist: symmetric and asymmetric cryptography. **Symmetric key cryptography** utilizes shared keys or secrets with fast ciphers to encrypt and decrypt messages. Asymmetric cryptography utilizes computationally complex math problems to enable encryption and decryption while communicating parties have different keys. The trade-offs of the two types is that symmetric encryption is fast, but requires some method of securely sharing the key material. Best practice methodology leverages the strengths of asymmetric cryptography to exchange the secret key material between communicating parties so that they may then use the faster symmetric cryptography for data exchange.

Symmetric Encryption

There are many different symmetric ciphers, some of the more widely known being the Advanced Encryption Standard (AES), Data Encryption Standard (DES), Triple DES (3DES), Rivest Cipher 4 (RC4). Ciphers can operate on data in blocks (block ciphers), where chunks of data are operating at once, or streaming (streaming ciphers), where operations are performed on each atomic piece of data. However, block ciphers can execute under certain modes to replicate characteristics of streaming mode ciphers. Table 2.4 displays the different common modes of operation for block ciphers.

Table 2.4 Modes of Block Ciphers

Mode	Description
Electronic Cipher Book (ECB)	Each block of plaintext is encrypted separately. The same plaintext produces the same ciphertext with the same key. This leads to significant information leakage in certain situations and, as such, ECB mode shouldn't be used for real applications.
Cipher Block Chaining (CBC)	Each plaintext block is XOR'ed (a binary operation for exclusive disjunction) with the ciphertext of the previous block such that it creates a chaining of the cipher blocks.
Cipher Feedback	Cipher Feedback is closely related to CBC but instead of XOR'ing before the encryption, plaintext is XOR'ed after the encryption to create the ciphertext. A random value is used as the initial input to the cipher. Cipher Feedback improves on CBC by allowing synchronization at smaller than block sizes if certain techniques are used.
Output Feedback	The key is used to generate blocks of ciphertext by starting with an encrypted initial random value and then encrypting the output of each subsequent encryption. The ciphertext is generated by XOR'ing the plaintext to the encrypted block. As the encryption is independent of the plaintext, this mode can behave like a stream cipher.
Counter	Similar to Output Feedback, Countermode encryption encrypts a value and generates the ciphertext by XOR'ing the plaintext to the encrypted block. Countermode differs by generating the input to the encryption by using half of the block as a random number and the other half is a counter that increments per encrypted block. Countermode also can operate like a stream cipher. Counter mode works well when lost information is possible in the communication channel as the counter tells the receiver, where, in the data stream, the message fits.

DID YOU KNOW?

As the community review and study of crypto-graphic algorithms has become one of the cornerstones of determining their strength, the U.S. government has begun using competitions to select the next standards for us. The Rinjdael algorithm was selected by U.S. National Institute of Standards and Technology (NIST) in the first competition, which become known as AES. More recently, U.S. NIST held another competition for an improved hash function, the Secure Hash Algorithm 3 (SHA-3). The Keccak algorithm, developed by Guido Bertoni, Joan Daemen, Michaël Peeters, and Gilles Van Assche was selected to become the SHA-3 standard. As of the writing of this book, NIST is contemplating a new competition for encryption algorithms that are secure against the capabilities of quantum computing.

Asymmetric Encryption

Asymmetric encryption uses computationally hard problems with a secret(private), and shared (public) key. With asymmetric encryption, a message encrypted with one's public key can only be deciphered by their private key and vice versa. Asymmetric encryption solves the problem of having to share without secure communication by enabling communicating parties to share their public keys and, using complex math, encrypt data such that an eavesdropper cannot decipher the message. Therefore, everyone can publicly share their public key so that others can communicate with them. Best practice behavior says you only encrypt data using the receiving party's public key, and you do not encrypt messages with your private key.

Asymmetric encryption also enabled the concept of digital signatures. If, instead of using a private key for encryption it is instead used for message authentication, one can sign a message. To sign a message one first hashes (hashes are described next) a message and then encrypts the hash. This encrypted hash is transmitted with the message. A receiver can verify the hash by decrypting it using the signer's public key and then compare the decrypted value to a computed hash of the message. If the values are equal, then the message is valid and came from the signer (assuming that the private key wasn't stolen of course).

Cryptographic Hash

A **hash function** is a computational method that can map an indeterminate size of data into a fixed size of data. Or more plainly, it provides a number quantity that represents the input data. A **cryptographic hash function** uses one-way mathematical functions that are easy to calculate to generate a hash value from the input, but very difficult to reproduce the input by performing calculations on the generated hash. One common way of generating cryptographic hashes is to use block ciphers. Some common hash functions are MD5 (which is broken and obsolete), SHA-1, SHA-2, and SHA-3.

Entropy

Entropy is the foundation upon which all cryptographic functions operate. Entropy, in cyber security, is a measure of the randomness or diversity of a data-generating function. Data with full entropy is completely random and no meaningful patterns can be found. Low entropy data provides the ability or possibility to predict forthcoming generated values. One measure of the quality of cryptographic functions is to measure the entropy of their output. Highly entropic algorithms are needed for encryption and hash functions.

Also entropy is crucial for the generation of random inputs, such as keys, nonces, initialization vectors, for cryptographic algorithms. These values need to be unpredictable or even completely secret to ensure the security of the process. Therefore, having and using high entropy sources of data is critical to security. Some common sources of entropy are keyboard/mouse input, drive reads, circuit voltage, and thermal readings. However, these sources are not always enough to generate the required material in the time needed, so **cryptographically secure pseudo-random number generators** (CSPNRG) are often used to generate additional entropy material. CSPNRG are mathematical functions that take a seed or some initial value, which needs to be highly entropic to prevent prediction, and produce highly entropic streams of numbers. The output of truly entropic resources are generally used to seed CSPNRG.

Cryptanalysis

Cryptanalysis is the process of studying cryptographic systems to look for weaknesses or leaks of information. Cryptanalysis is generally thought of as exploring the weaknesses of the underlying mathematics of a cryptographic system but it also includes looking for weaknesses in implementation, such as side channel attacks or weak entropy inputs.

DID YOU KNOW?

For his award winning 1999 science fiction novel, *Cryptonomicon*, Neal Stephenson enlisted famed cryptologist Bruce Schneier to develop an encryption cipher. The resultant cipher, Solitaire but called Pontifax in the novel, uses a full deck of cards with two jokers to create a cipher stream to encrypt and decrypt a message. The deck of cards is shuffled into a sequence that represents the key and is used to encipher the a message. The deck of cards is placed back into the order of the key and delivered with the ciphertext. The recipient use the deck to decipher the message.

Host Security

A **host** in cyber space represents an atomic unit of computational power. A host generally means a computer, but it can also mean an embedded device such as a smartphone, programmable logic controller, or it can mean logical constructs such as virtual machines.

Host security includes controls that provide monitoring and protection of hosts. This includes host firewalls, host intrusion detection systems (host-IDS), and authentication mechanisms. There are different event timings at which host security operates. Firewalls and host-IDS execute when packets are received on a network interface. Host IDS and antivirus operate when files are placed in the file system and when software is executed.

Software security can be performed during development using static and dynamic code analysis, which searches for possible locations of vulnerabilities. Fuzzing and penetration testing, both techniques for finding vulnerabilities, can be performed on an executable before used in operations. And finally, OSs have multiple techniques such as read-only sections of memory to provide operation time protection. Address randomization is a newer technique that, on each execution of an application, shuffles the layout of program memory space to prevent buffer overflows, a common exploit against software, jumping to known places within code.

Network Security

Network security encapsulates a suite of security controls that provide protections on cyber networks and when data is communicated between hosts. The processes and techniques of network security are very similar to host-based security, but instead of looking at a host it looks at a network. Just like host-based security, network security also has firewalls and IDS systems that monitor the data flow. Network security also has intrusion-prevention systems and application proxies that act like antivirus on a host but operate on the protocol level, or the process and format of exchanging data, to detect and prevent known bad behavior.

Network security is more confounding as the number and locations of sensoring are often limited in comparison to host security. While it is possible, it isn't often the case that every location on the network is observable. And as the number of sensors increases on the network, things such as synchronization and data merging and correlation become more of a challenge. Often host-based logs are merged with network logs to increase the visibility of the network.

Risk

Risk is a likelihood of potential for harm from a cyber attack. The commonly used formula is the probability of a threat attacking multiplied by the probability of a vulnerability be present multiplied by the size of the impact if the attack is successful. Or:

*Risk = Threat * Vulnerability * Impact*

The goal is to provide a measure of how secure a system is and to provide prioritization of where to spend resources to improve.

Risk can be handled in multiple ways. First, risk can simply be accepted. If a risk is too high to be accepted, then it can be mitigated through applying security controls that reduce the probability of vulnerabilities. Lastly, risk can be transferred through constructs such as insurance. The major problem with risk for cyber security is that it is currently impossible to measure the probability of a threat attacking or the probability of a vulnerability existing. Therefore, current risk measures are not generalized, but provide more of a localized ordinal measure. Even in spite of these shortcomings, current insurers have started providing policies for cyber security attacks.

DEFINING A SCIENCE OF CYBER SECURITY

At this point, you should have a good overview of what cyber space and cyber security mean and some common techniques and concepts. In the final section of this chapter, we will describe what it means to have a field of scientific study for cyber security. In this context, we provide our perspective of our guiding research questions and hypotheses.

Generally, the driving force behind a field of science is some unanswered, overarching research question. For example, if we look outside our field, scientists might have questions about the forces of interactions in a specific biological ecosystem for ecology or how dark matter relates to space and time for physics or the study of aberrant human behavior and cognition for psychology. To make research tractable, subfields of research are formed by studying derived, smaller questions, and around hypotheses that explain phenomena. While cyber security is still a young field, it is important to define the overarching objective so that we can frame our research.

The current view of the field is that cyber and physical space are analogous. This doesn't mean that the same laws exist but more that there are laws that exist, which we just need to find. From this perspective, the driving goal is to find the "physics of cyber space." By discovering these laws, principles, and theorems ("cyber physics") it would be possible to develop barriers in cyber space with predictive performance much like is possible today in physical space. From this knowledge of cyber physics, it would be possible to develop predictive models that would generate metrics for risk such that it would be possible to make sound decisions on cyber security application and posture.

There have been a few attempts over time to define a science of cyber security. A JASON report from Mitre[13] acknowledged that there currently doesn't exist any laws of cyber space and that other fields do not directly address the unique aspects of cyber security, like the possibility of infinite space and the quickly changing adversarial context. U.S. government-funded tablets at universities contextualized their science around a set of hard problems in cyber security.[14] A report from the National Science Academy provided a description of why a science is needed and a survey of research visions. Finally, a recent report from the National Science and Technology Council Networking and Information Technology Research and Development Program (NITRD)[15] states that we still need to develop some strong theories and laws that define cyber space.

Our Definition of a Cyber Security Science

All of the reports provide strong perspectives and well-formed ideas. However, we think the effort is slightly misplaced. Over the last 10 years, we have formed a new perspective about what a science of security means. We provide our definition to help cultivate the idea and foster thought within researchers. As was previously stated, the prevailing perspective is that cyber space has laws that we can discover and exploit. We don't necessarily agree. Our hypothesis is that there aren't any stable dynamics of cyber space. Or stated another way, cyber space is constantly in flux as new technologies, hardware, and software are developed. As such, each addition has the potential to alter the dynamics in some way. Therefore, you can't assume that there are stable laws for us to discover. We do believe that specific configurations of cyber space can exhibit laws of behavior. Therefore, it would be possible to find principles about how to construct cyber space to achieve resultant desirable attributes and principles within cyber space. These principles of construction would enable us to create logical systems with characteristics that cognitively/socially/logically constrain users to expected and predictable behavior. It follows from our perspective that cyber security is not a science of understanding cyber space, but instead a science of understanding how to construct cyber space to achieve desirable characteristics or laws. We can understand configurations of cyber space enough to determine when and where users will violate the logical laws constructed. Cyber security science is not for answering the question of *"what are the physics of cyber space,"* but instead *"what physics of cyber space would be necessary to achieve the behavior/response we want and how do we create that cyber space."*

To address this scientific vision, the definition of cyber space is critical. As we have defined previously, we believe that cyber space is a combination of the hardware, data, and humans. As such, each of these have a role in what characteristics are exhibited with cyber space. As each change in any one category could alter the system dynamics, the science lies in the interaction between these three areas. The hope is that the behavior or dynamics is consistent

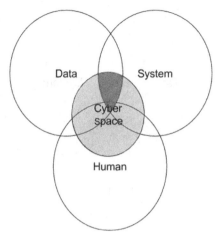

FIGURE 2.2
Intersection of Data and System in Cyber Space

between system interactions such that we can be predictive in what mechanics and dynamics would be formed under different configurations. Each interaction between two of the spaces of cyber space represent promising open areas of research (Fig. 2.2).

Intersection of System and Data

The intersection of system and data is the area of science in which there currently is the most fruitful research. This research subfield is looking to understand how to build logical boundaries in cyber space. The combination of Moore's Law with cryptography have achieved a reasonable model for predicting the appropriate strength of cryptographically derived logical boundaries.[16] However, even this result too is on the precipice of obsolescence as we get closer to a world with quantum computing that invalidates a lot of our understanding of the bounds of computational power.

Research under this subfield would focus on understanding the behavior of cyber space when constructed in different ways under different situations. With an understanding of how computational power is affected by the physical systems and software that operates will help us understand when, where, and under what designs logical bounds would exist. This knowledge would help drive system design with logical bounds suitable for security applications (Fig. 2.3).

Intersection of Social and System

The intersection of humans and the system is focused on understanding the behavior of people within cyber space. As we are learning over time, the

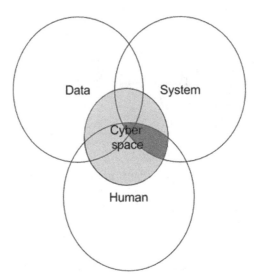

FIGURE 2.3
Intersection of System and Human in Cyber Space.

projection of oneself into cyber space loses some of the humanity in the transfer. Whether it is pirating music[17] and movies or cyber bullying, it seems that human beings behave physically and emotionally differently when interacting through cyber space versus physical space. Understanding these differences, what causes them, and what factors can be influential will help in defining a cyber space that can be secured based on/in spite of human behavior.

There have been recent studies[18] that suggest that if we make the synthetic real enough it will start to enable our normal physiological reactions. An interesting question is if we can construct cyber space to engage desirable physiological responses such as guilt and shame. This subfield also encapsulates the understanding of threats from a psychological and sociological perspective. With this understanding, it would be possible to construct cyber space to deter malicious behavior (Fig. 2.4).

Intersection of Social and Data
The intersection of social and data is focused on understanding the cognitive limitations and tendencies of people with data. It has been found that humans, regardless of socio-economic factors, generate the same weak passwords[19]. Researching human cognitive ability to store, interpret, and process data could lead to our ability to design and implement more systems that are more practical and secure. Research along these lines would include not only studying the

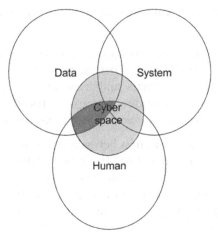

FIGURE 2.4
Intersection of Data and Human in Cyber Space.

direct interaction with security tools such as authentication or security notifications, but also understanding the best methods to present data for defenders to be more efficient and effective at finding and resolving attacks.

CHALLENGES IN ACHIEVING SECURITY IN CYBER SPACE

The interaction of the hard science of physical system behavior, the social science of human behavior and response, and the formal science of data encoding and information representation results is a completely unique field of study. Along with this uniqueness comes a set of challenging aspects that make performing research and applying results difficult. The following are a few common aspects that you may find when doing research.

First, cyber space, whose origins are entirely human, is an abstract, informational space defined by its code, elements, and interactions. Our current understanding is devoid of mathematical and physics-like foundations. From philosophy, it is a space though, as it conceptualizes the ability to move, act, create, and describe.

As we discussed when defining cyber space, there are multiple perspectives through which one can view research. There is the logical data and informational aspects that include the software, interfaces, and artifacts of cyber space to define and understand. Or you can study the physics that underlie cyber space and look at the electrons, wires, computers, and other physical phenomenology. Or you can study the behavior of people in cyber space.

Independently, these are challenging fields of study and together that are even more difficult.

While often it is easy to relate cyber space to physical space, it differs from our natural world in various ways. First, humans do not exist within cyber space. Instead people have avatars and leave artifacts within cyber space. Consequently, threats exist outside cyber space. Therefore, it is not always easy or even possible to sense all relevant information within cyber space.

A related challenge to the interaction between physical and cyber domains is that the ties are loose and dynamic. The cyber artifacts we tend to use to identify people, such as IP addresses and usernames, are nonbinding and not unique. IPs are dynamically assigned and it is easy to be proxied through other systems changing your IP. Also, usernames are generally self-assigned and are often different between different services. So the same username could represent different people on different platforms. In addition, it is easy for an attacker to assume the cyber identity of people to execute behaviors that appear to come from the victim.

The metaphysical nature of cyber space is also different than physical space as we still lack the mathematical constructs to define it. Geometry is a math of defining physical space where blocks of matter and mass can be mathematically described. We lack this ability to define cyber space. Length, distance, and other measures have no bearing in cyber space. In addition, concepts such as force in physical space also has no known corollary in cyber space.

What all of this means is that there has not been any discovered first principles of cyber space. Physical security is dependent on physical first principles. Through our understanding of force and material makeup, we can quantify and predict how much force it would take to break through a physical barrier or how long it would take with a given force. We currently have limited understanding of the mechanics and dynamics of cyber space. This leads to attackers often breaking the assumptions of the designers of cyber space components instead of attacking defenses head on. Owing to our lack of understanding of cyber space, robust treatment of cyber security is improbable and attackers currently have an advantage in finding weaknesses.

This leads to the last and one of the most challenging aspects of cyber security. One of the main variables under study is dynamic and intelligently changes as we learn, threats. Humans are the threats and they are intelligent and responsive, therefore as we learn their tactics and build defenses they change. Another analogy people like to use for cyber security is medicine. While viruses and bacteria do evolve and reduce the effectiveness of our immune systems and pharmaceuticals, they are not intelligent. Therefore, they change relatively slowly in comparison and it is possible to predict how they will change. Cyber security threats communicate, share, and sell exploits, and learn how cyber systems work just like we do. Therefore, there is a coevolutionary process that needs to be understood to help future proof knowledge gained from cyber security research.

FURTHER READING

While cyber security is a relatively young field of research, it already has a broad focus. There are countless numbers of journals and conferences surrounding different cyber security topics. While it would be difficult to completely summarize all subfields of cyber security research, below we provide a brief overview of some of the more common subfields to provide you with some ideas on where to look next for ideas and topics for your own area of research interest.

Attack Detection

The research field of attack detection researches patterns and behaviors of attacks to detect their occurrence. Use of statistical methods, expert systems, and machine learning are common in this subfield. Solutions such as antivirus and intrusion detection systems originated from this field of research.

Secure Mechanism Design

Secure design focuses on attributes of security and how to apply them to a system to achieve a level of security. This field encompasses multiple subfields such as formal methods, secure system architecture, and research into new applied security controls. Things such as firewalls and access control paradigms were a result of this field of research.

Software Security

Software security is a field of research that focuses on understanding why vulnerabilities in software exist, where they are commonly exhibited, how to detect them, and how to prevent them. Researchers in this field study topics such as secure coding practices, static and dynamic software analysis, and programming language and runtime design. Solutions such as sandboxing and static code analyzers came from this field of research.

Malware/Threat Analysis

Malware and threat analysis research focuses on understanding the behaviors and tactics of threats and the vectors of attack that they use. Subfields of this are cyber forensics, reverse engineering, and attack attribution. The continuous stream of signature updates for our various pattern matching attack tools are generated by this field of research.

Risk Management

Risk management research focuses on how to measure and quantify a state of cyber security. This includes quantifying the value of cyber security to an operation, how much of a threat is the operation exposed to, and scoring how mitigations and security controls affect the overall operational risk. Risk management researcher also includes what types of metrics and sensors are necessary if deployed security controls are effective.

Cryptography

Cryptography is a field of research focused on developing secure communication algorithms and protocols. A key part of this is cryptanalysis, which is the effort to study and discover ways to break cryptographic algorithms. Cryptography includes information theoretic and formal proof research as well as research into how to apply these techniques without vulnerability. Encryption and data integrity came from this field of research.

Our hope is that this chapter provides a sufficient introduction to cyber security to provide context for the rest of the book. As this book is more focused on providing information on the methods of rigorous research for researchers and practitioners, it is not a full introduction to the field of cyber security. There are many good books on the market that teach the theories of cyber security and fundamental concepts more in depth.[20,21,22] We also provided a list of seminal papers we think provide a strong foundation in cyber security in the Dig Deeper break-out box at the end of the chapter.

DIG DEEPER: SEMINAL CYBER SECURITY WORK

As with every scientific field there is research that is performed that is an inflection point for future research. Below is a list of seminal papers that will give you a solid foundation into cyber security research. This list includes research that had impacts that changed the way the field thought about topics. This list is not meant to be a list of just good research or interesting topics. A brief explanation of why the paper is seminal is provided per reference.

Title	Author(s)	Seminality
Communication Theory of Secrecy Systems	*Claude Shannon*	• First formal statement of modern cryptography • Defined secrecy system, cipher, and how to determine the strength of secrecy system from information theoretic perspective

The Protection of Information in Computer Systems	*Jerome H. Saltzer, and Michael D. Schroeder*	• Introduces seminal secure design principles • Descriptor-based protection systems • Historical insights into computer security
Moore's Law (Cramming More Components onto integrated circuits (1965) and Progress in Digital Integrated Electronics (1975))	*Gordon Moore*	• Defined a model of processor development and progression • Provided a way to project computing capabilities into the future • A fundamental concept that has enabled the quantification of encryption security strength
New Directions in Cryptography	*Whitfield Diffie and Martin Hellman*	• First idea for public-key cryptography • Defined Diffie–Hellman key agreement protocol
A Method for Obtaining Digital Signatures and Public-Key Cryptosystems	*Ron Rivest, Adi Shamir, and Leonard Adleman*	• Defined RSA public-key system • One of the most used public-key cryptographic systems
On Data Banks and Privacy Homomorphisms (1978)	*Ronald Rivest, Leonard Adleman, and Michael Dertouzos*	• First paper defined homomorphic encryption
Fully Homomorphic Encryption Using Ideal Lattices (2009)	*Craig Gentry*	• Second paper defined the first practical fully homomorphic encryption scheme
The Byzantine Generals Problem	*Leslie Lamport, Robert Shostak, and Marshall Pease*	• Theoretical exploration of agreement under adversarial threat • Defined limitations of trust in redundant systems • Does not solve the common vulnerability challenge
Smashing the Stack for Fun and Profit	*Aleph One (Elias Levy)*	• First widespread introduction to buffer overflows • Step-by-step discussion of the vulnerability and shell code • Exploration of the implications

On the Security of Public-Key Protocols	*Danny Dolev and Andrew Yao*	• Theoretical exploration of attacks on public key protocols • Defined Dolev-Yao threat model that has become the threat model used for cryptographic protocols
A Computer Virus and a Cure for Computer Virus	*Fred Cohen*	• First definition of a virus • Proof of undecidability of detecting a virus (counter proof) by mapping to halting problem
The Foundations of Computer Security: We Need Some	*Donald Good*	• Essay to complain about lack of strong foundations for engineering in computer security (cyber security not a concept yet) • Surveyed how theoretically secure systems are not really secure • Proclaimed we need more theories before being able to engineer "secure" systems
Programming Satan's Computer	*Ross Anderson and Roger Needham*	• Theoretical exploration of timing, ordering, and oracle attacks • Define principles for developing security protocols for integrity and authenticity using cryptography
The Base-Rate Fallacy and Its Implications for the Difficulty of Intrusion Detection	*Stefan Axelsson*	• Theoretical explanation of the problems we have with IDS • With extreme ratio of noise to signal (attacks = black swan events) even if you have a 100% detector you still need extremely low false-positive rate to not be inundated with false-positive detections
Red Pill (2004) Introducing the Blue Pill (2006)	*Joanna Rutkowska*	• Red pill demonstrated a method to detect that you were running as a guest virtual machine • Blue pill demonstrated malware becoming a hypervisor to running OS dynamically

The Science of Guessing: Analyzing an Anonymized Corpus of 70 Million Passwords	*Joseph Bonneau*	• Study that shows that regardless of subpopulation everyone choose equivalently weak passwords • An attacker is better off using a global password list

Endnotes

1. Glossary. (January 11, 2017). Retrieved February 25, 2017, from https://niccs.us-cert.gov/glossary.
2. Cyberspace and Security: A Fundamentally New Perspective, Victor Sheymov
3. Dux, E., Neale, M., Gibson, W., In Ford, R., Bono,., Sterling, B., Paine, C., ... New Video Group. (2003). *No maps for these territories: On the road with William Gibson.* United States: Docurama.
4. J. H. Saltzer and M. D. Schroeder, "The protection of information in computer systems," in *Proceedings of the IEEE*, vol. 63, no. 9, pp. 1278–1308, September 1975.
5. Secure Computer Systems: Volume I—Mathematical Foundations, Volume II—A Mathematical Model, Volume III—A Refinement of the Mathematical Model No. MTR-2547. (1973) by David E. Bell, Leonard J. Lapadula.
6. Integrity Considerations for Secure Computer Systems MITRE Co., technical report ESD-TR 76-372 (1977) by Biba.
7. Clark, David D. and Wilson, David R.; A Comparison of Commercial and Military Computer Security Policies, in Proceedings of the 1987 IEEE Symposium on Research in Security and Privacy (SP'87), May 1987, Oakland, CA; IEEE Press, pp. 184–193.
8. Lipton, Richard J.; Snyder, Lawrence (1977). "A Linear Time Algorithm for Deciding Subject Security" (PDF). *Journal of the ACM (Addison-Wesley)* 24 (3): 455–464. doi:10.1145/322017.322025.
9. G. S. Graham and P. J. Denning, "Protection–Principles and Practice," in *Proceedings of Spring Joint Computer Conference, AFIPS*, 1972, pp. 417–429.
10. Dr. David F.C. Brewer and Dr. Michael J. Nash (1989). "The Chinese Wall Security Policy". *IEEE*.
11. M. A. Harrison, W. L. Ruzzo, and J. D. Ullman, "Protection in Operating Systems," *Communications of the ACM*, vol. 19, no. 8, pp. 461–471, August 1976.
12. Endsley, Mica R. "Toward a theory of situation awareness in dynamic systems." *Human Factors: The Journal of the Human Factors and Ergonomics Society* 37.1 (1995): 32–64.
13. JASON. (2010, November). *Science of cyber-security.* Retrieved February 25, 2017, from https://fas.org/irp/agency/dod/jason/cyber.pdf.
14. Nicol, D. M., Sanders, W. H., and Scherlis, W. L. (November, 2012). *Science of security hard problems: A lablet perspective.* Retrieved from http://cps-vo.org/node/6394.
15. House, W. (2011). Trustworthy Cyberspace: Strategic Plan for the Federal Cybersecurity Research and Development Program. *Report of the National Science and Technology Council, Executive Office of the President.*
16. Barker, E. (January, 2016). *Recommendation for key management part 1: General.* NIST Special Publication 800-57 Part 1 Revision 4. Retrieved from http://nvlpubs.nist.gov/nistpubs/SpecialPublications/NIST.SP.800-57pt1r4.pdf.
17. Robert Eres, Winnifred R. Louis & Pascal Molenberghs (2016): Why do people pirate? A neuroimaging investigation, Social Neuroscience, DOI: 10.1080/17470919.2016.1179671.

18. "Touching a Mechanical Body: Tactile Contact With Intimate Parts of a Human-Shaped Robot is Physiologically Arousing," Jamy Li, Wendy Ju and Bryon Reeves; l International Communication Association Conference, Fukuoka, Japan, June 9–13, 2016.

19. Bonneau, Joseph. "The science of guessing: analyzing an anonymized corpus of 70 million passwords." 2012 IEEE Symposium on Security and Privacy. *IEEE*, 2012.

20. Charles P. Pfleeger, Shari Lawrence Pfleeger, and Jonathan Margulies. 2015. Security in Computing (5th Edition) (5th ed.). Prentice Hall Press, Upper Saddle River, NJ, USA.

21. Matt Bishop. 2004. Introduction to Computer Security. Addison-Wesley Professional.

22. William Stallings and Lawrie Brown. 2014. Computer Security: Principles and Practice (3rd ed.). Prentice Hall Press, Upper Saddle River, NJ, USA.

## CHAPTER 3

Starting Your Research

Knowing what science is does not make it clear how to perform research. Understanding the cyber domain and security thereof, does not enable a researcher to propose an experiment. While most of us were taught in primary school that science practice simply boils down to the scientific method, the reality of modern day research is more complicated than that. The scientific method is an abstract simplification of the processes researchers go through, but nothing is ever as straightforward or simple. Each research field has defined common methods of producing defensible and justifiable results. These methods change over time as technology improves and scientists find more efficient and effective ways. Each method is best suited to a class of research and it is good to follow each field's standards to enable comparative and easy reproducibility of results. In this chapter, we will introduce four categories of research: Theoretical, Observational, Experimental, and Applied Research. We will explain how to decide which form of research best suits the questions and problems the reader is confronting, and we provide pointers on how to begin the research process.

Science has provided the world with many answers. These answers are the foundation of our current technology and society. Inevitably, these answers and innovations will lead to new questions and new lines of inquiry. The field of cyber security is a nascent and fast-evolving domain. Currently, the scientific underpinnings of cyber security are lacking and we do not know how best to engineer systems to produce the results desired. Largely due to this, practitioners and researchers often cannot agree on terminology or core concepts. Two factors heavily contribute to the ever-changing nature of this subject; human agency and technological innovation. Cyber security, as introduced in Chapter 2, Science and Cyber Security, involves computing devices, networks, and users. The human element, both the user and the adversary, make for a complex and hard-to-study domain. Similarly, the rate of technological change, whether it is Moore's Law[1] or new mobile devices hitting the market, result in new paradigms, technological capacities, and heretofore unconsidered opportunities and security risks. Combined, the

Research Methods for Cyber Security. DOI: http://dx.doi.org/10.1016/B978-0-12-805349-2.00003-0

technosocial elements make cyber defenders and practitioners' job of understanding and protecting their systems all that much harder. Those who would endeavor to study, experiment, or theorize about the security of cyber systems face a commensurately hard challenge.

Deciding on what to research is as much art as anything else. There isn't a prescribed process that will lead to a good research topic. In school we are often presented with stories of falling apples[2] and accidental open windows.[3] However, let's dispel the eureka scientific achievements myth now. Research takes dedication and perseverance. Readers must realize that scientific progress is inevitably slow and steady. Eureka moments occur while doing slow and steady work that produces an unexpected result. Even if great discoveries are found, they must be validated, reproduced, and confirmed. The majority of scientists will only make progressive steps and do not make sudden leaps in achievements, unlike the portrayal of famous scientists we have all grown up studying. This is how science has always existed, while individually we may only make small steps, collectively we can make major forward progress.

Science, by its very nature, is a community effort. Classically, scientists would write letters to their colleagues to document their ideas and seek feedback, such as René Descartes' correspondences with Elisabeth, Princess Palatine of Bohemia, or Plato's letters to his contemporaries. In the modern era, the scientific community has embraced peer review, conferences, and journals as a means to not only review and validate work, but to share and communicate. Scientists strive to address biases, identify assumptions, and follow rigorous scientific methods. Practically, one of the ways scientists do this is by working in a team. Senior scientists will mentor and guide junior practitioners in universities, research laboratories, and similar institutions. This is not to say that science cannot occur in isolation or alone, but it will be hindered. However, with or without mentoring, science has evolved to include external validation. The peer review process, while not without its detractors, is purposefully designed to ensure competent, expert, impartial review of research. This is inherently a community effort. In addition, it is nearly inconceivable to have any field of research that does not build upon previous work or discovery. Even if researchers chose not to, or were precluded from publishing or communicating, the inspiration, foundations, and principles used in their research are predicated on an extant and vibrant scientific community.

Inspiration, insight, and questions for research can come from anywhere. While Hollywood depicts scientists at chalk boards or staring off into space to find inspiration, the real world is more prosaic. Often scientists are confronted by real-world problems or questions, such as the discovery of a new paradigm for command and control of malware, or a recent successful intrusion of a major corporation. And while their work might not be applying research to combat these problems, inspiration for theoretical and experimental research also comes from the world and perspective of the scientists. Linguistic and cultural paradigms will have profound effects on the type and approaches for research undertaken. Similar to how research is rarely performed in isolation, inspiration itself does not occur in a vacuum. Misunderstandings, previous failed research, and accidents can be as much inspiration as any other source. The critical step in conducting research is not the initial inspiration, but rather the follow through of it. A eureka moment is nothing without the diligent follow-through, review, dead ends, and stubborn dedication in adhering to an appropriate scientific method. Engineers cannot produce the next great intrusion detection system if you do not provide results that offer strong evidence and are understandable.

In this chapter we will discuss how to start your research. This includes the discussion of where to get and how to craft research questions. This flows into a discussion on an overview of the broad categories of research methods and what types of questions they are useful in answering. We then lay out a decision tree to help you pin down what category of research method is most appropriate for your current research. Once you have your research method decided we will guide you to the appropriate chapter that covers that research method category. While you can read this book in sequence it was designed to help you get answers and guidance on executing the research at hand.

CHAPTER OBJECTIVES

- Introduce the process of starting research
- Explain the different types of research, what they are best suited for, and how they fit together
- Help you decide which type of research via a branching decision tree
- Explain literature surveys and provide helpful resources
- Help define the next steps to executing your research

STARTING YOUR RESEARCH

Science is a journey of discovery and knowledge acquisition. Science seeks to answer questions and explain the riddles of the universe, as compared to engineering that seeks to design and develop solutions to address specific problems. In practice, the line between science and engineering is often quite blurred, as questions are answered in pursuit of solutions and engineering is required to even pose the questions needed. There are many people who comfortably perform roles as fully either scientists or engineers.

However, it seems that, especially in the field of cyber security, roles evolve and blend throughout a project or task. The principal investigator (PI) for a grant might design the experiment or study to address the pressing questions, but the PI might also lead design of a software system required to process or produce the datasets or analytics in questions. The key is to not get hung up on the roles of engineer or scientist, but to realize the appropriate application of engineering practices, or in our case scientific methods, to the work at hand.

The scientific process starts with a question. This question could be general or quite specific; it could be inspired by previous work, or events that are seemingly innocuous from your life outside of work. Whatever drives its inception, this question is core to what and how research is performed. What the question entails and how it is formed will have direct and indirect impact throughout the scientific process, so time spent refining and perfecting your scientific query can pay off significantly in reducing false starts and later on ensuring efficient execution. As Albert Einstein has been historically attributed as saying, "If we knew what we were doing it wouldn't be called research, would it?" In the process of your research, you may learn things that will require modifications to your question. Fear not, it's all part of the process. Acknowledging the imperfect and flawed nature of the pursuit of science is a crucial step in conducting research. The pursuit of the "perfect" scientific method or "flawless" approach to conducting research could quite easily blind the researcher to a partial solution, or worse prevent the researcher from discovering or acknowledging known flaws in the methodologies or analytical results. The end result of the scientific process is sharing the fruit of your efforts with others. This is very important to ensure that the rationale, limitations, and concerns are all documented from the start. This maintains scientific integrity, but moreover allows others to collaborate and build upon your work. There is truly no such thing as a scientific failure if you ensure that you follow these methods. Others will always be able to learn from your results. This diligence begins with the first step of creating a question.

The type of answer you are after will direct you to a different approach or category of scientific method. The practice of science is more complex than the simplistic framework taught in primary school. Owing to cyber security's hybridization of the social, natural, and formal sciences, it can get even more complicated than other fields. This book is designed to assist you in working through these complexities and define a rigorous research plan. The following sections will present a series of leading questions, with discussion and examples, that you should answer for your research. From your answers, we will direct you to another section of the book that is the next logical step for your research. Think of it like a Choose Your Own Adventure for research.

Hopefully, everyone has a eureka moment waiting for them as the culmination of the diligent application of cyber scientific methods from this book.

If at any time you feel that the text you are reading does not match your expectations for a research method, go back a step and reevaluate the path you have taken and the assumptions or expectations you have made. See if you can figure out if you answered a question ambiguously or did not understand our question. Try to determine why we think you should be doing one thing and why you think you should be doing something else. The authors clearly acknowledge that we are not infallible and we are distilling down a complex process. There is a real possibility you are doing something we could not have anticipated. If you do run into this situation, we suggest that you document your process and capture your assumptions, questions, and results along the way. There isn't really a wrong path as long as you clearly document what you are doing and your logic behind your decisions. Also, please feel free to reach out to us and we would be happy to discuss it with you. (Contact information is available in the authors' biographies.)

Initial Question Process

What is your research question?

Write it down. Think about it for a while.

Your question will lead you down a research path. We identify four categories of research in this book: Observational, Theoretical, Experimental, and Applied Research. These categories are separated around generalized scientific methods. Some may read these and think that some categories are "superior" to others. Know that we see them all as equally important and necessary components to the field. They are all complementary and essential.

Here is an example question and thought process. Recently the United States White House has been pushing for a passwordless society.[4,5] However, questions remain, like replacing the password with what, and is the password really all that worthless? These general ruminations could drive one to pose the following questions.

> What impact does poor motivation have on password strength? Alternatively are there inherent user limitations that prevent strong passwords viability?

The public articles about the so-called "death of the password," led rise to a line of questions about why passwords are so weak, and to what might we attribute the weakness. The next step after arriving at a question, like the one above, is to conduct a literature survey to explore this question. We will explore literature surveys in detail later in this chapter. After reviewing the research method options, perhaps the decision could be made to conduct an observational study with a group of university students, as an example.

In general, there really aren't any bad research questions as long as they are inquiring about a topic related to cyber security. However, the broader or more general a question the more difficult it is to answer. It is always best to attempt to break research questions down into as small atomic pieces as possible to help focus and guide your research. A question of "why are we bad at passwords?" is much easier to answer than "why is cyber security failing more frequently today?". This will happen naturally during the research process, but if you can do it sooner, it may help you target your research efforts sooner. And don't worry if, in breaking up your initial question, you generate a lot of research questions; that just means you have established a research plan for the foreseeable future (Fig. 3.1).

Research Progression

Often, when we are taught the research process, it is presented in its idealized form. The idealized model starts with the process of observing the world. When some phenomena of interest is noticed, a researcher then theorizes why that phenomenon exists and generates a hypothesis that would be present if the theory were true. To build evidence in support of or invalidate the theory, the researcher would then execute a test or experiment to generate evidence to determine if their hypothesis is true or false. With this newly gained knowledge, the researcher can go back to observing the world to start the process over and refine the knowledge.

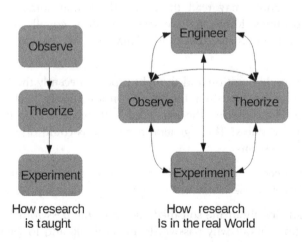

FIGURE 3.1
Idealized vs. Actual Research Progression.

DIG DEEPER: DEFINING HYPOTHESIS

A key concept to experimental data is the hypothesis. While we will go more in depth into how to handle a hypothesis and the characteristics of a good hypothesis in Chapter 9, Hypothetico-deductive Research, it is important that we define it now to help guide you in determining an appropriate research method.

A hypothesis is a predictive statement about how a system would behave under certain conditions. What this means is that, given current knowledge of a system, you will make a best guess on what will happen under certain conditions. A key differentiator from the research question is that is must be answerable, as in being able to, with evidence, conclude that the hypothesis is either true or false. Many hypotheses might be needed to fully answer a research question.

The idealized model really only works to answer the most basic of scientific questions. In reality, the research cycle is much more chaotic. The general steps between the idealized and real-world process are the same, although for completeness we added the application of knowledge in testing applied solutions as an additional step. However, the real-world model is more complex. A researcher can start in any of the steps, and the results of the step can lead to any of the other steps.

An observational study on user password behavior could lead to more questions that are directly answerable in a controlled experiment. A theoretical formalization of the progression of processing speed might only be corroborated by observation due to the inability to control the variables under study. Or, the results from an experiment could lead to a new understanding of a theoretical model that needs to be defined formally. Knowledge can be leveraged to engineer an application at any time, but what is highly prevalent in cyber security research right now, is the approach where a researcher engineers a system with an assumption of how cyber space works. Then, they will subsequently figure out how to test the theory, which is an approach we would not recommend. The better approach is to motivate your design and development with a foundation of theory or body of evidence from a study. You run the risk of an engineered failure or partial indeterminate success if you do not have the solid scientific foundations in place first. There are multiple factors that lead research to best fit in one of these steps. We will draw out a few answers around these variables to provide guidance and help determine what step best suits your current research.

In addition to the possibility of any path being taken between the phases, each one can be broken down into a set of research methods that include rigorous and methodical processes to achieve defendable results. The depths of each phase can be so deep for some cyber security topics that entire research programs can focus on executing just one step of the research process. As with each category, each research method is best suited to answer classes of questions. The heart of this book is broken up around the research categories, as Parts, and research methods, as Chapters. The rest of this chapter is focused on defining the different methods and guiding you to the most appropriate chapter to help you with your current cyber security research.

Observational Research

Observational research is useful when you are trying to understand a real cyber system (and the associated technosocial behavior). This type of research is best to answer open-ended or comparatively broad research questions. In general, **observational research** methods include sensing of real-world environments and data mining for discovery of interesting artifacts.

Observations are best for when you are trying to get a grasp of how a system behaves so you can generate theoretical models or learn enough to decide the most promising experiments upon which to expend your resources. For example, you may want to study cyber threat behavior in the wild to understand what types of targets and tactics the adversary will use. For example, a PI must first understand the adversary's behavior enough to comprehend they might detect or avoid virtual machines before they set up an experiment that includes a series of virtual honeypots. Then they might be able to validate a hypothesis that a category of threats target WordPress sites more than Django Framework sites.

The research methods from this category are also appropriate when you are trying to study something that is difficult to build around a controlled experiment. When studying things at the Internet scale, it is often difficult to create good representative experiments and it is impossible to create a replica, controllable Internet. Therefore, much like astronomy, this topic of research must try to understand phenomenology only from monitoring and then analyzing the real environment.

For the sake of organization, we have divided observational studies into three broad categories: exploratory, descriptive, and machine-learning studies. Throughout the years there have been several categorizations of research framework studies. And, we are confident that there will be more in the future. Our intent is not to introduce an end-all-be-all categorization of observational research. Instead, we are simply dividing the field into three manageable sections for the purposes of sharing methodologies with the reader.

Methods under this category of research:

- *Exploratory Study*: **Exploratory studies** consist of collecting, analyzing, and interpreting observations about known designs, systems, or models, or about abstract theories or subjects. These studies are largely an inductive process to gain understanding. When the experimental process goes from a general theory to an understanding in specific, exploratory studies observe specific phenomena to look for patterns and arrive at a general theory of behavior. The emphasis is on evaluation or analysis of data, not on creating new designs or models. The emphasis is on perspective and relative importance.
- *Descriptive Study*: The crucial distinction between a descriptive study and an exploratory study is the scope and generality of the observation. Where an exploratory study looks across a whole system, or many instances of a system, a **descriptive study** focuses in depth on a specific case of some system. For example, the larger exploratory study might look at adversarial behavior in general, and a descriptive study might focus on one hacker or one hacking team to understand their behavior in detail. There are also applied studies that look at effects of applied knowledge on specific cases of operational environments, but see the Applied Research section for more details.
- *Machine Learning*: **Machine learning** is a unique set of research methods that strives to automate the phases of the research cycle. Owing to the access to extraordinary amounts of data and the data science movement, machine learning has become a big part of the scientific process. While data is often hard to come by for certain endeavors in the cyber security field, machine learning is a useful and oft-used approach when there is sufficient data. Machine learning encapsulates a collection of mathematical techniques to detect correlations or generate models from data.

Theoretical Research

Theoretical research is a logical exploration of a system of beliefs and assumptions. This type of research includes theorizing or defining how a cyber system and its environment behave and then exploring or playing out the implications of how it is defined. This research is very valuable in understanding the bounds, edge cases, and emergent behaviors of a system. Often theoretical research is decried as out of touch with reality, so-called "ivory tower" research. Frankly, any research type or approach can run the risk of being irrelevant or out of touch if done incorrectly. In some scientific fields, theoretical research is so far ahead of engineering and technological progress that experiments to validate or refute them are hundreds of years away. In cyber security research, theoretical work often overlaps with mathematics, logic, or theory of computation; cryptography, of course, is a great example of this.

DID YOU KNOW?

Encryption, a fundamental building block of cyber security, is largely a theoretical field. All of the encryption algorithms we use today were designed around theoretical beliefs of computational power and its progression. Encryption works because those theories have remained consistent, but this may change as we are on the precipice of further technological breakthroughs, such as quantum computing.

In theoretical research, a scientist might postulate rules, conditions, and the state of a cyber system. This is the creation of a theoretical cyber model. This sort of approach is useful for cyber systems that are rare, expensive, or technologically infeasible today. These models can be used to help develop and inform questions for other types of cyber science. For example, while not the only way, theoretical models are a good way to develop hypotheses. A theoretical model will enable you to investigate how a cyber system would react under certain stimuli. Those theoretical reactions to the stimuli become strong candidates for hypotheses, which could subsequently lead to hypothetico-deductive experiments. Those tests could be used to generate a theoretical model on human usage of passwords of various sizes and then leverage an output from that model as a hypothesis to test against real-world cyber systems with controlled human subjects.

- *Formal Theory*: Formal theory and mathematical exploration are the basis for most of theoretical research. This is primarily due to the fact that theoretical work is in logical space where theories must be modeled and represented in some language. Mathematics is the perfect language suited to defining and exploring possibilities. As such, a lot of work involves formal proofs and internal validity. For example, most of the access control models that exist today are rooted in and derived from theoretical models that were formally proven. Formal methods is another example of formal theory. The field of Multiple Levels of Security (MLS) Operating Systems often uses formal methods to design, develop, and verify system performance and security.

  Formal theoretical research involves the definition of a formal theoretical space where formally tractable propositions, for example, lemmata and theorems and their proofs are described and developed. Generally, all cryptography and formal methods papers will fall into this class of research. But, of course, not all theoretical papers are cryptography and formal methods.

- *Simulation*: As cyber security research often explores very complex systems that are difficult to formally model, the rest of this category of research is covered by simulation. **Simulation** provides the ability to produce automated sampling of a large variable space to test and understand a theoretical model with enough confidence to move forward, while also reducing the test space enough to be computationally possible. New communication protocols and paradigms are often simulated to test their behavior in a broad range of cases before it becomes worth the cost to manufacture and test new communication devices.

Experimental Research

Experimental research covers what is often thought of when science is discussed: the experiment. This is the type of research where a scientist takes concepts and beliefs gained from observation and theorizing and creates targeted, controlled experiments in an attempt to generate evidence in support of, or in contradiction, to their premise.

DID YOU KNOW?

The term *hypothetico-deductive* was coined by William Whewell in the 19th century as a refinement of the inductive model that Francis Bacon started. Whewell was great at creating popular nomenclature and even coined the terms *scientist* and *physicist*, among others.

- *Hypothetico-Deductive*: The **hypothetico-deductive** type of research centers on hypotheses or predictions of behavior. The bulk of the work is the design of experiments and the rigorous collection of evidence for or against the hypotheses. This type of research is what is thought of as the traditional scientific method; formulate hypothesis or question, design and run the experiment to provide evidence for or against the hypothesis, revise the hypothesis, and repeat.
- *Quasi-Experiment*: A **quasi-experiment**, as the name indicates, is similar, but not identical to a formal experiment, as described previously. There can be several reasons for this. For example, imagine a researcher wants to conduct an experiment about secure communication over the Internet. She has a hypothesis about the performance behavior of the system under test. But because the researcher cannot control the network outside of her lab, let alone the Internet service provider (ISP), the Internet backbone, and various other steps along the way, she is not able to isolate, identify, and control the variables. The test can still be run, but without rigorous control of all independent variables, a true hypothetico-deductive experiment cannot be run, but instead a quasi-experiment can be conducted. The researcher will change the variables within her control, and acknowledge the variables outside of her control. An alternative

reason for a quasi-experiment is a researcher who can control all the known variables in the experiment, but does not have a specific hypothesis per se. For example, the same researcher previously wanted to study secure communication effects just within her lab, but she did not have a specific hypothesis to test at the time. Instead, she set up several experimental runs with various changes in various variables. The goal was to observe and study the quasi-experimental runs to gather enough information to create a hypothesis, that could be used in a subsequent hypothetico-deductive experiment.

Applied Research

Applied research is a little different that the rest of the methods described previously, which are all considered basic research. **Applied research** is the process of quantifying how well we applied the knowledge we have learned from basic science to solving some problem. Here we use similar techniques to basic research, but the goals of the research are different. **Basic research** is the process to rigorously explore and understand the interaction of variables in a system. However, applied research is a process to rigorously understand and quantify how effective an engineered system is at solving the problem for which it was designed. The key distinction is a preconceived "problem" that needs "solving." Applied research includes designing, implementing, and testing systems. Applied research often utilizes experimental rigor but is mostly focused on understanding the performance of an engineered system or application, like the true/false positive rate of an intrusion detection algorithm.

- *Applied experimentation*: An **applied experiment** is the execution of a controlled test to determine how a system performs. It is often beneficial for context to compare applied experiments to other solution options. These experiments include the use of benchmarks or validation tests to investigate the performance of engineered systems. For example, an industrial researcher is tasked with comparing the next-generation malware disassembler. He decides to conduct an experiment to evaluate the performance against the company's previous generation, as well as two competitor products. The results of the experiment would help developers and marketers prepare the technology for sales, and if released to the public, would help other researchers understand the performance of malware disassemblers.
- *Applied observational study*: The applied version of an **observational study** includes applied exploratory and descriptive studies. Applied exploratory study is the process of observing and studying how an engineered system behaves in different situations. For bounds testing the goal is to study how a system performs under extreme conditions.

Sensitivity analysis looks what inputs an engineered system are sensitive to and by what scale. Applied descriptive studies follow the deployment of an engineered system or process into a real-world situation to see how it performs. The researcher in an observational study tries not to inject, influence, or bias the observed system or phenomena. On the other hand, in an applied study the researcher deliberately introduces a change or perturbation into the system. This change, if it was in a controlled environment, could be an experiment, but in an open system is instead an applied observational case study. For example, imagine a scientist who would like to understand how a new password policy would affect an organization. After getting all appropriate approvals and Institutional Review Board (IRB) evaluation, she is able to convince the management at her university to implement the new policy. Without the ability to control the entire environment (university setting) the scientist is able to observe and collect information about the new password policy in an actual functioning system. Note that case studies can be used in both observational science and applied research.

RESEARCH BEFORE THE RESEARCH

Before setting up and running potentially expensive studies or experiments, it is prudent and necessary to first fully understand what is already known and where the research community stands on the topic. Scientific understanding is built up over time and it is important to understand what knowledge exists to produce useful and progressive results from new research.

Reviewing literature is helpful in providing insights into your cyber system of interest and also what knowledge already exists and through what means it was gathered, both of which are helpful in deciding where you should take your research. Ask yourself: is your topic already heavily researched or fairly untouched? Do you have a new perspective on the problem? Do you have a theory about the cyber system that is different than or contrary to current theories? At the end of this chapter, we will work through these questions and how they fit into how one decides what is the most prudent research path. However, it is critical that you have studied enough of the previous work to be able to answer these questions with confidence. If you are unsure of an answer, then you probably need to continue with your literature search.

There are a few ways to go about a literature search. The first is to perform a keyword search. Most publishers require a list of keywords in each paper to help with this process. To start, generate a list of keywords that surround your research question. Aim for a list of 5 to 10, and be as specific as possible with keywords that scope your topic. For example, if you want to understand user cognitive capacity for passwords, you might create a list of keywords such as cognitive load, password, computer security, authentication, and human factors. A good keyword is specific enough to limit the results to the topic of interest, but general enough to ensure that the resultant search includes a broad coverage of work on the topic and does not limit to a small subfield of research.

Online academic literature databases and search engines have made performing keyword searches quite easy. Publisher search capabilities such as IEEE Xplore[6] or the Association for Computing Machinery Digital Library[7] are good options or try search engines that query across multiple databases such as Engineering Village 2,[8] CiteSeerX,[9] CiteUlike.[10] Every database and search engine has a little different flavor and covers a different set of fields and topics, so it is good to search across multiple databases and make sure you pick the most appropriate set for the keywords and topic.

> **DID YOU KNOW?**
>
> Currently, a good set of computer science search engines are: Engineering Village 2,[8] ACM digital library,[7] IEEE Xplore,[6] ISI web of knowledge,[11] ScienceDirect,[12] CiteSeerX,[9] arxiv,[13] SpringerLink,[14] and Wiley Online Library,[15] but there are search engines and databases that cover other fields that may also include work of interest.

Going back to our example question of user cognition for passwords, it would be apt to search across traditional computer science and engineering, but also searching something like PsycINFO[16] would also be prudent, given the psychology aspect of the research question. Starting with a search using something such as ScienceDirect[12] or Google Scholar[17] is a good start, as it covers a broad range of journals and topics.

Other than a keyword search, another good method of finding papers to review is to look at recent papers on or around the topic of which you are already aware. From these papers you can then start to do an iterative, intelligent crawl of the references to look for additional papers (this is in essence snowball sampling, which we discuss in Chapter 4, Exploratory Study). Look at when the references are cited in the text and their titles to determine the best papers to review in the next cycle of papers. Also, pay attention to the quality of the paper as better papers will often be based on a stronger understanding of the literature. Iterating this way for five to seven times should give you a fairly large corpus of data with which to start.

We should mention that a lot of databases require a fee for subscription to read their papers. There is a strong and growing movement to provide free access to publications, and so more and more publishers are providing access to papers and new open paper portals such as arxiv. We support this movement to open access to research as understanding, building, and comparing to previous research is critical to the knowledge-building process. However, there is a business aspect to the scientific world that cannot be ignored, therefore some of the highest impact conferences are fee publishers, so it is important to weigh the potential impact of a paper. Additionally, there is a dark side to "free"/open publishing. Several publishers have started to charge sometimes exorbitant amounts to publish in return for allowing anyone to subscribe and read for free. The problem is that this essentially becomes a pay-to-publish scenario and the integrity of peer review comes into question. In general, well reviewed and regarded journals and conferences avoid these pitfalls but be on the lookout for such practices as open publishing continues to flourish.

The benefits of conducting a literature review or "lit search" are twofold. First and foremost, the review of previous work will help to inform your own approach, ideas, theories, or hypothesis, as explained previously. The second is to ensure a sufficient review of the landscape so that you can convince yourself, and any reviewer of your work, that you have diligently evaluated the work of others, to ensure that you are not accidentally duplicating, overlapping, or worst of all, fraudulently copying other work.

Once you have a corpus of papers to review, there are a few different objectives you want to gain from the information acquired from the literature survey analysis. The first and most obvious is to understand what research has been done and if the question you have posed has been sufficiently answered. The second is to help you determine what type of research you should be performing to best contribute to the community. This can include changing the research method to understand a different perspective of the question or attempting to reproduce a result to increase the confidence in a theory. The third objective of the literature survey is to prepare you for writing your results paper after the research is complete (we go into depth on how to write good research at the end of each research method chapter).

You will largely have to learn how to organize your papers to best suit these objectives and your work process. However, an approach to get started is to parse out the information from the papers along a few different categories: the research question they are asking, the conclusions, and the methods used to produce the result. Organizing the information from the papers in this manner enables you to quickly look to see what questions were asked and answered to determine if they have tried to answer your specific research. If you think any of them have, then you can assess the quality of the previous work. Ask if they have fully answered the question and if you believe they missed an assumption or had a bias. If there are multiple papers that answer your question, is there consensus? If not, then it might be worth proceeding to attempt your own research to answer the question. If yes, then is there a specific paper that makes a crucial statement that is worth reproducing? Reviewing how the work was performed and documented by the paper is just as crucial in determining the research path as the results of the papers.

DIG DEEPER: FALSIFIABILITY

A fundamental understanding in the philosophy of science is that, as limited observers subjected to the principles of the world we are trying to study, we cannot actually prove the existence of a model of the world. To achieve a more deductive process from our natural inferential operation, a falsifiable hypothesis is key. To read more into the philosophy of science look at *The Logic of Scientific Discovery*.[18]

SELECTING YOUR RESEARCH PATH

This section will help you select the appropriate category of research: Observational, Theoretical, Experimental, or Applied. Selecting the most appropriate type of research is a function of multiple factors. Some of these factors are tied to being scientifically rigorous, such as how much is currently known on the subject, your expectations of system behavior, the scale, and controllability of the system being studied. The rest include pragmatic issues such as the resources available to you and availability of realistic environments and data. Rigor and scientific validity are the most important aspects of science, but pragmatic issues with your career and research finances must also be considered. Realize that no science is conducted in an ideal vacuum (metaphorically) and that all research processes must include these real-world issues. We think it is important to acknowledge these practical factors that will impact how real research gets accomplished. While it is impossible to create a general process to select the appropriate research for all situations, in this section we will walk you through the process and provide a work flow that will lead you to a research method.

Fig. 3.2 is an attempt to boil this process down to a decision tree. Starting at the top of the tree, there are a series of paths that end at a category of research. The flow of each path intersects a series of questions. The answers to each question provide you with the direction of the path to follow to the next question, and ultimately, a proscribed research category. Later in the chapter, there are research category decision trees to help you discover ultimately which research method may be best suited for your research.

Walking the Decision Tree

The decision tree in Fig. 3.2 is an attempt to turn the many variables of deciding research methods into a pictorial question flow. By answering the questions in the tree and following the path of each answer, you will be directed to a category of research. However, there is context and thought behind each question that might need to be explained for you to fully understand and answer. This section explains each question and what issues might drive you down certain paths. At the end of this section, we will walk you through an example of using the decision tree to determine the appropriate research category for a question. Let's get started!

While there could be multiple starting points in deciding a research category, a good starting point is to first look at what you know and expect of the research question. Is your research question about a system that your team developed? Is your goal to understand the performance or ability of something in solving a problem? If the answer to any of these questions is yes, then this is applied research and you can already stop. If it is about other extant systems that you just want to better understand, then it is basic research and further questions require answering to determine the best-fit research category and method.

If your question is about an existing system, do you have a hypothesis about it? While we will describe what constitutes a good hypothesis in Chapter 9, Hypothetico-deductive Research, at this stage do you feel like you have a strong understanding of the system you want to study and confidence in how it will behave under a specific situation? If yes, then you have a hypothesis. Is your hypothesis looking at normal system behavior or at boundary and black swan, or very rare, event conditions that are hard to create in a real system? If you want to study unique cases and you have the resources to create and control them, then experimental research is a good path. On the other hand, if you do not have the resources, theoretical research is a better fit.

The field of cyber security is often about behavior and conditions at the edge. Adversaries strive to take advantage of emergent and poorly understood system behavior to gain advantage in pursuit of their objectives. While statistically the occurrence of black swan events are quite rare, when one studies the field of cyber security, whether you know it or not, you might be dealing with boundary conditions and black swans. This becomes quite important to understand and recognize because, as Dr. Talib describes in his book, *Black Swan*,[19] rare events are often retroactively explained, and the public, or indeed a researcher's ability to predict the likelihood of a rare cyber event is fraught with assumptions or failures. For the purposes of cyber security research, it is important to explore the idea of outliers. Determine if the

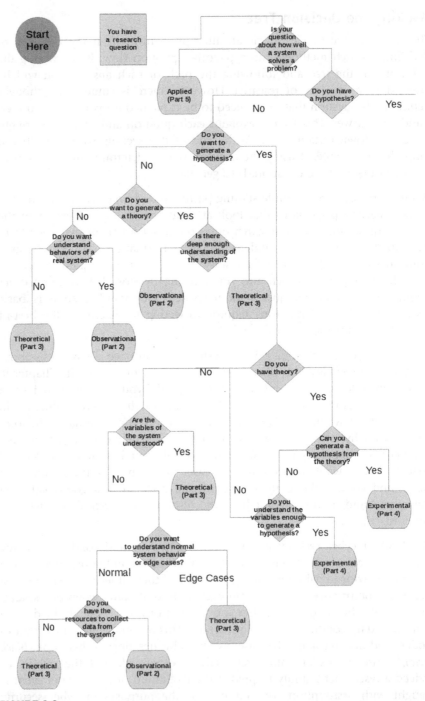

FIGURE 3.2

Cyber Security Research Method Decision Tree.

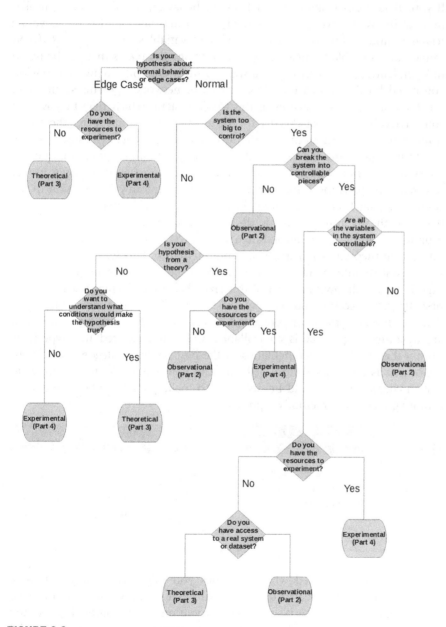

FIGURE 3.2
(continued)

question you are asking might fall within such a category and be open to the idea of reclassifying your question if the research progresses and seems like it might change, in either direction.

If your hypothesis is about normal system behavior, the scale and controllability of the system will determine the best research category. Do you have the resources and ability to control the different variables of the system? If you cannot, are you able to break the system into smaller pieces that can be tested independently? For instance, if you want to study enterprise network behavior, you could break it down into departments or network segments so that you can look at a smaller fraction of the whole system, which may be easier to control and be more cost-effective for the research. You could merge the results from each piece to get an understanding of the whole system (be sure to document this segregation and capture all steps along the way). If you cannot break the system up, but you have access to a real system or data, then observational research is perhaps most appropriate. You could explore your question in the context of your home institutions data or from open datasets of information that is publically available. If you do not have the resources or if you want to explore the ramifications beyond the realm of technological (or funding) feasibility, then theoretical research is a good alternative. Finally, if you can break up the system into smaller tractable pieces or you have the resources to run experiments with environments of this size, then experimental research is the best direction because you will be able to have the most control and confidence of the end results of your work. If, on the other hand, the system you are hypothesizing about is controllable, and you generated the hypothesis from a theory, then experimentation is the best research category. Yet if your hypothesis is not derived from a theory and you would like to explore what system characteristics would be necessary to make your hypothesis true, then exploring theoretical methods is prudent.

DID YOU KNOW?

While access to useful and validated data for cyber security research continues to be an issue, there are some publicly available sources such as:

https://www.predict.org/

http://www.data.gov/

http://www.caida.org/data/

http://www.pcapr.net/

So far, we have explored what categories you might select if you have a hypothesis for your research question, but what if you do not? If you have not yet posited a hypothesis, do you think you understand enough about the topic from previous research or the literature survey to generate a hypothesis?

If yes, is there a theory or set of theories that you or others have that you could use to generate a hypothesis? A theory that supports the generation of a hypothesis is one that is clearly stated or is a model that enables you to generate a prediction of behavior given some input. If there aren't any theories, or they are not developed enough to generate a hypothesis, do you think you understand the variables enough to create a hypothesis even without a general theory? In either case, if you can produce a hypothesis, then testing that hypothesis is potentially a good approach and experimental research is the path to choose. If there isn't a theory to help generate a hypothesis, is there deep enough understanding of the topic to enable you to generate a theory? If you don't have enough understanding, do you want to understand edge cases of the system? Or, if you want to understand normal behavior, are your resources limited such that you are unable to observe and collect data from the system you want to study? If you answered yes to any of these questions, then theoretical research is well suited for your research. Otherwise, observational research methods would be more effective.

Now that we have discussed each series of questions in the decision tree, let us walk through an example of selecting a category for a research question. A common starting place is a study. If you don't understand enough about the environment to make a hypothesis, or there is a lack of research covering your topic, a study will help gain initial insights and define a future research path to start nailing down theories defining the system. Let us revisit the password questions from the previous section to see how the decision tree will lead us to the observational research category.

> What impact does poor motivation have on password strength? Alternatively are there inherent user limitations that prevent strong password viability?

Given that question, what path might we take to arrive at the appropriate research category? Looking at Fig. 3.2, we will start at the very top. The first question asks if our question is about "how well a system solves a problem." We are definitely not that far along, so we answer "no." Next it asks, "Do you have a hypothesis?" We do not currently have a hypothesis about this topic, but we did start with some specific questions that we have narrowed down, so "no" for that one, too. The next question asks if we "would like to generate a hypothesis," and while we would like to go down the road, we decide that we are not quite ready for that step, and so select "no." The next question prompts us to consider theory, "Do you want to generate a theory?" This forces us to figure out what is meant by theory. After reviewing the section on Theoretical Research (Part III of this book) and our own investigation of theory (online searching and reviewing a few papers that discuss cyber security theory), we decide that we are also not ready to generate a theory. After following the decision tree down one more level we are confronted with the question that asks, "Do we want to understand the behavior of a real system?" And we quickly decide that we can answer this with an emphatic "yes!" All of our questions were motivated by a desire to study the process and system of password use in society. And there is nothing more real, or realistic, than actual human users. Finally, after answering "yes," we learn that indeed it seems like we should consider observational approaches, and we can turn to Part II: Observational Research to explore how we might design our study.

At this point, we have discussed a decision tree for category selection, along with an example of using it. If you have a research question selected, you should have been able to discover the category of research to investigate further. However, knowing a category does not give you a specific research method to utilize. Under each category there are sets of research methods that could be used. You will need to select the appropriate method that is most relevant to your work and is better suited to answer the questions to further your understanding of the topic. The following series of sections, divided by category, will provide further discussion of the trade-offs and capabilities of the different research methods to help you determine the most appropriate type of cyber security research to undertake (Fig. 3.3).

Observation Method Selection

As we discussed before, there are a few different research methods to perform observational research. Traditional exploratory observational studies leverage statistical methods to help collect data and to analyze the data to infer causal relationships between variables. Descriptive studies are good for studying specific instances of a system in operation. Finally, machine learning is useful when you have access to a lot of data and want to automate a model for prediction or hypothesis generation without fully understanding the causal inferences. Let us discuss some general issues that will help you in deciding the appropriate method.

If you already have a dataset, do you want to create a model to generate predictions or do you want to try to discover and understand causalities? Machine learning techniques are generally better at taking data and automatically or semiautomatically generating a model that can then provide predictions about future behavior. However, it is not always clear which salient data features caused the model to generate certain predictions. Traditional observational studies, on the other hand, use statistical methods to try to discover relationships between variables and infer causalities. With observational studies you might get strong beliefs about some variables, but not have a complete system model of behavior.

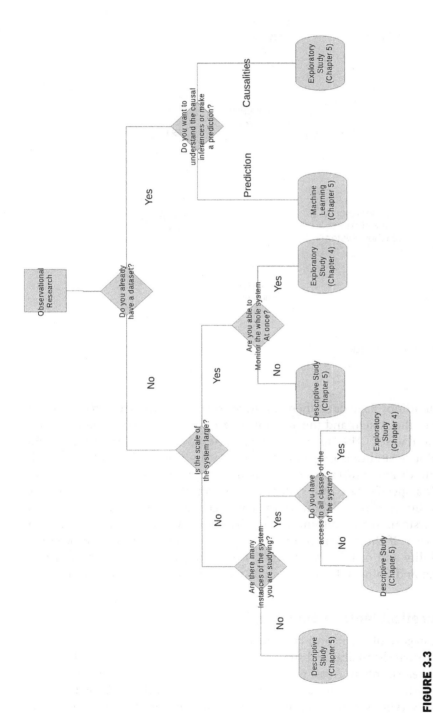

FIGURE 3.3

Cyber Security Observational Research Method Decision Tree.

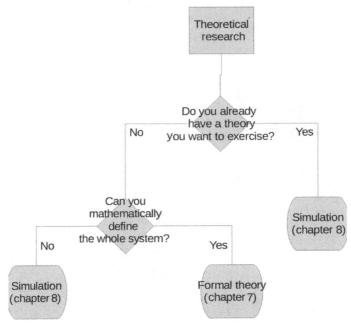

FIGURE 3.4
Cyber Security Theoretical Research Method Decision Tree.

If you do not have data, then you need to evaluate your research from the scale of the system and the amount of resources you have available to collect a dataset. The major difference from observational studies and descriptive studies is that an observational study attempts to observe a full system, or many instances of a system, and descriptive studies examine in depth a specific case of a system or a subset of a system. If you have the capability to collect data from the complete system, or from all classes of that system, then performing an observational study will be the best approach. If the system you want to study is large, you do not have the capability and/or resources to collect data, maybe finding a subset of that system and doing a descriptive study would be a better fit (Fig. 3.4).

Theoretical Method Selection

The category of theoretical cyber security research contains two main methods, formal theoretical and simulation. The theoretical aspects of cyber security research often cross over into other research fields. As mentioned previously, cryptography and cryptanalysis are research fields that involve not only cyber security, but also mathematics, theory of computation, and linguistics. The interdisciplinary nature can make theoretical cyber security research sometimes dissimilar to the other research categories. The key concepts in theoretical research are to define abstract concepts, either mathematical or computational models that define the cyber universe. From those self-contained, abstract universe questions, thought exercises and predictions can be made.

To decide whether or not you should conduct a formal theoretical approach or leverage a simulation method depends on both the interests and resources available to the investigator. First, if you are working with an existing theory, or are close to a having a defined theory and want to exercise it to evaluate how it holds up under various conditions you might not have considered, you could conduct a simulation. Alternatively, if you do not have a well-defined theory, but you can constrain and describe the situation with mathematical constraints or using mathematical nomenclature, such as formal methods, you could conduct a formal theoretical effort. Finally, if you do not have a theory, and you are unable to define the concepts in precise mathematical notations, you can create an exploratory simulation to flesh out your concepts and provide some early input to help determine where to take the research next (Fig. 3.5).

Experimental Method Selection

The experimental category is often what is most often considered "science," researchers with laboratory coats and test tubes performing well-documented experimental procedures in the pursuit of furthering science. While that is undoubtedly true, experimentation in cyber security is often messier and complicated by the unique characteristics of the cyber domain. Two methods of cyber security experimentation are possible in this category, the first is hypothetico-deductive and the second is quasi-experimental.

The key factors for determining whether or not you should pursue a hypothetico-deductive-based experiment are straightforward and twofold. First, do you have a sufficiently refined hypothesis that is ready for testing? Have you matured and revised the hypothesis such that it can be falsified? That is to say, can you conclusively reject your hypothesis if your experimental results provide sufficient evidence? Sometimes a researcher might want to write a hypothesis with enough "wiggle room" to enable future testing. This room for ambiguity means that little confidence can be ascribed to the end results. The more precise the hypothesis, the easier it is to understand if the results refute, or corroborate the line of inquiry. The second factor is one of control. You must have an environment with sufficient control to ensure that

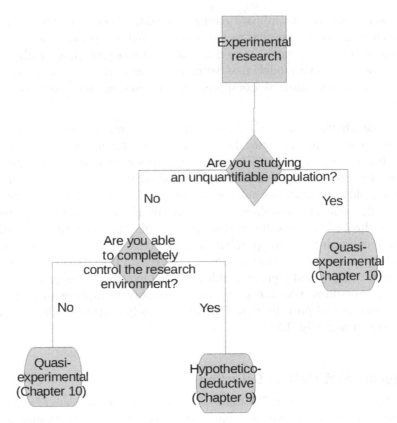

FIGURE 3.5
Cyber Security Experimental Research Method Decision Tree.

the system under test is only subjected to the planned variables, and not to other external factors.

The second type of experimentation that can be done in this category is called quasi-experimental. The reason that this line of inquiry cannot be rightly called hypothetico-deductive typically comes about for two reasons. The first reason is that the researcher cannot control the experimental environment with sufficient fidelity to ensure that only the variables are under test change, and that external factors do not accidentally confound the resultant output. A lack of full control is quite common. Factors such as Internet communication or issues with human subjects are often too complex to reproduce and sufficiently control in a laboratory setting, and as such warrant a different experimental approach (Fig. 3.6).

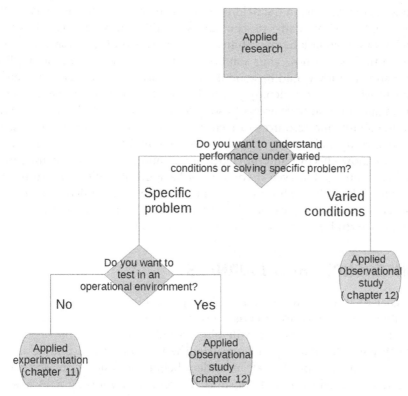

FIGURE 3.6
Cyber Security Applied Research Method Decision Tree.

Applied Method Selection

Applied research is largely when you are testing and evaluating an application of science to solve a real-world problem. There are two research methods that cover applied research: applied experiments and applied observational studies. Deciding between performing applied experiments or observational studies largely comes down to your expectations. If you want to understand how a solution performs against a specific problem, then applied experiments are the appropriate path. If instead you want to understand the performance of a system under varied conditions, then applied observational studies should be fruitful. For applied experimentation, if the field of comparable solutions already has and supports benchmarking, then it might be good to follow that standard so that you can compare your solution. For example, in the field of antivirus there are different benchmarks that people use annually to compare the different solutions. However, benchmarks often lack in their ability to cover real-world situations, so if you want to understand how your solution works in the real world, an applied observational study would be good if you have access to an operational environment where you can deploy your solution. If there aren't any established benchmarks, do you have access to some of the similar solutions, or do you have the ability and resources to recreate them? If you do, then it is best to execute a comparative study that showcases the results where you can easily determine how effective and different your solution performs in comparison to other solutions. But even if you do not have the ability to do a comparative study with other solutions, attempt to create a controlled test of your application. You want clear results so that others in the future can perform comparative studies with their solutions against yours.

CONFERENCES AND JOURNALS

The goal of this chapter is to introduce you the various types of research available to cyber security scientists along the way. When you progress into the subsequent chapters, we will also include an outline of a possible research paper for that type of research. The purpose of this outline is not meant to constrain, but to help provide a helpful scaffold upon which you can build your evidence and construct the results of your effort in a well-crafted and intelligible manner. The goal of research publications is to explain a finding or convince the audience of your conclusions. The more evidence you offer and questions you can anticipate will make your paper more effective. The outline is a template to help the reader understand what sort of evidence may be required for a paper in the field of that research method, and to assist in marshaling one's thoughts and evidence in an organized manner. We want to emphasize that the outlines are not meant to be prescriptive and limiting, but useful as a starting place when you begin to write your findings.

We believe it is worth noting that different scientific disciplines publish and disseminate information in different ways. Without speaking on behalf of other scientific fields, computer science, and cyber security, even more so, rely on conferences as a primary means of communication. This is often attributed to the dynamic and rapid pace of change in the cyber domain (as described in detail in Chapter 2, Science and Cyber Security). The speed of journal publications is often a slow and gradual process, whereas conferences and workshops are typically annual and have much quicker notification time frames. The claim is that the rapid change in the domain might render research publications obsolete or irrelevant by the time of publication.

Whether or not this is true, the field is indeed dominated by conferences. A list of a few top-quality venues might include:

- IEEE Symposium on Security and Privacy
- ACM Conference on Computer and Communication Security
- USENIX Security

There are also venues such as: Learning from Authoritative Security Experiment Results (LASER) and Workshop of Cyber Security Experimentation and Test (USENIX CSET), which focus on the science and experimentation of cyber security. Finally, there are large events such as DEFCON, CanSecWest, Black Hat, RSA conference, and many other enthusiast and general audience venues. For those interested in academic rankings, we have found Dr. Guofei Gu's,[20] and Dr. Jianying Zhou's[21] ranking websites useful in discovering and evaluating academic venues. Additionally, IEEE maintains a calendar with useful venues throughout the year.[22] The use of journals in cyber security is to share a larger corpus of work, perhaps a dissertation, or a collection of individual experiments (that perhaps would be worthy of a conference publication individually). The conferences are dynamic, with many competing ad-hoc positions and claims. Ideally, these claims would be substantiated and corroborated by the research field and documented in the slower moving and more consistent journals. To delineate between the two, conference papers are well suited to each iteration of research, but journals may include multiple interactions within or across fields of research to start forming a strong understanding and contribute as a whole to the field of work.

Endnotes

1. Moore, Gordon E., *Cramming More Components onto Integrated Circuits*, Electronics, Volume 38, Number 8, 1965.
2. Stukeley, William. *Memoirs of Sir Isaac Newton's Life*. Taylor and Francis, 1936.
3. Haven, Kendall. *Marvels of Science: 50 Fascinating 5-Minute Reads*. Libraries Unlimited, Inc., PO Box 6633, Englewood, CO 80155-6633, 1994.
4. "The White House Cybersecurity Czar Wants to Kill Your Password." *Five by Five*. N.p., October 09, 2014. Web. October 15, 2015. <http://blogs.rollcall.com/five-by-five/the-white-house-cybersecurity-czar-wants-to-kill-your-password/>.
5. Kemp, Tom. "Despite Privacy Concerns, It's Time to Kill the Password." *Forbes*. Forbes Magazine, July 18, 2014. Web. October 15, 2015. <http://www.forbes.com/sites/frontline/2014/07/18/despite-privacy-concerns-its-time-to-kill-the-password/>.
6. "IEEE Xplore Digital Library." *IEEE Xplore Digital Library*. Web. November 1, 2015. <http://ieeexplore.ieee.org/Xplore/home.jsp>.
7. "ACM Digital Library." *ACM Digital Library*. N.p., n.d. Web. November 1, 2015. <http://dl.acm.org/>.
8. *Engineering Village*. Elsevier B.V., n.d. Web. November 1, 2015. <http://www.engineeringvillage.com/>.
9. CiteSeerX Index. Pennsylvania State University, n.d. Web. November 1, 2015. <http://citeseerx.ist.psu.edu/>.

10. "CiteULike: Everyone's Library." *CiteULike: Everyone's Library*. Oversity Ltd, n.d. Web. November 1, 2015. <http://www.citeulike.org/>.

11. "Web of Science - Please Sign In to Access Web of Science." *Web of Science*. Thomson Reuters, n.d. Web. November 1, 2015. <https://www.webofknowledge.com/>.

12. "ScienceDirect." *ScienceDirect*. Elsevier B.V., n.d. Web. November 1, 2015. <http://www.sciencedirect.com/>.

13. "ArXiv.org." *E-Print Archive*. Cornell University Library, n.d. Web. November 1, 2015. <http://arxiv.org/>.

14. "SpringerLink." *Home - Springer*. Springer International Publishing AG, n.d. Web. November 1, 2015. <http://link.springer.com/>.

15. "Wiley Online Library." *Wiley Online Library*. John Wiley & Sons, Inc., n.d. Web. November 1, 2015. <http://onlinelibrary.wiley.com/>.

16. "PsychINFO." *PsychINFO*. American Psychological Association, n.d. Web. November 1, 2015. <http://www.apa.org/pubs/databases/psycinfo/index.aspx>.

17. "Google Scholar." *Google Scholar*. Google, n.d. Web. November 1, 2015. <https://scholar.google.com/>.

18. Popper, Karl R. *The Logic of Scientific Discovery*. New York: Harper & Row, 1968. Print.

19. Taleb, Nassim N. *The Black Swan: The Impact of the Highly Improbable*. New York: Random House, 2007. Print.

20. Gu, Guofei. "Security Conference Ranking and Statistic." *Security Conference Ranking and Statistic*. N.p., n.d. Web. October 7, 2015. <http://faculty.cs.tamu.edu/guofei/sec_conf_stat.htm>.

21. Zhou, Jianying. *Top Crypto and Security Conferences Ranking*. N.p., September 2015. Web. October 7, 2015. <http://icsd.i2r.a-star.edu.sg/staff/jianying/conference-ranking.html>.

22. "IEEE Cipher S & P Calendar." *IEEE Cipher S & P Calendar*. IEEE Cipher, October 20, 2015. Web. November 1, 2015. <http://www.ieee-security.org/Calendar/cipher-hypercalendar.html>.

Observational Research Methods

Truth in science is always determined from observational facts.

David Douglass

## CHAPTER 4

Exploratory Study

Observational research, of which exploratory study is a subset, is useful when you are trying to understand a real cyber system (technosocial behavior). This type of research is suited to answer open-ended or comparatively broad research questions. In general, observational research methods include sensing of real-world environments and data mining for discovery of interesting artifacts. If you were lead here from the previous chapter, it means you want to answer research questions or understand a system better but you don't necessarily have a preconceived conceptual hypothesis of behavior. Or you are trying to study an uncontrollable system. If this is accurate then this chapter will provide an introduction to research methods that will be helpful in executing your research.

In this chapter we will introduce the first category of observational studies, exploratory studies. Exploratory studies consist of collecting, analyzing, and interpreting observations about known designs, systems, or models, or about abstract theories or subjects. Studies are largely an inductive process to gain understanding. Where the experimental process goes from a general theory to an understanding in specific, studies look at specific phenomena to search for patterns and arrive at a general theory of behavior. The emphasis is on evaluation or analysis of data, not on creating new designs or models. This is often called a qualitative study in the social and health sciences. The emphasis is on perspective and relative importance.

Exploratory studies are often, but do not have to be, a starting place for research. When you have no expectations or beliefs about how a system operates but you want to study and understand it, exploratory study is a helpful method. By observing the world around us we can start to discover patterns and sequences of events that can lead to understanding the underlying principles and laws of behavior. Exploratory studies enable researchers to start developing models of system operation.

As some aspects of cyber security is practically uncontrollable, such as threats, when exploring topics and research questions around uncontrollable variables, exploratory studies are a useful approach to discover information

95

Research Methods for Cyber Security. DOI: http://dx.doi.org/10.1016/B978-0-12-805349-2.00004-2

about a system. Quasi-experimental methods discussed in Chapter 10, Quasi-experimental Research, may also be useful methods to investigate. In this chapter, we will discuss different exploratory research methods and when they are useful. Examples will be used to demonstrate concepts.

CHAPTER OBJECTIVES

- Discuss data collection as it relates to observational studies
- Introduce the different types of exploratory studies
    - Ecological
    - Longitudinal/Cohort studies
    - Cross-sectional
    - Case-control studies
- Explain analysis bias
- Discuss the design and presentation of exploratory studies

KNOWLEDGE BY INFERENCE

Among some in the community, observational research is held in a lower regard than hard experimental research. You can just turn on the television and comedic sitcoms will poke fun at psychologists, sociologists, and other so-called soft sciences. We take the view that science is just the process of gaining knowledge and there are a suite of methods that are the tools by which we perform science. Not every scientific question can be broken down into an experiment to be answered. Before we start discussing observational research methods, it is important to address these criticisms.

One of the first criticisms is that ascribing variables to resultant patterns is difficult. While this is true, pattern matching is widely used not only in machine learning (see Chapter 6, Machine Learning, for more in-depth discussion) but also in experimental research. Furthermore, patterns are useful with sufficient information and analytical techniques, and they can be used to identify causality.

Second, inductive reasoning seems to have fallen out of favor. While the purely rational modern scientific mind seems to favor hypothetico-deductive reasoning above all else, scientific observers of all kinds leverage their accumulated experiences and observations to inform their research. Taleb's Black Swan[1] scenario is sometimes used to argue against inductive reasoning. For example, if a field biologist spends his lifetime observing, documenting, and studying the characteristics, behavior, and life cycle of the North American white swan to only learn late in life that black swans exist in Australasia, this somehow refutes a lifetime of work. In reality, this couldn't be further from the truth. At worst, it becomes a footnote on the pages describing the various colors heretofore observed in North America. But the existence of a black swan, somewhere else, does not nullify the inductive research on mating habits, or migratory behaviors. Inductive reasoning is intrinsically uncertain. This uncertainty fits in very well with the complex cyber domain.

Third, observational studies are accused of being anecdotes, stories, or one-off observations. And yet the most interesting findings often start with, "and while this observation is anecdotal..." Observations need not be the end-all or final determinate, rather they should be used as a springboard and starting point for further exploration. The human narrative is already an intrinsic aspect of cyber space, from social media to reliable delivery of information. The point is not to place too much, or too little, stake in inductive evidence, but collections of evidence over time that can and should be quite persuasive. One need only look at the legal community to understand the powers of inductive (and deductive) reasoning in action.

DIG DEEPER: ON THE RELATIVE MERITS OF OBSERVATIONAL STUDY

Sagarin et al. provide an insightful discussion on the limits and strengths of observational research in their book "Observation and ecology: broadening the scope of science to understand a complex world."[2] Furthermore, they discuss the counter arguments and prejudices against observational research, such as does not use strong inference, and is not binary falsifiable. The book's authors summarize criticism into four types:

> (1) observation-based studies find patterns, but patterns can't be used to infer process; (2) observation-based studies rely on the flawed approach of induction, rather than the more precise deductive approach, to reach conclusions; (3) they are just a collection of unreplicated anecdotes; and (4) they rely too much on correlations between variables.[3]

Sagarin et al. continue to point out the utility of correlations and inductive reasoning.[4] While fully acknowledging the continued point that correlation does not indicate causation, it is possible with sufficient evidence (correlations) and sufficient analysis, to lead to a causal conclusion.

> The story of the massive K-T extinction event that brought the end of the dinosaurs is an especially elegant example of correlating many variables to determine the mechanism—a large asteroid impact and associated global cooling—that brought the demise. Here a highly interdisciplinary team that included Nobel Prize—winning physicist Luis Alvarez and his geologist son Walter correlated stratigraphic data, fossil data, and chemical data—most notably a thin layer of the rare element iridium found at the same level in multiple strata around the world—
>
> ...
>
> Correlation may not always imply causation, but in this case the correlations seem to have been strong enough to wipe out the dinosaurs!

Finally, observational research is said to rely too much on correlations. Indeed with all of these concerns this is an absolutely justifiable concern. One should not blindly assume the first pair of correlated events is causal. But it is equally true that one should not assume that there is never a correlated pair of events that are causal. The key for observational approaches is to ensure that you don't throw the scientific baby out with the bathwater in haste to find the "scientifically correct" thing. Correlations and their power will be explored next in greater detail.

Indeed, our continued mantra is to encourage the reader not to get caught up in the dogmatic debates on the relative merits of one particular scientific approach versus another. Indeed, pursue the avenue that best addresses your burning research questions and fits your resources, skill set, and even interests.

TYPES OF STUDIES

Observational methods are often used in the social, medical, political, and economic fields. To a greater extent, the physical sciences focus on the hypothetico-deductive experimental approaches to science. Keep in mind that all sciences, of course, have their own theoretical branches that are immune from the quantitative versus qualitative, and experimental versus observational debates.

Observational studies are a broad category of research that cover the inductive observation of phenomena, symptoms, or systems. Observational studies are distinct from experimentation in that no independent variable can (technically, ethically, or financially) be controlled. Both experiments and studies observe dependent variables in order to better understand the outcomes. For example, in astronomy, the ability to conduct celestial engineering to study the end of life of a star, is clearly, beyond our current abilities. More down to earth, a principal investigator (PI) who would like to study behavioral incentives for criminals online, would not be able to conduct an experiment encouraging or soliciting criminal behavior. Instead, an observational study would be necessary to discern the intent and incentives behind the cyber-criminal behavior. A final example might be a researcher who is interested in understanding the cyber behaviors of users on an enterprise network, because she is not able to design an experiment and control variables within the network, she will have to collect the network and host information at hand and conduct a study from the available resources.

Exploratory Study

The exploratory-based studies are generally characterized by the objective of greater understanding and insight into the phenomena or situation under study. Please note that exploratory studies are also called correlative. In addition, they are also characterized by the data collection method. Typically, exploratory studies are either datasets that are not in the immediate control of the investigator, or are collected after the fact. Often the scope of the study and the dataset is much larger (in size or space scale). On the other hand, descriptive studies, which are discussed in Chapter 5, Descriptive Studies, are focused on preconceived behavior and a goal of describing the phenomena. Additionally, descriptive studies typically have more interaction and control of the subject at hand.

In this section, a series of exploratory research methods will be introduced. An overview of some useful research methods for cyber security research is provided to set the stage for more in-depth discussions later in the chapter. A research example for each method will be walked through at the end of the chapter to help contextualize the information presented.

Case Control: A **case control** study is a type of observational study where a set of measurements can be divided into two groups. The first group is called the case group. The case group exhibits the signs or symptoms of the event or phenomena under study. The second group, the control group, does not exhibit these systems. In this style of study, the incident or event has already occurred and the study is looking back over time at candidates divided into the groups. This means that the investigator is examining a system after an initial vulnerability or flaw was disclosed or identified, after a subsequent infection or compromise on part of the population. While it is important to keep in mind that the size of the sample population for control and case need to be sufficiently large, the number of control (vulnerable, but not compromised) can be larger than the case population (vulnerable and compromised). Finally, this sort of study can be conceivably conducted at one institution or host network/system, if sufficient subjects can be identified to produce sufficient statistical rigor, but another more traditional approach would be an industry or regional-wide study that treats compromised networks as the subjects.

Ecological: **Ecological studies** explore the entire population in either geographic or temporal space (in a region or at a particular time). This means that the observations are taken at the entire population level, in addition to any specific or individual observations. The goal of an ecological study is to assess the risk factors confronting a cyber population by evaluating risk mitigations and the subsequent adverse outcomes that affect the population. Data collection for these types of studies will often be of a secondary nature. The primary purpose of the data collection might have served some other need, for example U.S. census data collected for Constitutional taxation purposes, might be used in a large-scale medical study. Similarly computer and network devices might be inventoried for asset management, financial controls, or another reason. However, that dataset could be used in a variety of cyber security studies. For example, a study looking at the effectiveness of workstation patching in preventative defense could use the asset list to identify the entire possible population at an institution.

Cross-sectional: This **cross-sectional** study is sometimes called a census. Cross-sectional studies are related to, and sometimes a branch of, ecological studies in that a time-slice sample is collected from a population. This technique is used in medical, social, and economic observations. In this style of study, a sample is collected from the entire population at a specific period of time. Cross-sectional studies are often used to describe the prevalence of certain characteristics of the overall population or enable deductive inferences to be made about the information at hand. Descriptive studies are useful in exploration of the correlation of events.

Longitudinal/cohort: A **longitudinal study** is a sequential observation of a cyber system or cyber behavior over time. This timescale could stretch into years or decades. The goal is to collect sufficient information over time to ensure the entire lifecycle or complete context of the system under evaluation is considered. This type of study could span generations. In medicine, a longitudinal study might look at genetic diseases that are inherent in offspring. In cyber security, one could study the evolution of viruses over time, if you could ensure that you are observing the same subjects for the duration, which could be a challenge. A **cohort** study is a type of longitudinal study that focuses on a specific group, over time, called a cohort. The cohort shares some common trait, like exposure to malware, similar manufacturing defect or same compiler version, and are monitored over a period of time. Finally, longitudinal (and cohort) studies can be retrospective, that is to say, that the investigator might instead start in the present and dive into the past if the corpus of data is sufficient to support this level of inquiry.

GATHERING DATA

At the point of data collection, a researcher should have a sufficient handle on the research questions and approach they will be undertaking. Undoubtedly, your specific questions or ways of both analyzing the data and coming to conclusions will change, but if you have insufficient clarity to start with, then you run the risk of gathering data that does not end up being relevant to your line of inquiry. An iterative approach is possible, and discussed later, but it is best for situations where the data collection process is under the researcher's control and is not too arduous.

The diversity in datasets is staggering. From questions about collection methodologies, to formats and syntax, the task of collecting sufficient data, or even knowing when to stop, can dwarf the labor involved in the subsequent analysis. To avoid this trap, as much as possible, a well-crafted research plan will alleviate several of these pitfalls. We suggest that you start by exploring a few questions to help identify the scope, objectives, and likely challenges in data gathering.

DID YOU KNOW?

Any research that is conducted using federal funding, or at most universities or research institutions, that involve human subjects require a review process. This process is often called an Institutional review board (IRB). The goal of the IRB is to ensure that the subjects are treated fairly and will not come to permanent harm. In the field of cyber security, physical harm is of course far less likely, but privacy, and mental state might be an issue. IRBs will review the research plan and recommend any protections for the human subjects. For a more detailed discussion, please see Chapter 15, Ethics.

Questions to address before collection:

- *Have you reviewed your idea with your IRB informally to seek guidance or feedback?*
- *What types of questions are you asking (qualitative vs quantitative, relationship, volume, one off/black swans, or routine occurrences)? Clearly the questions must be observable, but the dataset may not exist.*
- *How much data will you need? Do you know what amount will be statistically significant for the conclusions or answers you hope to address?*
- *Who owns the dataset? Privacy, access, control, dissemination, and other issues will need to be addressed beforehand.*
- *Can you easily recollect or recreate the dataset? Or are you stuck with the dataset from a single point in time? Are you able to come back and revisit your initial assumptions if they do not pan out?*
- *Are you sampling? Will you be able to collect the entire population or dataset? This is very common in network traffic. If you have to sample, what is the method? What artifacts or challenges might it introduce?*
- *Have you reviewed the full study plan with your IRB?*

Broadly speaking, there are two types of data, collected or leveraged. Collected datasets are generated by the investigator for the purposes of this particular study. Your team might install and manage network taps for the university IT department. Or you might hire a company to conduct an online survey of target recipients. Either way, you are the responsible party for generating and collecting the information that you deem relevant to the study at hand. Alternatively, many studies are conducted on "someone else's data." That is to say, you have authorized and legitimate access to data that was collected for other previously incidental purposes. This can happen in many different ways, and is quite common. Using the previous example, if, instead, the IT department had already installed network taps and collected the information for their own performance reasons, a researcher could gain approvals to access the data. However, in this example, the fact that the data was collected for other purposes than the researcher's study might introduce artifacts. Example artifacts could include downsampling (perhaps the IT department only sampled every 1000 packet), partial coverage (often IT will only instrument the core network, so traffic within segments or entire portions of the enterprise might not be instrumented), and partial data (because the data was collected for other purposes, it might not contain all relevant information, for example IPFIX [or Cisco NetFlow] only contains header information). Leveraged data can, of course, come from outside your home institution tool. For more in-depth discussion of the concept and issues with instrumenting a cyber environment, review Chapter 13, Instrumentation. For details on how to collect qualitative data, see Chapter 5, Descriptive Studies.

In addition to inherent issues of ownership and collection, the data in and of itself can be a challenge. How will you store, query, and manage the data must all be addressed. Furthermore, the Internet and sheer complexity of cyber space allows for an incredible amount of information to be generated. The size and scale of cyber security data can be daunting. Moradi et al., in "On collection of large-scale multipurpose datasets on internet backbone links," present an exploration of several online datasets, their collection methodologies, and the addressed scale and privacy issues.[5] Their paper presents an exploration of how to deal with such large-scale issues. Another issue especially relevant to cyber security research are the legal and danger-related issues. Every researcher will have to work with their home IRB, or similar organization, to ensure ethical and safe conduct. But the IRB might not be as familiar with cyber space and the risks and opportunities therein. A PI should take the time to ensure that the IRB is fully aware of the issues relevant to their research. For example, Stone et al., in "Peering through the iframe,"[6] describe the infiltration and monitoring of a criminal drive-by campaign called Merboot. The authors present an account of how they collected information for 4 months and were able for 1 week to collect information directly from a network tap that totaled over 300 GB. Possible ramifications could include the legal issues with infiltration (please note in this example the systems were under their legitimate authority), and danger (after publication would the criminals involved seek retaliation or reprisals).

Research Questions and Datasets

Depending on the research questions you are asking and what aspects of cyber space you are studying will lead to the collection of different types of data. As they say, not all data is created equal. Understanding the types of data you will be collecting and the implications on your analysis and what you can learn from it is important. Collecting the incorrect forms of data can limit your ability to answer questions. Broadly there are two types of data: qualitative and quantitative.

Qualitative research includes collection and analysis of descriptive data. Research involving humans often includes information about their emotional state and social characteristics. Qualitative data can be categorized and sometimes ordered but does not provide the ability to mathematically quantify the data.

Quantitative research involves the collection and analysis of numerical data. Quantitative research enables the quantification or statistical exploration and explanation of data. Quantitative provides the most flexibility in analysis and should be sought above qualitative when possible.

Scales of Data

When you are collecting data for a study there are scales that underlie the two types of data. Each scale determines what type of analysis and information you can extract. The scales of data are largely dependent upon what and how you are measuring. The scales of measurement represent how data is related and what mathematical functions can be applied. There are four categories of data by scales of measurement.[7] The following scales of data are listed in order of strength of evidentiary support. Nominal scale provides the least strength of evidence and ratio scale data provides the strongest. The progression down the list allows more mathematical manipulation and analysis.

Nominal

Nominal data is data that can be categorized but does not allow any quantitative, or mathematical, measures and comparison. Nominal data is often referred to as qualitative data. Examples of nominal data would be network protocol. If you collected a network traffic data, one way you could categorize it would be based what protocol was used. Alternatively, if you have samples of malware you could categorize them around the types of malware (see Chapter 2, Science and Cyber Security, for a list of types of malware). The samples of malware are binary blobs that are themselves not quantifiable. However, through categorization you can start to mathematically analyze them. Categorization or constrained questioning is a method of mapping qualitative data onto a nominal scale for analysis.

Ordinal

Ordinal data is data that can be ordered from relative comparisons. However, absolute comparisons are not possible, preventing application of mathematical functions. Therefore, you can determine that one value is greater than or higher ordered than another but you can't claim that it is some percentage more than the other. For example, the Common Vulnerability Scoring System[8] (CVSS) was developed as a means to score the risk of discovered vulnerabilities. The CVSS is an ordinal scale because it bases the score on different metrics such as how complex the vulnerability is to exploit, what privileges it enables, or what starting privileges are necessary to exploit it. As this score combines many different metrics that are orthogonal or incomparable, the resultant values only provide information on the order of severity. However, CVSS score of 6 is not twice as severe as a CVSS score of 3.

Interval

Interval data provides meaning for the differences between values. With interval data you are able to add and subtract measurements but with interval data a measurement with the value of zero does not mean nonexistence. This prevents the use of multiplication or division for interval data. The pinnacle example of interval data is temperature measurements on the Fahrenheit or Celsius scales. A 10 degrees of difference is the same between 10 degrees and 20 degrees as it is 90 to 100 degrees. However, you can't say that 100 degrees is 2 times as hot as 50 degrees.

Ratio

Ratio data provides the ability to multiply and divide measurements. In ratio data, the zero value represents nonexistence of the measured item. In addition you can compare quantities as ratios; for instance, the number of bytes in a network flow. Zero bytes in a flow means that no data was transferred. However, a flow with 100 bytes can be said to be twice as big as a flow that has 50 bytes. Ratio data is the best data for statistical analysis as it enables full mathematical manipulation.

Sample Size

While the easiest answer to how much data you collect would be all of it, that is generally not a possible. Instead it is necessary to measure a sample of data from the full population. Just as with all other aspects of research, a thoughtful and rigorous determination of the sample size leads to better results. In this section, we will provide an overview of different concepts and approaches to sampling with a finite population size. Sample size calculation with an infinite population is discussed in Chapter 9, Hypothetico-Deductive Research Methods.

> **DIG DEEPER:** DATA SAMPLING
>
> Statistical sampling is a deep field of research as the size and construction of samples have great impact on the strength of results from research. This book cannot do justice the full depths of knowledge and approaches to sampling. If you believe that your research will use a lot of observational studies requiring different forms of sampling, we recommend that you pursue further research with books such as Sampling Statistics.[9]

There are two categories of sampling that exist. Probabilistic sampling is when there is a well-formed population from which you are sampling. This is the general form of sampling that happens for most research. However, for fields researching hidden or not well understood populations, nonprobabilistic methods are often a better fit. As cyber security includes study of threat actors there is need for using nonprobabilistic sampling methods.

Probabilistic Methods of Sampling

A population can be viewed from different perspectives based on valued attributes, but each of these attributes form distributions. For instance, if you look at the population of the United States there is a percentage of male and females, percentages of people in each generation, distributions of ethnicity, and so on. The goal of **probability sampling** is to create a sample that is representative of the larger population.

Random Sampling

Once a sample size is determined, **random sampling** is simply selecting each sample randomly from the population. If you can envision putting every item or person from the population in a hat, a random sample would be blindly grabbing a sample from the hat until you have reached your needed sample size. For random sampling to be effective as generating a sample that is close to the representative of the population, the random process determining the selection must truly be random. Any bias in the random process can bias the representation of the sample taken.

Systematic Sampling

Systematic sampling is a sampling process that defines a process by which each sample is selected. If you put all of the population in a list, a systematic sampling would be to take every third item until you collect the desired sample size. To prevent inadvertent bias in ordering or selection, it is always good to randomize the starting place of the sampling in the list. Network flow sensors, which are discussed in more depth in Chapter 13, Instrumentation, are a common sensor that uses systematic sampling. To reduce storage requirements, flow sensors can be set to only sample one out of a user configurable number of flows.

Stratified Sampling

Stratified sampling is the process of defining subpopulations around a set of common characteristics to eliminate bias of a majority characteristic influencing the sample. For example, let's say we wanted to study the cyber security practices and tools used by businesses. If we did a systematic or random sampling, we would with high probability get most or all small businesses in our sample. Looking at U.S. Census data you can see that 99%[10] of businesses in the United States are small businesses and therefore you would likely get zero samples of medium or big businesses. Stratified sampling would instead have you break the business into their different sizes and then randomly sample from the subpopulations to ensure that one characteristic doesn't overwhelm the results.

Nonprobabilistic Methods of Sampling

When you are studying a question that relates to a population that is not easily observable or tries to hide, such as cyber criminals, performing probabilistic sampling methods will not work well. **Nonprobabilistic sampling** is a structural sampling when population distributions are unknown. As cyber security is often studying subcultures that do not want to be observed, these methods of sampling are useful tools.

Convenience Sampling

Convenience sampling is the most common form of nonprobabilistic sampling, mostly because it is misused. **Convenience sampling** is a method of collecting samples by taking samples that are conveniently located around a location or Internet service. We have all seen studies that leverage students in the computer science classes. This is convenience sampling improperly used. A proper use of convenience sampling would be sampling of craigslist, the Silk Road, or other black market services to study cyber-crime communication. Selecting a set of found communications would adequately represent other criminal communication where computer science students do not represent the general public very well.

Purposive Sampling

Purposive sampling is the selection of samples based on your knowledge of the population you are sampling. Going back to our sampling of businesses for cyber security practices and tools for example, we may know that the financial sector has the most advanced practices. In purposive sampling, you would collect samples from financial businesses because you know they are a special case and you want to cover it.

Quota Sampling

Quota sampling is an extension of purposive sampling to try to intuitively reproduce probability sampling. With **quota sampling** you subdivide the population you are studying around different relevant characteristics; that is job category, age, education level, and so on. For each category of subdivision you will then intuitively assign proportions. From these proportions you would then select samples so that your sample set fulfills these proportions or quotas.

Snowball Sampling

Snowball Sampling is a common method of finding data samples when initially you only have a few leads. **Snowball sampling** is the process of starting with sampling a few participants and, after completion, asking them for a list of potential participants to discover who else would be good to sample. You would then collect data from that list and get additional lists from this level.

Calculating Sample Size

Each sampling method has its own specific formula for calculating the sample size.[11] However, calculating the correct sample size is dependent on a few different parameters. In the context of calculating a randomly sampled size from a population, we will define the common parameters.

Population Size

A population defines the demographic you want to study. A population is defined by having shared characteristics that you are interested in studying. Populations can be defined along many different lines such as organizational (all the employees at a company or students at a university), geographically (citizens in a country or residents in a state), or demographically (all teenagers or females). The **population size** is the approximate or absolute number of members in a population.

Power

Power is the likelihood that a study will accurately detect a true effect. The higher the power the lower the probability of falsely concluding that there isn't an effect. Adequate power in an experiment means that the likelihood of achieving a false negative is sufficiently low. As with significance level, the power level isn't a hard-and-fast rule. The general rule is to use an 80% power. However, this again is a factor you need to think through. In the medical profession, it is typical to over factor the power analysis ($>80\%$) to ensure a very low false-negative rate; as it is better to incorrectly think you have a disease and do more tests than to incorrectly determine someone is healthy when they are actually sick. Cyber security in general shouldn't have this level of concern, but every situation is different so use your best judgment to construct the appropriate experiment.

Significance Level

The **significance level** is the likelihood of accurately believing that there is an effect when there is not one.

Standard Deviation

A **standard deviation**, often represented as the Greek letter sigma σ, is a statistic derived from a distribution that measures the dispersion of values. A low standard deviation means that values are tightly clustered around the mean or average value. A high standard deviation means that values are dispersed a distance away from the mean. In sampling formulas that use it, standard deviation accounts for how varied the dataset is to determine how big a sample is necessary.

As mentioned earlier, there are different variations on sample size formulas for each study method. We will walk through using one common formula of sample size with an example to demonstrate how it is done. However, the goal of this book is not to cover statistical methods in depth; we leave it up to the reader to search out the appropriate sample size formula for your research. There are also a lot of free online calculators available to help you, but make sure you understand what formula they are using and that it is appropriate for your use case.

The formula for calculating a cross-sectional study sample size is:

$Sample\ Size = (Z_{Score}^2 * \sigma^2)/(Absolute\ Error)^2$

where:

Z_{Score} is the standard normal variate of the significance level. In general, Z scores are measures of how many standard deviations away from the mean a value is. For this sample size formula it is the Z score for the statistical significance. Table 4.1 shows the Z scores for some common significance levels.

σ is the standard deviation of the value being studied. This value is normally not known so you can perform a small pilot study to estimate it.

Absolute Error is the amount of error or precision you want to ensure you are able to detect.

Let's use an example to contextualize the parameters of this formula. If we wanted to study the security practices of a university, specifically how well students keep their computers patched (updated) on average, this would be a good use for a cross-sectional study. For this study, we want to get a significance level of 95% and we want to be within ± 2 patches of the real value.

Table 4.1 Z Scores for Common Significance Levels

Significance Level	Z Score
0.70	1.04
0.75	1.15
0.80	1.28
0.85	1.44
0.90	1.645
0.95	1.96
0.99	2.58

From other case studies,[12] we can estimate the standard deviation of missing patches to be 6. With this information we can calculate the sample size.

Example sample size $= (Z_{Score}^2 * \sigma^2)/(Absolute\ Error)^2 = (1.96^2 * 6^2)/(2)^2 = 34.57$

To execute this study, we would need to randomly sample at least 35 student computers for their number of missing patches.

Dataset Sensitivities and Restrictions

When you are collecting data for a study, it is important to understand the sensitivity of datasets and the governing laws. To protect test subjects a myriad of protections, both ethically and legally, have been established. When you are designing your study and the method of data collection, it is important to think about things such as test subject consent, privacy and data anonymization requirements, and protection of test subjects.

For studies involving humans and that are either federally funded or required by the publication venue must be reviewed by an IRB. IRBs were developed to ensure that researchers behave ethically in their treatment of human subjects and to be an advocate for test subjects. They are a body of independent reviewers from the community. IRB's expect to see a fully defined study or experiment when research is reviewed. They will determine the sensitivities of data and what protections are required for approval to execute the research. For a more in-depth discussion of data sensitivities and IRBs, please see Chapter 15, Ethics.

EXPLORATORY METHOD SELECTION

As identified by the Center for Evidence-Based Medicine,[13] you can ask a sequence of questions to determine what type of studies, or research, should be conducted. First, is the goal of the study to describe or explore the system under test, or is it to quantify, associate, or measure the relationship between two factors (nonanalytic vs analytic). Then, if the study is following the analytic course were the independent variables, interventions, or controls randomly determined? If they were, then the experimentation (randomized control trial or otherwise) are more relevant than a study. Finally, you will need to ascertain when the observations of outcomes are collected. If you have access to a system under test or a population for a considerable period of time, and before the event or incident of concern occurs, you can conduct a longitudinal study. If you do not have access to a population for study over a longer period of time, then a cross-sectional study may be suitable to answer some research questions. However, the cross-sectional method limits the ability to understand sequencing or causality. An alternative, if the event or incident of concern has already occurred, is that you can conduct case-control (or retrospective) studies. Case-control studies allow you to identify a system or population with the characteristics (has installed a certain IDS, or was compromised by a particular malware strain) and compare them to similar analogous systems or environments without the events or factors in play.

Longitudinal studies provide the most in-depth understanding of a system. Longitudinal methods capture data on variables changing over time, which provides information on how individuals evolve and the time sequences of events. These help with inferring causality of variables. However, longitudinal methods require the most investment as you must be willing and able to track a population over the length of the study. A common challenge with longitudinal studies is participant attrition. The participants are often required to invest some effort into a longitudinal study also, which can have an impact on the internal validity of the results. The reason for some participants to quit the study might also be related to the results of the study. It is often useful to group participants into cohorts or groups of common traits to assist in the analysis.

If you are unable to execute a longitudinal study a backup option is using the cross-sectional method. Cross-sectional study only takes a snapshot of a population and therefore is much less labor- and cost-intensive. However, cross-sectional study limits the amount of information you can infer. Owing to a single period of data collection, it is difficult to determine temporal relationship of variables. This leads to issues with cohort effect. As the population will generally have participants who are from different regions, ages, and experience, it is hard to determine the effect of these differences on the data. The ability to measure over time, as in longitudinal, or to focus into a cohort or specific group eliminates this validity challenge.

If you do want to try to figure out traits that lead to a specific result, like a malware infection of a computer, you can utilize the case-control method. With this method you collect data about subjects that have the case, in this scenario have been infected by malware, and some that are the control, or have not been infected. Then you retrospectively look at the history of the case and control population with commonalities in traits and conditions. However, even if commonalities are found, it is not possible to ensure that there is a causal relationship as difficult to determine what events led to the result looking in the past. This is also an ineffective method if the case under study is rare and a sufficient sample cannot be collected.

Finally, ecological studies are useful methods when you lack data at an individual level but only have aggregate statistics around geography or time. This can be common due to the lack of information released by companies that have been attacked or the requirement of anonymization of data for study. With an ecological study you can study the population as a whole to detect groups that have common events. However, be careful attributed discovered ecological relationships back to individuals because they do not have to hold. These common improper associations are called ecological fallacy.

It is important to point out that in medicine and other domains, cohort studies are often conducted first by identifying initial infection or event, and then studying the population to determine the mortality and consequences. This is possible in cyber security, but it is also likely that the population (i.e., your home enterprise) will be identified and monitored, and the subsequent notification of infection will come later.

EXPLORATORY STUDY METHOD EXAMPLES

In this section, we will walk through examples for the three exploratory studies identified.

An observational study is a study where data is collected from a real-world system without any control mechanisms. More specifically, an exploratory study is generally performed when a system is too complex for a controlled experiment or when the goal is to learn the characteristics of a system without an expectation of performance. An example of the first is understanding phenomena at the Internet scale. The Internet is a large and complex system that is very fluid and dynamic. No entity controls the Internet and it is therefore impossible to perform a controlled experiment where a few variables are rigorously tested. In one example,[14] the researchers collected an Internet scale corpus of passwords to learn what factors had an impact on user password security. Another example would be evaluating a Computer Emergency Response Team (CERT). The goal is to understand how the human teams react and adapt to the system. For this example, the CERT would be evaluated with conventional tools and then compared to using next-generation resilient capabilities. The goal was not to evaluate the performance of the tools or technologies but to study human behavior in context.

Case-control Example

A case-control study identifies two systems or groups that are then compared to better understand the phenomenology or event under study. For example, a network with an active virus compromise could be compared to a network without one, or perhaps compared to itself, before the compromised event. The purpose of these studies is to assess and understand the factors that lead to the event or phenomenon under study. Cases represent elements or subjects with the desired traits or characteristics in the system. Controls should be similar elements or subjects that are representative of the whole, without the desired (or observed) traits. For example, in a study of virus propagation, cases would be currently infected machines, and controls would be a selection of machines that are not currently infected (with a representative number of operating system, version, and application diversity).

That premise will be the start of our example. A security company was massively breached by a drive-by malware campaign. An initial workstation was infected, but then the malware continued to spread around the entire organization, and yet not every workstation was infected. A security team eventually reverse engineered the source code and determined that the targeting portion was written in obfuscated opcode. But, they could not figure out how workstations were selectively targeted. A case-control study could be conducted to determine any characteristics or traits that might make a certain portion of the population more susceptible to the malware.

The PI reviews the observational data questions:

- *What types of questions are you asking (qualitative vs quantitative, relationship, volume, one off/black swans, or routine occurrences)? Clearly the questions must be observable, but the dataset may not exist.*
  - The purpose of this study is to identify characteristics of systems that make them predisposed to the malware identified. Finding some correlated characteristics would lead to a straightforward hypothesis and experiment to validate the study results. That is to say that the findings from such a study would be easy to verify with an experiment by taking the conclusions (specific trait) and running an experiment to corroborate or refute the hypothesis. But, by only looking at common characteristics and not specific variables, this leads to qualitative data.
- *How much data will you need? Do you know what amount will be statistically significant for the conclusions or answers you hope to address?*
  - As this is a qualitative study, we will need to use a sample size formula for a qualitative analysis. The PI is not sure at this point, but sufficient detail on every workstation will be required to determine which workstations are infected and which are not. This includes OS, applications, running processes, local files (not collected), host IDS

logs, host antivirus logs, application logs, browser history, Windows system logs, and live memory capture (not collected), incident response logs and forensic analysis reports. The PI is concerned that because he is using an existing dataset, he might not be able to get the bottom of this effort with only the limited data the company collected. But after review, the team is able to proceed with the information available.

- *Who owns the dataset? Privacy, access, control, dissemination, and other issues will need to be addressed beforehand.*
  - The company that got infected, in a spirit of furthering research, was very diligent in collecting as much information as they could during their response to aid the research community. As a security company, they saw the value in sharing their information as much as possible within the defensive community. The company has already proactively sanitized the information and made it ready for public release.
- *Can you easily recollect or recreate the dataset? Are you able to come back and revisit your initial assumptions if they do not pan out?*
  - No. The dataset is not under the control of the PI and no additional information is available. The PI is concerned that this might torpedo the entire case-control study. But after working with the company sufficient agreements are made to provide confidence that the research team can use the information, and will have sufficient access to conduct the study.
- *Are you sampling? Will you be able to collect the entire population or dataset. This is very common in network traffic. If you have to sample what is the method? What artifacts or challenges might it introduce?*
  - Same as above. The dataset was collected by the company and the PI hopes that any sampling that might have been conducted was annotated for the researcher's information.
- *Have you reviewed this with your IRB?*
  - After reviewing these questions the PI and his research team draft a study plan and share it with the IRB.

The PI collected the datasets from the company and divides the host-based information into three categories: operating system related (OS, Windows system logs, memory capture, if it existed, and local files, if it existed); application related (application logs, antivirus logs, running processes); and outside-facing related (IDS logs, browser history, incident and forensic information). The PI had originally intended to have three teams of graduate students go through the groups, but unfortunately, due to schedule challenges, only had one team on hand. This forced the team to use a sequential approach. With over 6000 workstations and around 6% infection rate, the teams had to pour over the 360 infected machine records and at least as many uninfected machines (they ended up looking at every single record) to ensure that had equal populations of case and control for this study. But, it was not until the third grouping of data, outside-facing (external focused), that they begin to find discernible patterns (upon review of external traffic 5 never used Domain Name System (DNS) lookups occurred to human unreadable domains, only for the infected machines. This coupled with specific sport websites set the infected apart). As it turned out, with all of the infected machines, the user had a habit of browsing a sports-related website throughout the day. The researchers conjectured that while the malware did not infect through the website (it was infecting peer to peer locally; local packet capture established that the malware was not coming from the Internet, but rather from peer systems within the network) the command and control was through the website and therefore only machines that had human-initiated browser traffic to the compromised sites, would ultimately become infected. In the end, this finding was born out by experimental results that duplicated the results in a controlled experimental setting.

Ecological Example

As we learned earlier in this chapter, ecological studies are a type of observational study where at least one measurement is made at the group level. This means the emphasis is less on an individual subject's health or performance, but rather the entire system in context. In biology, environmental science, and ecology (of course), the definition of the group and environment is well established, but for cyber security, this is decidedly less so. One researcher's environment might be another researcher's individual subject. This is easy to see, if a study is looking at process protections of individual executions, the entire environment would be a single operating system. Similarly, a single machine might be the lowest common denominator in an enterprise study, and even an enterprise might be an individual subject in a nationwide evaluation of incident response. Given the dynamic, human engineered, and adversarial nature of cyber space, the application and utilization of ecological studies will likely evolve over time as more researchers explore and use these techniques.

For our example, we are going to propose an ecological study of a municipal network. Our investigator is concerned that given all the risks to cyber defense, local municipal governments are likely overwhelmed and unable to cope with the demand of cyber network defense. Given this rough objective and topic area, the investigator reviews the list of questions to ask before collection.

- *What types of questions are you asking (qualitative vs quantitative, relationship, volume, one off/black swans, or routine occurrences)? Clearly the questions must be observable, but the dataset may not exist.*
  - Our PI is most interested in studying the cyber security practices of the various municipal agencies against each other within one city. For the first go around, the PI is very comfortable with a qualitative assessment given the limited time and resources available for anything more indepth. This could include system information (patch levels, change and configuration management details), network information (network topology), security counter measures used (SIEM, firewalls, network and host IDS, antivirus, antimalware, etc.), practices (CERT practices, network defense strategies, forensic and incident response practices, etc.)
- *How much data will you need? Do you know what amount will be statistically significant for the conclusions or answers you hope to address?*
  - Sufficient data will be required to generally answer our PI's questions. However, our PI is willing to tailor the study to the information at hand. Given the qualitative nature of this exploration, the statistical strength of the information will not be dictating the amount of data collected but rather based on the population and the variability of the attributes being studied. The PI hopes to be able to collect enough artifacts of different types to paint a complete picture of the environment and will use statistical power analysis to guide the gathering.
- *Who owns the dataset? Privacy, access, control, dissemination, and other issues will need to be addressed beforehand.*
  - After talking to the IRB, the PI is quite concerned that privacy and ownership of data will prevent her from even being able to conduct the study. But, after talking to the city's information director, it looks like, not only will it not be a problem, but the city council is very much in favor of open information and working with researchers. This turns out to be an unexpected advantage.
- *Can you easily recollect or recreate the dataset? Are you able to come back and revisit your initial assumptions if they do not pan out?*
  - The short answer is no. The PI will only have the information that the various municipal agencies have already collected. This effort is largely relying on information that has already been collected by others. If anything turns up during analysis, she could go back and see if there were other data streams that she did not think to include, but this is a long shot at best.

- *Are you sampling? Will you be able to collect the entire population or dataset. This is very common in network traffic. If you have to sample, what is the method? What artifacts or challenges might it introduce?*
  - The intent of this study is to paint a clear picture of the municipal cyber defense posture. Given the secondary collection nature (this study will use already collected data, and will likely sample from that) sampling will play a significant role. For example, sampling artifacts that the Information Management (IM) department might have done will, of course, persist.
- *Have you reviewed this with your IRB (again)? Has anything changed that might warrant a second review?*
  - Armed with the answers to the above question, and the revised questions (below), the PI is ready to discuss this research with the local IRB.

After answering these questions the PI is able to refine the questions to help scope the ecological study. Specifically, does municipal level of budgets and staffing adversely affect the city's ability to monitor their networks for cyber events? This explores the effects on the city-wide budget on the various municipal agencies and their individual IM and cyber defense teams. The PI gets approval from the IRB and approaches the city IM director and the various IM managers for the various municipal agencies. Each of the agency IM managers are in control of their own budgets. Now the PI can collect defense plans, network topologies, security tool equipment procurement lists, and staff lists. The IM director redacts any personally identifiable information (PII) and private information and turns the rest of the information over to the PI. At this point, the PI can start the data analysis phase. She consults a statistician at her university that recommends that she tries a linear regression test to first evaluate the trade-offs between budget and cyber defense. With this bit of advice, the PI is able to explore the interrelationship between budget allocation on staffing, procurement, and perceived cyber defense.

Cross-sectional

Cross-sectional studies are related to, and sometimes a branch of, ecological studies in that a time-slice sample is collected from the entire population. The purpose of conducting such a study is to ensure complete coverage of the entire population within your representation at one specific point in time. One convenient example is to consider this a cyber census. This means that the method of selecting the population must ensure sufficient coverage and diversity to meet the objectives of the research at hand. The purpose of the questions below are to help identify those objectives and ensure that the appropriate datasets are collected. In this style of study, a collection is made from the entire population at one specific point in time. Cross-sectional studies are often used to describe certain characteristics of the overall population or enable deductive inferences to be made about the information at hand.

Let's start with an example research study to highlight cross-sectional studies. Suppose that a team of researchers at a university would like to explore the correlation of time spent on specific websites compared to relative security posture. They could postulate that users at a university who spend time on security websites and forums would, perhaps, be the population least likely to be infected. Similarly those who spend time on technology-related sites and forums might be more savvy than the general population. Then, other topics could be identified as needed: sports, news, general entertainment, less-savory topics, if covered by the IRB. The goal is to understand if, in a given population, the security competency can be inferred from browsing habits.

Questions to address before collection:

- *Have you reviewed this with your IRB?*
  - The university research team meets with their IRB when they are first designing their study. This meeting ended up being very valuable, as the IRB was able to connect the research team with the University IT infrastructure team so they were able to immediately identify their data collection source.
- *What types of questions are you asking (qualitative vs quantitative, relationship, volume, one off/black swans, or routine occurrences)? Clearly the questions must be observable, but the dataset may not exist.*
  - The researchers wanted to utilize existing information streams and collections and not introduce any new data collection. This is in keeping with the cross-sectional collection style. Typically this style of research can be used as a first pass when studying a topic, given the utilization of existing information. The question the researchers would like to specifically answer: Is there a correlation between websites visited and user security? They have a hunch that security-minded browsing will have more secure systems, which can be inferred from browsing habits.
- *How much data will you need? Do you know what amount will be statistically significant for the conclusions or answers you hope to address?*
  - The study plans on collecting all DNS query information and as much HTTP get header information that leaves the university network over the course of two weeks. *In addition, an anonymous survey will be sent out to the university population to ask their self-assessment of their security awareness and a small test to evaluate their security competency. To ensure a high response rate, a printable coupon is provided at the completion survey for a free meal at the university cafeteria.*

- *Who owns the dataset? Privacy, access, control, dissemination, and other issues will need to be addressed beforehand.*
  - The information is collected by the University IT department. But given the IT department's past work with the IRB, and on the advice of the IRB, the IT department has procedures in place for collecting and sharing information with researchers. This process identifies mechanisms for protecting privacy, and dictates all relevant policies for access, publication, and utilization. (If you are in an institution that has not yet had to address these sorts of issues, you will have to become an advocate for all researchers, in ensuring that the relevant parties understand the importance and value of enabling this sort of research, regardless of the setting (university, government, industry).

- *Can you easily recollect or recreate the dataset? Are you able to come back and revisit your initial assumptions if they do not pan out?*
  - This sort of information can be recollected, but because it is a single snapshot in time (the whole purpose of this style of study) it is impossible to determine if this dataset will remain valid. However, the study should be reproducible if not repeatable.

- *Are you sampling? Will you be able to collect the entire population or dataset? This is very common in network traffic. If you have to sample, what is the method? What artifacts or challenges might it introduce?*
  - The advantage of this sort of research is that there is no sampling or downselection. The entire population of information will be collected as a single moment in time. However, it is important to point out that there are limitations even when collecting "everything." For example, if the IT department does not have sensor coverage over every college and department, than those users would be necessarily excluded. In this case, the collection point will be at the edge of the university network and will collect all outbound web traffic. Even then, however, this will not catch everything. For example, this will not get encrypted traffic (beyond the DNS queries), and will not get any internal traffic that does not traverse the outside. Any web browsing to forums or website hosted within the university would be excluded from this study, an issue that might become a problem in the future.

- *Have you reviewed this with your IRB again? Has anything changed that might warrant a second review?*
  - After all the preparation, the university team is ready to collect the HTTP and DNS information from the IT network perimeter.

Longitudinal Example

Longitudinal studies can come in several different varieties, but at their core they observe a population or system over an extended period of time. Two varieties are cohort and retrospective cohort studies. Cohort groups are identified based upon some common characteristics, that is all employed by one company or received a certain degree. Conventional cohort studies first identify the group, and then follow them through time to determine outcomes. Retrospective cohort studies identify the outcome, and then based upon existing records and evidence follow the common group back in time, to determine if there are any correlated or causal events. Regardless of whether there is a specific group (cohort) or not, these studies are typified by long time periods. However, much like ecological studies applied to cyber security, longitudinal studies applied to cyber security are still in their infancy. This means that there is no great body of evidence to say that 4 months is too short or too long for a longitudinal study. We could cite the previously mentioned Stone et al., in "Peering through the iframe"[15] paper, which observed a malware drive-by campaign for a period of 4 months as an example of a longitudinal study. Given the dynamic, human engineered, and adversarial nature of cyber space, the application and utilization of longitudinal studies will also likely evolve over time as more researchers explore and use these techniques.

In the following example, we will explore educational impacts of the U.S. National Science Foundation's Scholarship for Service (SFS)[16] on the cyber security posture of federal agencies where they are employed. The PI would like to determine the effectiveness of the SFS training and determine if it has an impact on the broader nation at large. This study will need to evaluate several classes of students over time. The PI first reviews the questions for study preparation.

- *Have you reviewed this with your IRB?*
  - The PI approaches his home institution's IRB to help shape his proposal. After discussing his plans, the IRB points out that measuring the security posture of an entire federal agency or the nation at large is quite overly broad, and it would be a good idea to narrow down the topic. After discussion with colleagues and the IRB, the PI decides to measure cyber hygiene penetration in federal agencies as measured by the results of annual internal email phishing tests. The premise is that SFS graduates will directly perform well on this assessment and might help influence and inform those around them to increase the overall cyber security savviness of the organization.
- *What types of questions are you asking (qualitative vs quantitative, relationship, volume, one off/black swans, or routine occurrences)? Clearly the questions must be observable, but the dataset may not exist.*
  - The PI is attempting to assess the relationship between SFS graduates employed in federal agencies and the results of employee email phishing. The problem will be the myriad of potential confounding

factors (education campaigns not attributable to the SFS program, widening public awareness of email phishing).

- *How much data will you need? Do you know what amount will be statistically significant for the conclusions or answers you hope to address?*
  - Given the previous concerns, the PI seeks input from colleagues again to determine if this sort of study would be even possible to conduct. After consulting with a few statisticians, they develop sufficient target numbers of students, employees, and additional factors that will need to be monitored. This information helps bound not only the study, but informs the data collection and analysis phases.
- *Who owns the dataset? Privacy, access, control, dissemination, and other issues will need to be addressed beforehand.*
  - SFS students are required to share their employment information with the SFS program. Furthermore, the PI will seek positive consent from the SFS graduates to ensure a sufficiently long study period. Additionally, because the PI is conducting a government-funded study, access to the results of the phishing campaign will be straightforward (covered under existing government use), but will still be required for each institution under study.
- *Can you easily recollect or recreate the dataset? Are you able to come back and revisit your initial assumptions if they do not pan out?*
  - The PI determines that this should not be a concern. But the confounding factors (what else could influence employee phishing results?) continues to be a concern.
- *Are you sampling? Will you be able to collect the entire population or dataset. This is very common in network traffic. If you have to sample what is the method? What artifacts or challenges might it introduce?*
  - Sampling is not an issue for this study as the PI will retroactively follow all consenting SFS graduates in federal service. The email phishing information is collected by the host agencies and not within the control of the PI (but the sampling rates of their phishing tests are noted by the PI). The historical information for phishing testing is also available.
- *Have you reviewed this with your IRB (again)? Has anything changed that might warrant a second review?*
  - With the answers to the above questions, the PI is able to return to the IRB for approval.

In the end, it took the PI a considerable amount of time and effort to track down the SFS graduates and their employed institutions. After looking at the distribution of graduates to more than 100 federal agencies and groups, the PI realized that he will need to downselect and sample, after all. His statistician suggested taking the top 10 most institutions (the ones with the most SFS graduates employed) and he also suggested using the same ranking, but with the most SFS graduates per 1000 employees and comparing the two. This is then compared to a sampling of institutions without SFS employees. With this guidance, the PI approached the relevant government agencies and collected the previous phishing test results for as long as they had conducted tests, and had SFS graduates employed. The PI also personally interviewed cyber security staff at the institutions to identify any confounding factors as suggested previously. In the end, the PI collected all the information needed to conduct the analysis. He graphed the results in a simple line plot to see the effects of number of SFS employees versus phishing results annually versus institutions without SFS employees. Ultimately, the research team agreed that the causal links between the employees of SFS to email phishing results could not be made, but the information proved useful in establishing educational correlations in the employed populus.

ANALYSIS BIAS

Data collection can introduce bias before work has even begun. If the study will be sampling (because the entire dataset is cost-prohibitive or restricted) the results will be downselected or sampled. The means of selection can introduce what is called sampling bias. If, for example, you divided computer systems into either server or workstation groups and treated those two groups equally, you would fail to account for the fact that there are typically far more workstations in an enterprise than there are servers.

Another form of bias is systemic bias. This form of bias underlies the entire research lifecycle. A classic example would be a drug company funding pharmacologists to conduct studies on their drugs to determine safety and effectiveness. In cyber security, the easy analogy would be an antivirus/antimalware or IDS vendor contracting a university or research institution to conduct a security/vulnerability or performance assessment. This is a common practice in applied research and a reader might be suspicious of the results of the pharmacological study evaluating the drug company's products as safe and effective, and should be equally suspicious of research that is funded by the subject or stakeholder under evaluation. Now this is not to say the research is automatically unscientific or invalid, but rather a subconscious, accidental, or deliberate tampering with the setup, the process, or the analysis might exist and should be corrected for or addressed in an appropriate manner. Examples might include having the study design and results reviewed by an independent third party, ensuring that personal profit or benefit are not coupled in any way to the outcome of the results, or establishing sufficient relationships so that the process addresses and controls for bias inherently.

Another form of systemic bias occurs at the very start of data selection. There is a trend for journals, conferences, and dataset repositories to be either pay-walled, or open access. The authors support this trend, as democratizing access to information ensures the broadest scientific discourse possible. However, a side effect of this proliferation is a selection bias toward open access publications and datasets for studies. If a researcher was conducting a study of average password size compared to password complexity, open and publically available datasets would likely be preferred to paywalled or hard-to-access datasets. While this might not inherently be a concern, the bias and shaping of the research, even at this preliminary level should be acknowledged and assessed. Perhaps, in this example case, it would be better to register at a paywalled or arduous site, to ensure access to the most relevant and useful data.

The last forms of bias that we will explore come from psychology. The observer (or experimenter) effect is an example of a subconscious bias where a human observer inadvertently influences or prejudices the subject. This type of bias is typically not deliberate tampering or fraud perpetrated by the survey, experiment, or study administrator, but rather subconscious, physiological, or other tells that influence the subject behavior. An amusing example, from the turn of the last century, with an animal subject, is the case of Clever Hans.[17,18] Hans was an intelligent horse that his owner Wilhelm von Osten would exhibit around Germany. For a crowd, Willhelm would ask his horse to perform addition, subtraction, multiplication, and even logic questions. The horse would invariably tap out with his hoof, the correct answer to the amusement of the crowds. This became such a spectacle that a commission was appointed to investigate. In the end, it turned out that the horse was watching his handler/owner who would become progressively more and more tense, until the right number of taps had occurred, and then he would relax. The horse simply tapped until the owner relaxed. This example of unconscious observer-expectancy even led to the bias being called the "Clever Hans effect," after the horse.

A similar bias, this time with the subject, is called the "lab coat syndrome." This time the subject in an attempt to please the authority or expert figure, often literally dressed in a lab coat, will provide the answer or outcome that they anticipate the observer would like to see. An extreme example of this is the Milgram experiment or study,[19] where participants are following the instructions of a lab-coated observer in providing shock to another human subject. A simpler example, would be answering a survey about password strength by lying and telling the survey taker that they never share passwords and always change them to new complex passwords (anticipating and assuming that the observer would like a more positive outcome). A final corollary of this is called "lab coat hypertension." In medicine, this is a syndrome when subjects are in a medical environment and have their blood pressure measured by a medical professional, experience higher blood pressures than they normally do in outside settings. This physiological response is explained by psychological pressure placed upon the subjects by being subjected to the medical environment and practitioner process. This is hard to control for because both the environment and the expert administering the blood pressure test must be removed, reducing the potential fidelity and trust at any at-home measurements.

THE SEARCH FOR A CAUSAL RELATIONSHIP

As we have mentioned, the objective of observational research is to discover patterns of data that could represent causal relationships. Interesting discoveries can lead to further research or, if the evidence is strong enough, new models of thinking. Patterns in data largely represents one or more variables following or reacting to the behavior of another set of variables, which is called correlation. Our intent is to provide you with an introduction to a few of the commonly used statistical tools for data analysis. However, there is a broad and deep amount of mathematical approaches to analyzing data to look for patterns or detect correlations. We are unable to cover statistical methods in detail in this book. Therefore, we recommend you seek out further texts, such as regression modeling strategies: with applications to linear models, logistic and ordinal regression, and survival analysis,[20] if you need more advanced data analysis methods.

Graph Summarization

The easiest and first method you should use in your analysis is to graph your data. Human beings have the best visual pattern matching capability as that is how our visual process works. By graphing your data in different ways you can look for interesting patterns that are worth exploring more deeply with the mathematical methods below. **Frequency graphs** are one of the most useful graphs as they show distributions of data and are applicable to all scales of data. Fig. 4.1 shows an example of a frequency distribution that could be created from a survey of user cyber security awareness.

Descriptive Statistics

Descriptive statistics are ways at evaluating and exploring the results of one variable at a time, which is called **univariate analysis**. Descriptive statistics provide a way to describe a dataset by a few parameters. Over time, a set of

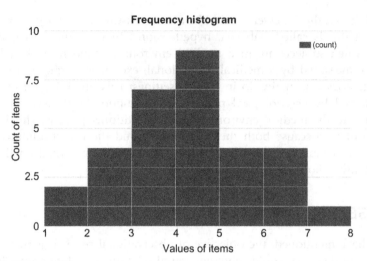

FIGURE 4.1

Example Frequency Histogram.

common reoccurring descriptions of data have been derived called distributions. There are many different distributions that are generated around different behaviors of data. The Gaussian or normal distribution is the most used
distribution as the central limit theorem states that if a sample is big enough
most datasets follow a normal distribution. The following are some parameters that can be determined from a normal distribution.

Central Tendency

Central tendency measures define aspects of a dataset that show a middle or
common value. Fig. 4.2 shows central tendency measures on a frequency histogram. A mean is a calculation of the average of all values. The **mean** is provided
by dividing the summation of all values with the total number of values. As
you can see on the figure, the mean is represented by the yellow line and does
not have to align with one of the values as it is 3.8 for a number of integer
values. A **mode** is the most frequently occurring value. On the figure, the mode
is the value of 4 as it occurs the most. The mode is represented by the red bar.
Finally, the median is the middle value of an ordered set of data. In the graph
the **median** is represented by the green square. If you align the values in ascend-
ing order, one of the items with a value of 4 would be the median. Without a
clear ordering sequence the median could be a set of numbers; in this case, any
of the four squares could be the median if we shuffled their order.

Regression Analysis

Regression analysis is the process of using statistical techniques to quantify
and understand the relationship between variables. While the overall goal is

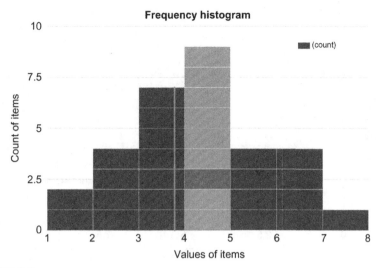

FIGURE 4.2
Examples of Central Tendency Measures Displayed on a Frequency Histogram.

the determination of a correlation between variables it also includes description of this correlation. For instance, the direction of the relationship (direct/
indirect, positive/negative), the dimensionality of the relationship, and the
strength of the correlation. Regression analysis, and inferential statistics in
general, is a very broad field of mathematical study. We are only presenting
overviews of the most common techniques here to provide an introductory
set of techniques for research. There are a multitude of other statistical methods,[21] if you find that the methods presented here do not adequately fit your
research.

Linear

Linear regression is a process of modeling a linear correlation between two
variables. With linear regression a best fit or trend line is found that models
a series of data. The line is found by creating a line that optimizes or finds
the smallest summation of deviations from every point. Fig. 4.3 shows a linear regression line on a set of data. The bars are the deviations from the
points. The line shown is the best-fit option to limit the total size of the deviation from all points. Linear regression can be applied to any set of data
even if it is not a good model. An easy way to determine the fit of a line is to
look at the R^2 value. The higher it is the better the fit of the line to the data.

Logistic

Logistic regression is a process of modeling the probability of a discrete outcome given an input variable. The most common logistic regression models

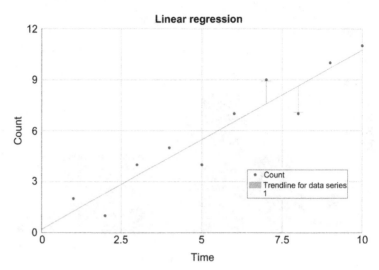

FIGURE 4.3
Linear regression example.

a binary outcome; something that can take two values such as true/false, yes/ no, and so on. Multinomial logistic regression can model scenarios where there are more than two possible discrete outcomes. Logistic regression is a useful analysis method for classification problems, where you are trying to determine if a new sample fits best into a category. As aspects of cyber security are classification problems, such as attack detection, logistic regression is a useful analytic technique.

REPORTING YOUR RESULTS

The final important step of an observational study is reporting your results. The greatest discoveries have little value if no one knows about it, cannot leverage the knowledge for further science or can engineer something with more predictable behavior. The two most prevalent forms of documenting study results are conferences and journals. These venues provide a path to insert your knowledge into the field's corpus. However, the quality venues all require peer-reviewed acceptance. Peer review provides a validation check against the topic of research, methods of research, and the quality of reporting the research to ensure that a certain level of quality is maintained. Ideally, the quality of the work should be the only metric of acceptance; in reality the novelty, groundbreaking, and popularity of the topic also play into the review process, so these things should be taken into account when you select your venue. In this section, we provide a general template for reporting observational studies, which will be applicable to most conferences and journals.

Sample Format

In the following we will provide you with a general outline for publishing your results. Every publication will provide their own formatting guidelines. Be sure to check your selected venue's submission requirements to make sure you follow any outline and formatting specifications. The outline provided here follows a common flow of information found in published papers and should meet the requirements of a larger number of publisher specifications.

Every paper is unique and requires some different ways of presentation; however, the provided sample flow includes all of the general information that is important to cover in a paper and is a general starting format we take when starting to write a paper and then modify it to support the topic and venue. We understand that every researcher has their own style of presentation, so feel free to use this as a jumping-off point. The discussions of each section are provided to explain what is important to include and why, so you can present the important information in whatever way best suits your style.

Another example outline can be found at the Strobe Initiative.[22] The Strobe Initiative goals are to enable the STrengthening the Reporting of OBservational studies in Epidemiology (STROBE).[23]

Title

This title section should be self-explanatory. Provide sufficient information to help audience determine if they should read more. Some authors enjoy clever or amusing titles, your mileage may vary. You should indicate what type of study you conducted.

Abstract

The abstract is a concise and clear summary of the paper. The goal of an abstract is to provide readers with a quick description of what the paper discusses. You should only talk about what is stated in the rest of the paper and nothing additional. Each submission venue will provide guidelines on how to provide an abstract. Generally, this includes the maximum length of the abstract and formatting instructions, but sometimes this will include information on the type and layout of the content to provide.

Introduction

The first section of a paper should always be an introduction for the reader into the rest of the paper. The introduction section provides the motivation and reasoning behind why the research was performed. This should include a statement of the research question and any motivating questions that were used for the research. If any background information is required, such as explaining the domain, environment, or context of the research, you would discuss it here. If the audience is significantly removed from some aspect of this topic, it may be worth it to create an independent background section.

Related Work

The related works section should include a quick summarization of the field's knowledge about this research topic. Are there competing theories? Have other experiments, studies, or theoretical studies been done? If there are a lot works in this field, cover the most impactful or influential work for you.

Study Methods

The study methodology section of your paper should clearly define the process you took to conduct your study. It is crucial that this section is clear and complete, such that a reader would be able to replicate it. In this section you should detail the specific observational methods, the setting/environment, and the size of the study. Additionally, the participants/subjects should be detailed. The variables under observation should be described including outcomes, quantitative values, and any confounding factors. Next, the biases should be acknowledged and also address how they were controlled and mitigated. Finally, you should define the statistics you used and the motivation for using them; you can also address if you have any missing data and how you dealt with that.

Study Results

In the results section of your paper, explain what you found after you performed your analysis. Lay out the significance, confidence intervals, and effect sizes for all of the study. Creating tables to show results is usually an efficient and effective method. You should address the participants in the study. Also, you could show pictures of interesting results, that is if a data anomaly occurred, or to display the distributions of the data samples. This should include descriptive data (the inputs) and outcome data (the outputs), and the analysis. If anything unexpected occurred, and shows up in the data, explain it in this section.

Discussion/Future Work

The discussion/future work section is for highlighting key results and results you found interesting or noteworthy. You should mention any limitations about which the reader should know. You can interpret and discuss any important correlations and discuss generalizability and causal relationships as relevant. Discuss where you think this work should lead next.

Conclusion/Summary
In the final section of the paper, summarize the results and conclusions of the paper. The conclusion section is often a place readers jump to quickly after reading the abstract. Make a clear and concise statement about what the ultimate results of the study were and what you learned from them.

Acknowledgments
The acknowledgments section is a place for you to acknowledge anyone who helped you with parts of the research. This is also a good place to acknowledge funding sources that supported your research.

References
Each publication will provide some guidelines on how to format references. Follow their guidelines and list all your references at the end of your paper. Depending on the length of the paper, you will want to adjust the number of references. Usually, the longer the paper, the more references. A good rule of thumb is 15—20 references for a 6-page paper. For peer-reviewed publications, the majority of your references should be other peer-reviewed works. Referencing web pages and wikipedia doesn't generate confidence in reviewers. Also, make sure you only list references that are relevant to your paper, that is don't inflate your reference count. Good reviewers will check references and this will likely disqualify and reflect poorly on you.

Endnotes

1. Taleb, N. N. (2007). *The black swan: The impact of the highly improbable.* New York: Random House.
2. Sagarin, Rafe, and Aníbal Pauchard. *Observation and ecology: Broadening the scope of science to understand a complex world.* Island Press, 2012.
3. Sagarin, Rafe, and Aníbal Pauchard. *Observation and ecology: Broadening the scope of science to understand a complex world.* Island Press, 2012, p. 118.
4. Sagarin, Rafe, and Aníbal Pauchard. *Observation and ecology: Broadening the scope of science to understand a complex world.* Island Press, 2012. p. 126.
5. BADGERS '11 Proceedings of the First Workshop on Building Analysis Datasets and Gathering Experience Returns for Security Pages 62—69.
6. Stone-Gross, B.; Cova, M.; Kruegel, C.; Vigna, Giovanni, "Peering through the iframe," in *INFOCOM, 2011 Proceedings IEEE*, vol., no., pp. 411—415, April 10—15, 2011.
7. Gravetter, Frederick J., and Lori-Ann B. Forzano. *Research methods for the behavioral sciences.* Nelson Education, 2015.
8. *FIRST Common Vulnerability Scoring System v3.0: Specification Document,* 2015, [online] Available: https://www.first.org/cvss/cvss-v30-specification-vl.7.pdf.
9. Fuller, W. A. (2011). *Sampling statistics* (Vol. 560). John Wiley & Sons.
10. Small Business and Entrepreneurship Council. (n.d.). *Small Business Facts & Data.* Retrieved February 25, 2017, from http://sbecouncil.org/about-us/facts-and-data/.
11. Charan, J., and Biswas, T. (2013). "How to Calculate Sample Size for Different Study Designs in Medical Research?" *Indian Journal of Psychological Medicine, 35*(2), 121—126. http://doi.org/10.4103/0253-7176.116232

12. Ross, C. (October 14, 2016). *Broken Cyber Hygiene: A Case Study*. Retrieved February 25, 2017, from https://blog.tanium.com/broken-cyber-hygiene-case-study/Tanium.
13. Centre for Evidence-Based Medicine. (March 7, 2016). *Study Designs*. Retrieved February 25, 2017, from http://www.cebm.net/study-designs/.
14. Proceeding WWW '07 Proceedings of the 16th international conference on World Wide Web Pages 657−666 ACM New York, NY, USA ©2007 table of contents ISBN: 978-1-59593
15. Stone-Gross, B.; Cova, M.; Kruegel, C.; Vigna, Giovanni, "Peering through the iframe," in *INFOCOM, 2011 Proceedings IEEE*, vol., no., pp. 411−415, April 10−15, 2011.
16. OPM. (n.d.). *CyberCorps®: Scholarship for Service*. Retrieved February 25, 2017, from https://www.sfs.opm.gov/.
17. Jackson, D. M. (2014). *The Tale of Clever Hans*. Retrieved from http://www.donnamjackson.net/PDF/Clever-Hans-Story.pdf.
18. Pfungst, O. (1911). *Clever Hans (the Horse of Mr. Von Osten) a Contribution to Experimental Animal and Human Psychology*. Retrieved February 25, 2017, from https://archive.org/stream/cu31924024783973/cu31924024783973_djvu.txt.
19. Behavioral Study of obedience. Milgram, Stanley *The Journal of Abnormal and Social Psychology*, Vol 67(4), October 1963, 371−378.
20. Harrell, F. (2015). *Regression modeling strategies: With applications to linear models, logistic and ordinal regression, and survival analysis*. Springer.
21. Harrell, F. (2015). *Regression modeling strategies: With applications to linear models, logistic and ordinal regression, and survival analysis*. Springer.
22. STROBE Initiative. (n.d.). *STROBE Statement*. Retrieved from http://www.strobe-statement.org/fileadmin/Strobe/uploads/checklists/STROBE_checklist_v4_combined.pdf.
23. STROBE Statement: Home. (n.d.). Retrieved February 25, 2017, from http://www.strobe-statement.org/.

## CHAPTER 5

Descriptive Study

For the purposes of organization, we have divided the discussion of observational studies into three separate chapters. In Chapter 4, Exploratory Study, we discussed exploratory studies. Those types of studies are broadly characterized by the scope and focus of the study. Exploratory studies often look at larger populations or trends across systems. In this chapter, Descriptive Studies, however, the focus is often more on an individual subject or more specialized target subject. Keep in mind, there is no grand dividing line, but this sort of classification is useful in understanding how large the scale of the study and the intent or goal of the research. Also note that there are applied observational studies, often in a descriptive style. This type of study will be covered in Chapter 12, Applied Observational Study. And finally, the next chapter in the observational research section will cover machine learning, the final style of observational research.

A study is the inductive process of gaining knowledge. The ultimate goal of a study is to detect patterns in data that could represent causal relationships between variables. Studies are usually performed as a starting point in understanding a problem, to observe a pattern or interesting event, and to direct further research or when studying a system that is too complex to control to a sufficient level for a hypothesis-driven approach.

The crucial distinction between a descriptive study and an exploratory study is the scope and generality of the observation. Exploratory studies may survey across a whole system or many instances of a system, and a descriptive study focuses in-depth on a specific case of some system. An exploratory study might look at adversarial behavior in general, but a descriptive case study might focus on one hacker or one hacker team to understand their behavior in detail. There are also applied case studies that look at the effects of applied knowledge on specific cases of operational environments; however, please see the Applied Research section for more details.

Research Methods for Cyber Security. DOI: http://dx.doi.org/10.1016/B978-0-12-805349-2.00005-4

CHAPTER OBJECTIVES

- Introduce descriptive studies
- Discuss descriptive study methods
  - Case study
  - Surveys
  - Case reports
- Address data collection as it relates to observational study in general
- Discuss the design and presentation of exploratory studies

DESCRIPTIVE STUDY METHODS

As we have learned previously, observational methods are often used in the social, medical, political, and economic fields. Usually, the physical sciences focus on the hypothetico-deductive experimental approaches to science.

As discussed in the previous chapter, observational studies are a broad category of research that cover the inductive observation of phenomena, symptoms, or systems. Observational studies are distinct from experimentation in that no independent variable can (technically, ethically, or financially) be controlled. Both experiments and studies are types of research that observe dependent variables in order to better understand the outcomes. For example, in astronomy, the ability to conduct celestial engineering to study the end of the life of a star, is clearly, beyond our current abilities. More down to earth, a PI who would like to study behavioral incentives for criminals online, would not be able to conduct an experiment encouraging or soliciting criminal behavior. Instead, an observational study would be necessary to discern the intent and incentives behind the cyber criminal behavior. A final example might be a researcher who is interested in understanding the effects of a next-generation intrusion detection system, deployed in a network that is not under her control. Since she is not able to design an experiment and control variables within the network, she will have to collect the network and host information at hand and conduct a study from the available resources.

Again, for the sake of organization, we have divided observational studies into two broad categories: exploratory and descriptive studies, (in addition to the automated machine learning approach). Throughout the years there have been several categorizations of research frameworks studies. And, we are confident that there will be more in the future. Our intent is not to introduce an end-all-be-all categorization of observational research, whatsoever. Instead, we are simply dividing the field into two more manageable sections. In order to do that, we have designated the first collection of studies as exploratory. The exploratory-based studies are generally characterized by the objective of greater understanding and insight into the phenomena or situation under study. Please note that exploratory studies are also called correlative. In addition, they are also characterized by the data collection method. Typically, exploratory studies are either datasets that are not in the immediate control of the investigator, or are collected after the fact. Often the scope of the study and the dataset is much larger (in size or space scale). On the other hand, descriptive studies are focused on preconceived behavior and a goal of describing the phenomena. Additionally, descriptive studies typically have more interaction and control of the subject at hand.

Sometimes in the various research fields, qualitative approaches are also called descriptive studies. For them, the goal of a qualitative style study is to provide more information and insight into the phenomenology and underlying behavior of the (cyber) system under test (whether that is human subjects or network latency). Analytic studies, on the other hand, strive to associate the relationship, frequency, or consequences between two events. These are the same objectives of an experiment, but without attempts at control like an experimental environment. This description, we have found, largely holds true, but you will occasionally find a case where a descriptive study is legitimately used to identify and establish causation. In the end, we would encourage readers to not get caught up in taxonomies or labels of science and scientific methods, whatsoever. Instead, use the information as a guide to conduct your own research and leverage as much as possible from those who have gone before you.

Observational descriptive studies are in-depth and detailed studies of specific cases of systems or environments in cyber space. Where exploratory studies attempt to study specific variables of larger populations, descriptive studies attempt to document all aspects of individual and interesting systems. As descriptive studies are subjective by nature, they often generate qualitative results that are informative but not mathematically quantifiable. The following are descriptions for three common methods for performing descriptive analysis.

Case Study: **Case study** is both a generic term, a so-called study of a particular event or situation, and also a useful type of observational study. While it is important to realize that a case study is not anecdotal evidence, it is very limited in scope and applicability. Case studies follow a formal process for collection and evaluation. A doctor in a hospital studying a single incidence of a previously unknown disease or malady does not make for a wide-spread and generalizable diagnosis for the entire field. In this example, this case study, in concert with other studies or evidence, will undoubtedly contribute to the foundational knowledge for medicine. Similarly in cyber security, individual evaluations and studies of cyber system behavior might not be generalizable, but they will contribute to the systemic body of knowledge. Indeed, seminal cases (think Stuxnet or APT1) often have widespread and profound influence on the field. As you may have seen in Chapter 1, Introduction to Science, case studies are low on the hierarchy of evidence.

Case studies are a common method when researching malware, threats, or implementations of new policies and procedures. It is common to see in-depth case studies covering a newly discovered piece of malware.[1] Much less common, but case studies have also been used in describing details about specific threat actors[2] or attack campaigns.[3] If you find yourself wanting to go into great detail about a specific event, then a case study is a good method of choice.

Elicitation Studies: **Elicitation** is the act of gathering information from human subjects. Examples include surveys and human subject interviews. Surveys are both a method of data collection and a means of observational study. PI's might want to elicit a response for a computer system, but the topic of elicitation studies will be limited to human subjects. This field has broad applicability from satisfaction surveys to focus groups and psychological analysis.

In cyber security research, there are often situations where we lack the necessary models or theories to inform us on how to interpret results or assess a scenario. It is often the case that it is necessary to elicit expert opinions when evaluating the results of experiments or studies. For example, when attempting to apply and evaluate risk models, it is generally necessary to elicit expert judgment on the relative risk of test events to determine how well a risk model performs.

Case Report: Case reports are lifted largely from the medical community. While in that field they are used (like case studies) to describe a specific incident of disease or occurrence; in cyber security, **case reports** are less rigorous than case studies. The topics of a case report in cyber security could be a detection method (similar to the medical community), the detailing of a new countermeasure, or even architectural setup.

Case reports are quite prevalent in the current cyber security literature. Case reports are commonly used to describe a particular new technology, without any associated performance or security experiment and without even a rigorous study of its behavior in context. Papers that simply describe a new solution without providing context or assumptions would be best described as a case report.

OBSERVATION METHOD SELECTION

Case studies are useful when you want to describe and discuss an in-depth study of specific scenario or item, such as a cyber attack, new malware, threat actors, or how cyber security solutions or policies are integrated at an organization. As this research is highly qualitative, it enables you to explore the concepts and reasoning around why something is the way it is.

Elicitation studies are useful when you need to collect the wisdom of a specific population. This is generally useful when you need expert knowledge on assessing the value of something that we lack the ability to directly measure, such as risk, security, or scenario probabilities.

Case reports are useful when you want to describe a new solution. These are good for white papers or other nonpeer-reviewed publications. However, while this is a common practice, we highly recommend against using this method for scientific publications as its scientific contribution is low. Extending a case report by doing exploratory study or applied experiment goes a long way to improving the value of publications to the community.

GATHERING DATA

Information collected for descriptive studies is often first-hand and purpose-gathered. For example, a case study or report will involve directly interacting with the subjects at hand and collecting the information for the specific descriptive study. Similarly, any interview or form of elicitation will also have direct interaction with the subjects and therefore first-hand dataset collection and gathering. Given the often live and interactive nature of data collection, special care must be taken to ensure that the observer/researcher does not bias or tamper with the data. See the Analysis Bias section in Chapter 4, Exploratory Study, for details. Additionally, care must be taken to ensure that the first collection is sufficiently broad and wide. For example, in a case study of a specific infected system, sufficient information needs to be collected from the host system before any treatment (wiping or rebuilding) occurs. After the treatment, any information that wasn't collected, will likely be lost. Appropriate care must be taken at collection to ensure, often for posterity, that sufficient data is collected to address not only anticipated, but also unanticipated questions that might arise in the future.

This can lead to the researcher's often knee-jerk reaction, of "collecting everything." Ultimately, there is no universal process or step for discerning what information will be relevant or irrelevant, and an approach of collecting "everything," for example a full disk image, might be the best practice. But this would raise at least two issues. First, the lack of critical thinking as to what is needed and not needed might breed sloppiness. If researchers think they can just collect everything and then perform their critical thinking and analysis later, they might miss key decision points early on in the process. And second, the blind mindset of collecting everything might lead into a dead end. For example, if we take our example of forensically cloning a disk image and copying it for offline use and subsequent analysis, we might miss the fact that for certain circumstances the relevant information is not, in fact, stored on the hard drive but persists only in system memory. This rush to collect, without critical analysis, might lead to mistakes. In the end, the gathering data for descriptive studies is often first-hand and immediate, so care should be taken to ensure appropriate and sufficient collection methods.

Another problem that becomes especially relevant for descriptive studies is human subject issues. These challenges lie largely in two categories. First, are issues dealing directly with human subjects. These types of observational studies (case report, case study, elicitation, etc.) deal directly with human subject interaction. We highly recommend involving researchers with experience in conducting studies involving human subjects from the very beginning. They can help identify challenges that the IRB will raise, as well as issues that are inherent with humans as subjects (incentives, falsehoods, etc.). IRB is obviously necessary, so we recommend working with them early, before any initial work has begun. The IRB is often comprised of the various experts that you would want to consult with in any event. While this is not a replacement for your own expertise, they can often help guide and inform the entire process from start to finish.

The second challenge of involving human subjects comes into play when you analyze the data, like how the hidden intelligence of the adversary confounding defense and making cyber security a complex and challenging field. Similarly, human subjects, whether willingly or not, often make for very challenging and elusive subjects, even when they don't want to be. We covered the "Lab Coat Syndrome" and "Clever Hans" in the previous chapter in the Analysis Bias section. The fundamental challenge is that in the social sciences, each and every subject is an intelligent, thinking, self-optimizing, emotional, (ir)rational being. As Alan Greenspan now famously stated in testimony to the United States Congress about the assumed rationality of the Western economic system:

> Those of us who have looked to the self-interest of lending institutions to protect shareholder's equity—myself especially—are in a state of shocked disbelief.... I still do not fully understand why it happened and obviously to the extent that I figure where it happened and why, I will change my views. If the facts change, I will change.[4]

Greenspan and others were extremely surprised at humanity's behavior, especially against its own self-interest. The more suppositions and assumptions you have about human interaction, whether from your own experience or interactions, or from idealized assumptions, the more chance you will make mistakes in the design collection and analysis of your results.

Data Collection Methods

Survey/Questionnaire
Medium

The medium through which a survey is conducted impacts the types of questions and answers you can use. Complex questions are not easy asked over the phone and complex answers are not often delivered well through paper or the Internet. While it may seem easy to just always use something like Internet-based surveys, it is important to think through your questions and expected answers to ensure that the selected medium provides the best ability in collecting your required data.

In Person In-person surveys are the most restrictive because they require someone on the researcher's team and the participant to be present. However, in person surveys are the best for open-ended questions as it allows you to ask follow-up questions to clarify and get more detailed answers. This also requires great care as it can become easy to inadvertently bias responses by using positive or negative language.

Paper Paper-based surveys are useful if you have a large number of closed questions. Paper provides the flexibility of mailing to a large number of participants or doing a more intimate in-person scheduled survey. Largely, paper-based surveys have given way to Internet-based survey collection methods due to ease of use and cost.

Phone Phone-based surveys provide the ability to easily communicate surveys to a large and, if needed, distributed sample, so it is less work than in-person interviews but more than paper or Internet-based surveys. Phone-based interviews need clear and succinct questions as they lack visual cues that can make long, complex questions difficult to understand, which can lead to answers that are incorrect for your intentions. Phone-based surveys have the same bias risks as in person, so be very thoughtful and careful in what you say and how you say it.

Internet The Internet has become a common medium for collecting survey responses. There are easy-to-use, inexpensive, and quick-to-setup tools online for creating surveys. The use of computers enables in the integration of visual and audio components to help explain or contextualize questions if needed. With the Internet it is easy to reach a large number of subjects. However, when doing broad Internet surveys, there can be subjects that purposefully answer untruthfully and you can get responses from only those with an extreme opinion. Therefore, your ultimate sample may not be representative of the larger population.

Developing Questions

One of the main concerns when developing a survey are the questions you ask. Understanding the what, how, and why for each question is important. The what relates to the specific question you want to ask. The how focuses on how best to represent and present the question to ensure that you get the data you want. The why is making sure you understand how a question maps to your overall research objectives. Underlying these three concepts are multiple issues to think about. The following are short descriptions of some of the characteristics and issues for which you should be aware.

Types of Questions There are multiple ways in which you can present a question. Each of them has their trade-offs and are useful in gathering data for different use cases. Open-ended questions provide the participant the ability to fully express their opinion and feelings. However, open-ended questions often lead to participants answering questions in different ways, which make using any mathematical methods for analysis difficult. Multiple choice questions limit the responses of participants to a specified set of answers, which lends to easy coding of answers to use statistical methods of analysis. However, the risk of using multiple choice is biasing the responses based on the set of answers provided or making questions tend toward a specific answer. Finally, rating scale questions provide a range of valued answers that range from low to high. These enable participants to express their feelings while still limiting the form of the answer. The challenge with ratings scale questions is that users generally avoid the extremes and clump answers in the middle of the scale.

Make Clear When developing questions attempt to use simple and clear language. You want it to be very clear what you are asking and leave little room for multiple interpretations. Use language appropriate for the set of participants, that is no technology lingo for nontechnical participants.

Short and Sweet Following closely along with making your questions clear, it is important to try to make them precise and succinct. You don't want to make your questions more complex than necessary. Try not to embed multiple concepts in one question. If a question is long you run the risk of participants glossing over it and not answering it the way you intend.

Biased Language It is important to understand that the words you choose and the way you phrase your questions can influence the answers. Use of positive or negative adjectives can send a message to participants of your views. Or using known connotations such as "hacker" to represent something can influence a negative response from participants. In addition, you need to be aware of the common filter used by people when answering questions to make themselves appear more socially acceptable. There are no hard and fast rules on how to avoid bias issues, other than think what emotions your questions invoke in yourself and get the perspective of others.

When designing a set of questions for a survey, it is good to do a pilot or peer review of the questions. You can become deeply ingrained with your research design and become blind to some of the mistakes you made in developing the questions. Getting a fresh perspective from independent third parties can go a long way to ensuring that you have a solid survey before sending it out.

Question Placement It is good to strategically locate questions to make your survey more appealing for participants. Try to place boring items such as general demographic questions at the end so participants don't give up on the survey before starting. Group categories and formats of questions together to reduce the burden of having to think about how to answer each question.

Interviews/Focus Groups

Surveys are good for structured information gathering but when you want to collect the impressions, thoughts, and feelings of individuals or groups interviews or focus groups are better collection tools. Interviews and focus groups gather information from a smaller set of subjects than with surveys but their open-ended behavior allows for more in-depth exploration of a few topics. It allows participants to explain themselves and why they answer questions the way they do. Interviews and focus groups limit the generalizability, or external validity, of the results.

Field Observation

The last type of qualitative data collection we will discuss is field observation. This data collection method is where the researcher is observing and documenting the behaviors of the system or participants being studied as they perform tasks. This can include shadowing a subject where you are integrated and able to ask questions as activities occur. Or this could include passive observation like using eye tracking[5] and screen-capturing software.[6] Field observation is useful as it lets you get first-hand experience with what you are studying, which eliminates confusion in results. You should take field notes as you go to insure you are able to capture your thoughts. It is important to think through your level of involvement when doing field observation. With interactive observation there is the potential of your interactions biasing the behavior of the subjects. On the flip side, if you are a passive observer, it can lead to situations where you are forced to subjectively interpret an event in which you do not understand the reasoning or motivation behind. For instance, if you were studying the behavior of cyber defenders and you observe them ignoring an alert, it may be the case that they believe the alert to be unimportant due to past experience or they simply have zoned out and haven't noticed the alert. It would be up to you to make a subjective judgment on why this behavior is occurring if you are unable to interact with the subject.

DIG DEEPER: CYBER SECURITY DATASETS

The first thing that researchers often complain about is the lack of data. While this can certainly be true, there are several efforts around the world to ensure that datasets that are collected are shared with the broader research community. A few examples are listed below, but many more exist and are worth searching for before contemplating collecting your own datasets.

- *MIT-LL Intrusion Detection Dataset* In 1998 and 1999 DARPA funded MIT-LL to generate datasets for the evaluation of intrusion detection. These datasets were seminal in the field of cyber security, and while containing limitations (as all datasets due) they continue to be referenced and used.[7]
- *DHS IMPACT program (formerly PREDICT)* The US Department of Homeland Security Science and Technology Directorate funds the systematic collection, review, and dissemination of cyber security datasets. A variety of current and historical datasets are available to all researchers. Several steps are required to share data, and use data but the program continues to grow as more information is added.[8]
- *Center for Applied Internet Data Analysis (CAIDA)* The Center continues to collect and share cyber (IT and network) data to the research community. Often this data is at the Internet scale. Not all of the data is available to the public and some will require an application (such as IMPACT). CAIDA makes it easy to pursue the available sets.

Many more datasets and sources are available and these are just a sampling of the currently available datasets that might be of relevance for future research.

DATA ANALYSIS

The issues associated with exploratory observational studies will also hold true for descriptive studies, as well. Issues with bias and sampling can inadvertently influence and even ruin the results of a study. Reviewing the Analysis Bias section of the exploratory study in Chapter 4, Exploratory Study, would be very beneficial. Without duplicating too much material, we will cover additional issues that are highly relevant to descriptive observational studies.

Descriptive studies generally produce qualitative data, which often falls in the nominal or ordinal scales of information (which were discussed in detail in Chapter 4, Exploratory Study). As these scales limit mathematical manipulation, there are less formal techniques for analyzing these data. Overviews of some possible analytical methods are provided here to help you in understanding your data. Graphically displaying is always a useful method, but it is not covered here because we discussed previously; therefore, please review that analytical method if you have not yet read Chapter 4, Exploratory Study.

Coding Unstructured Data

In observational studies you may find yourself with unstructured data, whether it is free form text answers to a survey, responses to an interview, or code of software. In their raw form, unstructured data does not lend itself to analysis beyond summarization. In order to analyze it you must convert it to a form of data able to be analyzed. The process of converting unstructured data into categorical or taxonomic data is called **coding**. The process of coding involves the selection of a common taxonomy or developing a new set of categories that answers will be coded with or assigned to. For instance, if subjects are asked how they feel about their computer security practices, which would get a spectrum of answers. A simple code for this could be high, medium, and low, and then making a determination on a code based on the language used (like "feeling okay" fitting into medium or "I'm terrible" fitting into low). Another example would be analyzing malware samples. There are plenty of taxonomies of malware, one of which we discussed in Chapter 2, Science and Cyber Security, based on the objective of the malware. We could analyze our samples of malware and make a determination if they are ransomware or worms. You can utilize multiple codes for a set of unstructured data. Once you have transformed your data into a set of codes you are then able to use the following methods of analysis for nominal and ordinal data.

Proportions

Nominal data is binned into categories. The categories naturally lend themselves to proportionality analysis. By analyzing the proportions of these categories you can gain understanding of trends of data based on the most common versus least common categories in comparison to other variables of data. A good example of proportional analysis is the Status of ISCM (Information Security Continuous Monitoring) Programs by Maturity Level for Chief Financial Officers (CFO) Act Agencies from the 2015 US Federal Information Security Modernization Act Report. As you can see in Fig. 5.1, when looking at the proportionality of the data on the federal agencies, approximately 90% have not sufficiently implemented an ISCM capability. About 65% have ad-hoc and informal processes and another 26% have defined a process but not yet implemented it. Only ~10% of the agencies have adequately implemented this but only as the minimal level where it is consistently running. None of the companies have a smoothly managed and monitored program let alone an optimized and efficient program. These proportions show that there may be some underlying cause, whether there is a difference of understanding of what constitutes an ISCM or something like a lack of available technology, is preventing the majority of agencies from meeting this cyber security defensive requirement.

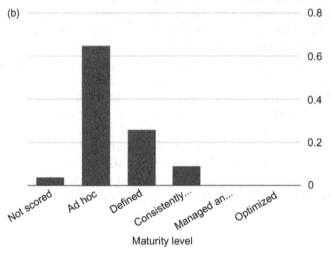

(a)

Maturity Level	No. of Agencies	Percentage
Not Scored	1	0.04
Ad hoc	15	0.65
Defined	6	0.26
Consistently Implemented	2	0.09
Managed and Measurable	0	0
Optimized	0	0

FIGURE 5.1

Status of ISCM Programs by Maturity Level (CFO Act Agencies).[9]

Frequency Statistics

Frequency statistics provide a method of analyzing data that can be counted. Both nominal and ordinal data can be counted, therefore frequency statistics is a useful tool in learning something about a dataset. Nominal data, which can be categorized, is possible to determine the mode of a dataset. A **mode** is the most frequently occurring value. If, however, you collect ordinal data in your descriptive study, this enables you to also determine a median value. The median is the middle value of an ordered set of data. For a visual representation of the mode and median, refer the central tendency section of Chapter 4, Exploratory Study.

DESCRIPTIVE STUDY METHOD EXAMPLES

We are going to use the same set of questions to help inform the planning and execution of the descriptive studies addressed. The purpose of these questions is to help identify shortfalls in the planning before you begin to conduct your research. The earlier you catch issues and problems, the less costly and impactful they are in the long run. Ultimately, some challenges might be infeasible to resolve (unable to ever get IRB approval, inflexible time window, etc.), but the sooner these issues are identified, the better off the research.

Descriptive studies are often focused on smaller-scale subjects. Elicitation studies cover interviews, surveys, and questionnaires. While these forms of study could grow quite large, they fundamentally are a one-on-one, or small-group investigation. Similarly, case reports (the simplest form of study) and case studies are focused on a single infection, incident, event, or subject. For example, a corporate incident report that documents the initial infection, spread, detection, and mitigation of the newest strain of malware would be an example of a case report (likely applied in nature if it was conducted for commercial reasons). Similarly, a case study could start with the same malware and follow a university team reverse engineering, studying, and dissecting the malware to understand its provenance, taxonomy, functionality, and perhaps authorship and objectives. This sort of research would be a foundational case study if conducted for the purposes of understanding and knowledge discovery. However, if, for example, a for-profit, antimalware company conducted a similar endeavor, with the purpose of advertising or to highlight the capabilities of their products, then this would be an example of applied case study.

In our examples, we will expand upon an example started in the Cross-sectional example section of Chapter 4, Exploratory Study. In this example, a team of researchers at a university would like to explore the correlation of time spent on specific websites compared to relative security posture. In the cross-sectional study, data was collected at the border of the university to see what websites are visited by students and a survey was sent across the campus to assess student cyber security competency. The goal is to understand if, in a given population, the security competency can be inferred from browsing habits.

DID YOU KNOW?

Certain universities have strong preference for professor-led research projects. If you are a part of a student team, and you have worked with the IRB, it would still behoove you to ensure you have a sympathetic professor who can run interference and even sponsor the research. This obviously varies from one university to another, but often, the mechanism, and sponsorship for research are geared to professors.

Case Study

Case studies are one of the most basic forms of observational study. They are typically used to focus on one scenario, event, or circumstance. Because of this specificity, they are limited in their generalizability and broader applicability. In the medical and social sciences, case studies are scientifically driven descriptions of a singular incident or disease. This is compared to the less rigorous case report, which is merely descriptive and is addressed later. Remember that a case study is limited in scope and applicability, but is also a useful type of observational study. For the purposes of this topic, we will describe an example case study. Let's propose that the previous university research team, in conducting the previous cross-sectional study, stumbled upon an active malware phoning home by making a sequence of suspicious DNS queries (that only their study previously would have noticed). The researchers mentioned this malware to some colleagues who specialized in malware reverse engineering. This led to a subsequent research project. The goal of this study is to describe the behavior and performance of this malware in detail. The researchers hope to figure out who wrote the malware, but at the very least they hope they can identify what family or style of malware it is.

Questions to address before collection:

- *What types of questions are you asking (qualitative vs quantitative, relationship, volume, one off/black swans, or routine occurrences)?*
  - Since this is a descriptive case study this topic will fall into the qualitative category. And ideally would be a unique or special occurrence worth documenting. The researchers would like to taxonomically identify this malware and figure out if they can determine country/organization of origin.
- *How much data will you need? Do you know what amount will be statistically significant for the conclusions or answers you hope to address?*
  - Given the limited nature of case studies, the researchers will likely have the information that they need. They started with the binary, but they were successful in decompiling the executable into source code. Given the limited scope of this study, the researchers are confident they have all the information they need for the preliminary study. Subsequent information they might need include other samples of similar code, related malware, or additional tools to reverse engineer, and deal with any antidisassembly controls the malware authors have included.
- *Who owns the dataset? Privacy, access, control, dissemination, and other issues will need to be addressed beforehand.*
  - Interesting question in the context of malware. However, since the software was running in a university setting, case precedent seems to indicate that the university can run, modify, and study the software. However, there might be licenses and international property issues that would contraindicate this. Their province has not yet been established in the courts. Additionally, all the notes and observations taken by the research team are of course their own property and would not have any ownership issues.

- *Can you easily recollect or recreate the dataset? Are you able to come back and revisit your initial assumptions if they do not pan out?*
  - Not directly relevant here. The initial dataset is a malware executable. This malware could be re-examined or it could be caught in the wild again. Subsequently caught samples might undergo evolution or modification, which would change the results but be an interesting analysis in its own right.
- *Are you sampling? Will you be able to collect the entire population or dataset?*
  - This is very common in network traffic. If you have to sample, what is the method? What artifacts or challenges might it introduce? Not applicable. And often, not as much of an issue for case studies that are focused in a narrow and specific topic, time, or area.
- *Have you reviewed this with your IRB again?*
  - After defining the steps to identify, disassemble, and study the malware, the IRB review determined that there were no human subject issues related to this effort.

Elicitation Studies

Elicitation studies gather information from human subjects. This is often directly from the researcher (or a research project) to the human subject at hand. This sort of study does not rely on indirect information collection (network or system behavior) as much as it does investigate the human element directly. Examples of this are surveys and human subject interviews.

Sticking with the same university, the initial team that conducted the cross-sectional study, would like to follow up with a simple questionnaire to users that represent the six groups they identified: security, technology, news, entertainment, sports, and other enthusiasts. The goal is to conduct an assessment of how people in those six categories rate their own cyber security savvy/ "hygiene." The PIs would like to determine if self-described security and technology users are more security savvy than the other groups.

Questions to address before collection:

- *Have you reviewed this with your IRB?*
  - This style of observational (descriptive) study will definitely require extensive involvement with your institution's review board. Given the direct and immediate interaction with human subjects, you will need to ensure that you are safely, humanely, and fairly interacting with the population, especially if they are a sensitive population such as children, prisoners, pregnant women, and others with an enhanced societal responsibility. Even if the subjects do not fall into these groups (the classic healthy, university student population), you still need to take

steps to ensure that you appropriately interact with the population. Secondarily, you will want to make sure you control for bias and error in your population itself. See the previous chapter with some forms of bias, but it is important to realize that when dealing with human subjects you will have additional sources of error and assumption that have to be managed and controlled. For example, some subjects will exaggerate or artificially inflate their answer, and this can occur subconsciously or deliberately. Similarly, other subjects might provide answers that they believe the interviewers or researchers are looking for, irrespective of the truth. These issues can be controlled for (explaining the anonymous nature, the necessity for truth, appropriate incentive structures, sufficiently large collections, robust population samples, etc.).

- *What types of questions are you asking (qualitative vs quantitative, relationship, volume, one off/black swans, or routine occurrences)? Clearly the questions must be observable, but the dataset may not exist.*
  - The researchers would like to ask both subjective and some quantitative questions of their participants. They start with self-assessment questions that cover subject perception of their own cyber security knowledge. They then share a few cyber security puzzle problems and challenge questions to attempt to control for subject matter competency. The subjects are asked to simply respond with what they know and not collaborate or look up answers. This balance of self-assessed and more empirical data is designed to provide a more complete picture.

- *How much data will you need? Do you know what amount will be statistically significant for the conclusions or answers you hope to address?*
  - The researchers work up a scheme that will sample from the total population spread proportionally over all six categories, but they will ensure sufficient coverage in every category. Additionally, they will utilize a Z score method to summarize the results, because it will help compare individual subject results with the average population overall (see Chapter 4: Exploratory Study, for description of the Z score method). The researchers will make sure it is clear what the raw data was that they summarized.

- *Who owns the dataset? Privacy, access, control, dissemination, and other issues will need to be addressed beforehand.*
  - The IRB worked with the researchers to address individual privacy issues by helping to craft an anonymous survey that has sufficient population size in the categories to preserve privacy.

- *Can you easily recollect or recreate the dataset? Are you able to come back and revisit your initial assumptions if they do not pan out?*
  - This sort of data would not be easily recollected and a new survey would need to be conducted. Because of that, the researcher enlisted

the help of other researchers from the social sciences with experience in conducting surveys to help avoid pitfalls.

- *Are you sampling? Will you be able to collect the entire population or dataset? This is very common in network traffic. If you have to sample, what is the method? What artifacts or challenges might it introduce?*
  - This effort will be sampled. The proctors will ensure that for each of the six groups they identified: security, technology, news, entertainment, sports, and other enthusiasts, that a sufficient number of population responds to ensure coverage, even if this requires multiple solicitations.
- *Have you reviewed this with your IRB again? Has anything changed that might warrant a second review?*
  - IRB was consulted throughout this effort and as such there were no final surprises and the research plan was approved on time.

Case Report

The fundamental difference between a case report and a case study is that a study attempts, even superficially, to answer a question or explain why. The researcher will have a hunch or initial expectation that a case study will explore. Case reports simply describe the scenario, infection, or phenomena. They are quite prevalent in the current cyber security literature when a particular technology is described, without any associated performance or security experiment and without even a rigorous study of its behavior in context. Those sorts of papers would be best described as a case report, simply describing, without providing context or assumptions. These case reports are commonly collected and even published in the medical community, but have not yet caught on in the cyber security field. However, unfortunately, the cyber security community often publishes papers that are little more than glorified case reports. Any paper that describes a technology, product, or algorithm without going into detail on the study or experiment that was conducted on the solution is essentially a straightforward case report, the lowest form of empirical research. Without information of the hypothetico-deductive experimental setup, or the controls and assumption for the particular study, the audience is left with the impression that results were collected, but with only the evidence of a case report.

Case reports are often artifacts of operations. Perhaps a research institution's IT department detects a malware infection that has compromised a dozen systems throughout their network. The standard practice for this institution is to write up the infection, the scope of impact, and the mitigation. This is done to document the impact and can be shared with the larger community in hope of helping to prevent the spread in the future.

REPORTING YOUR RESULTS

The final important step of an observational study is reporting your results. The greatest discoveries have little value if no one knows about them, and cannot leverage the knowledge for further science or can engineer something with more predictable behavior. The two most prevalent forms of documenting study results are conferences and journals. However, for observational research in this chapter (especially case reports), often peer-reviewed venues will not look favorably on those types of research. To that end, other venues such as letters, technical reports, public announcements, or other alternatives can be used to disseminate the information. These methods, while often not peer-reviewed, are often appropriate for the subject matter and ensure that the community gains access to the material.

If appropriate, conferences and journals provide a path to insert your knowledge into the field's corpus. However, the quality venues all require peer-reviewed acceptance. Peer review provides a validation check against the topic of research, methods of research, and the quality of reporting the research to ensure a certain level of quality is maintained. Ideally, the quality of the work should be the only metric of acceptance, in reality the novelty, ground-breaking, and popularity of the topic also play into the review process, so these things should be taken into account when you select your venue. In this section, we provide a general template for reporting observational studies, which will be applicable to most conferences and journals.

Sample Format

In the following, we will provide you with a general outline for publishing your results. Every publication will provide their own formatting guidelines. Be sure to check your selected venue's submission requirements to make sure you follow any outline and formatting specifications. The outline provided here follows a common flow of information found in published papers and should meet the requirements of a larger number of publisher specifications.

Every paper is unique and requires some different ways of presentation; however, the provided sample flow includes all of the general information that is important to cover in a paper and is a general starting format we take when starting to write a paper and then modify it to support the topic and venue. We understand that every researcher has their own style of presentation, so feel free to use this as a jumping-off point. The discussions of each section are provided to explain what is important to include and why, so you can present the important information in whatever way best suits your style.

Note: Technical reports would omit the study methods section and likely simply summarize the information in a single section. This could include a sequence of events and description of findings. The results section would be similarly different. No analysis would be conducted per se, rather a description of the exploration and findings would be presented.

Another example outline can be found at the Strobe Initiative.[10] The Strobe Initiative goals are to enable the STrengthening the Reporting of OBservational studies in Epidemiology (STROBE).[11]

Title
This title section should be self-explanatory. Provide sufficient information to help audience determine if they should read more. Some authors enjoy clever or amusing titles, your mileage may vary. You should indicate what type of study you conducted.

Abstract
The abstract is a concise and clear summary of the paper. The goal of an abstract is to provide readers with a quick description of what the paper discusses. You should only talk about what is stated in the rest of the paper and nothing additional. Each submission venue will provide guidelines on how to provide an abstract. Generally, this includes the maximum length of the abstract and formatting instructions, but sometimes this will include information on the type and layout of the content to provide.

Introduction
The first section of a paper should always be an introduction for the reader into the rest of the paper. The introduction section provides the motivation and reasoning behind why the research was performed. This should include a statement of the research question and any motivating questions that were used for the research. If any background information is required, such as explaining the domain, environment, or context of the research, you would discuss it here. If the audience is significantly removed from some aspect of this topic, it may be worth it to create an independent background section.

Related Work
The related works section should include a quick summarization of the field's knowledge about this research topic. Is this a follow-up case report? Are you repeating someone else's case study? Are you following a survey template or methodology?

Study Methods
This section will highlight the methods used in the case study, or the design of the questionnaire/ survey, or finally the reasons and objects of the case

report. Be sure to provide sufficient detail that a reader will understand the why of what you did. Leave the results (the what) to the next section.

Study Results

In the results section of your paper, explain what you found after you performed your analysis. For the survey results or case study results, lay out the significance, confidence intervals, and effect sizes for all of the study. Creating tables to show results is usually an efficient and effective method. You should address the participants in the study. Also, you could show pictures of interesting results; that is if a data anomaly occurred, or to display the distributions of the data samples. This should include descriptive data (the inputs) and outcome data (the outputs), and the analysis. If anything unexpected occurred, and shows up in the data, explain it in this section. For a case report, ensure to clearly document the finding and rationale for conclusions.

Discussion/Future Work

The discussion/future work section is for highlighting key results and results you found interesting or noteworthy. You should mention any limitations about which the reader should know. You can interpret and discuss any important correlations and discuss generalizability and causal relationships as relevant. Discuss where you think this work should lead next.

Conclusion/Summary

In the final section of the paper, summarize the results and conclusions of the paper. The conclusion section is often a place readers jump to quickly after reading the abstract. Make a clear and concise statement about what the ultimate results of the study were and what you learned from them.

Acknowledgments

The acknowledgments section is a place for you to acknowledge anyone who helped you with parts of the research. This is also a good place to acknowledge funding sources that supported your research.

References

Each publication will provide some guidelines on how to format references. Follow their guidelines and list all your references at the end of your paper. Depending on the length of the paper, you will want to adjust the number of references. Usually, the longer the paper, the more references. A good rule of thumb is 15–20 references for a 6-page paper. For peer-reviewed publications, the majority of your references should be other peer-reviewed works. Even if this paper is not peer-reviewed (technical report, or letter), sufficient citation and references are important. Referencing web pages and wikipedia doesn't generate confidence in reviewers. Also, make sure you only list references that are relevant to your paper, that is don't inflate your reference count. Good reviewers will check references and this will likely disqualify and reflect poorly on you.

Endnotes

1. Moore, D., and Shannon, C. (2002, November). Code-Red: A case study on the spread and victims of an Internet worm. In *Proceedings of the 2nd ACM SIGCOMM Workshop on Internet measurment* (pp. 273–284). ACM.
2. Mandiant. (n.d.). *APT1 Exposing One of China's Cyber Espionage Units*. Retrieved from https://www.fireeye.com/content/dam/fireeye-www/services/pdfs/mandiant-apt1-report.pdf.
3. McAfee® Foundstone® Professional Services and McAfee Labs™. (February, 2011). *Global Energy Cyberattacks: "Night Dragon"*. Retrieved from https://www.mcafee.com/us/resources/white-papers/wp-global-energy-cyberattacks-night-dragon.pdf.
4. Farrell, S. (December 31, 2008). Quotes of 2008: "We are in a state of shocked disbelief". *The Independent*. Retrieved February 25, 2017, from http://www.independent.co.uk/news/business/analysis-and-features/quotes-of-2008-we-are-in-a-state-of-shocked-disbelief-1220057.html.
5. Holmqvist, K., Nyström, M., Andersson, R., Dewhurst, R., Jarodzka, H., and Van de Weijer, J. (2011). *Eye tracking: A comprehensive guide to methods and measures*. OUP Oxford.
6. Imler, B., and Eichelberger, M. (2011). *Using screen capture to study user research behavior*. Library Hi Tech, 29(3), 446–454.
7. MIT-LL. (n.d.). DARPA intrusion detection data sets. *Cyber Systems and Technology*. Retrieved February 25, 2017, from https://www.ll.mit.edu/ideval/data/
8. DHS S&T CSD. (n.d.). *Trusted Cyber Risk Research Data Sharing*. The Information Marketplace for Policy and Analysis of Cyber-Risk & Trust (IMPACT). Retrieved February 25, 2017, from https://www.dhs.gov/csd-impact
9. United States of America, Office of Management and Budget. (n.d.). *Annual Report to Congress: Federal Information Security Modernization Act* (Vol. 2015).
10. STROBE Initiative. (n.d.). *STROBE Statement*. Retrieved from http://www.strobe-statement.org/fileadmin/Strobe/uploads/checklists/STROBE_checklist_v4_combined.pdf.
11. STROBE Statement: Home. (n.d.). Retrieved February 25, 2017, from http://www.strobe-statement.org/.

## CHAPTER 6

Machine Learning

Machine learning is a computational process to discover the underlying models of system behavior. Machine learning takes datasets, processes them, and attempts to discover causal variables. Machine learning techniques were big in the 1980s during the first artificial intelligence. Machine learning is having a major resurgence in the last decade because of the immense amounts of data available and the significant advancements in computational power.

The absence of a robust and unified theory of cyber dynamics presents challenges and opportunities for using machine learning—based data-driven approaches to further the understanding of the behavior of such complex systems. Analysts can also use machine learning approaches to gain operational insights. In order to be operationally beneficial, cyber security machine learning—based models need to have the ability to: (1) represent a real-world system, (2) infer system properties, and (3) learn and adapt based on expert knowledge and observations. Probabilistic models and probabilistic graphical models provide these necessary properties and are further explored in this chapter. Bayesian networks (BNs) and hidden Markov models (HMMs) are introduced as an example of a widely used data-driven classification/modeling strategy.

This chapter is organized as follows: We begin with an introduction of machine learning concepts and techniques. This is followed by a discussion of validating models derived through machine learning. Finally, we will explore using BNs and HMMs.

CHAPTER OBJECTIVES

- Introduce machine learning
- Discuss model validation
- Explore the use of Bayesian networks and hidden Markov models in cyber security research

153

Research Methods for Cyber Security. DOI: http://dx.doi.org/10.1016/B978-0-12-805349-2.00006-6

WHAT IS MACHINE LEARNING

Machine learning is a field of study that looks at using computational algorithms to turn empirical data into usable models. The machine learning field grew out of traditional statistics and artificial intelligences communities. From the efforts of mega corporations such as Google, Microsoft, Facebook, Amazon, and so on, machine learning has become one of the hottest computational science topics in the last decade. Through their business processes immense amounts of data have been and will be collected. This has provided an opportunity to re-invigorate the statistical and computational approaches to autogenerate useful models from data.

Machine learning algorithms can be used to (a) gather understanding of the cyber phenomenon that produced the data under study, (b) abstract the understanding of underlying phenomena in the form of a model, (c) predict future values of a phenomena using the above-generated model, and (d) detect anomalous behavior exhibited by a phenomenon under observation. There are several open-source implementations of machine learning algorithms that can be used with either application programming interface (API) calls or nonprogrammatic applications. Examples of such implementations include Weka,[1] Orange,[2] and RapidMiner.[3] The results of such algorithms can be fed to visual analytic tools such as Tableau[4] and Spotfire[5] to produce dashboards and actionable pipelines.

Cyber space and its underlying dynamics can be conceptualized as a manifestation of human actions in an abstract and high-dimensional space. In order to begin solving some of the security challenges within cyber space, one needs to sense various aspects of cyber space and collect data.[6] The observational data obtained is usually large and increasingly streaming in nature. Examples of cyber data include error logs, firewall logs, and network flow.

CATEGORIES OF MACHINE LEARNING

There are two dimensions around which machine learning is generally categorized: the process by which it learns and the type of output or problem it attempts to solve. For the first machine learning–based solution strategies can be broadly classified into three categories based on the mechanism used to perform learning namely, supervised learning, semisupervised learning, and unsupervised learning.[7] For the latter, machine learning algorithms can be broken into four categories: classification, clustering, regression, and anomaly detection.

The style of learning has an impact upon the question you are trying to solve. In some cases, you have data that you do not know the ground truth, other times it is possible to label data with categories or classifications. Sometimes you know what a good result looks like but you may not know what variables are important to get there. By categorizing machine learning techniques by the learning style can help you in selecting the best approach for your research. Table 6.1 discusses the different styles and provides a sample set of machine learning algorithms.

Supervised learning involves using a labeled dataset (e.g., the outcomes are known and labeled). Unsupervised learning is used in cases where the labels of the data are unknown (e.g., when the outcomes are unknown, but some similar measure is desired). Examples of unsupervised learning approaches include self-organizing maps (SOMs), K-means clustering, expectation—maximization (EM), and hierarchical clustering.[8] Unsupervised learning approaches can also be used for preliminary data exploration such as clustering similar error logs entries. Results of unsupervised algorithms are frequently visualized using visual analytic tools. An important caveat on using an unsupervised approach is to make sure one knows the numeric space that the data encompasses as well as the type of distance measure applied. Semisupervised approaches are a hybrid of unsupervised and supervised approaches. Such approaches are used when only some of the data is unlabeled. Semisupervised approaches are used when a portion of the data is unlabeled. Such approaches can be inductive or transductive.[9]

While it is sometimes helpful in picking algorithms based on what type of input data is available, it is equally helpfully to break them out along the

Table 6.1 Learning Style Categorization of Machine Learning Algorithms

Style	Definition	Example Algorithms
Unsupervised	In **unsupervised learning**, no extra or meta data is provided to the algorithm and it is forced to discover the structure data and the relationship of variables by observing a raw dataset.	K-means clustering, hierarchical clustering, principal component analysis
Supervised	In **supervised learning**, input data is annotated with expert information detailing what the expected output or answer would be. The process of annotating data for supervised learning is called **labeling**.	Neural network, Bayesian networks, decision tree, support vector machine
Semi-supervised	In **semisupervised learning** a small set of learning data is labeled but large gaps in labeling are present. This is largely used when it is known that a small number of variables led to a result, but the full extent of the variables involved is unknown. A special case of semisupervised learning is called **reinforced learning** where an expert informs the algorithm if its output is correct or not.	Expectation—maximization, transductive support vector machine, Markov decision processes

Table 6.2 Categories of Machine Learning Algorithms Separated by Problems they Address[10]

Problem	Definition	Example Algorithms
Classification	**Classification** algorithms take labeled data and generate models that classify new data into the learned labels.	Hidden Markov models, support vector machines (SVMs), random forests, naïve bayes, probabilistic graphical models, logistic regression, neural networks [9]
Clustering	**Cluster analysis** attempts to take a dataset and define clusters of like items.	K-means, heirarchical, density-based (DBSCAN)
Regression	**Regression** attempts to generate a predictive model by optimizing the error in learned data.	Linear,logistic, ordinary least squares, multivariate adaptive regression splines
Anomaly detection	**Anomaly detection** takes a dataset of "normal" items and learns a model of normal. This model is used to determine if any new data is anomalous or low probability of occurring.	One-class SVM, linear regression and logistic regression, frequent pattern growth (FP-growth), a priori

result types provided. Variables within a dataset can be numeric (i.e., discrete or continuous), ordinal (i.e., order matters), cardinal (i.e., integer valued), nominal/categorical (i.e., used as an outcome class name). Machine learning algorithms can also be categorized based on the type of problem they solve. An example of such a breakdown of algorithms is listed in Table 6.2.

Decision tree algorithms: classification trees (e.g.,C4.5) can be used in cases of a nominal class variable while regression trees can be used for continuous numeric valued outcome variables.

As discussed by Murphy et al.,[11] several issues affect the alternative learning schemes, including:

- Dynamic range of the features
- Number of features
- Type of the class variable
- Types of the features
- Heavily correlated features

In order to be operationally beneficial, cyber security machine learning–based models need to have the ability to: (1) represent a real-world system, (2) infer system properties, and (3) learn and adapt based on expert knowledge and observations. Probabilistic graphical models have wide applications for assessing and quantifying cyber security risks.[12,13] These models contain desirable properties including representation of a real-world system, inference about queries of interest related to the system, and learning from expert knowledge and past experience.[14] The probabilistic terms in these models may be estimated or learned from historical data, generated from simulation experiments, or elicited through informed judgments of subject matter experts.

DID YOU KNOW?

A common application of anomaly detection machine learning algorithms is credit card fraud detection. Machine learning is used to generate models of each customer's behavior and usage pattern. If the activity appears that is deemed anomalous by the model then a fraud alert is triggered. So when you go on vacation and get a fraud alert from using your credit card, you should know this means you deviated enough from your schedule such that it appears anomalous.

Owing to the adaptive nature of cyber threats, probabilistic cyber risk models need to accommodate efficient updating of model structure and parameter estimates as new intelligence and information becomes available. Also, understanding relationships between factors influencing the occurrence and impacts of such events is a critical task. Bayesian networks, or probabilistic directed acyclic graphs, have mathematical properties for characterizing relationships between dynamic event and system factors, can be updated using probabilistic theories, and produce inference and predictions for unobserved factors given evidence. Past research indicates the potential for the application of BNs along with attack graphs for real-world cyber defenses.[15,16,17,18] HMMs have been widely used to generate data-driven models for several cyber security solutions.

DEBUGGING MACHINE LEARNING

One of the challenges with machine learning is the problem of overfitting or underfitting called *variance* and *bias* respectively. **Model variance** or **overfitting** is when a machine learning developed model fits the training dataset very well but fails to generalize to new datasets. Model bias or underfitting is when the machine learning generated model has high error in fitting the training set. This can commonly occur when you are learning over too many features There are two general options to address overfitting: reduce the number of features or use regularization. **Regularization** is the process to reduce the magnitude of values of a large feature set.

If you find that a model you have developed through machine learning is making large errors in predictions what should you do? One approach is to develop a diagnostic. A **machine learning diagnostic** is a test designed to gain insight into what isn't working in an algorithm or how to improve its performance. Diagnostics can be difficult to build but they are well worth it in the long run.

Another good approach to validating your model is to use cross-validation. **Cross-validation** is a process to evaluate the generalizability of your developed model. The process of doing cross-validation largely starts with dividing your initial dataset into three; a training set, a cross-validation set, and a test set. You want to have a sufficient amount of data for your training set so a good rule of thumb is to make the divisions at 60% training, 20% cross validation, and 20% test. The cross-validation set is used to tune or find the best-fit model parameters. Then the test set is used to determine the generalizability of the generated model.

There are a few more tips for addressing. To fix high variance you can get more training data or try to learn around a smaller set of features or variables. To fix high bias try adding more features or polynomial features. In both cases tuning your parameters can help.

> ### DID YOU KNOW?
>
> In 2011 the IBM Watson super computer competed in two Jeopardy matches with Brad Rutter and Ken Jennings, two of the most successful Jeopardy players in history. The technology underlying Watson's ability to parse and answer questions, called DeepQA, leveraged over 100 machine learning algorithms.[19] But it wasn't just the algorithms alone but also the pipeline and structured sequence of using the machine learning algorithms that helped Watson best two of the best Jeopardy contestants.

BAYESIAN NETWORK MATHEMATICAL PRELIMINARIES AND MODEL PROPERTIES

A **BN** is a graphical model that represents uncertainties (as probabilities) associated with discrete or continuous random variables (nodes) and their conditional dependencies (edges) within a directed acyclic graph.[20,21]

BNs model the relationships among variables and may be updated as additional information about these variables becomes available. Mathematically, if nodes represent a set of random variables, $X = X_1, X_2, ..., X_n$ then a set of links connecting these nodes $X_i \rightarrow X_j$ represent the dependencies among the variables. Also, each node is conditionally independent of nondescendant nodes given its parent nodes and has an attached probability function. As a result, the joint probability of all nodes, $P(X)$ may be represented as: $\prod_{i=1}^{n} P(X_i \mid parents(X_i))$.

Strengths and Limitations
Key strengths and limitations of BNs are listed below:

- Models dependencies among random variables as directed acyclic graphs
- Allows probabilistic inference of unobserved variables
- Graphical representation may be intuitive for users

- Incorporate data/expert judgments and update structure/parameters as "new" data/knowledge becomes available
- Inferring structure of an unknown network may be computationally demanding from a scalability perspective
- Identifying reliable prior knowledge is a challenge

Data-driven Learning and Probabilistic Inference within Bayesian Networks

Structure learning within **Directed Acyclic Graphs** (DAGs) may be broadly classified as: (1) *constraint-based* and (2) *score-based*. Constraint-based algorithms use conditional independence tests using the data to build causal graphs that satisfy constraints. A challenge associated with constraint-based approaches is identifying independence properties and optimizing network structure. Also, these approaches do not account for a well-defined objective function and may result in nonoptimal graphical structures. Score-based algorithms assigns a score function to the entire space of causal graphs and typically use greedy search among various potential DAGs to identify the structure with the highest score. These approaches are optimization-based and tend to scale better.

Data-driven statistical learning methods (e.g., *Hill Climbing* and *Grow-Shrink* algorithms) may be adopted to infer Bayesian network structures for various parameters of interest across geographic regions. **Hill Climbing** is a score-based algorithm that uses greedy heuristic search to maximize scores assigned to candidate networks.[22] **Grow-Shrink** is a constraint-based algorithm that uses conditional independence tests to detect *blankets* (comprised of a node's parents, children, and children's other parents) of various variables.

DIG DEEPER: BAYESIAN NETWORK PROVENANCE

The probabilities and process underlying BNs was first defined by Thomas Bayes in mid-17th century. The Bayes rule determines the probability of an event by updating prior probabilities with new information. It wasn't until the 1980s that Judea Pearl made the distinction between evidence and causality. In the Bayesian network defined by Pearl, the nature and uncertainty of evidence is taken into account before updating probabilities.

Parameter Learning

Probabilistic parameters associated with these network structures may be estimated using *expectation maximization* and *maximum likelihood* estimation techniques. **Expectation maximization** is useful with not fully observed data, and is an iterative algorithm where in the "Expectation" step the probability of unobserved variables given observed and current parameters are estimated. Thereafter, in the "Maximization" step the current parameters are updated through log-likelihood maximization.

Maximum likelihood approach is useful with fully observed data and involves estimating probabilistic parameters θ, for each node in the graph such that the log-likelihood function, $log(P(X|\theta))$, is maximized.

Bayesian estimation is also an option, where θ is treated as a random variable, a prior probability $p(\theta)$ is assumed, and data is used to estimate the posterior probability of $p(\theta|X)$.

Probabilistic Inference

BNs apply Bayes' theorem for inference of unobserved variables. **Variable elimination** (by integration or summation) of unobserved, nonquery variables is a widely used exact inference method. Approximate inference methods include stochastic *Markov Chain monte Carlo (MCMC)* simulation, *logic sampling, likelihood weighting,* and others.

Notional Example with bnlearn Package in R

R, in conjunction with the RStudio integrated development environment, provides a powerful platform for data analysis. The default setup of R provides several libraries including the stat library. R and RStudio need to be installed separately.[23,24] The example described below uses the R package "*bnlearn*"[25] for structure learning, parameter learning, and probabilistic inference. The code begins by loading the "learning" dataset. This data has discrete levels for each of the following random variables: In a realistic cyber setting, these random variables (e.g., A, B, etc.) may represent the time-varying health of system components and the levels (e.g., a, b, c) may represent the discrete states of health.

```
#install.packages("bnlearn")
library(bnlearn)
data(learning.test)
str(learning.test)
##  'data.frame': 5000 obs. of 6 variables:
##    $ A: Factor w/ 3 levels "a","b","c": 2 2 1 1 1 3 3 2 2 2...
##    $ B: Factor w/ 3 levels "a","b","c": 3 1 1 1 1 3 3 2 2 1...
##    $ C: Factor w/ 3 levels "a","b","c": 2 3 1 1 2 1 2 1 2 2...
##    $ D: Factor w/ 3 levels "a","b","c": 1 1 1 1 3 3 3 2 1 1...
##    $ E: Factor w/ 3 levels "a","b","c": 2 2 1 2 1 3 3 2 3 1...
##    $ F: Factor w/ 2 levels "a","b": 2 2 1 2 1 1 1 2 1 1...
head(learning.test)
##   A B C D E F
## 1 b c b a b b
## 2 b a c a b b
## 3 a a a a a a
## 4 a a a a b b
## 5 a a b c a a
## 6 c c a c c a
```

Structure learning using *Hill Climbing* and *Grow-Shrink* results in the following.

```
raw <- data.frame(learning.test)
bn.h <- hc(raw) #hill climbing
bn.g <- gs(raw) #grow-shrink
bn.h
##
##    Bayesian network learned via score-based methods
##
##    model:
##     [A][C][F][B|A][D|A:C][E|B:F]
##    nodes:                                6
##    arcs:                                 5
##      undirected arcs:                    0
##      directed arcs:                      5
##    average markov blanket size:          2.33
##    average neighbourhood size:           1.67
##    average branching factor:             0.83
##
##    learning algorithm:                   Hill-Climbing
##    score:                                BIC (disc.)
##    penalization coefficient:             4.258597
##    tests used in the learning procedure: 40
##    optimized:                            TRUE
```

Bayesian Information Criterion (BIC) score above is a measure of relative model quality, and provides a mechanism for model selection by balancing goodness-of-fit and complexity through a *penalty term*. Lower *BIC* scores are preferred; however, these scores do not represent model quality in the absolute sense and must be interpreted carefully.

The resulting structures are given below. The dependencies among certain nodes learned solely from data may or may not make intuitive sense and can be updated based on expert inputs (e.g., *blacklist* or *whitelist*). *Blacklist* indicates an expert-provided absence of a relationship between nodes that is indicated prior to data-driven structure learning; and *Whitelist* is the presence of such a relationship. The different approaches can result in different outcomes including directionality or the lack thereof between nodes.

```
#source("https://bioconductor.org/biocLite.R")
#biocLite("Rgraphviz")
library(Rgraphviz)
##  Loading required package: graph
##  ## Attaching package: 'graph'
##  The following objects are masked from 'package:bnlearn':
```

```
##
##     degree, nodes, nodes < -
##   Loading required package: grid
par(mfrow = c(1, 2))
graphviz.plot(bn.h, main = "Hill climbing")
graphviz.plot(bn.g, main = "Grow-shrink")
```

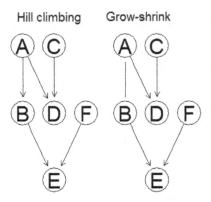

In this notional example, the *hill climbing* and *grow-shrink*-based BN structures above are similar except the directionality between nodes A and B. Grow-shrink results in an undirected edge between nodes A and B, whereas hill climbing results in the learning of a dependence of node B on node A. Once the network structure is determined, one can learn the model parameters (i.e., *conditional probability* tables (CPT) for the *discrete* case) associated with each node in the BN. The results below display parameters of node D based on maximum likelihood and Bayesian estimation methods.

```
fit.bnm <- bn.fit(bn.h, data = raw, method = "mle")
fit.bnm$D
##
##     Parameters of node D (multinomial distribution)
##
##   Conditional probability table:
##
##   , , C = a
##
##    A
## D    a         b         c
##   a 0.80081301 0.09251810 0.10530547
##   b 0.09024390 0.80209171 0.11173633
##   c 0.10894309 0.10539019 0.78295820
##
##   , , C = b
##
##    A
```

```
## D     a          b          c
##   a 0.18079096 0.88304094 0.24695122
##   b 0.13276836 0.07017544 0.49390244
##   c 0.68644068 0.04678363 0.25914634
##
## , , C = c
##
##   A
## D     a          b          c
##   a 0.42857143 0.34117647 0.13333333
##   b 0.20238095 0.38823529 0.44444444
##   c 0.36904762 0.27058824 0.42222222
fit.bnb <- bn.fit(bn.h, data = raw, method = "bayes")
fit.bnb$D
##
##   Parameters of node D (multinomial distribution)
##
## Conditional probability table:
##
## , , C = a
##
##   A
## D     a          b          c
##   a 0.80039110 0.09273317 0.10550895
##   b 0.09046330 0.80167307 0.11193408
##   c 0.10914561 0.10559376 0.78255696
##
## , , C = b
##
##   A
## D     a          b          c
##   a 0.18126825 0.88126079 0.24724285
##   b 0.13339591 0.07102763 0.49336034
##   c 0.68533584 0.04771157 0.25939680
##
## , , C = c
##
##   A
## D     a          b          c
##   a 0.42732811 0.34107527 0.13577236
##   b 0.20409051 0.38752688 0.44308943
##   c 0.36858138 0.27139785 0.42113821
```

The code below generates a plot of the CPT.

```
bn.fit.barchart(fit.bnm$D, xlab = "Probabilities", ylab = "Levels",
main = "Conditional Probabilities")
## Loading required namespace: lattice
```

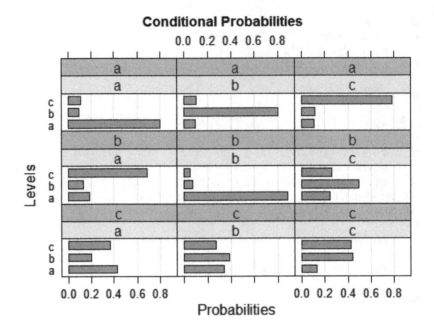

With the BN structure and parameters, we can perform probabilistic inference. *Logic sampling* and *likelihood weighting* are currently implemented options. For example, $P(B == \text{"b"} | A == \text{"a"}) \sim 0.025$.

```
cpquery(fit.bnm, event = (B == "b"), evidence = (A == "a"))
## [1] 0.02622852
cpquery(fit.bnm, event = (B == "b"), evidence = (A == "a" & D == "c"))
## [1] 0.02760351
```

BNs are also useful for in-sample and out-of-sample predictions. In-sample predictions are useful for model evaluation and out-of-sample predictions help with model testing and validation. An out-of-sample prediction example is given below with training and testing datasets and out-of-sample predictive performance of 90%.

```
train <- raw[1:4990, ]
test <- raw[4991:5000, ]
bn.train <- hc(train)
fit <- bn.fit(bn.train, data = train)
pred <- predict(fit, "D", test)
#library(xtable)
#print(xtable(cbind(pred, test[, "D"])), type= 'html')
#print(xtable(table(pred, test[, "D"])), type= 'html')
cbind(pred, test[, "D"])
##    pred
```

```
## [1,]    1 1
## [2,]    3 3
## [3,]    2 2
## [4,]    1 2
## [5,]    2 2
## [6,]    1 1
## [7,]    2 2
## [8,]    2 2
## [9,]    3 3
## [10,]   1 1
table(pred, test[, "D"])
##
##  pred a b c
##    a 3 1 0
##    b 0 4 0
##    c 0 0 2
```

HIDDEN MARKOV MODELS

In this section, we discuss HMMs,[26] which are a type of dynamic BN models. HMMs have found applications in biological sequence analysis for gene and protein structure predictions,[27,28,29] multistage network attack detection[30], and in pattern recognition problems[31] such as speech,[32] handwriting,[33] and gesture[34] recognition. HMMs model the generation of a sequence of states that can only be inferred from a sequence of observed symbols. The symbols can be discrete (e.g., events, tosses of a coin) or continuous. In a HMM, a hidden Markov process generates the sequence of states, which are in turn used to explain and characterize the occurrence of a sequence of observable symbols. Therefore, the generation of the observable symbols is probabilistically dependent on the generation of the unobservable Markov states.

To illustrate the process of generating the observation sequence in a HMM, let's denote a time-ordered sequence of observed symbols of length T, as $Y = \{Y_1, Y_2, \ldots, Y_T\}$, and the associated hidden sequence of Markov states, as $X = \{X_1, X_2, \ldots, X_T\}$. Each observed element, Y_i, can be a symbol describing the outcome of a stochastic process. Let $O = \{O_1, O_2, \ldots, O_M\}$ represent a discrete set of M such possible outcomes (observed symbols). Similarly let $S = \{S_1, S_2, \ldots, Y_N\}$ represent a discrete set of N distinct Markov states. Besides specifying the number of observed symbols, M, and the number of distinct Markov states, N, a HMM specification involves specifying three probability distributions: (1) the transition state probability distribution, A; (2) the probability distribution to choose the observed symbol from a state, B; and (3) the initial state distribution, π. The compact notation, $\lambda = (A, B, \pi)$, is normally used to represent an HMM.

Fig. 6.1 illustrates a general example of an HMM. The process of generating the observation sequence is described below.

Generation of observation sequence in HMM

1. Initialize time index, $t = 1$
2. Choose the initial state, X_t, according to the initial state distribution, π.
3. Choose the observed symbol, Y_t, according to the probability distribution, B in state X_t.
4. Choose a new state, X_{t+1} according to the state transition probability distribution, A for the current state, X_t.
5. Set $t = t + 1$
6. **if** $t < T$ **then**
7. **go to** step 3
8. **end if**

There are three types of problems that need to be solved, in order for HMMs to be useful in real-world applications:

- Problem 1: Given the observation sequence, $Y = \{Y_1, Y_2, \ldots, Y_T\}$, and the model parameters, $\lambda = (A, B, \pi)$, compute the probability

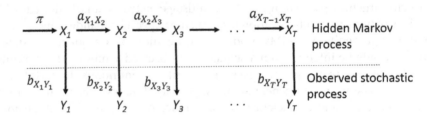

Notations

X – sequence of hidden Markov states
Y – sequence of observed symbols
S – set of N distinct Markov states ($S = \{S_1, S_2, \ldots, S_N\}$)
π – initial state distribution vector
O – set of M possible observed symbols ($O = \{O_1, O_2, \ldots, O_M\}$)
A – transition state probability matrix
$a_{X_t X_{t+1}} = A_{ij}; X_t = S_i, X_{t+1} = S_j$, for any $i = 1, 2, \ldots, N$ and $j = 1, 2, \ldots, N$

B – observation probability matrix
$b_{X_t Y_t} = B_{ik}; X_t = S_i, Y_t = O_k$, for any $i = 1, 2, \ldots, N$ and $k = 1, 2, \ldots, M$

FIGURE 6.1
General process modeled by hidden Markov models.

(likelihood), $P(Y|\lambda)$, that the observed sequence was produced by the model. Problem 1 aims to evaluate the model.

- Problem 2: Given the observation sequence, $Y = \{Y_1, Y_2, \ldots, Y_T\}$, and the model parameters, $\lambda = (A, B, \pi)$, determine the most optimal state sequence of the underlying Markov process, $X = \{X_1, X_2, \ldots, X_T\}$. Problem 2 aims to uncover the hidden part of the model.
- Problem 3: Given the observation sequence, $Y = \{Y_1, Y_2, \ldots, Y_T\}$, and the dimensions M and N, adjust the parameters of the model, $\lambda = (A, B, \pi)$, to maximize $P(O|\lambda)$. Problem 3 aims to find the best model that fits a training sequence of observed symbols.

Notional Example with HMM Package in R

This example uses the R package "*HMM*" for: (1) computing most probable path of states given a HMM and (2) inferring optimal parameters to a HMM. The Viterbi algorithm for state path estimation is implemented below:

```
#install.packages("HMM")
#source: https://cran.r-project.org/web/packages/HMM/HMM.pdf
library(HMM)
##Viterbi algorithm for computing most probable path of states given an
HMM
# HMM Initialization
hmm = initHMM(c("A","B","C"), c("o1","o2"), startProbs = matrix(c
(.25,.5,.25),1), transProbs = matrix(c
(.3,.4,.6,.4,.4,.3,.3,.2,.1),3), emissionProbs = matrix(c
(.5,.4,.9,.5,.6,.1),3))
print(hmm)
## $States
## [1] "A" "B" "C"
##
## $Symbols
## [1] "o1" "o2"
##
## $startProbs
## A    B    C
## 0.25 0.50 0.25
##
## $transProbs
##    to
## from   A   B   C
##    A 0.3 0.4 0.3
##    B 0.4 0.4 0.2
##    C 0.6 0.3 0.1
##
## $emissionProbs
##    symbols
```

```
##   states o1 o2
##      A 0.5 0.5
##      B 0.4 0.6
##      C 0.9 0.1
#  Sequence of observations
observations = c("o1","o2","o2","o1","o1","o2")
print(observations)
##   [1] "o1" "o2" "o2" "o1" "o1" "o2"
#  Calculate Viterbi path
viterbi = viterbi(hmm,observations)
print(viterbi)
##   [1] "C" "A" "B" "A" "C" "A"
```

The Viterbi-training algorithm for inferring optimal parameters is implemented below.

```
##Viterbi-training algorithm for inferring optimal parameters to an HMM
#  Initial HMM
hmm = initHMM(c("A","B","C"), c("o1","o2"), startProbs = matrix
(c(.25,.5,.25),1), transProbs = matrix
(c(.3,.4,.6,.4,.4,.3,.3,.2,.1),3), emissionProbs = matrix
(c(.5,.4,.9,.5,.6,.1),3))
#  Sequence of observations
a = sample(c(rep("o1",100),rep("o2",300)))
b = sample(c(rep("o1",300),rep("o2",100)))
observation = c(a,b)
#  Viterbi-training
vt = viterbiTraining(hmm,observation,1000)
print(vt$hmm)
##   $States
##   [1] "A" "B" "C"
##
##   $Symbols
##   [1] "o1" "o2"
##
##   $startProbs
##   A    B    C
##   0.25 0.50 0.25
##
##   $transProbs
##      to
##   from      A         B         C
##     A 0.0000000 0.2981928 0.7018072
##     B 0.4230769 0.5769231 0.0000000
##     C 1.0000000 0.0000000 0.0000000
##
##   $emissionProbs
##      symbols
##   states o1 o2
```

```
##    A 0.5 0.5
##    B 0.0 1.0
##    C 1.0 0.0
```

DISCUSSION

BNs and HMMs provide a probabilistic framework to infer, predict, and gain insights into the dependencies between components within a cyber system. The choice of random variables, their types (discrete or continuous), and state information are critical for designing and interpreting BN and HMM results. Within BNs, the strength and direction of component dependencies (represented as conditional probabilities) learned from data may vary across systems and time periods. Additional cyber intelligence information related to pre-event conditions and postevent impacts can be valuable for enhancing what-if and forensic analyses. Modeling extensions of interest may include the use of dynamic BNs that allow evolution over time and hybrid networks that can accommodate mixed discrete and continuous random variables as nodes. Further, validation approaches may be incorporated to test various data-driven learning models using appropriate training and testing datasets.

SAMPLE FORMAT

In the following, we will provide you with a general outline for publishing your results. Every publication will provide their own formatting guidelines. Be sure to check your selected venue's submission requirements to make sure you follow any outline and formatting specifications. The outline provided here follows a common flow of information found in published papers and should meet the requirements of a larger number of publisher specifications.

Every paper is unique and requires some different ways of presentation; however, the provided sample flow includes all of the general information that is important to cover in a paper and is a general starting format we take when starting to write a paper and then modify it to support the topic and venue. We understand that every researcher has their own style of presentation, so feel free to use this as a jumping-off point. The discussions of each section are provided to explain what is important to include and why, so you can present the important information in whatever way best suits your style.

Abstract

The abstract is a concise and clear summary of the paper. The goal of an abstract is to provide readers with a quick description of what the paper discusses. You should only talk about what is stated in the rest of the paper and nothing additional. Each submission venue will provide guidelines on how to provide an abstract. Generally, this includes the maximum length of the abstract and formatting instructions, but sometimes this will include information on the type and layout of the content to provide.

Introduction

The first section of a paper should always be an introduction for the reader into the rest of the paper. The introduction section provides the motivation and reasoning behind why the research was performed. This should include a statement of the research question and any motivating questions that were used for the research. If any background information is required, such as explaining the domain, environment, or context of the research, you would discuss it here. If the audience is significantly removed from some aspect of this topic, it may be worth it to create an independent background section. In machine learning papers, it is good to include the performance or learning criteria around which you will determine the quality of the machine learning application. It's also good to specify the category of machine learning you are describing in this paper; is it a new machine learning algorithm or an application of an existing machine learning approach to a new set of data?

Related Work

The related works section should include a quick summarization of the field's knowledge about this research topic. Are there competing solutions? Have other machine learning approaches been used in the past? Explain what is deficient about past applications. What was the gap in the solution space that motivated the use of the proposed machine learning approach defined in this paper.

Approach

The approach section of an applied paper is often the meat or largest portion of the paper. In this section you describe how your machine learning algorithm works and represents or systematizes knowledge. Describe your learning dataset and any processing or manipulation of the data to provide it to the algorithm.

Evaluation

In the evaluation explain how you are going to exercise the machine learning approach to generate a results dataset for performance characterization. Discuss what test datasets you will use. Explain if you do cross-validation and regularization.

Data Analysis/Results

In the results section of your paper, explain what you found after you performed your analysis. Present the performance and/or learning results around whatever metrics you define. Comparative analysis with past or competing applied solutions are very helpful in contextualizing your results. Without previous performance numbers it is difficult to understand the significance of your work. Creating tables to show results is an efficient and effective method. You can also show pictures of interesting results, that is if a data anomaly occurred or to display the distributions of the data samples.

Discussion/Future Work

The discussion/future work section is for you to provide your explanations for the results you received. Discuss additional tests you think should be performed. Discuss future directions in research that may result from the knowledge gained from the evaluation. If performance was less than expected should more observation research be performed?

Conclusion/Summary

In the final section of the paper, summarize the results and conclusions of the paper. The conclusion section is often a place readers jump to quickly after reading the abstract. Make a clear and concise statement about what the ultimate results of the experiments and what you learned from it.

Acknowledgments

The acknowledgments section is a place for you to acknowledge anyone who helped you with parts of the research that were not part of the paper. It is also good to acknowledge and funding sources that supported your research.

References

Each publication will provide some guidelines on how to format references. Follow their guidelines and list all your references at the end of your paper. Depending on the length of the paper you will want to adjust the number of references. The longer the paper the more references. A good rule of thumb is 15–20 references for a 6-page paper. For peer-reviewed publications, the majority of your references should be other peer-reviewed works. Referencing web pages and Wikipedia doesn't generate confidence in reviewers. Also, make sure you only list references that are useful to your paper, that is don't inflate your reference count. Good reviewers will check and this will likely disqualify and reflect poorly on you.

Endnotes

1. Weka 3: Data Mining Software in Java. (n.d.). Retrieved February 25, 2017, from http://www.cs.waikato.ac.nz/ml/weka/Weka.
2. Shaulsky, G., Borondics, F., Bellazzi, R. (n.d.). *Orange—Data Mining Fruitful & Fun.* Retrieved February 25, 2017, from http://orange.biolab.si/BioLab, University of Ljubljana.
3. Data Science Platform. *Machine Learning* (2017, February 22). Retrieved February 25, 2017, from http://www.rapidminer.com/rapidminer.
4. Tableau Software (n.d.). Retrieved February 25, 2017, from http://www.tableau.com/.
5. Data Visualization & Analytics Software—TIBCO Spotfire. (n.d.). Retrieved February 25, 2017, from http://spotfire.tibco.com/.
6. Sheymov, V., *Cyberspace and Security: A Fundamentally New Approach.* 2012: Cyber books publishing.
7. Chapelle, O., B. Schölkopf, and A. Zien, *Semi-supervised Learning.* 2010: MIT Press.
8. Murphy, K.P., *Machine Learning: A Probabilistic Perspective.* 2012: MIT Press.
9. Chapelle, O., B. Schölkopf, and A. Zien, *Semi-supervised Learning.* 2010: MIT Press.
10. Borgelt, C., *An implementation of the FP-growth algorithm,* in *Proceedings of the 1st international workshop on open source data mining: Frequent pattern mining implementations.* 2005, ACM: Chicago, Illinois, pp. 1−5.
11. Murphy, K.P., *Machine Learning: A Probabilistic Perspective.* 2012: MIT Press.
12. Ezell, B.C., et al., *Probabilistic risk analysis and terrorism risk.* Risk Analysis, 2010. **30**(4): p. 575−589.
13. Koller, D. and N. Friedman, *Probabilistic graphical models: principles and techniques.* 2009: MIT press.
14. Koller, D. and N. Friedman, *Probabilistic graphical models: principles and techniques.* 2009: MIT press.
15. Frigault, M., et al. *Measuring network security using dynamic bayesian network.* in *Proceedings of the 4th ACM workshop on Quality of protection.* 2008. ACM.
16. Xie, P., et al. *Using Bayesian networks for cyber security analysis.* in *2010 IEEE/IFIP International Conference on Dependable Systems and Networks (DSN).* 2010. IEEE.
17. Bode Moyinoluwa, A., K. Alese Boniface, and F. Thompson Aderonke. *A Bayesian Network Model for Risk Management in Cyber Situation.* in *Proceedings of the World Congress on Engineering and Computer Science.* 2014.
18. Shin, J., H. Son, and G. Heo, *Development of a cyber security risk model using Bayesian networks.* Reliability Engineering and System Safety, 2015. 134: p. 208−217.
19. https://www.aaai.org/Magazine/Watson/watson.php.
20. Team, R.C., *R: A language and environment for statistical computing.* 2013.
21. Nielsen, T.D. and F.V. Jensen, *Bayesian Networks and Decision Graphs.* 2007: Springer New York.
22. Bode Moyinoluwa, A., K. Alese Boniface, and F. Thompson Aderonke. *A Bayesian Network Model for Risk Management in Cyber Situation.* in *Proceedings of the World Congress on Engineering and Computer Science.* 2014.
23. Team, R.C., *R: A language and environment for statistical computing.* 2013.
24. *RStudio.* 2016: https://www.rstudio.com/.
25. Scutari, M., *Learning Bayesian networks with the bnlearn R package.* arXiv preprint arXiv:0908.3817, 2009.
26. Rabiner, L.R., *A Tutorial on Hidden Markov-Models and Selected Applications in Speech Recognition.* Proceedings of the Ieee, 1989. **77**(2): p. 257−286.
27. Yoon, B.-J., *Hidden Markov models and their applications in biological sequence analysis.* Current genomics, 2009. **10**(6): p. 402−415.
28. Krogh, A., et al., *Hidden Markov models in computational biology: Applications to protein modeling.* Journal of molecular biology, 1994. **235**(5): p. 1501−1531.

29. Eddy, S.R., *What is a hidden Markov model?* Nature biotechnology, 2004. **22**(10): p. 1315–1316.

30. Ourston, D., et al. *Applications of hidden markov models to detecting multi-stage network attacks.* in *System Sciences, 2003. Proceedings of the 36th Annual Hawaii International Conference on.* 2003. IEEE.

31. Fink, G.A., *Markov models for pattern recognition: from theory to applications.* 2014: Springer Science & Business Media.

32. Gales, M. and S. Young, *The application of hidden Markov models in speech recognition.* Foundations and trends in signal processing, 2008. **1**(3): p. 195–304.

33. Plötz, T. and G.A. Fink, *Markov models for offline handwriting recognition: A survey.* International Journal on Document Analysis and Recognition (IJDAR), 2009. **12**(4): p. 269–298.

34. Moni, M. and A.S. Ali. *HMM based hand gesture recognition: A review on techniques and approaches.* in *Computer Science and Information Technology, 2009. ICCSIT 2009. 2nd IEEE International Conference on.* 2009. IEEE.

Mathematical Research Methods

The science of operations, as derived from mathematics more especially, is a science of itself, and has its own abstract truth and value.

Ada Lovelace

## CHAPTER 7

Theoretical Research

Theory is a set of interrelated concepts, definitions, and propositions, which explains, predicts, and models relationships and outcomes. Formal theoretical cyber security research is the deliberate approach to developing these concepts, definitions, and propositions for cyber security. It provides a systematic way to coherently view phenomena, events, situations, and behaviors.

Moreover, theory is notionally generalized, often idealized, and broadly applicable, meaning not specific to any context or situation. However, this does not mean to say that theory is set apart or irrelevant to the cyber security field; theory should not be isolated. It should inform and develop other theory. Additionally, a key feature of good theory is that it is testable: theory should inform hypothesis, hypothesis are then used to design and conduct experiments to test their validity. Theory is neither fixed nor constant. Results of experiments are used to refine and update theory—or depending on the severity of the experimental outcomes, wholly discarded. The cycle continues in which, from revised theory, new hypotheses are formulated and tested, theory is refined, ad infinitum.

CHAPTER OBJECTIVES

- Define the terms and concepts of theory
- Provide a process to develop a strong theory
- Explore concepts through example research
- Proper presentation of theory research (paper outline)

BACKGROUND

A **theory** is a proposed model or inner working of why a system behaves in a specific way. The word is often used colloquially as to mean a guess. However, in science, a theory represents a foundational piece of knowledge around which research and even fields of research are built. A scientific

Research Methods for Cyber Security. DOI: http://dx.doi.org/10.1016/B978-0-12-805349-2.00007-8

theory follows the lifecycle of the scientific process. It starts as a belief based on observations. This belief is a **cognitive model** that can be formulated with language. Through iterations of research a cognitive model becomes a **formal model**. A formal definition of a theory is a mathematical representation of the behavior of a system. A theory that has significant empirical support and is widely accepted becomes a law. A law is a theory of a system behavior that is accepted as accurate.

Formal research is one method of formalizing a cognitive model. The mathematical techniques of formal theoretical methods enable you to define and then explore a formal model. Information theory, cryptography, cryptanalysis, and cryptology have strong theoretical underpinnings, supporting advanced mathematical analysis and evaluation. This is generally not true about all the disciplines that fall under the banner of cyber security science, especially disciplines focusing on adversarial behaviors.

DIG DEEPER: TERMINOLOGY

Theory, theorems, axioms, lemmas, and so on. Each research field develops it own specific terminology. Since cyber security is such a nascent field, there has not been sufficient time to mature a language to go along with the research. The field does, however, borrow from other domains, and in theory this borrows especially from mathematics. In mathematics, theory can be a body of knowledge, but for the purposes of this chapter, the concept of mathematical theory is more akin to a mathematical model, which uses the language and structure of math to describe a system. In mathematics and logic a theorem is a statement that has been or can be proven true. This is only applicable in deductive contexts. These statements can take the form of a hypothesis that can be (again mathematically, deductively) proven true. In observational and experimental research, the inductive analog is a scientific principle or law. An axiom is a concept or statement that is meant to be taken as true, this is similar to the explicit assumptions in experimental and observational research. A lemma is an intermediate step or component of a larger theory. There are analogs between theoretical and experimental/observational research, because both strive to achieve shared scientific objectives of reproducible, validatable, falsifiable, and so on.

The first question in pursuing theoretical research, that one should ask, is why not another research method? Can the topic or problem you are interested in exploring be refined into a testable statement that can lead to an experiment. Or, are you curious about behavior or phenomenology in cyber space that can lend itself to an observational study? If the answer to both is no (because you cannot get the data to study, and do not have enough precision or resources for an experiment), then theoretical research might be the right path. For example, if a researcher wants to explore a setting where the average person has access to a computer capable of 100 petaFLOPS, then theory would be the only practical approach. Simulation would likely not be able to keep up with every person having the computing power of the top supercomputer circa 2016. Another example might be research into engineering techniques for processing and memory storage that far surpass the engineering limits today. This sort of research is highly valuable, because, as innovation progresses, the engineering will catch up, and the designs and theory of today can be tested and implemented tomorrow. Another type of research that lends itself to theoretical research is one where experimentation is all but impossible. For example, extra-solar astronomy and cosmology, for the time being, have no applicable engineering or applied research possibilities. This leaves only observation and theory, and for that field the cycle of theory development observational refuting can be a very long cycle indeed. In cyber security, the challenge with engineering might still apply but typically the lifecycle can be much quicker.

As we have mentioned several times, one of the key challenges in cyber security research is the inherent adversarial nature. Other challenges include the dynamic nature of the environment (new devices, technologies, and configurations are introduced all the time). These characteristics make for a complex system to study, experiment, or reason over. Science is based on observation, experimentation, mistakes, and guesses. Similarly, the process of constructing a theory can use all of those as well. Often theorists are considered "Ivory Tower" elites who do not need to consider or interact with the real world, because their theories are "so far ahead" or "advanced" from the day to day. This myth like many might have some grounding in reality, but for most the truth is far more prosaic. A key observation might lead to a new theory, or a frustrating experiment might cause the experimentalist to revisit the motivating theories anew. Like real life, science is often messy and ambiguous, and the line between the various research methods can become mutable and blur over time, for one research effort, or one researcher.

The key to theoretical research is to better understand or predict cyber security. The distinction comes when observational or experimental methods cannot be applied, for whatever reason. The theorist, in the absence of these techniques must make do with what is at hand, from mathematical formalisms, to software simulation, to social models, to help explain and vet their theories.

Characteristics of a Good Theory

Good theory should be coherent, parsimonious, and systematic explanation or view of phenomena, events, situations, and behaviors. Beyond that, it must be predicative. It should encourage testing and the expansions and evaluations of hypothesis. Good theory is designed to be testable and should be able to be disproved through observations, experiments, and logical reasoning. Theory should be able to be refined and reformed through additional results, outcomes, and information. Good theory should focus on effects, not on causes. They should inform on the outcomes of the next step of the experiment, and so on. Theory is not statements of fact, but instead focuses on likelihood.

CHALLENGES IN DEVELOPMENT OF CYBER SECURITY SCIENCE THEORY

Similar to the cyber security science experimentation, progress on the development and advancements of general theoretical basis is stagnant. Contrast this to the strong foundations and rapid advancements of information theory, cryptography, cryptanalysis, and cryptologic. These fields find their basis in mathematics and mathematical sciences. Experimentation as we define it in this book doesn't regularly transpire; instead, advancements and arguments are mathematically derived and supported with structured proofs that demonstrate validity and correctness. Unfortunately, essential aspects of cyber security cannot be so readily formalized in mathematics.

Part of the difficulty in developing cyber security science is a consequence of the abstract nature of cyber space. While it fulfills generalized attributes of space—"space conceptualizes the ability to move, act, create, describe ..."[1]— it is not described by ordinary space concepts familiar to students and practitioners of modern physics. Present challenges in describing cyber space with ordinary space concepts include: virtual identities appear to be weakly binding objects and there isn't virtual equivalents of mechanics—set of laws describing how objects operate and interrelate. The former means that it is complex to understand the parties involved in conversation or mechanism and that parties may exchange identities and observers may not notice. While weakly binding identities do create complexities for cyber security, it is fundamental to many high availability technologies engineered for Internet infrastructure. The latter has consequences in that there doesn't exist fundamental relationships between virtual distance, velocity, acceleration, nor force. From a programmer's perspective of developing a networked application, all points in the Internet are abstracted to appear equidistant—and hence not a Euclidean space (some restricted subspace may satisfy requirements for Euclidean space, that is cyber physical systems[2]—and consequently, it takes the same amount of effort to communicate with an entity geographically near as an entity 40,000 kilometers away. Sheymov[3] noted other essential differences: cyber space has no natural limits; it is described by infinite and uncountable number of dimensions, with each dimension being infinite; and objects can belong to one or more subspaces.

The creation of a theory is about abductively reasoning over our given knowledge to produce the best fit description available. The process detailed below is hardly required, but it can be a helpful guide to help articulate cyber security theories.

Optional process for developing a formal theory:

1. Identify insight (from observation, previous experiment, or inspiration)
2. Determine relevant factors (key inputs, assumptions, or factors)
3. Formally define theory (pseudocode, mathematics, model, or laws)
4. Test for internal consistency
5. Test for external consistency
6. Refute (conduct experimentation or observational studies to validate or refute your theory)
7. Continue to seek refinements.

Identify Insight

The media, and even in school, people often think of theoretical researchers staring at a chalkboard or dry erase board until inspiration strikes and a sequence of impressive mathematical notations pour out. While this might work for some, it seems like an isolated and profoundly boring way to conduct theoretical research. Often, for even full-time theoretical researchers, they are involved in experiments or studies, at the very least they continue to read and study the developments in their subfield. Especially, in cyber security, the lines between theoretical research, versus experimental, or even applied research, or engineering, are blurred, and one person might take on many different roles. The key at this step is to identify (from previous experimental or observational research, literature, direction observation, or inspiration) a topic to explore. The more precise and well formed the easier the effort will be, but ultimately an explanation or prediction in cyber security will be of use.

A lot of theoretical research is focused on exploring why an observed phenomena exists or deriving the behavior of a system under specific assumptions. For the former this includes exploring the implications of something you have seen or an observation made by the field. For example, there is an observation that software monoculture can increase the risk to cyber space. With theoretical research, it would be possible to explore the optimal level or range of diversity to reap the most rewards or to investigate the trade-off of defender costs in developing and maintaining diverse defenses versus the cost and sharing of exploits by attackers. For the second common focus of theoretical research we could further investigate this diversity question. Through theoretical modeling it would be possible to assume different ways in which diversity could be developed into a system to explore how it would effect a theoretical attacker. This latter form of research is security protocol proofs fall.

Determine Relevant Factors

After fleshing out a rough idea, the research should consider relevant assumptions, implications, inputs, and contributing factors. For example, if an idea is intriguing, but no evidence will ever be able to be collected to refute or corroborate the position, and perhaps the topic should be abandoned, in favor of a more fruitful exploration. If your theory combines several different perspectives, domains, or bodies of work, review of relevant inherited factors should be conducted. And in unexplored domains, such as cyber security, the combinatorial factors are poorly understood (e.g., if I combine a social model, a physics-based model, what are the limitations, weaknesses, etc.).

Formally Define Theory

After the initial work is done, the formal definition of the theory can begin. This might be represented in mathematical notation. This often occurs in cryptography, theory of computation, and information theory. See Claude Shannon's "Theory of Communication"[4] or Diffie and Hellman's "New Directions in Cryptography"[5] for examples of mathematical descriptions of a theory.

While each theoretical research will require its own logic, in the general case you will want to mathematically define a system. To do this you should start from a set of axioms or evidentiary supported logical formulations. An **axiom** is a generally accepted or obviously true atomic piece of information. A **postulate** is an atomic piece of information that you are positing as true for the purposes of this theory. It is good practice to provide references that support postulates. For example, it could be postulated that current defensive solution support follows a geometric distribution as there are a few tools used by many with a long tail of boutique solutions used by smaller communities.

However, the goal is not to just define a theoretical model. The goal is to explore the implications of that model. This could be exploring the results of different situations, finding an optimal scenario, or even proving that a threat model is unable to break a security system. Through the use of the model you should document useful propositions or theorems. A **theorem** is a significant result proven through a logic chain from a starting set of axioms. Documenting the subject proves necessary to derive a theorem that is called **lemmata**.

DID YOU KNOW?

Formal Methods is a specific form of theoretical and applied research used in cyber security. The approach taken by formal methods is to explicitly define the requirements for a software or hardware system, design a system based on those requirements, implement the system, typically in software, but sometimes including hardware. Then the practitioner mathematically maps from the formal notation in the

(Continued)

requirements, to the programming language, to the implementation binary. This provides a rigorous mathematical proof of system performance and security. A Computational Logic for Applicative Common Lisp 2 (ACL2) is an example of a programming language, mathematical framework, and solver commonly used to formally design and implement computer systems. This level of rigor is required for high assurance systems (these are systems such as aircraft, safety critical, or national security, where the importance warrants the formal steps required in formal methods. The Common Criteria for Information Technology Security Evaluation or Common Criteria (CC) is a formal approach to providing security assurance for computing systems. The developers formally specify what the security system should be able to do (functional) and what it should and should not do (assurance). This approach grew out of the Rainbow series of development books published by the National Security Agency.

Alternative means of formal notation include pseudocode or software. Especially for application relevant theories, drafting pseudocode can aide in the understanding and translation from theory to implementation. Another way is to define a model in an existing taxonomy, or, if absolutely needed, develop your own. And if a model exists, a simulation of the model can be instantiated to allow testing and evaluation. Finally, predictive, confirmable, refutable statements can be made about the specific topic at hand. If these statements stand the test of time, substantial review, they can become so-called "laws." Alternative names might include rules, axiom, principles, and so on.

Test for Internal Consistency

To test for internal consistency is to ensure that the inherent theory does not contradict or invalidate itself. Depending on the sophistication of the theory (software can be tested, mathematics can have proofs) the approach will depend on the type of theory. The key is that internal consistency means that the entire theory is coherent and internally justified. This has no bearing on the theory's applicability or relevance to the world at large.

Theoretical research should largely ensure internal consistency. Theoretical research should follow a completely deductive process. A deductive process logically builds from accepted or logically supported information. Generally, these are the axioms. To ensure internal consistency formally prove or provide strong logical reasoning for each step in defining your theoretical model.

Test for External Consistency

External consistency evaluates how accurate, or relevant, the theory is to the observable experimental world. The means to test for external consistency include developing predictions or questions that can lead to hypotheses for experimental evaluation or observational study. The test for external consistency is a major hurdle for a theory to be accepted and used. As such some theories will never reach this phase, and that is ok, but all theories should be able to be tested, if sufficient data, computation, or resources become available.

Refute

In short, every effort should be made to disprove the theory. Every experiment, and observation should be able to identify results, that is found, would refute and therefore invalidate the theory. The fact that research continues but does not refute a theory is what makes it stronger. This means that the theory must result in a falsifiable testable statement, and be reproduced as needed.

Continue to Seek Refinements

Ultimately, if a theory is identified, that is not yet refuted, does not mean the work is done. Research in cyber security always seeks to understand and predict, for every theory a better, more comprehensive, clearly, or applicable theory, is still out there, and every theory can be refined and improved. Often theoretical research does not start from scratch, but it seeks to improve upon existing theories.

EXAMPLE THEORETICAL RESEARCH CONSTRUCTION

As we have mentioned many times now, one of the key challenges in cyber security research is the adversarial nature inherent. Other challenges include the dynamic nature of the environment (new devices, technologies, and configurations are introduced all the time). These characteristics make for a complex system to study, experiment, or reason over. Let us explore the human adversarial element in more detail. Our researcher has been reviewing reports about sophisticated Advanced Persistent Threats such as APT1,[6] Energetic Bear,[7] and others,[8] and would like to better understand the workplace context and motivation of such professional-seeming attackers. Evidence indicates that they work regular hours (given the relative time zones they are in) have organized teams, tool developers, recon, impact, persist, execute/exfil, and so on. This level of organizational structure indicates substantial funding and competence but it might be a means to better understand and categorize adversaries in cyber security. After a bit more research, this time in the social sciences, the researcher wonders how motivation theory could be used to explain, or even predict APT behavior. Looking at various social models, from the historical Maslow's Hierarchy,[9] drive, arousal, expectation, or incentive, the researcher postulates that incentives and expectations are quite different for different types of adversary in an attempt to **identify insight**. Governmental sponsored APT, versus hacktivists, versus criminal APT, will have different incentives and expectations. This concept in and of itself cannot be tested, but is still worth exploring, making it an ideal candidate for theoretical research.

Next the researcher looked more into the social models to determine if there are any limits or challenges with applying a hybrid of incentive-expectation theory to advanced cyber actors. This will help them **determine any relevant factors**. They had previously identified other assumptions such as western style employment, government service, patriotism versus economic gain, (and noticed that culture and politics are likely to have major influences on the research). This new issue will need to be explored in subsequent validation as the theory currently fits western models of motivation, as well as workplace environments, and personal fulfillment.

To more **formally define the theory**, the researchers posit a theory that nation-state actors are motivated by a communal good expectation. These are currently identified as a weak set of rules, or laws. They do their day job because they are (1) patriotic, (2) want to apply their technical skills, and (3) want to help aid their country by conducting their work. This is similar but distinct to criminal APT, which are fully incentive-motivated because they want (1) financial security, (2) want to apply their technical skills, and (3) are unburdened by committing crimes (either in foreign countries or in home country, or both). Finally hacktivists are similar to nation-state actors. The hacktivists are (1) ideological, (2) want to apply their technical skills, (3) and want to aid their specific group.

> *Nation State*: Are (1) patriotic, (2) want to apply their technical skills, and (3) want to help aid their country.
> *Criminal*: (1) Financial security, (2) want to apply their technical skills, and (3) are unburdened by committing crimes (either in foreign countries or in home country, or both).
> *Hacktivist*: (1) Ideological, (2) want to apply their technical skills, and (3) want to aid their specific group.

Testing for internal consistency can be done for simulation and mathematical efforts, but for this topic the researchers review their assumptions and statements to determine if there are any conflicting claims or issues. And they realize that the hacktivist is actually identical to the nation-state actor. They are both ideologically motivated. The researchers revise their rules to eliminate this redundancy. They still want to explore multiple types of motivation in advanced cyber groups. This leads them to add classical hackers to the list. Hackers are less and less the source or topic of cyber security attacks and defenses, but they continue to work and are a fascinating group to include. This new group is motivated because they (1) they are curious and (2) want to apply their technical skills. Curiosity lead the original phreakers and hackers to understand how the computing systems and communication networks worked, could be modified, and improved. Another motivation often attributed to hackers, especially the white hat hacker, is fairness and openness. Often white hat hackers will disclose information about a vulnerability to a company, but if that company fails to act they will often release the information to the public that they can take steps to protect themselves. However, this action sometimes opens up the white hat to punitive response from the company. Regardless, this sort of motivation is ideological in nature and falls into the first motivation role.

Finally this can be summarized as:

> *Role #1*: Are (1) ideological, (2) want to apply their technical skills, and (3) want to aid their specific group/organization/country.
> *Role #2*: (1) Financial security, (2) want to apply their technical skills, and (3) are unburdened by committing crimes (either in foreign countries or in home country, or both)
> *Role #3*: (1) They are curious and (2) want to apply their technical skills.

The next step is to **test for external consistency**. The researchers are not at a point where they can conduct an experiment involving nation-state actors, cyber criminals, and hacktivists. Alternatively, a direct observational study might be quite challenging a well. The researchers, however, do have an idea that the motivation role might affect the tools, techniques, and procedures (TTP), regardless of country, training, or experience. This hypothesis could be refined and existing observational data could be used to refute or corroborate the premise. See Chapters 4 and 5 (Exploratory Study and Descriptive Study) on observational studies for insights on how to conduct that style of work. The researchers will also have to first define the relationship between role and theTTP, before the causal relationship could be evaluated.

Finally, like any scientific theory, the researcher while using the theory to motivate research always seeks to disprove or **refute** the theory in use. Barring that the researcher can seek improvements and **refinements** to better describe and predict cyber security phenomenology. Ultimately, iteratively improving, even poor theories can help build a body of knowledge and foundation for the future of cyber security science, through a variety of research methods.

Another example of theoretical research could look at the interplay of attackers and defenders. The preferred a tool set to study adversarial relationships and interactions in game theory. The mathematical models of *game theory* have been successfully employed to understand behaviors and interactions of players in cooperation and in conflict. Two excellent texts on the discipline of game theory are "A Course in Game Theory"[10] and "Game Theory."[11] The standard example is the *prisoner's dilemma*.[12] The two-player game is presented as follows:

Two members of a criminal enterprise are arrested. Owing to insufficient evidence, prosecutors offer a deal to each member independently and in isolation. The deal is to fink on the other for a reduced sentence. The opportunity presents the following costs:

- If neither accept the deal, that is they both remain silent, they serve a 1-year sentence.
- If one betrays the other, the fink gets no penalty, while the other receives a 3-year jail sentence.
- If both accept the deal and betray each other, they receive a 2-year sentence.

Analyzing the model using standard game theoretic equilibrium concepts, the outcome is that both rational, self-interested individuals choose to betray and each receives a 2-year prison sentence. Note the outcome is preferred less by the players than the socially optimal outcome, where both players remain silent and receive a 1-year sentence.

Game theoretic analysis was employed by RAND to understand and predict Soviet use of nuclear armaments, which lead to RAND developing the idea of mutually assured destruction, the military strategy, and national security policy of retaliation using second-strike capabilities. Because of game theory's modeling of conflictual interactions and successes such as MAD, it is natural to want to apply it to cyber security problems. Much of the research interest aligns with modeling adversarial behavior and evaluating defenses.[13,14,15,16,17]

However, cyber security presents challenges to game theory. While game theory has analytical capabilities to handle incomplete (players do not have full knowledge about others) and imperfect information (not all aspect of the game play are observable), it has little support for unknown or partially known action sets. These action sets describe permissible "moves" by the game players. Designing these action sets are difficult for cyber security: either actions are forgone or highly abstracted and conceptualized, leading to outcomes that are inapplicable or unimplementable. Conventionally, game theory models are structured so that there are definite number of players well-versed in the game. This structure makes sense negotiating contracts, fighting war, and so on. But in cyber security, it can be conceived that a defender is simultaneously battling multiple attackers, with each attacker having its own agenda, objectives, and strategies. Attackers may willingly coordinate activities or be oblivious to the presence of others. Decisions by either defender or attacker influences all parties, either to the aid or detriment of other players. Owing to the structure of cyber space, cost of actions are not understood. Furthermore, cyber space's low barriers to entry and speed of information and knowledge transfer seemingly reduce cost faster for attackers than defenders. Recent work has addressed some of these challenges. Moayedi and Azgomi[18] consider widely diverse attacker communities, one possible method that can be used to overcome indefinite game structure.

Chatterjee et al.[19,20] address uncertainty in defenders and attacker's costs. One hurdle remains: tractability of game theoretical solution concepts. It is known that the Nash equilibrium, a stable system state in which no player will unilaterally deviate from, is computationally hard, both in computing a solution and verifying its correctness. While the problem is not NP-complete, as we know a solution exists,[21] it remains computationally hard and is tractable if and if PPAD subset of P.[22] Furthermore, equilibrium approximations are inadequate as once it is found, players immediately know how to deviate from it to achieve better payoffs.

REPORTING YOUR RESULTS

The final important step of scientific work is reporting your results. The greatest discoveries have little value if no one knows about it, can leverage the knowledge for further science, or to engineer something with more predictable behavior. The two most prevalent forms of documenting theoretical research results in conferences and journals. These venues provide a path to insert your gained knowledge into the field's corpus. However, the quality venues all require peer-reviewed acceptance. Peer review provides a validation check against the topic of research, methods of research, and the quality of the reporting of the research to ensure a certain level of quality is required. Ideally, the quality of the work should be the only metric of acceptance, in reality the novelty, ground-breaking, and popularity of the topic also play into the review process, so these things should be taken into account when you select your venue. In this section, we provide a general template for the general style of a theory-focused research paper, which will be applicable to most conferences and journals.

Sample Format

In the following, we will provide you with a general outline for publishing your results. Every publication will provide formatting guidelines. When you decide on a venue to submit your research, be sure to check their submission requirements to make sure you follow any outline and formatting specifications. The outline provided here follows a common flow of information found in published papers and should meet the requirements of a larger number of publisher requirements.

Every paper is unique and requires some different ways of presentation; however, the provided sample flow includes all of the general information that is important to cover in a paper and is a general starting format we take when starting to write a hypothetico-deductive paper and modify it to support the topic and venue. We understand that every researcher has their own style of presentation, so you can feel free to deviate from this outline. The discussion of each section is provided to explain what is important to include and why, so you can present the important information in whatever way suits your style best.

Abstract

The abstract is a concise and clear summary of the paper. The goal of an abstract is to provide readers with a quick description of what the paper discusses. You should only discuss what is stated in the rest of the paper and nothing additional. Each submission venue will provide guidelines on how to provide an abstract. Generally, this includes the maximum length of the abstract and formatting instructions, but sometimes this will include information on the type and layout of the content to provide. This should include the summary and impact of your theoretical research.

Introduction

The first section of a paper should always be an introduction for the reader into the rest of the paper. The introduction section provides the motivation and reasoning behind why the research was performed and should include a statement of the objectives or intent of the research. If any background information is required, such as explaining the domain, environment, or context of the research, you would discuss it here. If the audience is significantly removed from some aspect of this topic, it may be worth it to create an independent longer background section. It is important to establish what the theory you will be exploring is and where it comes from; that is why you are developing this theory. What information would this theory provide or what relationship does it attempt to document.

Related Work

The related works section should include a quick summarization of the field's knowledge about this research topic. Are there competing theories? Have other experiments, studies, or theoretical studies been done? If there are a lot work in this field, they cover the most impactful or influential work for you. If you are building upon a past theory provide a brief summarization here. If you are defining a competing theory, explain the deficiencies of the previous theories here. In theoretical papers you may find that you need to build upon past work to define your formalisms. As such, it is best to weave those references into the model definition section where they are leveraged instead of defining them in the related works section.

Theoretical Model Development

The theoretical research development part of your paper should clearly define the process you went through to develop your theory or theories. It is crucial that this section is clear and complete such that a reader would be able to understand the assumptions and logic behind the model you developed. In this section you need to define your premise, other theories, assumptions, and key inputs. Build your model from a set of axioms or reference-supported evidence. Prove additional theorems to build up your theoretical model. You need to be as complete in your documentation as possible. The goal is to be complete enough that a reader can understand how you arrive and your conclusions or results.

Proofs and Theorems

A theoretical research paper's results are the proofs and theorems generated. You should not document every proof; only highlight significant or interesting proofs as theorems. If it is necessary to build up a theorem then you need to specify any necessary lemmata. Often the contribution is the development and explanation of the theory. However, sometimes a theory can be exercised to produce or highlight results that are worth sharing with the wider audience. Often this is in the form of a model or simulation; see Chapter 8, Using Simulation for Research, for further details.

In the results section of your paper, explain what you found after you performed your analysis. Creating tables to show results is an efficient and effective method. You can also show pictures of interesting results, that is if a data anomaly occurred or to display the distributions of the data samples. Regardless of whether or not you are generating datasets, you should make sure and explain the impact, implications, and reach of the theoretical research. Are there any limitations of scope, impact, applicability, and so on.

Discussion/Future Work

The discussion/future work section is for general observations and comments on the entire research process, including the process itself. Provide your explanations for the results you received. If they are interesting, provide what you think happened? Discuss where you think this work should lead next. Is there any immediate or follow-on work planned?

Conclusion/Summary

In the final section of the paper, summarize the impact of the theory and conclusions of the paper. The conclusion section is often a place readers jump to quickly after reading the abstract. Make a clear and concise statement about what the ultimate results of the experiments are and what you learned from it.

Acknowledgments

The acknowledgments section is a place for you to acknowledge anyone who helped you with parts of the research that were not part of the paper. It is also good to acknowledge any funding sources that supported your research.

References

Each publication will provide some guidelines on how to format references. Follow their guidelines and list all your references at the end of your paper. Depending on the length of the paper, you will want to adjust the number of references. The longer the paper, the more references. A good rule of thumb is 15–20 references for a 6-page paper. For peer-reviewed publications, the majority of your references should be other peer-reviewed works. Referencing web pages and Wikipedia doesn't generate confidence in reviewers. Also, make sure you only list references that are useful to your paper, meaning don't inflate your reference count. Good reviewers will check and this will likely disqualify and reflect poorly on you.

Endnotes

1. Krippendorff, K. (2010). *The Growth of Cyberspace and the Rise of a Design Culture. Workshop on Social Theory and Social Computing.* Retrieved from http://manoa.hawaii.edu/ccpv/workshops/KlausKrippendorff.pdf.
2. Bayne, J. (2008). Cyberspatial Mechanics. *IEEE Transactions on Systems, Man, and Cybernetics, Part B (Cybernetics),*38(3), 629–644. Doi: 10.1109/tsmcb.2008.916309.
3. Sheymov, V. (2013). *Cyberspace and security: a fundamentally new approach.* North Charleston, SC: Cyberbooks Publishing.
4. Shannon, C.E. (1948). A Mathematical Theory of Communication. The Bell System Technical Journal, 27, pp. 379–423, 623–656. Retrieved from http://worrydream.com/refs/Shannon%20-%20A%20Mathematical%20Theory%20of%20Communication.pdf.
5. Diffie, W., Hellman, M. (1976). New Directions in Cryptography. IEEE Transactions on Information Theory, 22(6), 644–654. Doi: 10.1109/tit.1976.1055638.
6. Mandiant. (n.d.). *APT1 Exposing One of China's Cyber Espionage Units.* Retrieved from https://www.fireeye.com/content/dam/fireeye-www/services/pdfs/mandiant-apt1-report.pdf.
7. MSS Global Threat Response (2014). *Emerging Threat: Dragonfly/Energetic Bear—APT Group.* Retrieved February 25, 2017, from https://www.symantec.com/connect/blogs/emerging-threat-dragonfly-energetic-bear-apt-group.
8. Martin, S. (2016). *8 Active APT Groups to Watch.* Retrieved February 25, 2017, from http://www.darkreading.com/endpoint/8-active-apt-groups-to-watch/d/d-id/1325161.
9. Barnes, M. (1943). Classics in the History of Psychology—A. H. Maslow (1943) *A Theory of Human Motivation.* Originally Published in Psychological Review, 50, 370–396. Retrieved February 25, 2017, from http://psychclassics.yorku.ca/Maslow/motivation.htm.

10. Osborne, M. J., Rubinstein, A. (2007). *A Course in Game Theory*. Cambridge, Mass: MIT Press.

11. Fudenberg, D., Tirole, J. (1991). *Game Theory*. New Delhi: Ane Books.

12. Kuhn, S. (2014). *Prisoner's Dilemma*. Retrieved February 25, 2017, from https://plato. stanford.edu/entries/prisoner-dilemma/.

13. Ryutov, T., Orosz, M., Blythe, J., Winterfeldt, D. V. (2015). A Game Theoretic Framework for Modeling Adversarial Cyber Security Game Among Attackers, Defenders, and Users. Security and Trust Management Lecture Notes in Computer Science, 274–282. Doi: 10.1007/978-3-319-24858-5_18.

14. Jajodia, S. (2013). *Moving Target Defense II: Application of Game Theory and Adversarial modeling*. New York: Springer.

15. Gueye, A. (2011). *A Game Theoretical Approach to Communication Security*. Retrieved February 25, 2017, from https://www2.eecs.berkeley.edu/Pubs/TechRpts/2011/EECS-2011-19.html.

16. Carroll, T. E., Grosu, D. (2010). A game theoretic investigation of deception in network security. Security and Communication Networks, 4(10), 1162–1172. DOI: 10.1002/sec.242.

17. Carroll, T. E., Crouse, M., Fulp, E. W., Berenhaut, K. S. (2014). Analysis of network address shuffling as a moving target defense. 2014 IEEE International Conference on Communications (ICC). DOI: 10.1109/icc.2014.6883401.

18. Moayedi, B. Z., Azgomi, M. A. (2012). A game theoretic framework for evaluation of the impacts of hackers diversity on security measures. Reliability Engineering & System Safety, 99, 45–54. doi:10.1016/j.ress.2011.11.001.

19. Chatterjee, S., Halappanavar, M., Tipireddy, R., Oster, M., Saha, S. (2015). Quantifying mixed uncertainties in cyber attacker payoffs. 2015 IEEE International Symposium on Technologies for Homeland Security (HST). DOI: 10.1109/ths.2015.7225287.

20. Chatterjee, S., Halappanavar, M., Tipireddy, R., Oster, M. (2016). *Game Theory and Uncertainty Quantification for Cyber Defense Applications*. SIAM News. Retrieved February 25, 2017, from https://sinews.siam.org/Details-Page/game-theory-and-uncertainty-quantification-for-cyber-defense-applications.

21. Nash, J. F. (n.d.). Equilibrium Points in n-Person Games. DOI: 10.1515/9781400884087-007.

22. Daskalakis, C., Goldberg, P. W., Papadimitriou, C. H. (2009). The complexity of computing a Nash equilibrium. Communications of the ACM, 52(2), 89. DOI: 10.1145/1461928.1461951.

## CHAPTER 8

Using Simulation for Research

While computers and our understanding of humanity's interaction with them is core to this book, computers provide additional benefits to research. While fundamental exploration of abstract theoretical models can provide powerful knowledge, it is often insufficient. Cyber space by itself is a very complex space, which means mathematically modeling every aspect is impossible. Adding human behavior into the mix makes it even more untenable. Computers provide another option to explore these abstract models.

Using computers to simulate complex models can help explore system interactions, component performance, and theoretical limits. Setting up complex models and letting a computer investigate the effects of setting different parameters allows exploring the possible effect space without having to manually compute the optimal or perfect solution beforehand. Simulations can provide a glimpse into future systems to understand how they would operate and work with existing systems. Simulation is a powerful tool for theoretical research and as an initial step before the expensive or effort of a larger experiment or observational study.

Simulation is also a useful tool for empirical research. Instead of generating the data from a real system that is expensive or very difficult to control, simulation can provide a good proxy. Simulated systems enable strong control and ability to investigate multiple scenarios quickly. However, the results are only as good as the models used in the simulation. In this chapter, we will discuss model fidelity and the importance and process of model validation.

Finally, simulations can help generate hypotheses for experimentation. If a theoretical model is instantiated and simulated, the resulting output can be treated as a hypothesis. If the theoretical model is accurate, the behavior of the simulation should match the behavior of the real system. Treating the outcome of a simulation as a hypothesis provides a powerful way of starting the experimental process.

In this chapter, we define simulation and when it can be a useful tool. The different ways in which simulation can fit into research will be explored and

193

Research Methods for Cyber Security. DOI: http://dx.doi.org/10.1016/B978-0-12-805349-2.00008-X

the various aspects to consider will be discussed. In addition, we will provide an overview of different categories of simulation tools and provide some ideas on how they could be useful for cyber security research.

CHAPTER OBJECTIVES

- Define simulation and explain model validation
- Caution reader on appropriateness of simulation, and common pitfalls
- Expose reader to simulation-specific methodologies
- Provide taxonomy of types of simulation commonly used in cyber security
- Provide guidance on cyber security–specific simulation practices, opportunities, pitfalls
- Provide a brief use-case study of simulations for cyber security

DEFINING SIMULATION

Computational power has been a boon for scientific exploration, providing the ability to analyze more data, leverage more statistical algorithms, and explore theoretical models. We will discuss this in more detail, later in this chapter. In this section, we will define the various concepts involved in designing and executing models for research. This includes defining simulation, emulation, virtualization, and discussing how they differ.

A **simulation** is a computer process or application that imitates a cyber or physical process by generating similar responses and output. The creation of a simulation requires an abstract model of the actual process or object. Using a computer, this model is instantiated into an executable program that generates data, mimicking the behavior of the real system. The computational overhead of a simulation is often dependent on the complexity of the system and how abstract the model. For instance, it would be very computationally expensive to model the trajectory of a thrown rock by modeling the behavior of every atom, but a cell phone could easily handle the simulation when using Newton's second law of motion. Multiple gradations have been named to capture the different levels of simulations.

Traditional simulations simply attempt to achieve realistic output of a system. In Fig. 8.1A you can see that the simulation is essentially a black box that produces realistic-looking data. However, there is another level of higher fidelity simulation: emulation. **Emulation** is the process of simulating the inner workings of a system to produce realistic output. In Fig. 8.1B you can see that the emulation simulates the function of the inner gears of the box, which interact with real processes to produce the output. The hope with emulation is that you will gain higher fidelity of output. As emulation is simulating a finer aspect of a

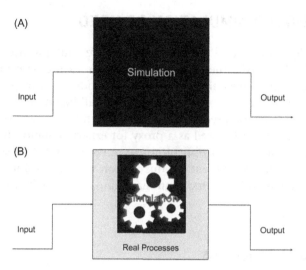

(A)

Simulation

Input

(B)

Simulation

Input

Real Processes

FIGURE 8.1
Difference between simulation and emulation.

system, it is often more computationally expensive and can be harder to adequately model, as there are generally more parameters incorporated.

A specific type of emulation that is quite widespread is virtualization. **Virtualization** is emulation of the relevant subset of a computer such that operating system and application-level software can run. Containerization is a lightweight form of virtualization that creates multiple containers within a single operating system to provide applications in their own namespace. This means that it appears to each containerized application that they are in their own operating system. The next level of virtualization is **paravirtualization**, which provides a virtualization of the hardware environment through an API. Paravirtualization requires modifications to the guest or virtualized operating system to operate within a paravirtualized environment. The final and highest fidelity of virtualization is **full virtualization**, where the full hardware is emulated such that guest operating systems can operate without change. Overall, virtualization is a very useful tool in cyber security research and which type one selects is dependent on the research question and its required level of fidelity. In the next section, we will discuss the various use cases for simulation.

DID YOU KNOW?

Some have hypothesized that our reality could be a simulation of a more advanced species.[1] The thought is, if there can be highly advanced civilizations that can model and simulate a universe, then the number of simulated universes would far outweigh the number of real universes. Therefore, the probability of our universe being simulated is much greater than the probability of it being real. Experiments have been devised and executed to determine if this is a possibility.[2]

WHEN SHOULD SIMULATION BE USED

Simulation is a useful tool for science. There are multiple use cases under which it is well suited. One being that it provides a mechanism to explore the boundaries and constraints of theoretical models. It can provide a tool through which predictions of how real systems will behave can be evaluated, which can ultimately be used for experimental setup or operational decision support. Finally, it can be used as a proxy for experimentation to enable the study and understanding of difficult-to-control systems before spending the resources on a true experiment. In this section we will explore all of these uses, as well as providing some cautionary guidance on when simulation is inappropriate.

Theoretical Simulations

Simulation is useful for exploring theoretical models. While it is possible to mathematically prove some models as we discussed in Chapter 7, Formal Theoretical Research, some systems are too complex to formally model every variable perfectly or compute the full input space. In these situations, simulations are a great tool to investigate how high fidelity components interact in a system or how lower fidelity systems would behave. Exploring theoretical models helps gain knowledge in a few useful ways. First, it enables understanding of the behavior of systems at extremes that are not easily tested or often seen in real systems.

For example, simulating behaviors and propagation of different malware through networks is hard to recreate in real systems so simulations can provide an initial level of understanding. If a theory is posited that malware is transmitted in social networks, via the same method as a communicable disease, simulation would be a useful tool to explore the boundary conditions of this belief. You could model the behavior of communication and then model the transmission of malware as if following a disease such as influenza. Then, you could explore how fast the malware would transmit under different conditions. Perhaps a user needs a certain number of social contacts in a given time to cause a pandemic level transmission. Or maybe herd immunity concepts are exhibited, so a patch campaign in a short time frame would be effective. Exploring a theoretical model with simulation lets you understand what would be the outcomes of different scenarios if the theory is accurate. It is crucial to understand that this does not prove or disprove the theory. Rather this is simply an instantiation of the theory to understand the results and output. To validate a theory, the same scenario would need to be experimented under real-world conditions to generate evidence of the accuracy of the model, and therefore the underlying theory.

Simulation for Decision Support

Another good use for simulations is generating predictions of system behavior. If a system is accurately modeled, a simulation can provide a method of playing what-if games. What if a 10 Richter scale earthquake hits a city? What if a high pressure air system moves across the mountains? What if an attack is targeted at substations in the power grid? All of these situations are basically experiments that are, for a variety of reasons, impossible to perform. Therefore, simulations provide a good decision support tool to run through the different scenarios of interest to see the result. In addition, this method can provide a way to investigate the effectiveness of solutions. However, as we will discuss later in this chapter, this tool is only as accurate as the model used in the simulation. Understanding the limits of your model is critically important when using simulation for decision support.

Empirical Simulation

Similar to decision support, predictions from simulations can be used as a starting place for experimentation. If a theoretical model is used instead of an empirical model, or a model generated from data like the one discussed in Chapter 6, Machine Learning, like in decision support use cases, the outcomes of simulations represent different types of predictions. Instead of representing how a real system would behave, a theoretical model represents how a system would behave based on our understanding of it. In a perfect world, all theoretical models would be accurate and would equal empirical models. However, it is necessary to validate our understanding of systems before theoretical models can be considered empirical models. They require validation. If you want to validate your theoretical model, using simulation to generate hypotheses for experimentation is a good approach. When you test a theoretical model using specific conditions in a simulation, the outcome represents a hypothesis. This hypothesis is a statement that the behavior of the real system will produce the same output if controlled in the same way as the simulation. Therefore, executing a controlled experiment validates if the model is accurate under these conditions or not. If the data generated from the experiment is statistically close to the simulation-generated data, then this represents evidence that the theoretical model is accurate. However, if the data is statistically different, then there is strong evidence that your theoretical model has inaccuracies. This may mean that the underlying theory is flawed, but it does not have too. Perhaps the simulation implementation introduced the flaws. This distinction would need to be explored before throwing out the theory.

In addition to starting the hypothetico-deductive process, simulation can also be used as a proxy for some experimentation. Cyber space is a complex and expansive space. And its interfaces and interactions with physical space make it immensely more complex. Therefore, there are plenty of research questions that involve aspects of cyber and physical space that are either very expensive, impossible, or unethical to control for experimentation. Simulation can provide a means to study a system that is uncontrollable or provide a filter on which experiments are the most promising when expenditures are high. If, for instance, you hypothesized that a 1 terabyte Distributed Denial of Service (DDoS) that persisted for 48 hours would take down the Internet's DNS service, it would be unethical and, for most, too expensive to carry out an experiment of this scale. Simulation provides a good proxy to see how likely this hypothesis is. As we will discuss later in this chapter, there are good network simulators that enable you to model a network with high fidelity, including using real protocol implementations. However, simulation should not be used as a replacement for experimentation, which we will discuss in the cautionary section.

DIG DEEPER: MIRAI DDOS ATTACK

While the example DDoS attack on Internet DNS was provided in this section, it was created as an off-the-cuff example idea, we recently got to observe the answer to this. After a draft of this chapter was written, the Mirai bot attack on the Dyn DNS service occurred.[3] The Mirai botnet, which consists of subverted Internet of Things devices, deployed a massive DDoS on the Dyn DNS service. Some believe the attack reached bandwidth magnitudes of 1.2 terabytes. While this attack caused serious outages to major portions of the Internet for the East Coast United States, it did not have an effect globally and Dyn was able to remediate and recover from it within a few hours.

Synthetic Conditions

There exists one last beneficial use of simulation for research. When performing experiments, it is not always possible to naturally create all conditions for the different control scenarios. When performing studies it may be necessary to create synthetic conditions to observe user reactions. Simulations are a technique by which conditions can be prepared for experiments and studies. For instance, one of the most common techniques to study attacker and malware behavior are honeypots, which we will discuss in the Types of Simulation section of this chapter. Honeypots simulate some vulnerable aspect of a system to lure in attackers to study what actions they take and the process they follow. For experimentation, creating the "noise" of a cyber system would be prohibitively expensive if you wanted real people to sit and perform actions on a computer. To solve this problem, multiple tools have been created that model users to generate traffic for fundamental and applied experimentation. Traffic generators will also be discussed briefly in the types of simulation section of this chapter. There is further discussion on these topics in Chapter 13, Instrumentation.

Cautions of Simulation Use

Thus far we have discussed all of the appropriate uses of simulation. However, simulation is not a panacea and is not appropriate in all situations. As we described in Chapter 3, Starting Your Research, you should start with your research question and from that decide the best approach, both in rigor and cost, to finding an answer. Too often researchers have a shiny tool at hand and build their research around using it. This leads to bad methods used and weak or questionable results. Simulation is a useful tool, but its use should be driven by the research.

First, simulation is not a replacement for experimentation. Yes, executing hypothetico-deductive research is hard and can be time-consuming and expensive. Yet it provides the strongest evidentiary support for claims and hypotheses. Just because a simulator exists doesn't mean it should be used. As we stated before, the results of a simulation can only be as good as the models used. If models are used that do not have sufficient empirical support, then it is expected and appropriate to question the applicability of the results.

This leads to the second cautionary statement on using simulations. Make sure you have appropriately validated models. Before you start using a simulator, you need to understand how underlying models were created and how they operate. You should also understand if and how the models were validated. The best models are empirically validated through data collected from real systems through study or experimentation.

This chapter is an introduction to the concepts of simulation for research. The history and knowledge of using simulation for science is broad and deep. There is too much to cover on the finer points of simulation and modeling for research. However, there are multiple books covering general simulation[4] and cyber space.[5]

DID YOU KNOW?

Most of the world's supercomputers are developed for executing complex simulations. For example, the Titan and future Summit supercomputer at Oak Ridge National Laboratory[6] are used for atomic and molecular modeling, among others. The Luna and Surge supercomputers operated by the US National Oceanic and Atmospheric Administration is used to simulate and predict weather patterns.[7] Germany's SuperMUC and France's Curie, their top supercomputers at the time, were used by MIT researchers to simulate the universe.[8]

DEFINING WHAT TO MODEL

To run a simulation, you must first have a model. And that model is foundational to the results generated. As a model is an abstraction of a real system, each component or variable of the model could range from very abstract to very high fidelity. Determining what level of abstraction is appropriate is based solely on your research question and what information or knowledge you hope to gain from the research. Fidelity and some applications are explained in detail in Chapter 13, Instrumentation, but we will explore the relevant aspects to simulation here.

As cyber space is digital, it is possible to have complete fidelity when simulating aspects of the system. However, simulation is generally done because the real system is too big to experiment with or a new idea is being tested before the expense of creating a real system. As such, it is important to scope down to what are the critical variables of the simulation and at what fidelity it is necessary to model them. If you are studying human response to phishing, you only need to simulate the content of an email message. However, if you want to understand fundamental patterns of communication, you may instead want to model the communication interaction, duration, and direction, but the content is less important.

When modeling analog systems, the discussion of fidelity takes on a different flavor. As analog values can be infinitely more precise, setting the fidelity level of all variables is important. For instance, if we wanted to model a physical process to study the interactions of cyber space with physical processes, we would need to understand our research question and the requirements it belies. If our research question was about a Supervisory Control and Data Acquisition (SCADA) system, the model of the physical process could be at the second fidelity, as that is the speed at which those systems communicate. However, if we instead wanted to study the interactions of a new protective system, then the model would need to have a millisecond fidelity to accommodate protective system speed of operation. Fig. 8.2 shows this

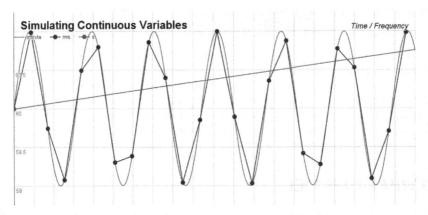

FIGURE 8.2
Simulating data at different fidelity levels.

model choice with drawing a sine wave to represent the power grid frequency. The blue line shows a perfect fidelity sine wave if we sampled it infinitely fine. The red line shows the next fidelity of drawing a sine wave. The red dots represent when the simulation samples the information from the model. Finally, the orange line shows the SCADA fidelity sine wave, which is even more coarser. Again, the orange dots represent when the simulation samples the information from the model, which, in this case, is so coarse that the second sample point falls outside the scale of this graph. As you can see, the dots all align with the perfect fidelity sine wave. From the simulation's perspective, the waves it is sampling from are perfect sine waves even though they are not.

Model Validity

When using simulation for decision support or as a proxy for experimentation, it is important that the models used have been validated. As we mentioned before, the results of a simulation are only as good as the model used. Results from using unvalidated models should be questioned, as there is no evidence of the model producing the generation. **Model validation** is the process of determining if a model is accurate and sufficiently representative of the real system such that it fulfills its requirements of use. To ensure that models are accurate, they need to be validated through empirical study. However, not every model requires the same level of validation. For instance, Newton's laws of motion are sufficient to predict the path of a thrown baseball, but the higher fidelity theory of general relativity is necessary for GPS positioning. There are largely two general methods of validating models, through observation and experimentation.

The first method of model validation is the use of observational studies. By using observational studies you can collect data about a system. There are two ways to use this data to generate a valid model. The first is to use statistical methods to ask and answer questions of the data. The second is using machine-learning techniques over the dataset to generate a model directly from the data.

Traditional observational studies are designed to answer research questions. However, using observational methods to validate simulation models is slightly different. Instead, the purpose of the questions you are asking are to validate the model instead of directly answering research questions. These questions corroborate (or disprove) the output of the model and indicates what is valid (or invalid). First, using statistical methods you can derive distributions of behavior that underlie processes. If it is found that the data fits certain distributions well, these distributions can be used within the model to recreate similar behavior. Second, you can look through the data for specific scenarios. Using simulations of your current model, you can recreate these scenarios. Comparison of the simulation and real system data will inform you how well your model captures the unique aspects of the system. If the data matches, then the model is valid. If there are significant deviations, then the model is inaccurate. By studying the real dataset for factors, which may have caused the deviations, you might be able to discover and fix the invalid aspects of your current model. Refer Chapter 4, Exploratory Studies, for guidance on how to execute different types of observational studies that may be useful for validating models.

Traditional observational studies can be manually intensive. However, the increased computation power available to researchers has enabled the field of machine learning to expand and become a useful technique. With machine learning techniques, you can feed collected data to an algorithm that will learn distributions and correlations to generate a model. There are many different machine learning techniques and each one has a class of mode it is good at learning. It is worth pointing out that it is believed that a single method cannot be developed that can learn every model.[9,10] Therefore, you need to select the right algorithms for the models that underlie the data you collect. See Chapter 6, Machine Learning, for an overview of machine learning methods.

The last approach for validating a simulation model is experimentation. Validating a model via experimentation is the same process as using a simulation to generate and test a hypothesis. To validate a model you can define a series of test cases that you know you can experimentally execute. You then execute the test cases in the simulation to generate data results. To validate the model, you execute the same test cases experimentally on a real system. By comparing the results of the simulation against the experiments, you can determine the accuracy of your model. For more in-depth discussion of hypothetico-deductive research methods, see Chapters 9, Hypothetico-deductive Research and 10, Quasi-experimental Research.

Using simulations as a proxy for experimentation still requires some empirical study. As they say, there is no free lunch. You can't just use simulation independently of empirical methods. Some level of confidence, based on data, is necessary in models used for simulation. Executing research methods to validate simulation models provides the foundation of trust that is transferred to the simulation results.

INSTANTIATING A MODEL

As we have previously mentioned, a model is an abstract or conceptual representation of a system. Models in and of themselves are not executable. Instead, a tool is needed to turn a model into an executable process that generates data. Simulation is the process by which a model is turned from descriptive into informative. Simulations require a programming framework through which a model can be specified and then an executable platform that can run the model under various specified conditions. A simulation runs through scenarios of inputs with a model to generate data about the state of the model and the output that would be produced. For example, one of the common types of simulators we will discuss is a network simulator. Network simulators take a model of a network and allow the simulation of behavior as communication passes through it. Network simulators enable researchers to study new protocols such as how a new wireless protocol will function under different configurations of a network.

Types of Simulation

There are several ways to define a model and different simulation platforms. **Agent-based simulation** uses models of agents that operate independently. These types of simulations are good for discovering emergent behavior when there is distributed control of a system. **Process-based simulations** use a mathematical definition of a system to generate behavior from a process. Process-based simulations are good for simulating physical processes that can be defined with continuous mathematics. **Trace-based simulations** execute small-scale applications to generate logs of real behavior, and then the simulation framework interpolates these logs to a much bigger scale. Trace-based simulations are good for understanding scalability performance of systems. Finally, **Monte Carlo simulations** execute a number of tests to determine the likelihood of outcomes. Monte Carlo simulations are good for decision support or when there is a large amount of uncertainty on the input parameters.

Each of these approaches have trade-offs. Some provide easier modeling. For instance, modeling independent agents is easier than modeling a full system with interdependencies. Decisions you make on models affects the performance and scalability. A matrix-based model like the power grid is not easy to decompose into sub problems, which makes it difficult to scale.

While these are general ways of simulating systems, there are specific types of simulation that are useful for cyber security research. The following list provides a good overview of different types of simulation that might be useful in helping answer your research questions.

Network simulators

- *Container-based simulators*: Container-based simulators leverage lightweight virtualization to enable the generation of a network of communicating nodes on one or a small number of physical computers. Container-based simulators are good at looking at new network protocol behaviors. However, as all containers will leverage the exact same communication stack, they are not a good simulator for tests of heterogeneity of unique response behavior. These simulators have been created for software-defined networking,[11] wireless applications,[12] and general networking.[13]

■ *Discrete event simulators*: Discrete event simulators generate sequences of discrete events. As cyber space is a discrete space, discrete event simulators are well suited for simulating aspects of it. In particular, discrete event simulators have been the main method of simulating networks and protocols. There are multiple discrete event network simulators; commercial[14,15] and open source.[16,17] Each have unique characteristics such as configuration and analysis graphical user interface (GUIs), network emulation features for hardware-in-the-loop, and various supported protocol and physical models.

DIG DEEPER: HARDWARE-IN-THE-LOOP

Hardware-in-the-loop is a special kind of simulation that fuzzes the lines with experimentation. Hardware-in-the-loop simulation provides emulation capabilities that enable the integration of real equipment into the simulation. Generally a larger system is simulated with a few real devices to enable the high fidelity response of real equipment while enabling the scale of the simulation. One of the main reasons behind the redesign of ns-2 into ns-3 was to enable hardware-in-the-loop testing to enable quicker progression of evaluating real implementations.

Traffic Generators

Where network simulators attempt to model and capture the realistic behavior and output of communication networks, traffic generators are generally only concerned with modeling and simulating the communication packets and payloads that would be produced by devices on a network. Or stated another way, traffic generators simulate many devices on a network and the communication they would produce, but they are not concerned with measuring that traffic across the network. Traffic generators are often used for applied experimentation to investigate the performance of network infrastructure, sensors, and security controls. There are general traffic simulators that generate various protocols and behaviors.[18,19] Specifically for security applications there are various traffic generation tools that generate attack behaviors.[20,21,22] There are also higher fidelity traffic generators that, instead of simulating traffic, emulate user behavior to generate real traffic from real applications.[23,24] Emulated users are useful both for applied experiments and fundamental experiments to provide background noise for attackers and defenders.

Target Simulation

As understanding attackers is a big part of research for cyber security, tools for testing them are important. While it is possible to perform studies on real cyber incidents, the number and frequency of them is still relatively low and may not provide definitive answers to open questions. Target simulation capabilities are designed to provide a controlled way of stimulating attackers for study. Target simulation tools (aka honeypots) provide a way to create vulnerable targets to entice attackers into exploiting them. These tools are often named on some variation of honey, based on the concept of honey trapping, which is a spy technique of using a physically enticing target to lure assets into divulging secrets. Target simulation tools often provide extra sensoring to monitor the actions of attackers. There are target simulators for host-based systems,[25] networks of honeypots,[26] browsers,[27] and, even data.[28]

DID YOU KNOW?

The term *honeypot* has a basis in the espionage world. Honeypotting or honey trapping referred to using sexual seduction to recruit assets. Cyber honeypotting techniques were named the same by using "appealing," based on easy vulnerabilities, systems to lure in attackers.

Threat Simulation

Threat simulation attempts to recreate threats and hazards to a system to observe and analyze how the systems or users of the system react. The suite of tools that fall under threat simulation have varied uses. Some are useful for applied studies to understand systems, others provide useful tools for experimentation, and finally others provide capabilities to support validation of solutions. There are multiple categories of threat simulation tools that are useful in modeling the different tasks and behaviors of an attacker. Failure simulators, vulnerability scanners, and exploit testing platforms are discussed in this section but refer to Chapter 14, Dealing with the Adversary, for a more in-depth discussion on modeling attackers.

- *Failure simulators*: **Failure simulators** simulate hazards to a system or faults in a system. Failure simulators degrade or impede the performance of some part of the test system. This provides ability to test and evaluate remedial actions and robustness measures. Netflix created a suite of tools to test cloud infrastructure's resilience to failure.[29] Other tools provide mechanisms to test degraded network conditions.[30] Finally, there are a special type of failure simulator, called fuzzers, that use protocols or APIs improperly to test for robustness of solutions in receiving bad input. Fuzzers are a common tool for studying the security of software implementations looking for possible vulnerabilities. Fuzzers come in all types of flavors; fuzzer frameworks,[31,32] file format fuzzers,[33,34] protocol fuzzers,[35,36] and application fuzzers.[37,38,39]

- *Vulnerability scanners*: **Vulnerability scanners** are tools that search for software and service signatures to determine if they have vulnerabilities. Vulnerability scanners simulate the process of attackers in finding system vulnerabilities for exploitation. However, it is important to note that vulnerability scanners are often designed as audit tools and are not designed to accurately model the stealth tactics of attackers. The results of these tools can provide a reasonable collection of knowledge that would be gained by an attacker. There are open source[40] and commercial[41] vulnerability scanner tools.

- *Exploit testing platforms*: **Exploit testing platforms** provide packages and a framework to execute exploits against known vulnerabilities. Exploit testing platforms provide a reasonable means of simulating the capabilities of attackers for performing studies or experiments. However, by the time exploits are added to exploit test platforms, they are generally far from being zero days anymore. Therefore, exploit kits are often not a good fit for modeling cutting-edge attacker tactics. Metasploit[42] is a well-known open source exploit framework, which has spawned some add-ons.[43,44] Canvas[45] and Core Impact[46] are the major commercial exploit frameworks.

DID YOU KNOW?

Zero days are vulnerabilities that are known by attackers, but unknown by the public or developers. Their term *zero day* originated in the warez community, which were a group of people that shared pirated software. Zero day warez software referred to software that was as yet unreleased to the public. The warez and hacker communities were cross-pollinated, which led to the term being applied to vulnerabilities.

General Simulation

The rest of the simulation tools we have discussed have been specifically focused on cyber space and security. However, there are a plethora of general purpose and domain-specific simulators that could be useful depending on your research topic. Engineers use MATLAB and Simulink to model physical processes. Modelica is an integrated modeling platform for modeling many different processes. There are tools such as Portico,[47] Ptolemy,[48] and FNCS[49] that are designed to integrate and bridge different simulators of different types. Pick the right simulator for the research you are doing. Just because some simulators are not designed for cyber security does not mean they are not the best fit to answer your research question.

EXAMPLE USE CASE

As we have discussed, there are multiple ways in which simulation can be useful in executing research. To help explore these ideas in this section, we will walk through example research using simulation. Our example will be an experiment to show the effects of attack on a power grid. This example will showcase how simulation can be used as a tool for experimentation.

Critical infrastructure security has become a hot topic in research in recent times. One critical question that most people want to answer is what affects cyber attacks can have on physical infrastructure. As electricity underpins all societal processes, it is often on the top of the list of infrastructure to study. So one may ask, can a cyber attack cause a significant event on the power grid? Simulation can help us answer this question.

As with most operational systems, cyber security experimentation is not allowed. The power grid has extremely high availability requirements, so studying how to cause an outage is unacceptable and unethical for the operational system. Also, the power grid is too big and complex to recreate large portions. As such, answering this question requires a way to study and understand what would happen on a large power grid. As the physics that underlie the operation of power grids are well understood, simulation provides the most reasonable path in answering this research question.

As modeling one of the US power grids is too complicated, it is necessary to pick test cases. IEEE has defined a series of models that have been validated for different generalized scenarios of power grids. For our example, we will select a smaller test case, such as the 39 bus transmission system. Fig. 8.3 is a one-line power diagram of the IEEE 39 bus system.

First, we need to select a method of simulating this model. As we want to answer if a cyber attack on this system will have a negative effect, it is important to understand our fidelity requirements. As we are unsure what effect an attack would have on individual devices, let alone the full system, it is important to have high fidelity models for the attack portion of the system. As such, having real field equipment upon which real cyber attacks can be targeted is a fidelity requirement for our research question. This requirement forces us down an experimental path using simulation as a tool.

Hardware-in-the-loop testing is a technique that combines executing hardware with a synchronized simulation. By using real hardware for the pieces of the system involved in the attack, we are able to see the direct effects of the cyber attack. And, by simulating the rest of the grid, it is possible to see the greater system effects, given the local effects. This simulation is a tool that supports our experimental environment by extrapolating what would

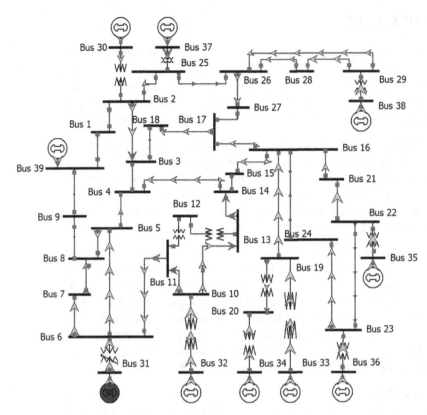

FIGURE 8.3

IEEE 39 Bus Transmission System.[50] *Source: Figure provided by the University of Illinois at Urbana-Champaign, using the PowerWorld visualization and analysis tool, and based on the IEEE 39-bus reference case.*

happen if the local system behaved in experimental ways. There are a few different simulation capabilities[51,52,53] that support hardware-in-the-loop simulation of power grids.

At this point, it is necessary to determine what pieces of our system model should be hardware and what should be simulated. This decision should be driven by our research question and as such we have to put ourselves in the role of an attacker. If our objective is to cause as widespread a power outage as possible, this would lead us to determine the highest value target for a cyber attack under these circumstances. In this scenario, substation 17 seems to be a likely target, as it is centrally located to the larger model and if lost would create three power islands as shown in Fig. 8.4.

To model substation 17, we just need 5 physical relays for each of the bus interconnects. For simplicity's sake, in this scenario, we will assume that

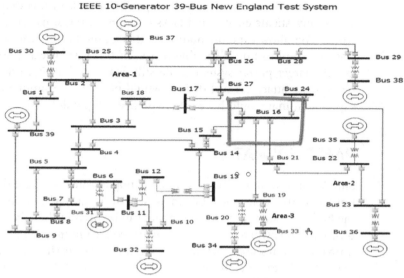

FIGURE 8.4

Target bus, for example, attack experiment.[54] *Source: Courtesy of the Pacific Northwest National Laboratory, operated by Battelle for the US Department of Energy.*

protective logic such as reclosing and system lockouts are not implemented. To interconnect these systems with the larger simulation, Goose and Sampled Measured values from the IEC 61850 protocol suite of standards[55] are used to pass system events and state. The DNP3 SCADA protocol[56] is configured for the communication protocol used to monitor and control the system from a utility control room. The rest of the system model for the simulation is filled in with simple relay logic overlaid on the physics model of the IEEE 39 bus system. To inject the attack, a simple replay of commands to open the breakers in the 5 substation 17 relays is sufficient. The goal of the attack is to open and close the breakers such that a system instability is caused, leading to sections of the power grid experiences an outage.

Executing this experiment multiple times leads to an understanding that the outage effect is driven by time and the drifting of frequency between the three islands. Once the first stage of the attack is executed, the three islands of power are formed. Over time, while being disconnected, the island's frequencies begin to drift. If the frequencies have not drifted very far apart when the second phase of the attack is executed and the breakers are closed, then the system will recover. While some thrashing, or sections going in and out of power may be experienced, ultimately the system will recover. However, if the frequencies are far enough apart, then some or all of the power system will experience an outage. See a demonstration of this example on YouTube.[57]

As you can see simulation can be a powerful tool. In this example, we were able to investigate effects on attacks on a power transmission system. No one would ever allow experimentation of this nature on the real power grid, so it was necessary to find a suitable proxy. In this case, it was possible to simulate the larger power system while still enabling the high fidelity needed to see how an attack on real devices would behave. The simulation enabled an experiment that would have otherwise been impossible.

PAPER FORMAT

Simulation is a tool to be used in executing research. While it does have some unique issues that must be addressed, it is largely not its own research method. Instead, it is a technique that can be used in the other research methods. Therefore, when documenting your research results you should follow the format of the research method you are doing. For each of the different methods, we will explore the unique aspects you should cover in a paper. You should always follow the formatting and outline guidelines of your publication venue first. These recommendations are generally good practices.

For theoretical research you should follow the format specified at the end of Chapter 7, Formal-Theoretical Research. However, where you normally discuss theoretical formula and axioms, you would describe the models used in the simulation. For research to train a model for simulation, you should follow the format specified at the end of Chapter 6, Machine Learning. For research to experimentally validate a model or using simulation as a proxy for an experiment, use the format specified in Chapter 9, Hypothetico-deductive Research. The hypotheses will be generated from the simulations instead of stated from observation.

Endnotes

1. Koebler, J. (June 2, 2016). Elon Musk Says There's a 'One in Billions' Chance Reality Is Not a Simulation. Retrieved February 19, 2017, from https://motherboard.vice.com/read/elon-musk-simulated-universe-hypothesis
2. Emerging Technology from the arXiv. (October 22, 2012). The Measurement That Would Reveal the Universe as a Computer Simulation. Retrieved February 19, 2017, from https://www.technologyreview.com/s/429561/the-measurement-that-would-reveal-the-universe-as-a-computer-simulation/
3. Hilton, S. (2016, October 26). Dyn Analysis Summary of Friday October 21 Attack. Retrieved February 19, 2017, from https://dyn.com/blog/dyn-analysis-summary-of-friday-october-21-attack/
4. Jain, R. (1991). *The art of computer systems performance analysis techniques for experimental design, measurement, simulation, and modeling.* New York: Wiley.
5. Banks, J., Carson, J. S., Nelson, B. L., and Nicol, D. M. (2010). *Discrete-event system simulation* (5th ed.). Upper Saddle River, NJ: Pearson.

6. Titan, World's #1 Open Science Supercomputer. (2012). Retrieved February 19, 2017, from https://www.olcf.ornl.gov/titan/

7. NOAA Completes Weather and Climate Supercomputer Upgrades. (January 11, 2016). Retrieved February 19, 2017, from http://www.noaanews.noaa.gov/stories2016/011116-noaa-completes-weather-and-climate-supercomputer-upgrades.html

8. Koebler, J. (2014, May 8). It Took a Pair of Top Supercomputers Three Months to Simulate the Universe. Retrieved February 19, 2017, from https://motherboard.vice.com/read/it-took-a-pair-of-top-supercomputers-three-months-to-simulate-the-universe

9. Wolpert, D.H. 1996. The Lack of a Priori Distinctions Between Learning Algorithms. Neural Computation 8, 7 (October 1996), 1341−1390. DOI = http://dx.doi.org/10.1162/neco.1996.8.7.1341

10. Wolpwert, D.H., Macready W.G, 1997. No Free Lunch Theorems for Optimization. *IEEE Transactions on Evolutionary Computation*, 1(1), 67−82.

11. Mininet Team. Mininet. Retrieved February 19, 2017, from http://mininet.org/

12. Common Open Research Emulator (CORE). Retrieved February 19, 2017, from http://www.nrl.navy.mil/itd/ncs/products/core

13. IMUNES. (July 11, 2015). Retrieved February 19, 2017, from http://imunes.net/

14. Tetcos. NetSim Standard. Retrieved February 19, 2017, from http://tetcos.com/netsim-std.html

15. Riverbed. OPNET Technologies − Network Simulator. Retrieved February 19, 2017, from http://www.riverbed.com/products/steelcentral/opnet.html?redirect=opnet

16. Ns-2 Main Page. (December 19, 2014). Retrieved February 19, 2017, from http://nsnam.sourceforge.net/wiki/index.php/Main_Page

17. Ns-3. Retrieved February 19, 2017, from https://www.nsnam.org/

18. Ostinato Network Traffic Generator Network Traffic Generator and Analyzer. Retrieved February 19, 2017, fromhttp://ostinato.org/

19. A. Botta, A. Dainotti, A. Pescapè, A Tool for the Generation of Realistic Network Workload for Emerging Networking Scenarios, Computer Networks (Elsevier), 2012, 56(15), 3531−3547.

20. Ixia. (n.d.). BreakingPoint. Retrieved February 19, 2017, from https://www.ixiacom.com/products/breakingpoint

21. Candela Technologies. (January 19, 2017). LANforge-FIRE Stateful Network Traffic Generator. Retrieved February 19, 2017, from http://www.candelatech.com/datasheet_fire.php

22. Spirent. Avalanche - Testing the Security of App Aware Devices and Networks. Retrieved February 19, 2017, from https://www.spirent.com/Products/avalanche

23. Skaion Corporation. (n.d.). Retrieved February 19, 2017, from http://www.skaion.com/

24. Blythe, J. DASH: Deter Agents for Simulating Humans. Retrieved February 19, 2017, from http://www.isi.edu/~blythe/Dash/

25. The Honeynet Project. Retrieved February 19, 2017, from http://www.honeynet.org/project

26. Spitzner, L. (2006). Know Your Enemy: Honeynets, What a Honeynet is, its Value, Overview of how it Works, and Risk/Issues Involved.web, May.

27. Wang, Y. M., Beck, D., Jiang, X., Roussev, R., Verbowski, C., Chen, S., and King, S. (February, 2006). Automated Web Patrol With Strider Honeymonkeys. In Proceedings of the 2006 Network and Distributed System Security Symposium (pp. 35−49).

28. Spitzner, L. (2003). Honeytokens: The Other Honeypot. http://www.securityfocus.com/infocus/1713, Security Focus

29. Izrailevsky, Y., & Tseitlin, A. (July 19, 2011). The Netflix Simian Army. Retrieved February 20, 2017, from http://techblog.netflix.com/2011/07/netflix-simian-army.html

30. Clumsy 0.2. Retrieved February 20, 2017, from https://jagt.github.io/clumsy/

31. Peach Fuzzer. Discover Unknown Vulnerabilities. Retrieved February 21, 2017, from http://www.peachfuzzer.com/

32. OpenRCE. (October 17, 2016). Sulley. Retrieved February 21, 2017, from https://github.com/OpenRCE/sulley

33. Grubb, S. (January 25, 2009). Fsfuzzer. Retrieved February 21, 2017, from https://github.com/sughodke/fsfuzzer

34. Caca Labs. (May, 2015). Zzuf - Multi-Purpose Fuzzer. Retrieved February 21, 2017, from http://caca.zoy.org/wiki/zzuf

35. Esparza, J. M. (April 25, 2013). Malybuzz. Retrieved February 21, 2017, from https://source-forge.net/projects/malybuzz/

36. Trailofbits. (May 19, 2016). Protofuzz. Retrieved February 21, 2017, from https://github.com/trailofbits/protofuzz

37. Software Engineering Institute. Failure Observation Engine (FOE). Retrieved February 21, 2017, from http://www.cert.org/vulnerability-analysis/tools/foe.cfm

38. American Fuzzy Lop. Retrieved February 22, 2017, from http://lcamtuf.coredump.cx/afl/

39. OWASP. (November 9, 2014). JBroFuzz. Retrieved February 23, 2017, from https://www.owasp.org/index.php/JBroFuzz

40. OpenVAS. Open Vulnerability Assessment System. Retrieved February 23, 2017, from http://www.openvas.org/

41. Tenable. (January 30, 2017). Nessus Vulnerability Scanner. Retrieved February 23, 2017, from https://www.tenable.com/products/nessus-vulnerability-scanner

42. Rapid7. Penetration Testing Software, Pen Testing Security. Retrieved February 23, 2017, from https://www.metasploit.com/

43. Strategic Cyber. Armitage - Cyber Attack Management for Metasploit. Retrieved February 23, 2017, from http://www.fastandeasyhacking.com/

44. Strategic Cyber. Adversary Simulation and Red Team Operations Software - Cobalt Strike. Retrieved February 23, 2017, from https://www.cobaltstrike.com/

45. Immunity. Canvas. Retrieved February 23, 2017, from https://www.immunityinc.com/products/canvas/

46. Core Security. (December 01, 2016). Core Impact. Retrieved February 23, 2017, from https://www.coresecurity.com/core-impact

47. The Portico Project. Retrieved February 23, 2017, from http://www.porticoproject.org/comingsoon/

48. Johan Eker, Jorn Janneck, Edward A. Lee, Jie Liu, Xiaojun Liu, Jozsef Ludvig, Sonia Sachs, Yuhong Xiong. Taming heterogeneity - the Ptolemy approach, Proceedings of the IEEE, 91 (1):127−144, January 2003.

49. Ciraci, S., Daily, J., Fuller, J., Fisher, A., Marinovici, L., and Agarwal, K. (April, 2014). FNCS: A Framework for Power System and Communication Networks Co-Simulation. In Proceedings of the Symposium on Theory of Modeling & Simulation-DEVS Integrative (p. 36). Society for Computer Simulation International.

50. T. Athay, R. Podmore, and S. Virmani, A Practical Method for the Direct Analysis of Transient Stability, IEEE Transactions on Power Apparatus and Systems, PAS-98(2), March/April 1979, 573−584.

51. Opal-RT Technologies. Electrical Simulation Software ⊠ Electrical Engineering Test. Retrieved February 23, 2017, from http://www.opal-rt.com/simulation-systems-overview/

52. RTDS Technologies. Real Time Power System Simulation. Retrieved February 24, 2017, from https://www.rtds.com/real-time-power-system-simulation/

53. DSPACE. (n.d.). SCALEXIO. Retrieved February 25, 2017, from https://www.dspace.com/en/inc/home/products/hw/simulator_hardware/scalexio.cfm

54. Edgar, T. W., Manz, D. O., Vallem, M., Sridhar, S., and Engels, M. (September 29, 2016). PowerNET. Retrieved February 25, 2017, from https://www.youtube.com/watch?v = x9hqdJxvYtI&feature = youtu.be

55. ABB. The IEC 61850 Standard. Retrieved February 25, 2017, from http://new.abb.com/sub-station-automation/systems/iec-61850

56. IEEE Standard for Electric Power Systems Communications-Distributed Network Protocol (DNP3), in IEEE Std 1815-2012 (Revision of IEEE Std 1815-2010), vol., no., pp.1-821, Oct. 10 2012

57. Edgar, T. W., Manz, D. O., Vallem, M., Sridhar, S., and Engels, M. (September 29, 2016). PowerNET. Retrieved February 25, 2017, from https://www.youtube.com/watch?v = x9hqdJxvYtI&feature = youtu.be

PART IV

Experimental Research Methods

We have to learn again that science without contact with experiments is an enterprise which is likely to go completely astray into imaginary conjecture.

Hannes Alfven

## CHAPTER 9

Hypothetico-deductive Research

Hypothetico-deductive research covers what is largely considered the traditional scientific method; experimentation. Experimentation is one of the strongest methods we have to understand the behavior and response of a system under varied conditions. Through hypothetico-deductive research, the strongest evidentiary support can be accumulated for.

If you are here, you have a research question and hypothesis, you want to design a series of experiments, or tests, to generate evidence, and you want determine if the hypothesis is false. You will need to have access to a representative environment that you have the ability to control.

In this chapter, we will discuss the different aspects of experimental research and how you perform each step in executing an experiment. To demonstrate the ideas, we provide ongoing examples for cyber security research. In this chapter we will explain topics such as what experimental research is good for, what constitutes a good hypothesis, how to design an experiment, how to analyze the results to determine if the hypothesis is false, and how to document your results.

CHAPTER OBJECTIVES

- Introduce hypothesis-driven research
- Discuss what a hypothesis is and the characteristics of a good one
- Explain the different aspects of experimental design
- Introduce different methods of analysis to determine effect
- Provide an approach on presenting your results for publication

PURPOSE OF HYPOTHESIS-DRIVEN EXPERIMENTATION

In general, hypothetico-deductive experimentation is good for eliminating or reinforcing prior knowledge about a system. For instance, discovering a new

215

Research Methods for Cyber Security. DOI: http://dx.doi.org/10.1016/B978-0-12-805349-2.00009-1

network communication behavior in an update to OS software or reaffirming the known behavior of a class of malware. Experimentation serves a different purpose for knowledge acquisition than observational studies and theoretical exploration. Experimentation is great for digging deeper into an observed behavior to determine more about what is causing the behavior and how the variables of a system influence each other. If abnormal network traffic is detected by network sensors, experimentation is a good way to isolate the cause to determine it the network stack changed when you updated your OS recently. Experimentation is also good for testing your theoretical models. If you have theoretically explored how a new bot network might behave and from that exploration you hypothesized that the bots would converge on a similar network characteristic, you could then experiment with the bot within a controlled environment to see if the converged behavior exists and if you have a good theoretical model. Experimentation is really good when you want to gain specific knowledge about a system and how a few set of variables relate to each other to help answer a research question. **Hypothetico-deductive research** focuses on designing experiments to reduce the influence of other variables so you can, with confidence, determine how the variables of interest interact. As you saw in Chapter 1, Introduction to Science, controlled experiments provide the strongest evidence for causal knowledge. While the main purpose of experimentation is to understand a system better there are some other purposes and benefits of hypothetico-deductive research:

Turn Inductive Process into Deductive Process

As we are observers within the world, it is impossible for us to deduce an accurate model of the world. The initial empirical foundations of science generated from Galileo and Bacon are naturally inductive. As we observe we can infer what processes are occurring to produce the behaviors observed. However, starting around the turn of the 19th-century scientists such as Charles Pierce and Whewel started to derive a new philosophy of science, that to improve our ability to understand the world, creating falsifiable hypotheses would provide more conclusive statements. This method was made most famous and mainstream by Karl Popper in the 1950 s as falsifiability. Simply stated, as observers of the world we can never prove a theory true; however, if we define a hypothesis that is falsifiable we can, through observation, prove a theory is false and therefore have gained a concrete understanding. The experimentation we discuss in this chapter is the process of defining an experiment to achieve the goal set forth by Popper and the other scientists of the past.

DIG DEEPER: KARL POPPER

Karl Popper is one of the greatest scientific philosophers of the 20th century. His thoughts on the scientific process have influenced much of how we think about science today. Popper's *The Logic of Scientific Discovery* is a good place to read more into his philosophy and why falsification is a good property for experimentation.

Reject a Theory or Build Evidence Strengthening

In the context of the previous goal, experimentation is good for rejecting a theory or building evidence for a theory. Theories are a representation of the knowledge we think we have about a field of study. Therefore, a strong goal of science is to refine and improve our theories such that they enable us to make better predictions of how a system will behave. Experiments are one of the best ways to target a theory and generate evidence to prove it is false or further strengthen the confidence in the theory. One good method of generating a hypothesis for an experiment is generating a prediction of behavior from the theory and running through the experiment to see if the same behavior exists in the real system. Going back to the bot example, if a theory of a botnet includes a distributed convergence of a command and control channel through negotiated parameters among peers, this would then make us think that a prediction of an initial flurry of hierarchical communication before stabilizing on the communication of the command-and-control channel is likely. You could define a hypothesis around that prediction to then go and test in an experiment to see if that communication pattern is exhibited.

Specify What You Think is Involved; Challenge Assumptions

A critical step in setting up an experiment is to clearly state all of your assumptions and what possible variables could have an influence on the dependent variables. As such, experimentation is a good way to define what our current understanding of a situation is. This forces you to methodically think through what may be happening and how everything could be involved. As a response to the philosophy of falsifiability, the Quine–Duhem thesis[1] documented that it is, in effect, impossible to truly test a hypothesis in isolation as they are formulated under the context of a larger set of assumptions we get from our other currently accepted theories. By rigorously defining your assumptions in preparation for an experiment, you are laying bare your thought process and the context under which your experiment was designed and your hypothesis was derived. This provides readers and future researchers the ability to understand and challenge your assumptions or replicate experiments in the future with new presiding. Or, if you are replicating previous research, you can highlight what assumptions you are challenging.

Define a Process by Which Others can Replicate and Reproduce the Effect; To Test and Ensure That Your Own Approach is Valid

To enforce a rigorous process, an experiment needs to follow a design. An experimental design lists the variables involved (both independent and dependent), the experimental setup, what equipment, people, and resources involved and how they are configured, the processes and manipulations to control the independent variables, and finally, the methods in which the data will be analyzed for effect. Documenting this provides reviewers and other researchers complete insight into what was done and why. One of the key tenets of scientific progression is the independent reproduction and verification of results. While it is never the intent, it is always possible that a poor assumption was made, a failure in process occurred, or something within an experiment failed. Enabling the independent replication of experiments to reproduce results is the community's method of ensuring if there was effect or not from past experiments. A rigorously defined and executed experiment provides the documentation and steps necessary for independent verification.

The Goal of Hypothetico-deductive Experimentation is Different than Applied Experimentation

When discussing experimentation, it is often the case that there is confusion between basic and applied experiments. Applied experimentation is focused on understanding the performance of some engineered solution in solving a problem or addressing a challenge. In essence, applied experimentation is a method to quantify how well we applied the knowledge we gained from basic science. The hypothesis for an applied experiment is often implied; the solution will improve upon addressing a challenge. This is different than basic hypothetico-deductive experimentation. With basic experiments the objective is to gain knowledge about another system, event, and so on, not to conduct the validation and verification of a system you designed/built. Basic experiments help generate evidence for or against causal relationships. It studies the interactions of an existing system. The lines get blurred because all of cyber space is essentially engineered. Therefore, a good rule of thumb is if you are trying to understand how a system behaves, it is basic experimentation and if you are testing for performance it is applied experimentation. Chapter 11, Applied Experimentation, discusses applied methods in more detail.

A PROPER HYPOTHESIS

The hypothesis is the key implement that turns the inductive observational process into a deductive logical process. A **hypothesis** is a falsifiable and testable prediction of how a system will behave under clearly defined conditions or how a dependent variable will react when independent variables are controlled. This prediction turns an inductive question into a deductive statement that, through experimentation, can be concluded as false or supported by evidence.

While, in general, a hypothesis is a statement about how you believe a system of variables interacts, not all statements make good hypotheses. As your hypothesis is the foundation upon which you will design your experiment, it is important that you have a well-formed hypothesis. A poor hypothesis can lead you to answer the wrong question, not account for the variables of a system that really matter to you, or prevent you from conclusively answering the hypothesis. A good hypothesis has the following characteristics:

- Observable and testable[2]
- Clearly defined
- Single concept
- Predictive

Observable and Testable

The observability trait means that it is a hypothesis about something that is possible to measure in some fashion. Without the ability to observe the hypothesized behavior, it is impossible to create an experiment to generate evidence for or against it. An example of a hypothesis lacking the observability:

Attackers who target Amazon Web Services (AWS) do it with the intent for monetary gain

It is impossible to measure the intent of the someone attacking AWS by monitoring the network. You may be able to get access to a few attackers, but you would never be able to track down and ask every attacker their motivation for attacking AWS. A more tractable hypothesis looks at the observable data of an attacker like this:

Public attack surface (number of publicly addressable components) is linearly correlated with the number of observed attacks.

However, not all observable hypotheses are also testable. The testability trait means it is possible to test, or create an experiment, to see if it holds true or not. Nontestable hypotheses generally include variables that are uncontrollable or cannot be managed to reduce bias. Some of these issues can be addressed through quasi-experimental methods covered in the next chapter, but when they can't, you have a hypothesis that can't be evaluated with experimentation.

The internet will collapse if 60% of the backbone is successfully denial-of-service attacked.

While it is possible to set up monitoring stations to determine if the Internet fails (although a specific definition of what a collapse means is needed), it is not ethically, legally, or, for most researchers, economically feasible to denial-of-service attack the Internet. Untestable research questions are bettered suited for theoretical exploration. Through understanding the effects under the theory would then allow designing observational studies to see if the casual situations ever happen naturally. If you find you can't alter your hypothesis to become something testable, you may be better served by looking into the observational and theoretical research methods.

Clearly Defined

With a good hypothesis, it should be easily discernable if the evidence is or is not supporting it. In support of this trait, all terms, variables, and metrics used in the hypothetical statement should be clear and concise. Usage of unclear measures is a sign of a bad hypothesis. Statements of measure such as better/worse than, more/less than, or improved/degraded are unclear without further definition. It must be clear in the hypothesis what it means for a variable to be in an improved state or when it is clear that a variable is in a state that is more than a previous state. A clear statement of measure makes it easily discernable if the collected evidence supports the hypothesis or not. For instance, instead of saying "better than" when measuring performance, you could say something like performance increases by at least 10% from the current operation (note: this would require a clear definition of how to measure the operation).

In addition, clear and quantifiable definitions must be provided for any unique, domain-specific, or imprecise words used in the hypothesis. There are a lot of branding/marketing type words that are used to generally categorize things in the cyber security field. Words such as "advanced-persistent threat" (APT) and "script-kiddie" are used a lot to define attacker skill and experience, but these terms aren't accompanied with widely accepted definitions. So having a hypothesis like:

An APT has a 20% higher ratio of successful to failed exploitation attempts against wordpress sites than script kiddies

is a bad hypothesis because your definition and ours of what constitutes an APT and script kiddie is probably different. To make this into a useful hypothesis you would need to define APT and script kiddies. Using specific terms makes it clear to readers what is being predicted and what data to expect to invalidate it. This is a more specific hypothesis:

The 2016 National Collegiate Cyber Defense Red Team will have a 20% higher ratio of successful to failed exploitation attempts against wordpress sites defended by new NCCDC teams versus wordpress sites defended by NCCDC teams that participated in the previous year.

DIG DEEPER: NATIONAL COLLEGIATE CYBER DEFENSE COMPETITION

The National Collegiate Cyber Defense Competition is an annual event that challenges the ability of teams of university students to compete in defending a cyber environment from professional red teams. The Collegiate Cyber Defense Competition started in 2005. It includes a scenario where teams are taking over managing a corporate environment where they have to secure systems while ensuring that services are active and being responsive to business needs. Professional pen-testers are leveraged to provide red teams against the teams to subvert and manipulate team cyber resources.

Single Concept

A hypothesis is supposed to be a succinct prediction of an effect in response to a cause. If x occurs, then y will happen. The intent of the hypothesis is to understand if there is truly a causal effect from x to y. Therefore, it is critical to limit the number of variables involved to determine what is causing an effect if there is one. A good hypothesis should be limited to testing one concept at a time. If, for example, you were investigating effects of defensive attributes you could hypothesize:

IP address hopping and software diversity increase the time to a successful attack.

Trying to test both ideas at the same time would confound the results. If there were a significant increase in attack time during experimentation you wouldn't know if it was caused by the IP address hopping, the software diversity, or both. Also, testing both IP address hopping and software diversity together might make it more difficult to control other variables that might compound the confusion more. This means it is better to break the hypothesis up into distinct statements to test:

The time to a successful attack is increased as the speed of IP address hopping is increased.

The time to a successful attack is increased as the amount of software diversity within a target is increased.

IP address hopping and software diversity increased in tandem will exponentially increase the time to a successful attack.

As you can see, breaking the original hypothesis into multiple hypotheses made it easier to target the specific stimuli and effect we wanted to test in each case. Breaking down a hypothesis into its most basic components enables you to clearly delineate what needs to be tested. In addition, given the often limited resource constraints of research, breaking research questions into multiple small hypotheses provides a clean way to scope and bound what answers you can expect to achieve and leave those beyond your resources for you or someone else to investigate in the future.

Predictive

A hypothesis needs to be a statement of what will happen, given a stimuli; that is a statement of effect, given a cause. A hypothesis helps define an experiment to test an idea and answer a research question. If the hypothesis is merely a statement of fact or a tautology, developing an experiment is unnecessary and wasted resources. For example, a hypothesis that states:

All malware, when transmitted over a network, is converted to digital signals.

is a tautology and doesn't need experimentation because networks operate by transmitting digital signals. Therefore it would lead to the fact that if malware was transmitted over a network it would have to be converted to digital signals.

Generating a Hypothesis from a Theory

A hypothesis can come from anywhere; a thought, a research question, an observation, and so on. However, a large driving factor of science is to encapsulate knowledge into a well-established theory or law. A scientific law is a model of understanding of some interaction within the world. For a theory to become established, accepted, and turn into a law it must be tested rigorously and have many pieces of observed or experimental evidence that it makes correct predictions. A good way to generate hypotheses for experimentation is to produce predictions of behavior from a theory.

Ultimately, a theory uses current knowledge to define an abstract conceptual model. For instance, a theory such as defense-in-depth is a model of the world where the relative cyber security is increased by layering the number and types of security controls. The theory is predicated on the fact that if one layer does fail, one of the additional layers will not fail and will detect or prevent the attack.

To generate a hypothesis from a theory, you just need to configure an input scenario and produce the effect that would occur from the model. For instance, taking the defense-in-depth theory, it should follow that an increase in the number and diversity of layered defenses should increase the relative security of a specific system. From this statement, we can generate multiple hypotheses good for evaluating the defense-in-depth theory. The first interesting concept is that the relative security should increase as the number of layers increases.

The relative security of a test system will increase as the number of layers of security controls increases.

However, there are a few problems with this hypothesis; it uses unclear, nonmeasurable terminology. How does one measure the relative security? What does it mean to layer security controls? To improve this hypothesis, we need to address these issues. For measuring relative security, we could state that a system is more relatively secure if it prevents (failed attempt) or detects an attack, which we will define as an attempt to exploit a vulnerability. When people layering security controls for defense-in-depth, they generally mean applying different categories of defenses; that is firewall, NIDS, HIDS; to monitor the same data. We will use this definition of layering for our hypothesis. Now we have a testable hypothesis.

The defense-in-depth theory can easily generate other hypotheses to test, such as increased diversity increases the relative security of a system. Or, the combination of diversity and layering security controls increases the relative security more than alone. These hypotheses would need more explicit defining as the first, but they are also good candidates for hypothetico-deductive research.

Our use of the defense-in-depth theory as an example was pretty naive, as the theory suggests some more complicated interactions. Through experimentation, some are starting to discover that, in fact, not all combinations of layered defenses produces the relative security increases theorized.[3] The cyber security field is ripe with a lot of largely anecdotally supported theories; moving target defenses, adversaries that take the path of least resistance, attacker asymmetric advantage, and so on. To ensure that we build our security applications upon a sound foundation, it is important that we validate our theories through hypothesis-driven experimentation. While a hypothesis can come from anywhere, if you are in need of one and have a theory you are interested in, generating one from it is a good, worthwhile approach.

EXPERIMENTATION

With a well-formed hypothesis in hand, it is now necessary to design an experiment to generate data to evaluate the truth of the hypothesis. As we discussed in the previous section, a hypothesis is a testable prediction that can be measured. A hypothesis is largely a guess, hopefully an educated guess, but a guess all the same. Until evidence for or against a hypothesis is generated, it will stay as such. To turn a hypothesis into bonafide knowledge, it has to pass the test of experimentation. An experiment is a test specifically designed to determine if a hypothesis is false under the conditions stated in the hypothesis.[4]

In the earlier chapters we discussed studies, where the process is to observe and collect data from an operating system for inferential analysis. An experiment changes this process. Instead of just watching as a system operates, an experiment controls the system to ensure that only specific variables or inputs of the system are altered to determine the response effect. Good experiments isolate the variables of interest in a system to have high confidence if the intervention produces the expected result.

An **experiment** is a rigorously defined and executed procedure to investigate how the control of a set of variables affects the behavior of another set of variables in a system of interest. A good experiment exhibits the following characteristics: **Clear, Precise, Repeatable, Reproducible**.

- *Clear*: A good experiment includes a clear design. This includes clear explanations of assumptions, the procedure to be executed, the analytical method used to detect an effect, and the logic behind the choices made. And, it should be clear to anyone reading the experiment what was performed in an experiment and why every action was taken.
- *Precise*: A good experiment also needs to be precise in its definitions and the procedures. There should be no possible alternate interpretations. All people participating in the experiment need the same understanding of the experiment and what exact process should be followed to ensure that the results are not confounded by inaccurate execution of the experiment.
- *Repeatable*: An experiment needs to be documented fully, such that it is repeatable. A test against inaccurate execution is to repeat an experiment a number of times to see if the result is similar. To support the repeatability, an experiment needs to be documented from the design through the execution and the analysis performed, so you or others can redo the experiment.

- *Reproducible*: A key aspect of science is reproducing results to validate peer results. Much like repeatability, the experiment needs to be fully documented; however, the difference is that peers reproduce experiments independently. Therefore, an experiment needs to be documented with the intent that others can read, follow, and reproduce the experiment. Reproducibility often means including more information in the documentation, such as your beliefs and intentions, software developed to execute and analyze the experiment, and even the data produced for comparison.

As you may have noticed, none of the characteristics of a good experiment are tied to the results of the experiment. It is key to understand that all results of experiments are good. All knowledge is good. While science is usually presented from the perspective of major finds, in reality there is a lot of work that happened before those major discoveries. While not every experiment will lead to a major breakthrough, the only real way to get to breakthroughs is to methodically test our beliefs until a surprise is found.

The statistics or mathematical approach often informs what goes into the design and analysis of an experiment. There are various philosophies of statistics for experimentation. We do not have a strong opinion on what statistics are used, as we see them as tools to achieve our objectives, and as tools they are better suited for different situations. However, in this chapter, we will be approaching the experimental design from a frequentist perspective as that is the statistics that is often taught in the context of hypothesis testing.

In this section, we will discuss what goes into the definition, design, setup, execution, and analysis of an experiment. Various examples will be provided to explain the concepts. Some of the examples may be simple or clearly false, but we use them to explain the subject, and not because they are experiments that should actually be executed. To demonstrate these concepts we will leverage the following hypotheses examples:

1. *Control system communication is deterministic enough that a MitM attack is detectable.*
2. *The time to a successful attack is directly proportional to the amount of software diversity within a target.*
3. *Public attack surface (number of publicly addressable components) is linearly correlated with the number of observed attacks.*
4. *Users are able to generate and remember passwords with higher complexity when using sentence-based password schemes over random character password generate.*

Dependent Variables (Measured Variables)

The first step in setting up an experimental design is defining the dependent variables from your hypothesis quantitatively. What this means is that you must take your prediction and break it down into one or more measurable observables. Each of these observables are dependent variables.

A **dependent variable** is an observable and measurable variable that is expected to show if there is an effect from the intervention applied in an experiment. To define a dependent variable you need to specify what the observable is, how you will measure it, a definition of the possible range, and the expected result values. It is also important to explain how the dependent variables tie back to the hypothesis as it may not always be clear.

Let's define the dependent variables for our examples:

1. *Control system communication is deterministic enough that a MitM attack is detectable.*
   In this hypothesis, the claim is that a MitM attack is detectable through looking at the deterministic behavior of a control system communication. Determinism is a characteristic of network traffic that means it is more consistent or has less variation over each instance. Therefore, we can break down the observables and measurements for network communication determinism into the latency and jitter of the communication. The hypothesis makes the claim that the latency and/or jitter will noticeably increase when a MitM attack is occurring.
   To collect these measurements we have a few options: (a) on the boxes in the system, (b) create a machine in the path of the communicating devices, (c) span port a network switch, or (d) tap the communication line. Since we are measuring the latency and jitter, which are both measurements of the delay of the communication, it is important that our measurement technique not have the possibility of contributing to the network communication delay. Putting the sensor on the boxes in the system or spanning a network switch port could both add processing performance that could add delay to the communication of the systems under test, so neither of those are optimal choices. Putting a machine in the path of communication would increase the delay because it would have to forward the communication, which is also not a good choice. A passive network tap that provides the ability to tap the communication without affecting the communication of the system is the best choice and what we would choose as the method for measuring the dependent variables. Let's take a look at our next hypothesis.

2. *The time to a successful attack is directly proportional to the amount of software diversity within a target.*
   In this hypothesis, time to a successful attack is the variable we want to measure to determine if the software diversity impacts the time for an attack to succeed. While at first blush, it would seem that this dependent variable is pretty straightforward, but in fact it is a little more complicated. If you think about how attackers operate, they generally leverage a suite of tools to execute attacks. What tools are provided for attackers to use and how experienced they are in using them, and how effective they are in successfully attacking different types of software, all could affect the speed of a successful attack. While controlling to make sure they are fairly applied is part of the design of the experiment, coming up with someone to measure and normalize time when they are used in different combinations is important to come to a final account of how much time was included in the attack. To accurately measure time in this example would require having synchronized time across the systems under test to ensure that the actions are logged in comparable time. Synchronizing boxes from the same local network time protocol (NTP) server would probably be sufficient.

   Looking at our third hypothesis:

3. *Public attack surface (number of publicly addressable components) is linearly correlated with the number of observed attacks.*
   The observable under this hypothesis is the count of attacks seen per IP address. The definition of this dependent variable is simply the attacks seen. The interesting part of this hypothesis is how to determine to measure this observable. As the IPs we want to use are previously unused, we can assume that all traffic is inadvertent and attack traffic. As the IP's are all new and unused previously, then it can be assumed that there is equal probability of getting random inadvertent traffic. Then only the amount of attack data can fluctuate. Therefore, just counting the amount of traffic to each IP is a good proxy for counting the number of attackers.

   And, now for our final example:

4. *Users are able to generate and remember passwords with higher complexity when using sentence-based password schemes over random character password generate.*
   In this hypothesis, the obvious observable is the complexity of the password selected. The statement is that sentence-based schemes will

help improve the complexity of passwords. If we measure the complexity of passwords as the entropy in the password, we have a method to observe and quantify the complexity of passwords generated by the users.

However, random passwords have the highest entropy possible (if the random function has entropy) so this wouldn't be a good hypothesis without a bounding variable. In this case, the second, bounding dependent variable is the memorability aspect of the passwords in relation to the complexity. Memorability of a password could be measured by time until forgotten. To determine if this hypothesis were true, a comparison on both the complexity and how long a password could be remembered.

As you can see from these examples, it is important to think about how you will look for the hypothesized effect. Sometimes the dependent variable can be observed directly, but sometimes you need to find proxy variables to observe the effects. And, it is also important to think through what the observed values mean and when they would explain the hypothesis. A clear understanding of the dependent variable is crucial to setting up an experiment such that it will provide the needed evidence to conclusively answer the hypothesis. Chapter 13, Instrumentation, discusses capabilities, issues, and processes for collecting data from a cyber system in more depth.

Independent Variables (Controls)

One of the first critical steps in developing your experimental design is defining all of the variables you think could have an influence on the dependent variables. **Independent variables** are the inputs to a system that have the potential to cause an effect or variation in the dependent variables' output. The starting set of independent variables is those variables you plan to have an intervention around. However, the final defined set of independent variables does not have to be, and probably is not, limited to the variables of intervention. There are often a lot of variables in a system that have a potential for impact on the dependent variable. However, due to various reasons: hypothesis, interest, resources, and so on, it is often the case that not all independent variables are intervened against within an experiment.

When documenting independent variables, it is important to be as complete as possible. The reason is twofold. First, it lists all of your assumptions and understanding of the system. Documenting this information is important for peer review and reproducibility to provide the context to readers of your work. Second, fully documenting the independent variables that could have an impact defines the set of variables that you will design control processes around for the experiments. In support of these reasons, it is also important to define what each variable is and why you believe it could have an impact when documenting them.

The list of possible independent variables can often be long. As such, we will only work through one example in this section. For example, we will define and discuss the independent variables for hypothesis 1: *Control system communication is deterministic enough that a MitM attack is detectable*. The following is an example list of independent variables for the example hypothesis.

- *Man-in-the-middle attack*: This is the main variable around which we want to create trials of interventions. The method of achieving the MitM attack could alter the behavior seen. Therefore, for the purposes of this example we could list the possible test cases as a bump-in-the-wire (physically insert an attacker box in communication lines) or address resolution protocol (ARP) poisoning attack.
- *Topology/architecture*: The number of machines communicating and the infrastructure supporting the communication can alter the behavior of the communication. The topology could both increase the overall amount of latency and jitter and also the noise range to make detecting a MitM attack more difficult.

  The topology of the system will be manipulated by adding or reducing the amount of machines on the network.
- *Equipment type/vendor*: The make and model of the types of computers and control system equipment could alter the deterministic behavior of the communication. Different vendors and equipment could be developed under different assumptions, utilize more efficient techniques, or be designed to meet higher determinism requirements.
- *Communication medium*: The communication medium by definition alters the minimum latency and bandwidth possible for communication. Wired (copper wire, fiber, Serial) and wireless medium (WiFi, 802.15.4) all have very different characteristics that could impact the way in which equipment communicate. This variable will be bounded by the communication medium supported by the equipment selected.
- *Bandwidth*: Closely related to the communication medium, the bandwidth selected/supported could impact the communication behavior of the system. Bandwidth selection is limited to a subset of communication medium such as different types of Ethernet or the Baud Rate selection of serial communication. The speed at which

communication occurs could slow down interactions or cause devices to become overwhelmed.

- *Fault events*: Faults do occur within control systems that require safety systems to react or control operators to enact corrective procedures. These off-normal behaviors could alter the communication behavior of the system enough to make it harder to detect a MitM attack.

- *Communication method*: In this context, communication method refers to whether the SCADA network has been set up as a master/slave or peer-to-peer. This includes whether devices are only allowed to talk to the "master," or whether they can contact each other, if necessary. In the architectures we have developed, it is likely that the main change would be configuring the Ethernet switch to allow peer-to-peer communications, if that is possible. Changing the communication method will likely affect the network topology, as virtual connections will be formed between machines in a peer-to-peer, which do not exist in master–slave networks. And, it may also affect the type of equipment we are able to use, as some may not be able to support peer-to-peer communications.

- *Scheduling*: Scheduling will be effected in the initial configuration of the devices. From this state, the operator can control schedules, such as the order in which devices report or change how they are reading the system. Using this, we can change the order in which the devices execute their actions, and study whether this has any impact upon determinism.

  Changing the scheduling of the system should not affect any of the other manipulation variables, except perhaps the type and vendor of the equipment, which have to be configurable.

- *Version of firmware/software*: Much like the equipment type and vendor, the software applications or firmware version used on the hardware could impact the determinism of the system. Some versions of software could have bugs that create different characteristics of behavior or newer versions of software could be designed with more efficient techniques or more feature bloat that makes it slower.

- *Protocol*: The protocols used can have an impact on determinism. For example, Modbus over Serial uses time-based framing so its latency will be bounded by how it operates. Or TCP provides reliable, ordered communication, which will continue to retransmit packets that are not received, where UDP is unreliable and will only send a packet once.

The different characteristics of each protocol used in the stack could alter the systems communication behavior.

- *Test monitoring equipment*: The method of monitoring could impact the latency characteristics. Adding additional equipment to the system to observe the communication could require adding equipment into the communication path (such as a bump-in-the-wire device) or increase the processing requirements on equipment within the system (such as a span port on a switch).

- *Geographical distance/disturbances*: Distance is a contributing factor to the latency. Altering the distance that communication must travel will alter the latency, but it might not be a direct correlation of distance to effect. This variable is tightly tied to the communication medium and topology architectures as the communication medium can travel different distances before requiring repeaters or routers, which alters the topology of the system.

- *Hardware condition*: The age and condition of equipment used in the system could impact the communication behavior. As equipment ages or becomes damaged, its probability of failure rate increases and it is not deterministic in what way it will fail and how the failure will impact its ability to communicate. Partially failed equipment could greatly impact the behavior of the overall system.

You may be thinking to yourself that we missed a variable that would have a probability of impacting the results. That is an important part of the independent variable list; documenting your own understanding of the system so that it can be reviewed, studied, repeated, and challenged by others. Each researcher shouldn't be required to understand everything. Science is a team sport. The goal of research is to provide enough information that the next researcher can take your work, augment it, and find the next discovery. Providing the independent variable list is an important step in documenting your assumptions about the system you are researching.

You may also think we covered some variables that you doubt would really have an impact in a significant way. To reiterate, at this stage, in the experiment design we are just documenting our understanding of the system of interest in the context of the hypothesis we posed. In the next section, we can pair down the list of variables around which we will provide interventions. However, this list defines all the variables we will have to control in some fashion across each trial of the experiment, whether it is as part of an intervention or to hold it stable to ensure that it doesn't impact the results. Finally, after you have exhaustively listed independent variables you are ready to start designing the experimental control scheme and trial procedures.

Experimental Design

Experimental design is the process of defining the methods, controls, and trials of an experiment to generate the data necessary to determine the accuracy of the hypothesis. Developing an experimental design includes a definition of the number of trials and what is varied between each trial, the processes and procedures performed within the trials, how the trials are organized and the statistical approach to quantify an effect, and a definition of the analytic process. An experimental design should document every step of the execution plan such that there is no ambiguity.

An experiment generally consists of two or more trials. An experiment **trial** is one runthrough of an experiment, which includes varying one or more independent variables to generate a dataset to statistically analyze for an effect compared to other baseline or other trials. The number of trials is a function of the independent variables you want to investigate, the control methodology selected, and the analytical method, which will be discussed in the next sections. In each trial, one or more interventions is applied to test the effects of an input state of the independent variables of interest. An **intervention**, or what some call a **treatment**, is a specific control of an independent variable to observe and measure the effect on a dependent variable.

The objective of an experimental design is to ensure a rigorous application of the hypothetico-deductive process. There are two desirable characteristics you should strive to achieve when designing an experiment: internal and external validity. An experiment that achieves full validity is rigorous, consistent, and broadly applicable.

Internal Validity

Internal validity is a measure of the internal consistency of the process that produces empirical evidence. Only experiments that maintain internal validity can conclusively provide evidence of a causal relation between independent and dependent variables. Achieving internal validity is a process of eliminating the systemic or process errors that diminish the confidence in the results.

There are threats to internal validity that you need to think about when you are designing your controls and control methodology. These threats are outlined in the following table and some control mechanisms to account for and mitigate them are provided (Table 9.1).

Table 9.1 Threats to Internal Validity

Threat	Description	Controls	Example
Confounding Variables	Confounding variables are independent variables, or variables related to the independent variables, that are not being sufficiently controlled within an experiment such that it is difficult to determine if the interventions or the variability of the confounding variables are causing an effect.	The best way to mitigate confounding variables is to be as comprehensive and rigorous as possible in documenting your independent variables and then design your experiment to ensure that only one variable at a time is changing. If you have an independent variable you know you can't control for, move to the next chapter (Chapter 10: Quasi-Experimental Research) for guidance on how to proceed.	We already discussed confounding variables in the independent variable selection. If from our example we didn't know that monitoring the communication by putting a machine in line could affect the resultant timing of communication, this would create a confounding variable.
Bias	Experimental bias is when something about the experiment design or operation that causes a control to fail and allow influence that could cause an unwanted effect. There are multiple ways in which bias can sneak into an experiment. **Selection bias** is a type of bias that occurs when you select the participants or interventions experimental trials. **Configuration bias** is selecting the experimental setup such that it unknowingly creates a stronger/weaker effect than would happen in the general case. Finally, **experimenter bias** is when the way the experimenter interacts with and operates the experiment influences the results.	Selection bias can be controlled for by using randomization to select participants. Randomization can't fix problems if the starting pool is biased, so make sure the initial selection pool is representative of the larger population. Configuration bias can be avoided if you define and use a logic of why you are configuring the environment and system for the experiment. This will limit the internal validity issue but does not solve external validity problems. Experimenter bias can be solved by using blind controls. A single blind control prevents the subjects from knowing about the treatments and adjusting their behavior. A double blind control prevents the experimenter from knowing when the interventions occur to prevent them from altering their behavior and inadvertently providing signals or cues that impact the results.	A common example of selection bias is using computer science students for experiments, but treating them as representative of the general population, which they are not in most cases. An example of configuration bias would be to only use old versions of a piece of software because it is what you have access to and treating it like it is representative of current technology. Finally, an example of experimenter bias would be giving additional/preferential time to the trial candidates of a similar background or interest as yourself. This could unduly affect the performance of the recipients and the overlooked participants.
History	Threats to internal validity due to history occur when external technological, political social, natural, etc., events occur that alter how the system under test, or participants, would respond to the interventions.	Controlling for historical changes is difficult. If you are aware of something that has changed that could have an impact on further trials you can rerun the trials so far to see if they did change before continuing through the rest of the trials.	Some examples of history threats to experiments could be the discovery of a new major vulnerability such that it would alter how an attack would play out, the release of a new technological paradigm that would change the underlying communication of a system, or a law or

Continued

Table 9.1 Threats to Internal Validity *Continued*

Threat	Description	Controls	Example
		If you are trying to build upon previous results, it is also good practice to replicate the previous experiment before performing your new experiment. We acknowledge that resource limits can prevent accounting for this validity threat, so acknowledge the possibility when documenting the results so others can account for it.	regulation being passed that would alter the way users or defenders would behave in different situations.
Maturation	Maturation is a problem that occurs when subjects of an experiment mature and learn over the course of the trials such that it is difficult to tell if an effect is due to the intervention or to the gained knowledge and experience of the participants.	To protect against maturation threats you can use pre-experiment training processes to ensure that participants don't have large experience gains in the trials. Or you can ensure, through trial sequencing or broadening group selection, that only unaffected groups participate in the trials where maturation could have an impact. Or you can ensure balance by randomizing the order of access for the participants to distribute the experience among the population.	Examples of maturation could be when you are testing defenders' abilities to make decisions under different conditions. If a training regime is not put into place, the effects could be impacted by the improvement of the defender in being able to use the tools at her disposal.
Instrumentation	Instrumentation threats to internal validity occur when the measurement instruments are imprecise and the effect could be an artifact of the measurement. For example, if the sensitivity of the instrument is insufficient to detect the effect or if the act of instrumenting the environment alters the effect the end result cannot be associated with the independent variable.	To control for imprecision, following a strict documented calibration process for all instruments used in the experiment will ensure that they all meet an equal and acceptable level of precision. Understanding the sensitivity requirements due to the expected size of effect will help you determine what instruments, and in what configuration are necessary to sensor the environment. Finally, understanding how the sensor works and could impact the environment you apply it to is important to prevent the act of observing from becoming a confounding variable.	Instrumentation is a threat that you have to be very cognizant of in cyber security research. Often the instrumentation is provided from within the system being studied. For example, if system logging is set to its highest level will that impact the behavior of anything else in the system that is relevant to the hypothesis? Also, there is a lot of complexity to cyber systems, so you need to have sufficient understanding of the systems you are instrumenting and how you are instrumenting them. Issues such as buffer bloat and kernel jiffy frequency could impact the timing of measurements that could prevent you from accurately detecting an effect.

DIG DEEPER: CONFOUNDS OF NETWORK INTERFACE CONTROLLER

A common form of measurement in cyber security experiments is network sensors that generate full packet captures. There are aspects of general computing devices that can confound your sensing. The first is Network Interface Controller (NIC) behavior. The drivers of some NICs will offload processing and buffer data such that it will impact the timing of when the operating system and your application will receive it. Turning off features such as TCP Segment Offload[5] (TSO) and Large Receive Offload[6] (LRO) is important for timing situations. Also operating systems operate at a frequency of operations, measured in jiffies. The jiffy size limits the speed at which an application can interrupt and subsequently calculate time. In Linux kernels prior to 2.6.0, the jiffy was set at 0.01 seconds. After 2.6.0, the jiffy was increased to 0.001 seconds. As this setting limits your measurement sensitivity, it is important to be aware of and configure appropriately.

External Validity

External validity is a measure of the generality of the knowledge gained from the execution of an experiment. An experiment that is fully externally valid applies universally. This means that the experimental design accounted for the variability across all of the independent variables such that it is representative of all situations. While external validity is the ultimate goal of experimentation because it fully validates theories, it can often be at odds with internal validity. In order to adequately control for all the confounding variables and bias, you can be forced to select a system definition that is specific and lacking external validity. In these situations it is best to prioritize internal validity to maintain confidence in the results.

There are a few different dimensions around which you can think about experiments being externally valid.

- Generalizability across environments
- Generalizability across situations
- Generalizability across actors

External validity is often a problem in cyber security research. Most networks are unique with different architectures, procedures, and policies. Recreating user behavior at scale and recreating how different threat groups behave is difficult. National and cultural conventions and laws are different and difficult to be completely inclusive of all perspectives. Since the cyber domain is so fluid and rapidly developed it is hard to predict what capabilities, functionality, and paradigms will exist so designing experiments that have future generality is also very difficult.

Control Methodologies

Putting together the independent variables in a fashion to achieve internal and external validity is a control methodology. The distribution of the data, the number of independent variables with intervention, and the analytic method can all play into the control method. The selection of a control methodology determines how you will control the independent variables, the ordering, and the number of trials. There are many different control methodologies available depending on how you want to investigate your hypothesis and the statistical analysis choice you want to use. As such we will only cover some of the more common control methodologies. In the next section, the various statistical methods that can be used with these control methodologies will be discussed.

Comparison

The most popular and common control methodology is a **two-sample comparison** test. This type of test compares, using a statistic that matches the distribution of the data or a nonparametric statistic, the distributions of two samples of data. Generally, the null hypothesis, or the inverse of your hypothesis, is a baseline or a sample from an un-intervened system. However, the two samples can be two levels of an independent variable compared for a variance or difference for effect.

An example of a direct comparison from our ongoing example of hypothesis 1 would be if we just wanted to first test if altering the bandwidth of the SCADA system caused an effect before testing the MitM attack effect. The hypothesis would therefore be that the change in bandwidth would cause a difference in the latency behavior of the system. From this, the null hypothesis would be that the bandwidth change does not cause a difference in latency. So the two trials would be one with a 100 Mb switch and the second would be 1 Gb switch. All other independent variables we discussed would be held constant, that is use the same hardware (same vendor, firmware, configuration), use the same software (same version and configuration), use ethernet as the medium for both trials, use DNP3 over IP for the protocol, and assume that the equipment will not degrade between trials (there are studies on mean time to failure[7] that could be used to back this assumption up) (Table 9.2).

Table 9.2 Trials for an Example Two-sample Comparison Test	
Trial #	**Bandwidth Intervention**
1	100 Mb
2	1 Gb

For this, and most experimental trials that include comparing computer behavior, we would strive for a balanced design. A **balanced design** is an experimental design where each trial has the same number of observations. Since it is "fairly" easy to generate the same number of events when computers are involved, it is good to do balanced designs such that the comparison is on more equal terms.

Factorial Design

A **factorial design** is a control methodology where you test each independent variable selected for intervention in every combination of possible intervention value. Factorial design requires that you define each independent variable into discrete states. A fully factorial design creates a trial for every possible combination of independent variables of interest at every level. A partial factorial design will downselect on how to vary some of the independent variables to optimize the results versus the number of trials necessary to execute. For example, for the bandwidth independent variable in the MitM attack research, we know that the majority of users are using 10 Mb and 1 Gb, but very few are using 100 Mb and nobody is using 10 Gb. To save resource we could do a partial factorial design and only perform trials at 10 Mb and 1 Gb. An important aspect of factorial design is that it can create the conditions to do analysis of variance (ANOVA) statistical methods to compare groups of trial results instead of doing many pairwise comparisons. We will discuss the statistical comparison concepts more in the next section.

Blocking is the concept of creating multiple copies of the test environment such that they are equivalent so that you can test the different interventions on common ground. For cyber security, when dealing with cyber systems this is normally a fairly trivial problem. Resetting systems, using virtual machines, or restarting applications to recreate the same initial conditions is common practice and should be easy to achieve for most situations. However, when performing experimentation in the context of human subjects, it is important to create a pool of participants and then using random selection to ensure uniform placement. You can do this by selecting subjects for each trial equally around variables of interest such that there isn't a bias in any of the trial blocks of participants.

DID YOU KNOW?

The term *blocking* comes from agricultural experimentation. As a means to avoid variability in the environment for testing agriculture treatments, blocks of land are portioned off for the different treatments. As it can be assumed that the land in a local region has the same characteristics, breaking a plot of land into blocks provides safety from confounding variabilities of the environment.

Table 9.3 Example Blocks for a 2 × 3 Factorial Design

	No Attack	In-line Attack	ARP Poisoning
100 Mb	Trial 1	Trial 2	Trial 3
1 Gb	Trial 4	Trial 5	Trial 6

Table 9.4 Example Blocks for an Orthogonal Design

	No Attack	In-line Attack	ARP Poisoning
100 Mb	Trial 1	Trial 2	
1 Gb	Trial 3		Trial 4

A simple 2 × 3 factorial design from our example would be to expand the experimental design we discussed in the comparison to include two types of MitM attack. Now we have the two bandwidth settings and now two MitM levels, physical in-line attack and ARP poisoning. Again, all other independent variables would be held to the same configurations across trials. For a full factorial design we would need to do six trials as laid out in the following table (Table 9.3).

Orthogonal Design

Orthogonal design is a control methodology where you know that some independent variables are unrelated, or orthogonal, such that you can create trials that include intervention in multiple dimensions or independent variables at the same time. Unlike factorial design, we would not need to test every combination of every independent variable, but would only need to test each intervention in one of the trials. So, if we make the assumption (which is a false assumption but for the interest of an example we will ignore this) that bandwidth and attack type will not have an effect on each other, we can alter our design to an orthogonal design with the trials setup as shown in the following table (Table 9.4).

Sequential

A **sequential design** is a control methodology where a sequence of trials is designed such that the next trial can be dependent on the results of the previous trial. This type of design is most useful when experimenting for applied research and trying to project the future effectiveness of defensive technologies and techniques. This can help model the co-evolutionary nature of cyber security and determine how effectiveness of red teams increases as they learn more about a system. We will cover this type of research more in Chapter 11,

Applied Experimentation, and methods of modeling and controlling for adversaries in Chapter 14, Dealing with the Adversary.

ANALYSIS

The process of analyzing your data is a crucial step in determining if your evidence supports your hypothesis or not. Just as with the rest of the experimental process, establishing and defining an analytical process needs to be rigorous and reasoned. In this section, we will discuss what you need to do in the process of setting up the experiment for analysis and to dig into the data after you collect it from running the experiments.

Hypothesis Testing

Statistical hypothesis testing is the process of generating evidence for or against a hypothesis by measuring samples. Generally, hypothesis testing is a comparison of two or more samples of data to see if there is a difference or effect. One of the samples of data is often taken from a baseline or untreated environment. The test is to try to determine if there isn't an effect or difference between the baseline and the data samples containing an intervention. The statement that there isn't an effect is called the **null hypothesis**. The frequentist approach to hypothesis testing provides the probability of observing the sampled data, given the null hypothesis is true.

The p-value is the key statistic for frequentist hypothesis testing. A **p-value** provides the probability of a result equal to or more extreme than the observed value if the null hypothesis is assumed to be true.[8] The p-value is a measure of the strength of evidence against the null hypothesis. To determine if the null hypothesis should be rejected or not, a significance level is selected. Historically, the traditionally accepted significance level is 0.05.[9] However, due to some challenges in some of the reproducibility of results in some fields, there are those calling for an increase to a significance of 0.005.[10] As cyber security is still young, there hasn't been an agreed-upon significance level, so we suggest you start with 0.01 but use your own judgment based on the question and form of the data.

The key is to understand what a p-value result tells you, as there is often a lot of confusion about it. First, a significantly low value means that either the null hypothesis isn't true or a low probability event happened. If, going into the research, you have a strong belief in the null hypothesis, then getting a low p-value should cause you to question arriving at a low p-value. This is the basis of the famous XKCD comic strip comparing bayesian and frequentist statistics,[11] where a sensor that detects if the sun has exploded rolls two dice and will lie if two sixes are rolled. While there is a low probability of the sensor being faulty, (in this case lying) the prior probability of the null hypothesis (the sun not exploding) is so overwhelming that you should question a significant p-value. Also, while a low p-value means the null hypothesis can be rejected, it doesn't mean the original hypothesis is highly probable or true. A p-value is defined in terms of the null hypothesis only, so just because you have confidence that there was an effect, it may not have any relation to what the underlying cause was. What this means is that being a good researcher is being a skeptic of everything, even the statistics. Statistics are a tool and not a panacea. If the result seems odd, question it.

DID YOU KNOW?

P-hacking is an unethical behavior that occurs in experimentation. P-hacking is the process of manipulating a dataset, dropping trials or reframing the research, to find a statistical significance. P-hacking is one of the main methods that leads to the distrust of statistics and believe that statistics can be used to show any answer you want.

P-hacking is not always done maliciously. You may think that just not including some trials of data in your results but it affects the statistics and probabilities, so it is unethical and highly frowned upon. Just remember that no result is bad and always report on all the data you generate.

However, the p-value is important for determining to reject the null hypothesis and believe that there is an effect, it isn't where the story ends. Also important is to think about and report a confidence interval and effect size. A **confidence interval** represents a range that with a probability derived from the significance level will include the true fixed value of interest. Stated another way, if 100 sampled datasets were taken from the system under test, 95 of the 100 confidence intervals would include the value of interest. The confidence interval provides a measure of the uncertainty of the process of sensoring and a way to bound where the true value may actually fall. The **effect size** is a measure of the practical effect of the intervention. Where the p-value measures if there was a difference, or the statistical effect, the effect size measures how big of an effect was seen. As the size of the data sample increases, the p-value test becomes more sensitive, which means it will detect smaller and smaller effects until the measured difference is an absolute zero. From this follows that you may find results that are statistically significant but, in the context of the research question, are practically so small that they are insignificant. From our example, this would represent finding statistical significance of the latency changing between the baseline and the MitM attack, but the practical difference is 1 ns, which is practically unmeasurable and therefore not useful.

The way of determining that we have the appropriate sample size to determine an effect with high confidence is power analysis. **Power analysis** is a process to estimate the appropriate sample size to achieve confidence in detecting an effect size. Adequate power in an experiment means that the likelihood of achieving a false negative is sufficiently low. As with significance level, the power level isn't a hard-and-fast rule. The general rule of thumb is to use an 80% power. However, this again is a factor you need to think through. In the medical profession, it is typical to set a very high power (>80%) to ensure a very low false-negative rate;[12] as it is better to incorrectly think you have a disease and do more tests than to incorrectly determine someone is healthy when they are actually sick. Cyber security in general shouldn't have this level of concern, but every situation is different, so use your best judgment to construct the appropriate experiment.

The sample size to meet the specified power is a function of the underlying distribution of the process, the estimated effect size (or acceptable error size), and the confidence level (1 − significance level). As we will discuss next, there are times when we don't know the underlying distribution, but in order to calculate the sample size picking a distribution is necessary. A common rule of thumb is to select a parametric distribution, calculate the sample size, and then add an additional 15% to it.[13] We discussed calculating a sample size in more depth in Chapter 4, Exploratory Study, and there are a lot of online resources to assist in calculating power and sample size. In most situations it is acceptable to leverage them,[14] but make sure they are using formula suited for the research method and data type in your research.

All of these statistics require some understanding of the distribution, or the lack thereof, underlying the data. There are different statistical tests that are more efficient and powerful (require less samples to achieve a confident result), but they have different assumptions on the type of underlying distribution and if you use them in the wrong situations you limit their effectiveness and power. The list below describes some of the more common parametric and nonparametric tests and their uses.

Parameterized Tests

- *t-Test*: The *t*-test is one of the most-used hypothesis test statistics. This is useful when comparing the parameters of two samples. The *t*-test operates on the assumption that the underlying population distribution is a normal or Gaussian distribution. There are many different uses of the *t*-test. The most common is Student's *t*-test where you test a null hypothesis such that the means of two samples are equal. You can use *t*-tests, called Welch's *t*-test, to perform paired tests where the intervention is executed on the same system and the before and after means are different. The *t*-test can also be used for regression testing to see if the fitted line's slope is far from 0.

- *ANOVA*: Analysis of variance (ANOVA) is another commonly used test. The test is used to see if there is an effect across multiple interventions. The null hypothesis is that there is zero effect between the different samples, or the means of multiple samples are the same. For this test, it is important to understand that the rejection of the null hypothesis only states that at least one of the samples is different than the others. This does not provide information on which sample sets are those that represent the effect or by how much. As with the *t*-test, ANOVA assumes a normal distribution for the population and adds an assumption that the variances among the samples are similar.

Nonparameterized Tests

- *Mann–Whitney test*: The Mann–Whitney test (also call the Mann–Whitney–Wilcoxon test) is the nonparametric version of the Student's *t*-test. This is useful when the population distribution is not known or not normal. The Mann–Whitney test requires that the data is at least ordinally measurable.
- *Wilcoxon Signed-Ranks test*: The Wilcoxon Signed-Ranks test is the nonparametric version of the paired test. This can be used largely in place of Welch's *t*-test when the distribution is unknown or not normal. The Wilcoxon test requires that the data is at least ordinally measurable.
- *Kruskal–Wallis and Friedman's test*: Kruskal–Wallis and Friedman's tests are both nonparametric versions of ANOVA tests. Kruskal–Wallis tests are used for the normal ANOVA situations where you want to determine if many samples are equivalent. Since it is nonparametric, the median is used as the measure of test since the mean is tied to a distribution. Friedman's test is a special test to see if there is a difference between the measurement across multiple samples. For instance, if you wanted to study the effectiveness of agreement of multiple cyber security analysts, you could provide a series of system alerts to the analysts to rank and then use the Friedman's test to see if any of the analysts' ratings are consistent

Example

Let's put all this statistical analysis information together with one of our examples. If we go back to the MitM attack and wanting to test the effect of changing the bandwidth of the system on the latency of the communication. If you recall, we had two samples to draw, one where the system communicates over a 100 Mb network and the other with communication over a 1 Gb network.

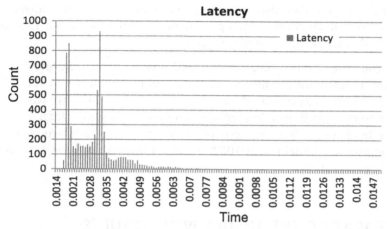

FIGURE 9.1 Network Communication Latency Histogram.

In this situation our null hypothesis is:

$h_0: s_1 = s_2$ where s1 is the 100Mb samples and s2 is the 1Gb samples

In order to determine the rest of the values to set up our statistical analysis, we first have to perform a pilot data collection. We collected data for an hour using the 100 Mb communication and found this distribution of latency (Fig. 9.1).

Clearly, you can see that this dataset is not pulling from a normal distribution, which means we will be using the Mann–Whitney test instead of Student's *t*-test. Also using this initial dataset we can estimate the rest of the values needed. We can leverage the standard deviation from this dataset, which we will say is at 0.01484. We also need to estimate the expected effect size, and from looking at the dataset we may notice that most of the fluctuation occurs at or above 0.001 of a second. To make sure we capture those effects, we can set the effect size to that value.

For this example, we can stay with convention and use a 95% confidence value or a 0.05 significance level. We will also set the power to 90%.

Using the following conservative sample size calculation for a quantitative hypothesis test:[15]

$$\text{sample size} = (2 * \sigma^2 (Z_\alpha - Z_\beta)^2)/\Delta^2 = (2 * (0.01484)^2 (1.96 - 1.645)^2)/(0.001)^2 = 43.703$$

where σ is the standard deviation, Δ is the level of significance, $Z\alpha$ is the Z score of the confidence value, and Z_β is the Z score of the power.

From this we calculate that we need 44 samples for each test. However, we remember that when using a nonparametric test it is good to add 15% to the sample size, so the final sample size is 51.

After collecting the two datasets, it would now be time to calculate the test statistic to determine the likelihood of the null hypothesis or no effect. If the Mann–Whitney test produced a p-value of 0.759382047434, we would compare it to our significance level of 0.05. Our p-value is greater than our significance level, so in this situation we cannot reject the null hypothesis that running the experiment with 100 Mb and 1 Gb does not have an effect on the communication.

INTEGRATING THE THEORY WITH RESULTS

If you derived your hypothesis from a theory, it is important to go back to determine how your results integrate with the theory. If the results of the experiment confirm what you expected from the theory, then you just need to document that the evidence supports the theory. However, if the results run counter to the theory, you have to think through what this means. While it would be easy to say the theory has been falsified, things aren't generally that simple. You should reevaluate your independent variable list, evaluate your sensors, and look at your statistics. Any one of those could have been set up to bias the results. As we discussed earlier in this chapter, you are always testing your assumptions just as you are testing your hypothesis. If the theory is old with strong evidentiary support, then you should question your process. Maybe one of your assumptions is incorrect. Perhaps it could be a problem with how you sensored the environment. Or, it could be you set up an incorrect statistical approach. You should definitely check your process, up to and including repeating some experiments, before attempting to falsify a strong theory.

However, if you rigorously review your approach and you still have the same belief or if the theory you are testing is fairly new without a lot of evidentiary support from other research, then questioning the theory is prudent. You might have found an edge case that the theory doesn't support. If you can modify the theory to support your situation, it is important to go back and validate previous results to ensure that the theory still holds for past evidence. The goal of experiments is to generate strong, general theories of the world, so taking the extra step to integrate your results into the field's corpus of knowledge is important.

DID YOU KNOW?

The discovery of Neptune occurred because observations didn't match Newtonian models. Using Newton's model, there was an attempt to predict the paths of, at that time, the eight planets in the solar system and they found irregularities with Uranus. Instead of throwing out Newton's gravitational models, which had significant confirmatory evidence to that point, researchers began investigating assumptions that could be false. Another planet in the solar system being present would explain Uranus's path, which led to the discovery of Neptune (which had actually been observed multiple times before, only no one knew what they were seeing).

REPORTING YOUR RESULTS

The final important step of scientific work is reporting your results. The greatest discoveries have little value if no one knows about it, can leverage the knowledge for further science, or to engineer something with more predictable behavior. The two most prevalent forms of documenting experimental results are conferences and journals. These venues provide a path to insert your gained knowledge into the field's corpus. However, the quality venues all require peer-reviewed acceptance. Peer review provides a validation check against the topic of research, methods of research, and the quality of the reporting of the research to ensure that a certain level of quality is required. Ideally, the quality of the work should be the only metric of acceptance, in reality the novelty, ground-breaking, and popularity of the topic also play into the review process, so these things should be taken into account when you select your venue. In this section, we provide a general template for reporting hypothetico-deductive research, which will be applicable to most conferences and journals.

Sample Format

In the following, we will provide you with a general outline for publishing your results. Every publication will provide formatting guidelines. When you decide on a venue to submit your research, be sure to check their submission requirements to make sure you follow any outline and formatting specifications. The outline provided here follows a common flow of information found in published papers and should meet the requirements of a larger number of publisher requirements.

Every paper is unique and requires some different ways of presentation; however, the provided sample flow includes all of the general information that is important to cover in a paper and is a general starting format we take when starting to write a hypothetico-deductive paper and modify it to support the topic and venue. We understand that every research has their own style of presentation, so you can feel free to deviate from this outline. The discussion of each section is provided to explain what is important to include and why, so you can present the important information in whatever way suits your style best.

Abstract

The abstract is a concise and clear summary of the paper. The goal of an abstract is to provide readers with a quick description of what the paper discusses. You should only discuss what is stated in the rest of the paper and nothing additional. Each submission venue will provide guidelines on how to provide an abstract. Generally, this includes the maximum length of the abstract and formatting instructions, but sometimes this will include information on the type and layout of the content to provide.

Introduction

The first section of a paper should always be an introduction for the reader into the rest of the paper. The introduction section provides the motivation and reasoning behind why the research was performed and should include a statement of the research question and hypothesis used for this research. If any background information is required, such as explaining the domain, environment, or context of the research, you would discuss it here. If the audience is significantly removed from some aspect of this topic, it may be worth it to create an independent longer background section. The provenance of the hypothesis should be explained if it was generated from something. If you used a theory or simulation to generate the hypothesis provide that information. If you are starting from observation explain the initial premise as well.

Related Work

The related works section should include a quick summarization of the field's knowledge about this research topic. Are there competing theories? Have other experiments, studies, or theoretical studies been done? If there are a lot work in this field cover the most impactful or influential work for you.

Experimental Design

The experimental design part of your paper should clearly define the process you will take to execute your experiment. It is crucial that this section is clear and complete such that a reader would be able to replicate it in their environment. In this section, you need to define your dependent and independent variables and your reasoning for them. You need to define the experimental control methodology and which independent variables are going to have interventions. Each experiment trial that will be run and how the independent variables will be varied between them should be defined. This should include the controls you will use both to provide the interventions and how you will control for the other independent variables to prevent confounding. Finally, you should define the statistics you used and the motivation for using them.

Experimental Configuration

The experimental configuration section should discuss the system under test and the laboratory environment you used to execute the series of experimental trials. You need to be as complete in your documentation as possible. Include information covering hardware (vendor/model of servers with configurations, firmware), software (type, version, configuration), network configuration (physical connectivity, logical connectivity including IP addresses, etc.), and instrumentation (location, frequency, etc.). As with the experimental design section, the goal is to be complete enough that a reader could replicate the setup. As papers have space limits, this is often a first place to cut as it isn't as important as the results. If you find yourself in this situation, it is good to fully document and add this to your paper as an appendix as you can often provide an appendix with explanatory information without counting against your word count.

Data Analysis/Results

In the results section of your paper, explain what you found after you performed your analysis. Lay out the significance, confidence intervals, and effect sizes for all of the experiment trials. Creating tables to show results is an efficient and effective method. You can also show pictures of interesting results; that is if a data anomaly occurred or to display the distributions of the data samples. If anything unexpected, like a device failure, occurred during testing and shows up in the data, explain it in this section.

Discussion/Future Work

The discussion/future work section is for general observations and comments on the entire research process, including interesting results. Provide your explanations for the results you received. If they are interesting and affect a theory, provide what you think happened, and if you think a modification to the theory would cover this result. Discuss where you think this work should lead next. Is there any immediate or follow-on work planned?

Conclusion/Summary

In the final section of the paper, summarize the results and conclusions of the paper. The conclusion section is often a place readers jump to quickly after reading the abstract. Make a clear and concise statement about what the ultimate results of the experiments are and what you learned from it.

Acknowledgments

The acknowledgments section is a place for you to acknowledge anyone who helped you with parts of the research who were not part of the paper. It is also good to acknowledge any funding sources that supported your research.

References

Each publication will provide some guidelines on how to format references. Follow their guidelines and list all your references at the end of your paper. Depending on the length of the paper, you will want to adjust the number of references. The longer the paper, the more references. A good rule of thumb is 15−20 references for a 6-page paper. For peer-reviewed publications, the majority of your references should be other peer-reviewed works. Referencing web pages and Wikipedia doesn't generate confidence in reviewers. Also, make sure you only list references that are useful to your paper, meaning don't inflate your reference count. Good reviewers will check and this will likely disqualify and reflect poorly on you.

Endnotes

1. Curd, M., and Cover, J. A. (1998). Philosophy of Science: The Central Issues. New York: W.W. Norton & Co.
2. Peisert, S., and Bishop, M. (2007). How to Design Computer Security Experiments. In Fifth World Conference on Information Security Education (pp. 141−148). Springer US.
3. Frei, S. (May 23, 2013). Correlation of Detection Failures (Tech.). Retrieved February 25, 2017, from NSS Labs website: https://www.nsslabs.com/research-advisory/library/infrastructure-security/data-center-intrusion-prevention-systems/correlation-of-detection-failures/
4. Dror G. Feitelson. Experimental Computer Science: The Need for a Cultural Change. Internet version: http://www.cs.huji.ac.il/~feit/papers/exp05.pdf, December 2006.
5. Wireshark. (October 30, 2013). CaptureSetup/Offloading. Retrieved February 25, 2017, from https://wiki.wireshark.org/CaptureSetup/Offloading
6. Gordon, S. (November 3, 2014). Segmentation and Checksum Offloading: Turning Off with ethtool. Retrieved February 25, 2017, from https://sandilands.info/sgordon/segmentation-offloading-with-wireshark-and-ethtool
7. Jones, J.V. 2006. Integrated Logistics Support Handbook, 3rd edition. New York, NY, USA: McGraw Hill.
8. Biau, D. J., Jolles, B. M., and Porcher, R. (2010). P Value and the Theory of Hypothesis Testing: An Explanation for New Researchers. Clinical Orthopaedics and Related Research, 468(3), 885−892. http://doi.org/10.1007/s11999-009-1164-4
9. Cowles, M., and Davis, C. (1982). On the origins of the .05 level of statistical significance. American Psychologist, 37(5), 553.

10. Johnson, V.E. (November 11, 2013). Revised Standards for Statistical Evidence. PNAS 2013 110(48) 19313–19317; http://doi.org/10.1073/pnas.1313476110

11. Munroe, R. Frequentists vs. Bayesians [Cartoon]. Retrieved February 25, 2017, from https://xkcd.com/1132/

12. Sample Size and Power in Clinical Trials (Tech. No. 1.0). (May, 2011). Retrieved February 25, 2017, from North Bristol NHS Trust website: https://www.nbt.nhs.uk/sites/default/files/attachments/Power_and_sample_size_in_clinical_trials.pdf

13. Erich L. Lehmann. Nonparametrics: Statistical Methods Based on Ranks, Revised, 1998, ISBN = 978-0139977350, pages 76–81.

14. Australian Bureau of Statistics. (n.d.). Sample Size Calculator. Retrieved February 25, 2017, from http://www.nss.gov.au/nss/home.nsf/pages/Sample size calculator

15. Charan, J., and Biswas, T. (2013). How to Calculate Sample Size for Different Study Designs in Medical Research? Indian Journal of Psychological Medicine, 35(2), 121–126.http://doi.org/10.4103/0253-7176.116232

## CHAPTER 10

Quasi-experimental Research

Cyber space is expansive and growing. Every day there are more cyber devices being activated and more functionality is being added to the domain. The scale and complexity of cyber space can make controlled experiments difficult like discussed in the previous chapter. Fully controlled experiments are the ideal. However, they are not always possible. Whether it is due to some environment that is not fully controllable or a subject population that is small or hard to study, you will run into situations where performing a fully controlled experiment will not be feasible. In this chapter, we will discuss quasi-experimentation methods to help when you can't fully control all variables.

If you were directed to this chapter, then you have a hypothesis but you suspect you have some variables that will be difficult to control. Quasi-experimental methods are designed to help under these conditions. While they don't provide a strong evidence, quasi-experiments are very similar to and share a lot of the same concepts with full experiments. As such, this chapter will not retread the same ground as the previous chapter. Only new concepts and differences with true experiments will be covered in this chapter. To fully grasp the concepts in this chapter, it is important for you to have read and understand the concepts of the Chapter 9, Hypothetico-deductive Research, when reading this chapter.

This chapter will cover the differences between true and quasi-experiments, including general factors for quasi-experiments and what we include under quasi-experimental as different from the social sciences. Common factors in cyber security research that lead to using quasi-experimental approaches are then covered. These factors are helpful in providing a starting list of potential issues to look for that may lend to quasi-experiments. Finally, we will walk through research methods using example experiments to showcase the concepts of each method, as well as showing how they can be used in practice. After reading this chapter you should have a good understanding of what quasi-experiments are, when they are appropriate, and some knowledge of how to use them under example circumstances.

251

Research Methods for Cyber Security. DOI: http://dx.doi.org/10.1016/B978-0-12-805349-2.00010-8

CHAPTER OBJECTIVES

- Define and explore the differences between a true and quasi-experiment
- Discuss the challenges in cyber space and security that compel quasi-experimental research
- Explore quasi-experimental methods through examples

TRUE VERSUS QUASI-EXPERIMENT

As was defined in the previous chapter, an experiment is the study of system behavior through a controlled environment and process such that all independent variables are accounted for, either through control methods or interventions. Experiments provide some of the strongest evidence for phenomenology and causal relationships. Through the methodical varying of independent variables you can determine, with confidence, which will affect the dependent variables. However, being able to control all independent variables is often beyond a researcher's capabilities.

It is important to know that in situations where you have uncontrollable independent variables all is not lost. **Quasi-experiments** are experiments where one or more independent variables are not fully controlled. Quasi-experiments are generally used within the social sciences when the subject population cannot be sufficiently randomized for some reason. This commonly occurs where the studied group is small or the treatment is medical and can only be applied to a specific subpopulation; that is, with an illness. Quasi-experimental methods were developed to enable researchers to continue to experiment under these conditions with an understanding that the results are less strong and contain internal validity issues, (i.e., differences between the control and treatment groups being responsible for measured effect).

While due to the social aspect of cyber security, an insufficiently randomized, small sample size type of situation is still possible, which we will cover later, it is not the only situation for a quasi-experiment. For this book, we expand the definition of quasi-experiment to mean any experiment where a small number of independent variables are not completely controlled. Some of the common factors that lead to uncontrollability will be discussed in the next section. Generally, this occurs when a controlled experimental environment intersects with a natural or operational environment. As was discussed in the previous chapter, operational environments are generally not good for experimentation due to the inability to control all independent variables. In Chapter 13, Instrumentation, we discuss experimental testbeds and provide some example environments that are potentially available resources.

It is important to note that quasi-experiments don't necessarily mean that independent variables are completely uncontrolled. As true experiments represent the process to generate the strongest evidence of phenomenology, you should always try to strive toward being as close to a true experiment as possible. Therefore, if there are opportunities to control, to some degree, hard-to-control variables, then you should do so. In the next section, we will discuss some common variables of cyber security research that lead to quasi-experiments. The research methods discussed in this chapter represent some ways to handle experimentation with these challenges.

CYBER DRIVERS FOR QUASI-EXPERIMENTAL DESIGN

The quasi-experimental path should not be viewed as an easy way out when performing a true experiment is difficult. However, quasi-experiments are justified under specific conditions. As with other fields, there are some commonly reoccuring factors that drive the use of quasi-experimental designs. In this section, we will discuss some of the commonly occurring situations where complete experimental control is not feasible.

- *Uncontrollable variables*: A common factor that drives quasi-experimental research is uncontrollable variables. A variable can be uncontrollable for various reasons, such as it is large scale or it can't be reproduced within a laboratory environment.
  - *Internet*: The Internet is one of the most complex and vast systems ever created, bringing together many different systems that produce emergent behavior. The ability to replicate or simulate the complexity of the Internet is very difficult. As such, when you have research questions that involve the Internet, it is often the case that you can't come up with a controllable method to experiment. In these situations, it is prudent to use the Internet in your experiment and move forward with a quasi-experiment.
  - *Users (as background noise)*: Human behavior is one of the most challenging behaviors to model and replicate. The entire field of Artificial Intelligence/Machine Learning/Deep Learning, and so on are focused on recreating pieces of how humans think and behave. For complex experiments, users are likely needed (as subjects, or more likely as part of the background environment behavior). Users will provide the fidelity of realistic behavior (they make mistakes, click on links, and behave sometimes irrationally).

- *Population limitations*: The main use of quasi-experimental methods in the social sciences is when there is an insufficiently sized test population to enable the use of randomization as a control technique. As cyber security science includes a significant social aspect, this situation is present. There are a few common populations of research that often run into this scenario.
  - *Threats*: Threat sources are a small population to start, but they also are a population that is often highly opposed to being researched. As they generally want to stay undiscovered and they want to protect their methods, it is difficult to get participating threats for research. Red teams can be a suitable replacement, but it is still a small population and difficult to get a large enough sample to be powerful. Therefore, quasi-experimental methods will often be used when experimenting with threats.

DIG DEEPER: DARK WEB

There is a thriving e-commerce market for threats and their tools and exploits called the dark web. As anonymity is highly valued due to the illegal nature of most threat activity, the dark web has become a common place for selling illicit materials including hacking services and tools. The dark web is a network that runs hidden over the Internet. Onion routing, which was developed to assist in anonymous communication, provides layers of encrypted routes that makes it very difficult to determine the location or identity of communicating parties. Major dark web ecommerce sites such as the notorious Silk Road were established to provide black market dealing over the Internet. Threat actors sell their expertise, services (DDoS botnets), and tools (exploit kits) on the dark web. The dark web both hampers the ability to study threats and also provides a place to watch threat activities. However, it is important to be careful when using these sites as they can lead to serious acts of retribution.[1,2]

- *Cyber environments*: Every cyber environment is a snowflake. There is practically an infinite way of architecting together hardware, with a nearly infinite amount of software types, so that the number of cyber environments for testing is a huge space. The effort to set up and test cyber environments limits how many you can realistically test. As such, quasi-experimental methods can be used to help with the limited number of test environments.
- *Users*: While getting general end users who are unbound to any specific environment is fairly easy, getting access to a large set of users tied to a specific use case can be very difficult. Under these circumstances, quasi-experimental methods will often be used when dealing directly with users as subject.

QUASI-EXPERIMENT RESEARCH METHODS

With some ideas in mind of what types of situations cause challenges for hypothetico-deductive experiments, we will now discuss quasi-experimental research methods. Our list of methods is not comprehensive of all quasi-experimental methods used across the social sciences because there are a lot of variations of methods developed for special cases. The list we present here are some of the more common methods and the methods we have found useful in our research. As always, examples of research will be used to help contextualize and explain the reasoning behind choices in designing these quasi-experiments.

Difference-of-differences Design

One of the most commonly used quasi-experiments is the difference-of-differences method. A recurring technique of modeling threats within controlled experiments is to use penetration testers, also known as red teams. This is a natural turn because red teams are used operationally to model threats to determine what vulnerabilities are found and how they can be exploited. In research, red teams can be and are used to investigate metrics and measures of security, behaviors of attackers under different scenarios, and, from an applied use case, to see how effective security applications are or compare to current practice.

Using red teams in research presents a control challenge, however. There are not a lot of red teams and they require considerable expense. For example, when conducting an experiment with red teams, having a high enough number of teams, and sufficient amount of people on each team can be a problem for achieving a sufficiently powerful sample size. Therefore, it is generally the case a small red team sample is used. When using a small sample size, setting up controls to account for differences between the red teams can become a challenge as well. These differences can be from different expertise, experience level, tool access, and comfort level, or may be uniquely tuned to the experimental setup. All of these potential differences must be accounted for to have any confidence in the results.

Techniques, such as providing preexperiment training, can be utilized to help manage some variance in users. However, there is only so much difference that can be handled with small training modules for users to equally prepare them for the experiment. Generally, this technique is insufficient to generalize red team experience and capabilities. This technique is more appropriate when users are unaware of something in the experiment, like training the red teams on the test environment.

Red team differences in this situation cannot be controlled to the extent of true experiments and here is where quasi-experimental methods are useful. In this case, the difference-of-differences research design is helpful. The **difference of differences** is a research method that enables you to evaluate the relative difference in response in test cases to account for differences in baselines. This method is useful when you have to test subjects that are potentially not starting at the same place. Without a common baseline, it is impossible to directly compare the treatment effects. Having two or more red teams is a great example of this. The expertise, tools sets used, techniques, training, all vary from team member to team member. Additionally, the team itself might be new, lacking a strong leader, and so on; this makes the starting reference point hard to assess.

The general measure of results from repeated samples in true experiments is to measure the difference in the resultant effect after a treatment. Yet, as this is not possible in this situation because of differing baselines, the difference of differences measures the relative effect difference instead. To do this, a pretest and a posttest are taken for all of the red teams. A **pretest** is a test given to each subject before any interventions are made to quantify a starting value or place. These initial test results can be used as a starting achor value to determine an effect. As the pretest result will probably be different for each red team, and it is unknown what factors drive the difference, this measurement is not useful. A **posttest** is a test given after an intervention in the experiment to take a measurement to determine the effect, if any, of the intervention. The posttest, for this example, too, will most likely result in different answers for each red team, and again, a direct comparison is inconsequential. However, as the only factor that changed between the pretest and posttest results was the intervention, it is reasonable to attribute with some confidence that the intervention drove the change in results. Therefore, measuring the relative difference can provide a measure of how different interventions affect the results.

Let's work through an example experiment to explain this research method. As in previous chapters we will use moving target defense as our example. As a reminder, moving target defense is a concept that if the cyber environment continually shifts in some fashion, it will impede an attacker's ability to target and execute successful attacks. This solution naturally leads to a research question of "How are attackers' abilities to understand and reason about a cyber environment affected when moving target techniques are present?" One may hypothesize that the number of true positive vulnerabilities detected or vulnerabilities that persist will decrease when moving target defenses are utilized. We can design and execute an experiment to test this hypothesis.

DID YOU KNOW?

Moving target defense is an idea that grew out of the success of attackers utilizing techniques to continuously alter their attack profiles to avoid detection. Methods such as polymorphism, packing, and encryption have enabled attacks to be quickly shifted to confuse and deceive detection. This has established an asymmetric relationship where defenders have to find every possible construct while attackers can reuse a small set of attacks. Moving target defense is hoped to provide the reverse asymmetry, whereby the defenders can shift the cyber environment such that it is difficult for the attacker to understand and accurately target cyber vulnerabilities.

To simplify the example for this discussion, we are purposely being naive and focusing just on different moving target approaches. As the intervention, in this example, we will use memory (Linux ASLR (Address Space Layout Randomization) and No-Execute (NX^3), and Windows ASLR and Data Execution Prevention (DEP^4)) and network (Network Address Space Randomization ($NASR^5$), OpenFlow Random Host Mutation ($OF\text{-}RHM^6$)) address randomization. Fig. 10.1 depicts an abstract design to explain this concept. Let's start with an example with three red teams. The first team, who is the baseline test without a treatment, will attack a traditionally secured environment that follows best practices, the second red team attacks an environment that follows best practice security plus all applications, where available, utilize memory

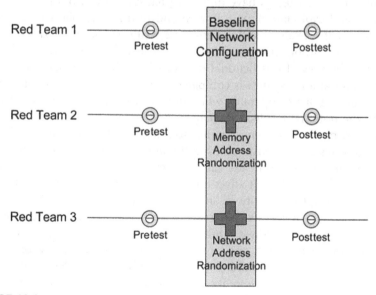

FIGURE 10.1
Moving target defense difference-of-differences design.

address randomization, and the third red team attacks an environment that follows best practice security plus deploys network address randomization.

Difference-of-differences Execution

To enable the difference-of-differences test, we must first assess the pretest capability of each red team. As the treatment is exposing the red teams to copied environments with different defensive strategies and technologies deployed, it is important to not use this environment without defensive technologies to control for maturation effect. The maturation bias exists when using the treatment environment because one red team could gain more understanding about the environment during the pretest environment that could make them more effective in the posttest, regardless of the defensive strategy. To ensure that the experimental design doesn't influence the results, the pretest needs to be designed with adequate controls. This could include testing on a similar, but different, pretest environment with some baseline set of security implemented. Alternatively, what we would choose instead, is to create a series of tests that relate to the posttest environment. For example, if the environment has services such as web servers or databases, then tests on exploiting some prebuilt, vulnerable web servers and databases can be given to each red team such that you could have a comparable pretest result.

Difference-of-differences Analysis

Notional results from this example are shown in Fig. 10.2. As you can see, all three of the red teams have different pretest scores in both vulnerability discovery and exploitation, and they all end in different places in the posttests. Visually this leads to an indeterminate result. However, these raw values are not the result, but instead, the relative measures are. Fig. 10.3 shows the relative differences of this fictional dataset where the difference between the baseline pretest and posttest is compared to the difference of the other tests. As you can see, it's comparable when driven down to this one set of numbers. In the notional results, the memory address randomization didn't have much effect on the discovery of vulnerabilities, but did have an effect on the exploitation results. We created this notional dataset to show what we would expect the results to be. In the case of memory address randomization we would expect that it doesn't affect the discovery phase of an attack, but does attempt to disrupt the ability of an exploit to succeed. This is shown in the data by the size of relative difference. The results are nearly reversed for the notional network address randomization. We would expect an effect in the vulnerability detection and only a minimal effect on the exploitation. Our logic is that network address randomization is intended to move the logical location of services to make them harder to target. However, the hope is that it would also affect the ability to exploit too if the network shuffling occurred too fast for the execution of an exploit.

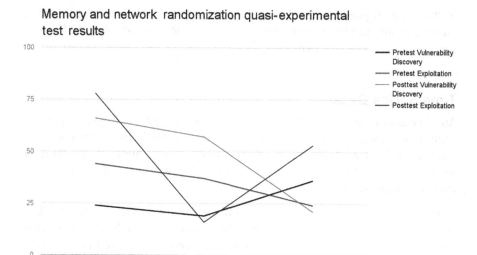

FIGURE 10.2

Notional example of trial results for a moving target difference-of-differences quasi-experiment.

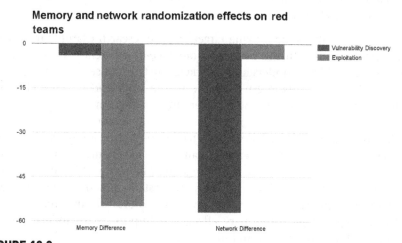

FIGURE 10.3

Notional example of relative difference of effect of memory and network randomization on red teams.

From this example, you can see that difference-of-difference tests can be very useful for cyber security research. You will often find research questions where it is difficult-to-impossible to get adequate test cases to produce the power needed for a true experiment. Difference-of-difference tests are the perfect solution to provide some answers. As the same factors affect all test subjects, this method has strong internal validity and you can have confidence in the results it produces. However, the key factor that drives its use is having an inadequate number of test subjects. As such, the external validity of results from this method are not strong.

Time Series Design

Another useful quasi-experimental method is *time series design*. Generally, time series design is a method where you take multiple measurements over time to see how an intervention effect persists. This method has its basis in medical treatment testing. However, it is just as useful in understanding the coevolutionary nature of cyber security.

A desired outcome of science is the predictability of understanding, not just at the current time, but projected into the future. This predictability is what will enable operational decisions like how to best to allocate funds to adequately mitigate cyber risks. However, this is also where one of the most challenging aspects of cyber security shows its face. Defenders and attackers evolve and change over time based on the actions of one another. Understanding this relationship is crucial to providing predictive understanding. Using time series quasi-experimental designs enables the integration of this maturation effect into experiments.

We can leverage the same moving target defense research example to explain time series concepts. In the previous difference-of-differences experiment, it would be possible to understand attackers' first response to moving target methods. However, this doesn't tell the whole story and is insufficient for predictive modeling. If, say, the attackers in that experiment were found to be significantly impacted or were made less effective, due to the moving target defense, one may conclude it is a technique worth applying. However, this may be a mistake. As adversaries gain more experience with new defensive techniques, they will learn and change their behavior. What if it were the case that attackers were able to quickly understand moving target defenses and with this knowledge, they became even more effective than before. Understanding the coevolutionary effects are important to understand the ultimate usefulness of new techniques.

If you recall, the difference-of-differences design was set up with a pretest and posttest, as shown in Fig. 10.1. If we want to study the coevolutionary effects, we need to add more tests across time. Traditional time series design allows evolution to occur naturally, which could be done in our case. However, the resources necessary to let a red team learn only through discovery can be extreme. Therefore, we like to add controlled information release to understand how an adversary would behave when they gain increased levels of knowledge. The current difference-of-differences design posttest is

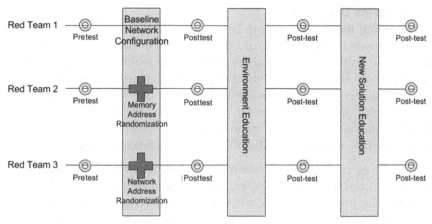

FIGURE 10.4
Revised moving target defense time series design.

on an environment with defenses about which the adversary lacks any knowledge. For predictability it is necessary to know how an adversary would behave differently when they have knowledge of the environment and when they have knowledge of the new defensive solutions. (Fig. 10.4)

Given those two additional questions, how might we create a design to answer them? We can simply add two additional posttests for each knowledge gain. Now our design looks like Fig. 10.4. The second posttest is to understand the effects of the treatment when the red team has knowledge of the test environment. The final posttest is when the red team is aware of the operation of the defenses to see if they can derive a strategy that is effective against the defense. The amount of time between these posttests is up to the designer and is often bound by resource constraints. It is important to give the red teams adequate time to absorb the information on the environment and the defensive strategies such that they can plan and derive an offensive strategy. As such a few weeks up to a few months should be allowed between posttests to allow for this maturation to occur.

Going back to our example, we now have three time series designs: baseline defense, memory address randomization, and network address randomization. In this example, it is useful to keep the difference-of-differences design, so that we can compare the effects across the three defensive approaches and three red teams. It is valid and often useful to combine research designs to achieve your goals. In this scenario we want to understand both how the adversary coevolves with defensive strategies, while also maintaining the ability to compare the results across the defensive strategies. Therefore, a multiple time series difference-of-differences design is perfect for our needs.

Times Series Execution

At this point, the experiment can be executed. In the rest of this section, we will use notional results to explain the outcomes of the example experiment and how to go through the analysis of the results and think about the implications. As we already covered the analysis of difference-of-differences experiments in a previous section, we will only focus on the time series analysis issues in this section. This means we will treat the results as if they are directly comparable even though in reality they would not be, because you would need to continue using the difference-of-differences calculation.

During the execution of this experiment, the red teams needs to be provided additional knowledge of the experimental system configuration before each posttest. The first posttest is a test with no knowledge of the experimental system design. The second posttest is after the red team is provided with information about the environment, that is, what services are running, network topology, what types of communication is occurring, what types of data are present, and so on. The final posttest is after explicit detail is provided to the red team about the defenses used in the environment. This includes which versions and types of services are operating, what types of defenses are deployed and their configuration, that is, if a firewall is deployed what rules are configured or if a Snort IDS (intrusion detection system) is deployed what rulesets are being used and in the case of the memory and network address randomization information on what they are and how they operate should be provided.

DID YOU KNOW?

The Snort, one of the biggest name open source intrusion detection systems, was named because it was a network sniffer with a little extra.[7] The funny name convention has burgeoned into a suite of tools with these names. Squil (pronounced squeal) is a situational awareness tool that helps collect and show Snort data and alerts. Snort is a packet generator tool that uses Snort rulesets as input for the packet formats. Pulledpork is a tool for automated installation and management of community snort rulesets. Barnyard is a tool to transmit snort data captures to a centralized data collector. Snort has a strong community that, as you can see, is clever in naming tools.

Time Series Analysis

The graph in Fig. 10.5 shows notional results from the example. As you can see, the red team's effectiveness in detecting and utilizing vulnerabilities increases following an exponential curve as they gain information. This would be an expected result as the attackers' knowledge of the system and defenses enables them to be more accurate and efficient in finding and targeting vulnerabilities. As you can see from the network address

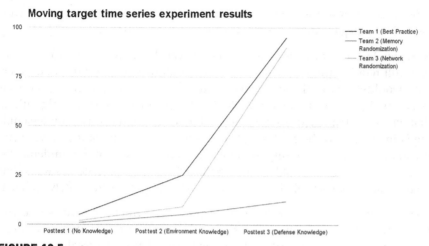

FIGURE 10.5

Notional time series results for example moving target research.

randomization, the second posttest was slightly more effective than the first, but the third test showed that the red team was nearly as effective as with the baseline. With knowledge of how the IP shuffling worked, the red team was able to generate an effective strategy. For the memory address randomization, the second and third posttests are only slightly higher than the first posttest. This means the red team was unsuccessful in generating an effective strategy against memory randomization. Again, these are only notional results to help explain concepts and effective strategies like return-oriented programming have already been developed that exploit memory randomization techniques. However, we used memory randomization in this example for a reason. ASLR, the common implementation of memory randomization, did withstand attempts to exploit it for around a year. This is the goal of research; it is hoped we can find through experimentation techniques that have time series results that follow a logarithmic growth instead of exponential growth. This represents a technique that maintains its security attributes as knowledge is gained about it. This would be a defense that is robust to disclosure and continues to provide benefit to defenders even after attackers learn about the technology.

It is important to understand some limitations to this experimental design. First, there is potential bias on the experience and expertise of the red teams in relation to the defensive strategies. While we are trying to control for that with the difference-of-differences design, it is important to understand that it is not perfect and it could be the case that the outcome could vary. For example, if the ordering of red teams were shuffled or another set of red teams were used, different results might be produced because they may have experience or expertise that is particularly well aligned or misaligned with defensive strategies utilized in the time series quasi-experiment.

Next, while theoretical defensive strategies can be sound and should work they still require implementation, which can allow vulnerabilities that otherwise wouldn't exist. Those familiar with the field of cryptography are well aware of this factor as there are plenty of fundamentally secure algorithms that when implemented become vulnerable to exploitation. This understanding is important to the analysis of the results as you will want to investigate if you think any vulnerability found is due to the strategy or the implementation of the strategy. It could be the case that the implementation is weak, but there could be ways to fix it such that the strategy is more accurately realized.

The last potential bias we will discuss is the measurement of maturation. The time series design is intended to enable the study of this maturation effect, but it, too, is not perfect. Attackers and red teams leverage a wealth of knowledge generated by the community and industry. This knowledge is often represented in tools and techniques used by attackers, which potentially encapsulate years of study and effort. Therefore, the time series design doesn't provide this level of maturation to occur. We will discuss thoughts on how to generate a normalized quantification of effort or resource usage for attackers in Chapter 14, Research with an Adversary.

Cohort Design

A *quasi-experimental cohort design* is similar to the traditional cohort study, except in this case, experimental interventions are used to study effects. As was discussed in Chapter 4, Exploratory Study, a cohort study is one in which cohorts, or a set of test subjects that are grouped based on some common factor or factors, are monitored to study some factor over time. One of the most commonly used situations for cohort studies is the study of subjects exposed to a disease. There is a comparable situation within cyber security: systems and users being exposed to malware or attacks. The main difference between the exploratory study discussed previously and quasi-experimental cohort designs is that in quasi-experiments the experimenter either intervenes to cause the separation of subjects into cohort groups or by providing interventions to study the differences in response of naturally occurring cohorts. This is considered quasi-experimental because the cohorts are often defined naturally and outside the control of the experimenter and becomes an uncontrolled variable in the experiment. Cohort studies are effective research designs to help with these situations.

Let's walk through a cohort quasi-experimental design example for answering the question, "Is cyber security training more effective for subjects that have been exploited recently?" Our guiding hypothesis for this example is that subjects that have been exploited more recently will be more motivated to improve their behavior and thus training will be more effective. We want to study right after the training and in the future to see if the effects of the training persist or if the effectiveness decreases over time. As it is out of our control in selecting who is or is not exploited, we are limited to testing with those subjects that are. This limitation in control makes using a quasi-experimental cohort design a good choice.

Let's assume that we have access to a collection of employees at a small company. We could wait for some employees to fall prey to real attacks over time, but that may take months and you may not be able to get a sufficient number of victims in a time frame sufficient to consider them all "recently" exploited. Instead, we can design in a phishing exercise into the design to generate a set of employees that are exploited at the same time frame. To control for experimental bias, the enterprise incident response team will respond to those successfully phished as if they are real exploits so that users believe the exploit is real. The users will be informed that this was simulated after the conclusion of the experiment. Two cohorts will be formed from this phishing exercise, those that are successfully exposed to the exploit and those that are not. Following the phishing exercise, a training regime will be applied to both cohorts. To measure the effect, a cyber security test will be applied before and after the treatments to see how their knowledge and understanding changes. There will be three posttests to measure how the effect of the training persists over a year. The first posttest is applied right after the training, the second posttest is after 6 months passes, and the final posttest is 1 year after the first posttest. Fig. 10.6 shows the cohort design for this experiment.

Cohort Design Analysis

Recall that our hypothesis is that training will be more effective for those who have been recently exploited. And we had a secondary question; if there are effects, do they persist over time? Fig. 10.7 shows notional results of this experiment. As you can see in this fictional dataset, there indeed was an effect and the pre- to posttest increase in test score is significantly bigger for the exploited cohort. However, this is quasi-experimental because the victims are not directly selected and as such all independent variables can't be completely controlled. Therefore, there is potential bias that there is a common factor that is lending to the user being a victim and their ability to absorb training. Since the cohort was selected based on the proclivity of the test subjects to be successfully exploited by a phishing email and the pretest scores were, on average, significantly lower than those not exploited, it could be the case that initial low knowledge is the factor that led to the exploitation and is also the factor that led to the increased improvement from the training. This means the low scores could be the factor that led to the increased effect and not the exploitation. This notional result would mean

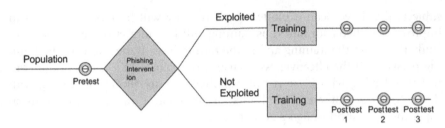

FIGURE 10.6
Example cohort experiment design.

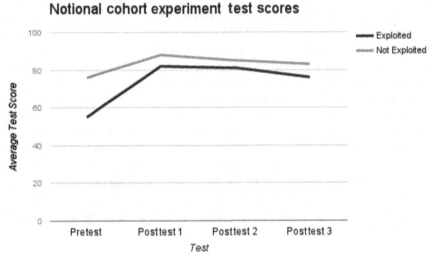

FIGURE 10.7
Notional results for example cohort experiment.

there is a possibility that exploitation is a factor improves effectiveness of training, but it is insufficient to definitively answer the question. Further experimentation where ranges of test scoring subjects are trained and retested would help answer this question more definitively and figure out of if, in fact, low knowledge is a contributing factor or compromise is a positive learning factor like our hypothesis posits.

As for the secondary question, if we perform linear regression on the results we get Fig. 10.8. As you can see, it does seem that in this fictitious example the effects of training do degrade over time. The generated functions do not appear to be significantly different, therefore, this provides evidence that benefits of training degrade equally for all subjects regardless of their past experiences. However, it should be noted that this result has some external validity challenges in that the subjects all came from the same company and only

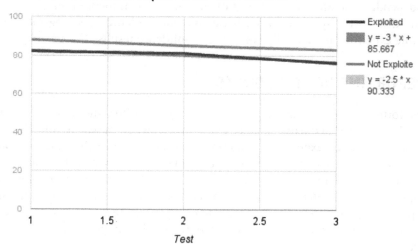

FIGURE 10.8
Linear regression on notional results for example cohort experiment.

one training method was used so it doesn't necessarily mean these will hold up in all cases. Further experiments and studies would be necessary to gain confidence in the generalizability of these results.

We simplified the results of this for the example but there is much more that could be explored for such an experiment. There could be subtopics of knowledge that are tested and you could look for correlations withinsub categories of knowledge and a propensity to falling for exploitation. As the exploit was phishing-based, it would be logical to think that those exploited would be lower scorers in phishing and email security based knowledge than those who were not susceptible to targeted emails. Second, we simplified the resultant data to a single cohort average test result. However, there will be a distribution of values for each subject in the cohort. Statistical methods should be used to determine if there is significance in the result. Looking at these distributions could provide additional evidence for or against test scores being a factor or not. If the cohorts were very disjoint then it would still be an open question. However, if there were a good deal of overlap then you could perform analysis to see if there was a difference in training increase from those with similar scores in both cohorts to determine if the pretest score does in fact drive the change. Our objective was to explain the cohort design concepts in this section but you should still ensure that you follow the rigorous processes needed for statistical validation, peer review of results, and publication.

Cohort quasi-experimental design can be useful when you are forced to use naturally occurring subpopulations to answer your research questions.

However, being quasi-experimental, it leaves open possibilities for bias as all independent variables are not controlled. This research method may not provide definitive results; however, it can provide evidence of strong cases for future experiments that will lead to high confidence results.

REPORTING YOUR RESULTS

The format for a quasi-experimental paper should follow the same format as the hypothetico-deductive paper. Quasi-experimental research follows the same flow as true experimental research. You pose a research question, pose a hypothesis, design, and execute an experiment, and analyze the results. As all of these actions are very similar for all experiments, the same general paper format is suitable for most papers. Therefore, if you are using quasi-experimental methods in your research and want to write a paper, you should read through the paper outline presented in Chapter 9, Hypothetico-deductive Research.

As is the case with all research, it is important to acknowledge any biases that may be present in the results. As there are, by definition, biases in using quasi-experimental research methods, it is important to discuss them and their implications. More often than not they lend to future research directions, which is the goal. You should not be afraid to present quasi-experimental research because of the biases present or perceived weaknesses. Instead see quasi-experimental research as a way to kickstart knowledge of a difficult research question that can lead to more firm results later.

Endnotes

1. Krebs, B. (March 15, 2013). The World Has No Room For Cowards. Retrieved February 25, 2017, from http://krebsonsecurity.com/2013/03/the-world-has-no-room-for-cowards/
2. Krebs, B. (September 21, 2016). KrebsOnSecurity Hit With Record DDoS. Retrieved February 25, 2017, from https://krebsonsecurity.com/2016/09/krebsonsecurity-hit-with-record-ddos/
3. Boelen, M. (October 24, 2016). Linux and ASLR: kernel/randomize_va_space. Retrieved February 25, 2017, from https://linux-audit.com/linux-aslr-and-kernelrandomize_va_space-setting/
4. Howard, M., Miller, M., Lambert, J., and Thomlinson, M. (December, 2010). Windows ISV Software Security Defenses. Retrieved February 25, 2017, from https://msdn.microsoft.com/en-us/library/bb430720.aspx
5. Antonatos, S., Akritidis, P., Markatos, E. P., and Anagnostakis, K. G. (2007). Defending Against Hitlist Worms Using Network Address Space Randomization. Computer Networks, 51 (12), 3471-3490.
6. Jafarian, J. H., Al-Shaer, E., and Duan, Q. (August, 2012). Openflow Random Host Mutation: Transparent Moving Target Defense Using Software Defined Networking. In Proceedings of the First Workshop on Hot Topics in Software Defined Networks (pp. 127-132). ACM.
7. Fisher, D. (July 31, 2013). Martin Roesch on Snort's History and the Sourcefire Acquisition. Retrieved February 25, 2017, from https://threatpost.com/martin-roesch-on-snorts-history-and-the-sourcefire-acquisition/101510/

Applied Research Methods

The aims of pure basic science, unlike those of applied science, are neither fast-flowing nor pragmatic. The quick harvest of applied science is the useable process, the medicine, the machine. The shy fruit of pure science is understanding.

Lincoln Barnett

## CHAPTER 11

Applied Experimentation

Applied research is a major aspect of cyber security. Security is largely an application of knowledge to achieve desired results. And cyber security is the application of security to cyber space. Therefore, the results of the basic research methods we have covered to this point help to gain the knowledge of cyber space needed to inform how to design security control and apply them more effectively. Applied research is the step in the research lifecycle in which we understand how well we used our knowledge to engineer a system to solve a pressing problem and generate predictable outcomes.

If you have found your way to this chapter, it should mean you want to understand the performance or effectiveness of a solution you or someone else developed. In this chapter, we will cover experimental methods for performing applied research to quantify the effectiveness of applying scientific knowledge to a problem. The methods in this chapter determine performance as related to a specific problem where the observational methods covered in the next chapter are more suited for understanding the bounds of performance in general. All applied experimental methods leverage controlled tests that attempt to capture real-world behavior to determine how the applied system behaves. Applied experimental research largely covers what some call validation testing to see if "the right system was built" for the problem.

As applied research is mostly determining how effective solutions are at solving a problem, it is often desirable to compare results to other solutions. Since finding an optimal solution is challenging, there are always different approaches to solving a problem. (And researchers should always be aware of what peers at other institutions, and what commercial industry is doing, related to their efforts). By standardizing one's testing processes and measurements, it becomes possible to evaluate the best solution under different conditions. This provides decision makers actionable and measurable information on what approaches to invest and deploy in real-world situations.

Research Methods for Cyber Security. DOI: http://dx.doi.org/10.1016/B978-0-12-805349-2.00011-X

CHAPTER OBJECTIVES

- Introduce applied research methods for quantifying performance
- Explain benchmarking as an applied research method
- Explain applied experimentation and its similarities and differences from hypothetico-deductive experiments
- Provide good paper outlines for applied experimental research
- Discuss comparison studies

BUILDING FROM A THEORY

Before jumping into a discussion of the different methods for applied experimentation, it is important to first discuss how basic science and applied science should interact. For many, the current research progression is currently locked in the black hat cycle, where every year a group of researchers discover a new vulnerability and other researchers develop defenses to prevent last year's vulnerabilities. None of this research is directed toward discovering the underlying phenomena nor using it to develop solutions that will extend beyond the specific vulnerabilities they are attempting to solve. As such, this cycle can continue ad infinitum without making any real progress. This is not to trivialize this important work, simply to point out the coevolutionary nature of the cyber arms race, and point out the limitations of defense-attack-defense's research and development.

Developing a solution without understanding the problem and the system's behavior is generally not the most effective approach. Without knowledge of the causal relationships in a system, it is difficult to develop an effective solution that controls variables to achieve the desired result. For instance, if users' practice of cyber security hygiene is more dependent on ease of use and transparency of cyber security tools and practices, then spending hundreds of thousands of dollars to demonstrate a proprietary education program might be wasteful because it is targeting the wrong variable.

Basic science provides the knowledge to enable the design and engineering of more effective solutions to our problems. The conceptual models we build from the results of basic science provide the ability to project how solutions would fare in controlling the environment. However, only in the ideal future will we ever have a complete understanding of the universe and our conceptual, scientific model will exactly match with reality. Therefore, our scientific understanding should drive which solutions to try but applied research is still necessary to determine if our knowledge was sufficient and the solution does indeed work as expected. If the solution doesn't meet the requirements of the problem, then it may be necessary to go back to basic science research to learn more.

Applied research results can feed back to basic science also. Solutions studied with applied research will generally not perform optimally or perfectly solve the problem. When and where they are suboptimal provides important information. Either the results inform on a missing piece of scientific understanding or point in a direction of basic research that would be fruitful. In both cases, the information provided through applied research can feed back into basic science to improve our understanding of the world. If the money to test the user education as a solution to poor cyber hygiene did proceed, and it produced poor results, this would inform us that education may not be a driving variable in why users have poor cyber security hygiene.

METHODS OF APPLIED EXPERIMENTATION

When we have developed a solution, from some knowledge generated through basic science, that can be applied to a problem in time for applied experimentation. **Applied experimentation** is the process of evaluating the performance or effectiveness of an engineered system in solving a problem under rigorously controlled conditions. The fundamental characteristics of applied experimentation are the metrics for quantifying performance from measurements and the rigorous process and application of controls to determine the effects. The characteristics that differentiate applied experimentation from basic hypothetico-deductive experimentation are the hypothesis, the dependent variables, and the objective of understanding. If you recall from basic experimentation discussed in Chapter 9, Hypothetico-Deductive Research Methods, hypotheses are focused on making predictions of behavior that can be falsified and the dependent variables are targeted to provide evidence for the hypothesis. With applied research, there is always an implied hypothesis of the solution being tested, which will solve some problem. The dependent variables for applied experimentation are always defined around performance or the effectiveness of the system under test in solving the problem. Finally, applied experimentation is about understanding the behavior of a system that exists where applied research is understanding an engineered system and how well it meets its design requirements.

Applied experimentation isn't the only set of methods for applied research, though. Applied observational study is also a method to understand how effective an application of science performs. The key differentiation between the two sets of methods is the control and objective of the testing. Where applied observational studies are more targeted to less controlled situations, meaning synthetic values are used to derive a spectrum of responses or an uncontrollable operational environment is used, applied experimentation use specific control environments and tests to understand how a solution performs. Another good differentiator is that the results of applied experimentation methods are comparable to determine if one solution is better suited for a use case or not. Generally, applied observational research provides information that is unique to a use case or solution that is difficult to use in comparative analysis. Refer to Chapter 12, Applied Observational Study, for more in-depth discussion of those methods.

Two methods of applied experimentation are benchmarking and validation testing. **Benchmarking** is the process of using a set of atomic test cases to evaluate the effectiveness of a solution. Usually, the test cases leverage or are facsimiles of real-world data or processes. For example, real instances of malware are used when benchmarking antivirus products. Benchmark testing is good for when you have a situation that has atomic test cases of which you can easily sample. While benchmarks use real data, they do not attempt to replicate real conditions. Therefore, benchmarks are not the best solution when you want to understand how a solution behaves under more realistic operational conditions.

Validation testing, on the other hand, is for evaluating solutions in controlled environments to see how they behave under varied but realistic conditions. As you will see, validation testing is very similar to basic experiments as discussed in Chapter 9, Hypothetico-Deductive Research. Validation testing is a good method for understanding how solutions will fare when presented with different situations. Some of the challenges with applied research is the difficulty to recreate realistically modeled environments and situations. The rest of this chapter will discuss the use cases, benefits, and challenges of these two methods of applied research in more detail.

BENCHMARKING

A **benchmarking** is a tool or measurement process through which things can be compared. Benchmarks are a common tool used across industries to provide an approachable and easy method for comparing solutions. Think of it like a ruler for whatever performance metric you wish to test solutions against. The ruler remains fairly constant, so you can measure each new approach or solution and see how it fares compared to past solutions.

DID YOU KNOW?

The term *benchmark* has provenance from the history of surveying. A notch would be cut into a stone face or wall to provide a means by which they could provide a consistent reference for measure. Angle rods would be slotted into the notch and leveling rods hung from the rods, which acted as a "bench" so that leveling rods could be consistently created.

Benchmarking is used across the computing domain. Whether it is measuring the petaflops[1] of supercomputers, the battery life of laptops,[2] or testing your graphics processing unit (GPU),[3] benchmarks are a pervasive applied testing tool for measuring performance. Largely, this is because benchmarks provide a simple way to specify how to test something that provides a universal measure that can be shared and compared.

To use a benchmark, it is important to understand what makes a good benchmark and how to execute it. A **benchmark** is a standard set of data, algorithm, or process that is used to generate performance measurements. The form the benchmark takes really depends upon the problem and solution you are trying to measure. If the problem is detecting malware, then the benchmark will include a dataset of malware. Or if the problem is incident response, the benchmark could be a set of test scenarios that an incident response team must work through in responding to a cyber attack based on their procedures and techniques. This consistently used set of test scenarios would help enable comparison of performance across different teams.

From performance measures, one or more metrics are derived. A **metric** is some derivation of the performance measures that is a standard for quantifying some. In a lot of cases, the metric is a direct application of a measurement. In the case of Linpack (a standard measure of computing power for floating point computation), the metric is the number of floating point operations per second (GFLOPS). In other cases, the metric can include multiple measures using a formula to normalize and combine them into a single number, such as how 3DMark provides a single performance score for GPUs. To enable comparison, the metric by which classes of solutions should be measured need to be agreed upon and standardized. Otherwise, you result in everyone reporting different benchmark results that are not directly comparable.

Let's discuss an example to help put all these concepts in context. Cellular phones have become commonplace. Everyone has a cell phone and these devices have expanded cyber space significantly. While antivirus for workstations are fairly ubiquitous, their dispersion in the mobile phone arena is limited.[4] There are, potentially, many factors to this but one question that is pertinent is how effective are these antivirus applications at detection? One characteristic of malware that is common and important to measure are packers. Generally, there are major families of malware that represent common techniques employed, exploits used, and malicious objectives.[5] Developing a new base of capability for a new family of malware is complex and expensive, so attackers find simple ways of changing the signature of their attacks to bypass antivirus. **Packers** are techniques to compress executables to be more storage-space efficient and protect them from piracy. Packers also alter the binary representation of malware, which can impact the performance, sometimes dramatically, of detection methods. Therefore, a benchmark of packer handling for cellular phone antivirus would be useful. This is the example we will use through the rest of the benchmark section to help demonstrate the concepts of the method.

DIG DEEPER: SOFTWARE PACKERS

Packers have become a mainstay of malware.[6] They provide a low-resource method of varying the signature of malware to bypass signature analysis-based detection methods, which are the most common means of detection. They illustrate the continual arms race between defender and malware developer. Two example packer tools are PEID[7] and ExeInfo[8] that can be used to help identify malware that has used been packed. However, more sophisticated adversaries will pack their own malware making detection with off-the-shelf tools more challenging.

Collecting or Defining a Benchmark

To define a benchmark, you must collect a dataset or suite of processes that can be used to exercise your test cases. The objective when finding a dataset or test suite is to provide sufficient coverage of the problem space. If you think of the problems from a basic science perspective, the parameters are the independent variables that have a practical effect on outcome. Notice, we said the *practical* effect and not *significant* effect. As we discussed in Chapter 9, Hypothetico-Deductive Research, statistically significant results don't always translate to practical results. For applied research, we only care about variables that have a practical effect. For our example, we may know that using certain interfaces with the hardware affect how software is packed, then we should include a sampling of apps that use the different hardware interfaces. On the other hand, if we know that the phone model does not affect the packing behavior we can test with any platform. For variables without strong evidence in either direction, it is best to include them in the benchmark, if possible.

The best benchmarks are based in reality. Benchmarks are supposed to measure how the solution would perform in realistic conditions. Which is why using real datasets, like real malware for detection solutions, is the best benchmark, as it informs you of real performance. However, there are downsides to this approach, which we will talk about a little later. If real data isn't possible, representative data is good or worst case data. But the overall goal is to understand how effective a solution would perform when operational. A benchmark that provides a metric completely devolved from reality doesn't provide you with much information.

Going back to our example, this means our benchmark would be best derived from a sampling of malware packed by real packers. As the point of this benchmark is the ability to detect known malware that has been packed,

Table 11.1 Malware List for Example Benchmark

Android Malware for Benchmark	iOS Malware for Benchmark
FakeInst	FindCall
SMSSend	LBTM
Eropl	Oneclickfraud
Boqx	PawnStorm.A
GinMaster	Toires
QdPlugin	YiSpecter
Droidkungu	
Smsagent	
SmSpy	
FakeApp	

the selection of malware for this benchmark should be based from more common, well-known malware that should be generally detected when not packed. As mobile malware is generally specific to the platform/operating system, it would be good to create a benchmark suite that covered the different platforms: Android and iOS (there are a small niches that we will ignore for this example). iOS has very few malware instances, so the six[9] that exist for unmodified software (i.e., nonjailbroken) would have to suffice for the benchmark. Android, on the other hand, has hundreds of families of malware from which to choose. However, there are 10 families that account for approximately three-fourths of infections.[10] Those being the most commonly found, it would be reasonable to assume that any respectable malware detection capability should be able to detect them. Therefore, a common variant of those families would be good for using in the benchmark. An example list of malware for the benchmark is shown in Table 11.1.

DID YOU KNOW?

While the Android platform has hundreds of families of malware, iOS still has barely been hit with malware, only numbering in the teens, most of which only work on jailbroken phones. This has led to iOS becoming one of the highest priced and sought after, by far, platforms, for zero days on the black market.[11]

The malware list is only the input to the benchmark, but is not the benchmark. The benchmark is the packed malware that will be used to test the detection capabilities of the antivirus cell phone applications. Therefore, we need an additional list of packers to process the malware instances. There are a few common packer services and applications for cellular devices (in addition to more fringe capabilities). Table 11.2 shows the list of packers we

Table 11.2 Packer List for Example Benchmark

Android Packers	iOS Packers
Ijiami	Morpher
BangCle	Metaforic
DexGuard	Arxan
LIAPP	LLVM Obfuscator

could choose for this benchmark, as they cover the majority of packer use. Some of the fringe packers should be sampled for the benchmark, but for simplicity of this example, we will not locate the full population of packers for sampling. In addition, each packer will have a set of settings that affect the behavior of the packing.

As with other forms of experimentation, when generating a benchmark, you need to be aware of bias. You really need to think through what exactly you are trying to measure and where you want to draw the line with your benchmarking. If, in our case, there was a possibility of the type of malware, a technique of coding, the type of packer, or any other independent variable could significantly alter the way the packed output presents for analysis, it is important to include in the benchmark. The goal of the benchmark is to provide good coverage of the possible operational situations to compare solutions. If a significant method is missed, it would bias the results to those solutions that handle one category better. We are not going in-depth into the technical details of malware and packer technology for this example, but you would need to when generating a benchmark.

At this point, in our example, we have defined the sets of data we need: the list of malware and packers we will use for our benchmark. One more item needed is the configuration of the packer, as the settings could bias our results. For example, an encrypted packed malware would look drastically different than one that just has its variables and method names obfuscated. Therefore, we need to include the different configuration possibilities of each packer in our list. If we say each packer has 10 possible settings, the number of combinations of our selected packed malware for Android and iOS is 400 and 240, respectively.

The population size for benchmarks can be large, as in our example. A benchmark is meant to be something that is relatively easy to apply to a solution. Therefore, it is often beneficial to downselect to a reasonable, representative size. This can be done in a few ways. As we discussed about bias, there may be categorizations around which you cluster the population. This can be technology, objective, and so on. You really have to understand your situation to know the best way to do this. As we discussed with malware, you can categorize them around their objective/goal or families of malware that share code bases. You can then sample from those categories to downselect. Or, in our case, we have a large population of combined options. In this situation, you can sample from the combination. Whatever method you choose for sample downselection, fully think through and document your logic.

To downselect our example benchmark, we could sample our set of packed malware. If you recall from our discussions of sampling from previous chapters, sampling is the process of selecting a subset of a population such that its characteristics reflect the populations to your specified level of confidence. If we selected a 95% confidence level, or population coverage, and 10% confidence interval, or margin of error, the sample size for our example bookmark would be 79 for Android and 69 for iOS. To generate our benchmark, we would randomly select that amount from each set of packed malware.

Removing Benchmark Bias

As we mentioned, you need to make sure you don't bias the benchmark so we have one more step in developing our benchmark. It could be the existence of packing that analytic approaches are detecting. Therefore, they may have great results in detecting packed malware but they will also detect all packed items, including nonmalware apps. To ensure that this isn't happening, it is important to include some tests in the benchmark for false positives. Just like the malware selections, we want to select common files that should be expected to not be flagged as malware. A simple way to do this is to select the top five free apps in the Google Play and Apple store, which both provide a listing of top downloaded free apps. Then, we would want to replicate the rest of the process by using the same packers in the various configurations to generate a population of nonmalware packed apps. Finally, we would sample that population to reduce the number of tests necessary for the benchmark.

Running the Benchmark

Running a benchmark against a solution is essentially a simple experiment, which is why it is categorized in this chapter. Therefore, the execution of the benchmark needs to be methodical, well thought through, and rigorous. A benchmark, by definition, needs to be repeatable. Therefore, any variability in the process is bad.

In a lot of cases, the process of executing a benchmark is pretty straightforward. You have your benchmark dataset and a tool that operates on data, apply the latter to the first and record the results. Finished. However, it isn't always that simple. For more complex situations, like organizational performance metrics, such as incident response or cyber security policy, you have to develop the processes to consistently and accurately gather the measures you need to calculate your metrics.

As with any experiment, it is important to clearly define the process to execute a benchmark. You want all steps to be defined without any ambiguity, so others can execute the benchmark to replicate your work and leverage it to benchmark other solutions. In the case of our example, the process to execute the benchmark is straightforward. The files are provided to the antivirus solution test applications, by placing them on an emulated phone's file system, and having them scan the benchmark test files. The report information produced by the test applications are used to determine if the test files were detected as malware or not.

Analyzing the Results

As we mentioned previously, you should have defined a set of metrics by which you can measure the effectiveness of a solution in addressing a problem. The definition of performance is very subjective to the problem space. This could mean the effectiveness of detection for antivirus, intrusion detection systems, vulnerability scanners; duration for incident response, forensics cloning/searching, penetration testing; or number of attempts for password cracking, or cryptanalysis. Each situation could have more than one metric with some being of higher importance or weight than others. It is important to define these metrics before defining a benchmark, as the benchmark really needs to be developed around these metrics.

With multiple metrics, you need to think about how to present your results. While it is always an option to just present the metrics as they are observed, this can present a problem. When you have multiple metrics, it may not be clear how to combine or normalize the values. As the point of benchmarking is to provide a method of measuring the effectiveness of solutions, being able to provide a single number helps quickly show the difference. If viewers are left to combine the values independently, they might do it differently and thus counteract the benefits of a benchmark. It is still important to provide the metrics independently as each use case comes with its own requirements, so there can be situations where one metric's performance greatly outweighs the others in addressing a specific problem. Therefore, while one solution is best in the general case, another solution with defects in some metrics is the best solution for a specific problem because it has the best score in the metric that matters in this specific case.

Let's go back to our example to explain these concepts. Posit that we ran the benchmark against 5 Android antivirus applications. As our performance is

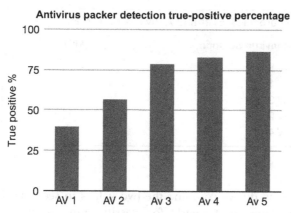

FIGURE 11.1
Percentage of true positive packed malware detection.

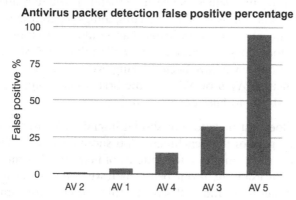

FIGURE 11.2
Percentage of false positive packed malware detection.

based around detection, our metrics are the true- and false-positive rates. If you recall from our previous discussion, a true positive is when a detector or classifier accurately detects a subject. In the case of our example, a true positive is when an antivirus solution detects a packed malware app as malware. A false positive is when the detector inaccurately detects a subject. A false positive for our example is when the antivirus detects a packed nonmalware app as being malware. Fig. 11.1 shows possible true-positive percentage results for our example. In this situation, a longer column is better, meaning that AV 5 is the best solution according to this metric. Fig. 11.2 depicts possible false-positive percentage results from our example. Shorter columns are better in this situation, which means that AV 2 is the better solution. As you can see, by just looking at either metric you would select a different antivirus

Table 11.3 Example Antivirus MCC Metric

Antivirus Solution	MCC
AV 5	−0.14
AV 1	0.43
AV 3	0.46
AV 2	0.62
AV 4	0.68

solution. But how do we combine the two values to see what is the overall best solution? One good metric for classification problems is Mathew's Correlation Coefficient (MCC). It incorporates the number of true and false positives as well as the true and false negatives in case the test set is lopsided. It also normalizes the values between −1 and 1 where values closer to 1 mean that the solution is good at detecting things without false positives, a 0 value means the solution is no better than random selection, and −1 is a poor solution that doesn't detect things well. Table 11.3 shows the MCC values for the example we have been working. As you can see from this combined metric, neither AV 5 or AV 2 are the best overall solutions but in fact AV 4 has the best true-to-false-positive ratio.

Your analysis does not have to, nor should it, end with just the metrics that are the ultimate goal of the benchmark. You should also treat the dataset as an observational study and look for patterns of behavior that might be useful or interesting. For example, if our benchmark were looking at just detecting malware, the FakeInstall and SMSSend families account for almost 80% of reported events. Therefore, if you executed a case control study (see Chapter 4: Exploratory Study, for details) on the dataset to just look at how effective antivirus solutions were at detecting these families of malware, the results may have a stronger weight on how effective a solution is because it would have a broader effect. Or, it would be interesting if some antivirus solutions were unable to detect any malware packed by one or more packers. This would show a potentially serious weakness in a solution that could be exploited to render it completely ineffective.

While it is not always possible due to the dynamic nature of the problem space, which we will discuss in a moment, it is good to standardize benchmarks in communities. A **standard** is a community agreed upon, accepted, and supported idea or concept. There are many different types of standards within the cyber domain and cyber security field, such as communication protocols, encryption methods, random number generation, and so on. However, for our purposes, we are only interested in benchmarking standards. Standardizing a benchmark should include the dataset or process used to generate it, the method of execution, and the process to measure and calculate the metrics.

DIG DEEPER: CYBER SECURITY BENCHMARKS

While the cyber security field doesn't have a great deal of standardization for benchmarking, there are several to start with and to use as inspiration. A listing of some cyber security benchmarks:

- https://www.owasp.org/index.php/Benchmark
- https://code.google.com/archive/p/wavsep/
- https://benchmarks.cisecurity.org/
- https://www.securityforum.org/tool/the-isf-benchmark-and-benchmark-as-a-service/
- http://dl.acm.org/citation.cfm?id = 1978683
- http://www.eembc.org/benchmark/dpibench_sl.php
- https://www.eicar.org/download/eicar.com.txt
- http://energy.gov/oe/cybersecurity-capability-maturity-model-c2m2-program/ electricity-subsector-cybersecurity
- https://www.praetorian.com/nist
- https://www.ipa.go.jp/files/000011796.pdf

Problems With Benchmarking

While benchmarking is a useful tool, it isn't without some challenges that currently limit its utility. First, cyber space evolves very quickly. Technology of today will soon be outdated and replaced by something else. Think about how different the world was merely 10 years ago. We wouldn't have been able to do our example benchmark, because neither the iPhone or Android had been released. The speed of progression means that benchmarks must be changed and updated frequently, which takes resources and community agreement.

As part of these changes, attackers are always trying to do something that hasn't been seen before to continue being successful. **Zero days** are exploits that have not been publicly identified or seen by the defender. Benchmarks are easy to define for things that have been seen, but it is difficult to generate tests for unknown situations in the future. Benchmarks that only include what is already known limits the future predictability of the results. Minutes after a benchmark is run, the results could be invalidated by the release of a new technique or tactic.

A third issue is that cyber security is by definition a competed domain. So attackers are always trying to find ways of getting around defenses. If defenses are developed to benchmarks, attackers can leverage the benchmarks as tools to determine if their attacks can defeat defenses. Benchmarks can also provide a false sense of security. As with other fields, vendors can also develop to benchmarks. Therefore, solutions can become biased to what a benchmark measures.

Finally, you need to understand a benchmark to use it appropriately. There have been cyber security benchmarks in the past[12] that, while developed with the best intentions, have become unsupported by the community due to bias or problems. Using these datasets can impair the acceptability of your results up to and including having your papers rejected.[13] It is always important to skeptically view benchmark datasets you didn't generate. Understanding how they were developed and what they were developed to measure, is important to determining if they will test the solution of interest in the method you are interested. As the cyber space domain changes quickly, we all need to be continuously reevaluating any benchmark to see if it no longer suits the goal.

REPORTING YOUR RESULTS

When using benchmarks, the results are often just documented as white-papers and technical reports. You likely have seen them before on the Internet.[14] Benchmarks are often used as the evaluation of a new research tool. These types of paper focus most of their space on describing their solution. If a benchmark is used, it is mentioned as the method of analyzing the performance and the results are discussed. As the benchmark should already be well defined, only brief discussion about the benchmark is necessary with a reference to its full documentation. Another type of paper for benchmarking is one in which a new benchmark is generated. The line between benchmark generation and experimentation is fuzzy. Generally, these papers will follow the same format and similar content categories. Below we provide a discussion of a good general format for a paper that uses an existing benchmark to study the performance of a developed solution. We refer you to the Validation Testing section in the second half of this chapter for a paper format suited for generation of a new benchmark.

Sample Format

In the following, we will provide you with a general good outline for publishing your results. Every publication will provide formatting guidelines. When you decide on a venue to submit your research, be sure to check their submission requirements to make sure you follow any outline and formatting specifications. The outline provided here follows a common flow of information found in published papers and should meet the requirements of a larger number of publisher requirements.

Every paper is unique and requires different ways of presentation. The provided sample flow includes all of the general information that is important to cover in a benchmarking paper and is a general starting format. We start with this outline when writing an applied research paper that uses a benchmark and modify it to support the topic and venue. We understand that every researcher has their own style of presentation, so you can feel free to deviate from this outline. The discussion of each section are provided to explain what is important to include and why, so you can present the important information in whatever way best suits your style.

Abstract

The abstract is a concise and clear summary of the paper. The goal of an abstract is to provide readers with a quick description of what the paper discusses. You should only discuss what is stated in the rest of the paper and nothing additional. Each submission venue will provide guidelines on how to provide an abstract. Generally, this includes the maximum length of the abstract and formatting instructions, but sometimes this will include information on the type and layout of the content to provide.

Introduction

The first section of a paper should always be an introduction for the reader into the rest of the paper. The introduction section provides the motivation and reasoning behind why the research was performed. For benchmarking research, it should introduce what new solution is being tested, what it is designed to solve, and at a high level what performance metrics you will use in evaluating the solution.

Related Work

The related works section should include a quick summarization of the field's knowledge about this research topic. Are there competing solutions? Explain what is deficient about past applications. What was the gap in the solution space that motivated the solution defined in this paper. This should include discussion of past benchmarks that were performed.

Guiding Theory/Science

For a benchmark this section is optional. If you are benchmarking a new system you designed, then having this section is highly recommended. If instead you are benchmarking one or more solutions developed by others then you will likely lack the information to write this section.

If you do decide this section is appropriate then, it is good to discuss what theories or basic science is the foundation for your approach. In this section you should provide the background of your approach. Explain what knowledge of the problem and domain you used for creating your solution. For example, if from an observational study we knew that attacker techniques had shifted and were using a new style of packer unlike anything before. And we knew that a specific machine learning method was good at finding the patterns this new packer would generate from previous literature; we would have sound scientific basis on which to develop our new antivirus solution. It is important to provide confidence in your reasoning for developing a solution and explaining what science you are applying. The goal of this section for you to provide evidence on why your application of science in a solution is justified.

Test Cases/Approach

This section covers different materials depending on if you are benchmarking a solution developed by yourself or solutions developed by others. If the former, the approach section of an applied paper is often the meat or largest portion of the paper. In the approach section you describe your solution. This includes any relevant details: algorithms, functions, code, and so on. If instead you are testing others solutions you should have a test cases section that discusses how and why you have selected the solutions you are benchmarking.

Methods

In the methods section you discuss the benchmark you are using and why you chose this benchmark. Explain briefly what testing the benchmark involves, what performance metrics it evaluates, and the procedure you followed to execute it. If the testing requires specific system or environmental configuration, document how you setup the test environment. The goal of this section to clearly state how you generated the benchmarking results such that someone else could independently replicate your testing.

Data Analysis/Results

In the results section of your paper, explain what you found after you performed the benchmark evaluation. Discuss the metrics of the benchmark and how the solution scored. Compare it to the results of other solutions. Creating tables to show results is an efficient and effective method. You can also show pictures of interesting results, that is, if a data anomaly occurred or to display the distributions of the data samples. As discussed previously, if during exploration of the results anything interesting is found beyond the metrics, explain them here.

Discussion/Future work

The discussion/future work section is for you to point out any work that you were unable to execute before this paper, any follow-up work you would like to conduct, and general suggestions for those who might follow after you. Provide your explanations for the results you received. If they are interesting and affect a theory, provide what you think happened, and if you think a modification to the theory would cover this result. Discuss where you think this work should lead next.

Conclusion/Summary

In the final section of the paper, summarize the results and conclusions of the paper. The conclusion section is often a place that readers jump to quickly after reading the abstract. Make a clear and concise statement about what the ultimate results of the benchmark testing are and what you learned from them.

Acknowledgments

The acknowledgments section is a place for you to acknowledge anyone who helped you with parts of the research that were not part of the paper. Here is a good place to acknowledge any funding sources that supported your research.

References

Each publication will provide some guidelines on how to format references. Follow their guidelines and list all your references at the end of your paper. Depending on the length of the paper, you will want to adjust the number of references. The longer the paper, the more references. A good rule of thumb is 15–20 references for a 6-page paper. For peer-reviewed publications, the majority of your references should be other peer-reviewed works. Referencing web pages and Wikipedia doesn't generate confidence in reviewers. Also, make sure you only list references that are useful to your paper, that is, don't inflate your reference count. Good reviewers will check and this will likely reflect poorly on and disqualify you.

VALIDATION TESTING

Validation Testing is a rigorously controlled process to investigate the performance of an application of science to solve a problem. Applied experimentation is sometimes called the process of validation. Validation testing is the process of determining how well an engineered system solves a problem. Where benchmarks are really more predetermined and generated suites of one-off tests, validation tests are fully controlled environments to ensure that only certain aspects of the problem and solution are studied together.

Validation testing is very closely related to hypothesis-driven experiments (covered in Chapter 9: Hypothetico-Deductive Research). Both use the same terminology, very similar processes, and requirement for rigorous and methodical application. However, the major difference between the two is the objective or focus of the research. Where hypothetico-deductive experimentation focuses on gaining a basic understanding of a system and how it behaves under varied circumstances, applied experimentation focuses on how well an engineered system solves a problem. This line can be blurry because cyber space largely consists of engineered systems. A simple way of determining if research is applied is to ask if the dependent measurements are performance-based. That is to say, is there an expectation of meeting or exceeding some performance measure (faster, more, efficacy, cheaper, etc.). If the lines of inquiry are more behavior-based (what happens, why), then it is a basic experiment.

Since validation testing is so similar to hypothesis-driven experimentation, which we already covered, this section will only cover the major differences between the two. Instead, we will walk through an example—validation testing. An applied research topic that is becoming quite popular is moving target defense.[15] The basis for this approach comes from the well-documented cyber kill chain[16] of an attacker. Attackers generally go through a series of steps to perform an attack, the first of which is reconnaissance to determine what to attack. The theory underlying moving target defense is that if the defensive cyber space shifts or changes in some way quickly enough, it will prevent the attacker from ever being able to hold a target long enough for a successful attack. For our example, let's imagine we want to test the performance of a new moving target defense.

DIG DEEPER: MOVING TARGET DEFENSE

Moving target defense is a broad topic but generally refers to defensive techniques that "move" cyber assets around such that it is hard for attackers to find vulnerabilities. One of the most successful defensive techniques developed over the last decade is a moving target defense. Address space layout randomization (ASLR) is a technique that randomizes the location of executables in memory space. This prevents attackers from knowing where in memory vulnerabilities like buffer overflows are located. ASLR, along with Data Execution Prevention (DEP), have raised the difficulty bar on exploiting buffer overflow vulnerabilities.

A difference with validation testing is the hypothesis or lack thereof. Hypotheses are a critical component of basic experimentation. However, they are more forced or implied with applied experimentation. The research question for applied experimentation is always how effective is the solution? And, the implied hypothesis is always the new solution will solve the problem equal to or more than previous (competing) solutions.

INDEPENDENT VARIABLES

Independent variables should be handled the same as they are with basic experimentation. You need to fully document your assumptions. Anything that could impact the performance of the solution should be listed and explained. This list, of course, includes the solution being tested and its competitors, but it also covers extraneous variables. Table 11.4 lists the independent variables for our example.

DEPENDENT VARIABLES

Like independent variables, dependent variables are handled mostly the same in applied experimentation as they are in basic experimentation. Recall from

Table 11.4 Validation Testing Example Independent Variables

Variable	Description
Hardware	The hardware characteristics of brand, model, and configuration could impact the baseline security of a system.
Software	The software characteristics of brand, version, and configuration could impact the baseline security of a system. This includes the operating system as well as additional running applications.
Architecture	The architecture, or how the hardware and software is interconnected, could impact the baseline security of a system.
Security sensors types	The types of security sensors used could impact the baseline ability of the system to detect attacks.
Analytic tools	The types of analytic tools, such as SIEMs, used could impact the baseline ability of the system to detect attacks.
Sensor placement	The location of the sensors used could impact the baseline ability of the system to detect attacks.
Attacker experience	The experience of the attacker could impact the baseline ability of the attacker to be successful in attacking the test environment. Especially challenging when running multiple tests. How do you ensure the attacker does not learn or change between tests?
Attacker objective	The objective of the attacker will alter what the attacker will target and how complex the attack must be, which could impact the baseline ability of the attacker to be successful in attacking the test environment.
Attacker strategy	The strategy used by the attacker could impact the baseline ability of the attacker to be successful in attacking the test environment. Especially challenging when running multiple tests. How do you ensure the attacker does not learn or change between tests?
Attacker tools	The tools used by the attacker could impact the baseline ability of the attacker to be successful in attacking the test environment.
Attacker social factors	The culture, nationality, and organization could impact the baseline ability of the attacker to be successful in attacking the test environment.

Chapter 9, Hypothetico-Deductive Research, that dependent variables are the observables that are monitored to determine the effect of the experiment. In the case of applied experiments, dependent variables are always observations of some performance measurement. The method of measuring performance for security applications is not always straightforward. As of yet, nobody has found a way to measure the actual security of a system. Therefore, it is generally the case that you will have to find some form of proxy for the measure of security.

Going back to our example, we can show how to handle measurement by proxy. Our ultimate goal is to measure the security of a system. As we said there isn't a direct way to measure the security of a system. So instead, we will develop some proxies to determine how effective is the security. There are two main measurements that can determine how effective security is against an attack: ability to perform designed objectives and how successful the attacker is. Designed objectives are highly environment-specific, but generically the observables are some quantification of how many critical actions were completed. Our experimental environment, will be modeled after an e-commerce site. The designed objectives measures can be mapped to business functions for the webserver and other applications, which we will discuss in greater depth in the next section. The number of sales and revenue are the critical aspect of the sales department; lines of code and up time for the software engineering department; and time cards and paycheck depositing for human resources (HR) department. For the threat success category, the dependent variables are: time to exploitation, amount of data exfiltrated, and the percentage of objective completed.

EXPERIMENTAL DESIGN

With the experimental design, we need to select which independent variables are the treatment variables and which are the extraneous variables that need to be controlled to have no effect. In the case of our example experiment, the two variables we will select for the treatment are the threat objectives and the selection of defensive tools. In the following section, we will discuss the control strategy of the extraneous variables followed by the block design of the treatment variables into tests.

As all of the environment variables are extraneous, we will use the same environment through all of the tests. We will build an environment model based on our software e-commerce site. Each department, HR, sales, and product development, has business processes that drive the actions of roles within the company. We will simulate this behavior with agent-based software. The environment will be outfitted with the best practice security tools and placement. The environment architecture will follow a common Cisco network architecture with a core network that splits the departments and a server center that host all of the internal services. A demilitarized zone (DMZ) hosts the external-facing services, including the e-commerce website. For a real experiment, the necessary level of specificity for documenting this environment would be significantly greater. However, for the purposes of our example, we want to get the point across that we need to define a realistic enough experimental environment and hold it steady between experimental tests.

To compare the effectiveness of the moving target defense it is necessary to have the alternative hypothesis. Remember that the implied hypothesis is that the new approach will improve the security performance. Therefore, it is necessary to have some other configuration in the test to provide a comparison of results. This could be a different moving target defense, or some other new approach but for simplicity sake we will designate it as following cyber security best practice. In this example, we would follow the NIST 800 series[17] guidelines to set up traditional security controls within the environment. These same security controls will be present in the moving target environments as well to control that we can see how much change the addition of the technique makes.

For the threat-based extraneous variables, we will have three red teams to be our experimental threats. While it would be better to randomly select a larger set from a population of red teams, the cost in resources is too high to make that a practical solution. Additionally, we will attempt to control for their experience by providing them both with a week-long training camp. To understand if the moving target only has an impact against specific types of attacks, three attack objectives will be included: a DoS, data exfiltration, and data integrity manipulation. We will have each team perform all three of the attack objectives to enable us to detect any effect from the difference; experience, approach, or tools, of threat team. We will randomize the order and which defensive tools are the target of each attack run to control for maturation effects and provide the comparative information necessary to determine an effect. Table 11.5 depicts the blocked tests we would perform in this experiment example.

The experiment plan blocks listed in Table 11.5 enables us to rigorously measure the performance of our new moving target defense. As you can see, in

Table 11.5 Control Blocking for Applied Experiment Example

Threat Team	Best Practice		Moving Target Defense	
Team 1	Exfiltration	DoS	Integrity	
Team 2		Integrity	DoS	Exfiltration
Team 3	Dos		Exfiltration	Integrity

order to deal with the practical limitations of having a limited supply of red teams, it was necessary to design additional controls to both get enough trials while handling maturation effects and differences in experience level and strategy. By measuring how effective the red teams are and how much downtime the various business processes had, we have designed a method to quantify the performance of our new moving target defense. We purposely selected this example to showcase the issues of validation testing and how to resolve them with thoughtful design, as validation experiments often run up against limitations in our ability to experiment and measure. The next section will go into more detail on some of the challenges you may face in validation testing.

DIG DEEPER: VERIFICATION AND VALIDATION

Verification and validation are common processes for evaluating engineered systems. Verification is testing to make sure what was developed meets the specification requirements. Validation is testing to make sure that it solves the problem it was created to address. Or as it is often more bluntly stated, verification is determining if you built it right and validation is determining if you built the right thing. By performing verification and validation with scientific rigor you can ensure that strong evidence will be generated to determine if the solution is suitable. As you have seen in this chapter, validation is largely an experimental process. Verification can be approached from a more exploratory perspective and the bounds testing and sensitivity analysis methods described in the next chapter are useful techniques.

After executing these experimental trials you would need to analyze the data to determine the effect. The same statistical analysis approaches that can be used for hypothetico-deductive experiments can be used here. On brief introduction to some of these analytical methods is provided in Chapter 9, Hypothetico-Deductive Research, along with some further reading recommendations.

PROBLEMS WITH VALIDATION TESTING

There are some challenges to keep in mind when doing validation testing. First, modeling realistic environments is very challenging. There aren't any accepted general cases of how a cyber environment is architected. There are typically multiple capabilities required (IT systems, users, applications, networks, etc.) to instantiate a model of a cyber space for validation testing. Unfortunately, we still lack the science on how to quantify how "real" an environment is even with an exhaustive list of included capabilities. We discuss these testbed capabilities in more detail in Chapter 13, Instrumentation. However, these capabilities are expensive and difficult to operate.

Operational systems are almost never open for experimentation. Given that operational environments serve a purpose, it is generally accepted as bad practice to perform potentially disruptive experiments in them. And even if you could experiment with real environments, you lack the ability to control the environments to a sufficient level. This leads to innumerable confounds such that it is very difficult to determine what events actually occurred and what actions are responsible for effects. All of this leads to operational environments being ineffective for most validation testing.

The final challenge is the ability to model attackers. Attackers don't like to be studied, and when their techniques are discovered, they change them so they aren't caught. This makes developing a model of attackers for experimentation very difficult. This leads to using real people as attackers, hence the red teams in our example. Red teams are expensive and it is difficult to quantify their expertise. Finally, real attacks can take months to execute as threats attempt to stay below the radar. With experiments, hosting month-long attacks can become impractical really quickly.

While these are big obstacles to executing validation tests they should not deter you. Validation testing is a strong form of understanding the effectiveness of applications of science. Without performing validation tests, as a society we will lack the objective knowledge on how best to invest in defenses and repel attacks. Validation testing is difficult but it is a noble pursuit.

REPORTING YOUR RESULTS

The final important step of scientific work is reporting your results. The greatest discoveries have little value if no one knows about it or can leverage the knowledge for further science or to engineer something with more predictable behavior. The two most prevalent forms of documenting experimental results are conferences and journals. These venues provide a path to insert your gained knowledge into the field's corpus. However, the quality venues all require peer-reviewed acceptance. Peer review provides a validation check against the topic of research, methods of research, and the quality of the reporting of the research to ensure a certain level of quality is met. Ideally, the quality of the work should be the only metric of acceptance, in reality the novelty, groundbreaking, and popularity of the topic also play into the review process, so these things should be taken into account when you select your venue. In this section, we provide a general template for reporting validation testing research, which will be applicable to most conferences and journals.

Sample Format

In the following, we will provide you with a general good outline for publishing your results. Every publication will provide formatting guidelines. When you decide on a venue to submit your research, be sure to check their submission requirements to make sure you follow any outline and formatting specifications. The outline provided here follows a common flow of information found in published papers and should meet the requirements of a larger number of publisher requirements.

Every paper is unique and requires some different ways of presentation; however, the provided sample flow includes all of the general information that is important to cover in a paper and is a general starting format we take when starting to write an applied experiment paper and modify it to support the topic and venue. We understand that every research has their own style of presentation so you can feel free to deviate from this outline. The discussion of each section are provided to explain what is important to include and why, so you can present the important information in whatever way suits your style best.

Introduction

The first section of a paper should always be an introduction for the reader into the rest of the paper. The introduction section provides the motivation and reasoning behind why the research was performed. For applied research it should discuss the problem domain; that is, what is the rest of the paper's work trying to solve.

Related Work

The related works section should include a quick summarization of the field's knowledge about this research topic. Are there competing solutions? Explain what is deficient about past applications. What was the gap in the solution space that motivated the solution defined in this paper.

Guiding Theory/Science

As it is good for applied research to be based upon knowledge gained from basic science, it is good to discuss what theories or basic science is the foundation for your approach. In this section, you should provide the background of your approach. Explain what knowledge of the problem and domain you used for creating your solution. For example, if from an observational study, we knew that attacker techniques had shifted and were using a new style of packer unlike anything before and we knew that a specific machine learning method was good at finding the patterns, this new packer would generate from previous literature we would have sound scientific basis on which to develop our new antivirus solution. It is important to provide confidence in your reasoning for developing a solution and explaining what science you are applying. That is the goal of this section of the paper.

Approach
The approach section of an applied paper is often the meat or largest portion of the paper. In this section you describe your solution. This includes any relevant details: algorithms, functions, code, and so on.

Experimental Design
The experimental design part of your paper should clearly define the process you will take to execute your experiment. It is crucial that this section is clear and complete such that a reader would be able to replicate it in their environment. In this section, you need to define how you will measure the performance of the solution and independent variables that could impact the performance, both relating to the solution and extraneous. You need to define the experimental control methodology and which independent variables are going to have interventions. Each experiment trial that will be run and how the independent variables will be varied between them should be defined. This should include the controls you will use both to provide the interventions and how you will control for the other independent variables to prevent confounding. Finally, you should define the statistics you used and the motivation for using them.

Experimental Configuration
The experimental configuration section should discuss the system under test and the laboratory environment you used to execute the series of experimental trials. You need to be as complete in your documentation as possible. Include information covering hardware (vendor/model of servers with configurations, firmware), software (type, version, configuration), network configuration (physical connectivity, logical connectivity including IP addresses, etc.), and instrumentation (location, frequency, etc.). As with the experimental design section, the goal is to be complete enough that a reader could replicate the setup. As papers have space limits, this is often a first place to cut as it isn't as important as the results. If you find yourself in this situation, it is good to fully document and add this to your paper as an appendix as you can often provide an appendix with explanatory information without counting against your word count.

Data Analysis/Results
In the results section of your paper, explain what you found after you performed your analysis. Layout the significance, confidence intervals, and effect sizes for all of the experiment trials. Comparative analysis with past or competing applied solutions are very helpful in contextualizing your results.

Without previous performance numbers it is difficult to understand the significance of your work. Creating tables to show results is an efficient and effective method. You can also show pictures of interesting results, that is, if a data anomaly occurred or to display the distributions of the data samples. If anything unexpected, like a device failure, occurred during testing happened and shows up in the data, explain it in this section.

Discussion/Future work

The discussion/future work section is to provide your explanations for the results you received. Discuss additional tests you think should be performed. Discuss future directions in research that may result from the knowledge gained from the validation testing. If performance was less than expected should more observation research be performed? Did something odd happen during the testing that could be investigated by executing a hypothetico-deductive experiment?

Conclusion/Summary

In the final section of the paper, summarize the results and conclusions of the paper. The conclusion section is often a place that readers jump to quickly after reading the abstract. Make a clear and concise statement about what the ultimate results of the experiments and what you learned from it.

Acknowledgments

The acknowledgments section is a place for you to acknowledge anyone who helped you with parts of the research that were not part of the paper. It is also good to acknowledge and funding sources that supported your research.

References

Each publication will provide some guidelines on how to format references. Follow their guidelines and list all your references at the end of your paper. Depending on the length of the paper you will want to adjust the number of references. The longer the paper the more references. A good rule of thumb is 15–20 references for a 6-page paper. For peer-reviewed publications, the majority of your references should be other peer-reviewed works. Referencing web pages and Wikipedia doesn't generate confidence in reviewers. Also, make sure you only list references that are useful to your paper, that is don't inflate your reference count. Good reviewers will check and this will likely disqualify and reflect poorly on you.

Endnotes

1. The Linpack Benchmark. Retrieved February 25, 2017, from http://www.top500.org/project/linpack/

2. Futuremark. PCMark 8. Retrieved February 25, 2017, from https://www.futuremark.com/benchmarks/pcmark

3. Futuremark. 3DMark Benchmarks. Retrieved February 25, 2017, from https://www.futuremark.com/benchmarks/3dmark/all

4. Consumer Reports National Research Center. (April, 2014). Where's My Smart Phone? [Digital image]. Retrieved February 25, 2017, from http://www.consumerreports.org/content/dam/cro/news_articles/Electronics/CRO_Electronics_Lost_Stolen_PhoneV6_04_14.jpg

5. Carrera, E., and Silberman, P. (April 14, 2010). State of Malware: Family Ties. Speech presented at Blackhat EU in Spain, Barcelona.

6. Ugarte-Pedrero, X., Balzarotti, D., Santos, I., and Bringas, P. G. (May, 2015). SoK: Deep Packer Inspection: A Longitudinal Study of the Complexity of Run-Time Packers. In 2015 IEEE Symposium on Security and Privacy (pp. 659-673). IEEE.

7. Aldeid. PEiD. Retrieved February 25, 2017, from https://www.aldeid.com/wiki/PEiD

8. A.S.L. (February 21, 2017). Exeinfo PE (Version 0.0.4.4) [Computer software]. Retrieved February 25, 2017, from http://exeinfo.atwebpages.com/

9. Spreitzenbarth. (May 12, 2016). Current iOS Malware. Retrieved February 25, 2017, from https://forensics.spreitzenbarth.de/current-ios-malware/

10. Mobile Threat Report (Tech. No. Q1 2014). Retrieved February 25, 2017, from F-Secure Labs website https://www.f-secure.com/documents/996508/1030743/Mobile_Threat_Report_Q1_2014.pdf

11. Greenberg, A. (November 18, 2015). Here's a Spy Firm's Price List for Secret Hacker Techniques. Retrieved February 25, 2017, from http://www.wired.com/2015/11/heres-a-spy-firms-price-list-for-secret-hacker-techniques/

12. McHugh, J. (2000). Testing Intrusion Detection Systems: A Critique of the 1998 and 1999 Darpa Intrusion Detection System Evaluations as Performed by Lincoln Laboratory. ACM Transactions on Information and System Security (TISSEC), 3(4), 262-294.

13. Brugger, T. (September 15, 2007). KDD Cup '99 Dataset (Network Intrusion) Considered Harmful . Retrieved February 25, 2017, from http://www.kdnuggets.com/news/2007/n18/4i.html

14. Rubenking, N. J. (February 21, 2017). The Best Antivirus Protection of 2017. Retrieved February 25, 2017, from http://www.pcmag.com/article2/0,2817,2372364,00.asp

15. Jajodia, S., Ghosh, A. K., Swarup, V., Wang, C., and Wang, X. S. (Eds.). (2011). Moving Target Defense: Creating Asymmetric Uncertainty for Cyber Threats (Vol. 54). Springer Science & Business Media.

16. Lockheed Martin. The Cyber Kill Chain. Retrieved February 25, 2017, from http://www.lockheedmartin.com/us/what-we-do/aerospace-defense/cyber/cyber-kill-chain.html

17. NIST. Computer Security Special Publications 800 Series. Retrieved February 25, 2017, from http://csrc.nist.gov/publications/PubsSPs.html#SP 800

## CHAPTER 12

Applied Observational Study

Applied observational study has the chance of being a skipped over or neglected chapter, perhaps in favor of other topics such as experimentation or theory. A reader might assume that applied observational study is just like fundamental observational study. However, this assumption would be a substantial mistake. In point of fact, applied observational studies are likely the most common type of research conducted in the field of cyber security. Like computer science, and allied fields, researchers in cyber security are often focused on presenting their technology, solution, algorithm, or process to the public. This approach ensures that information is shared between researchers in a timely matter. But it does not always address the scientific rigor needed for an experimental publication or follow the observational process of a case control study, for example. This does not, however, mean that authors are given a free pass where they expound without limit.

An **applied study** observes a new solution to understand how it performs under different conditions. Often this is a new defensive feature or system change. Furthermore, this is accompanied by an assumption or prediction. This is to say the researcher has an expectation or unwritten assumption of how the subject should behave. A designer of an applied study seeks to understand the effect of some change or effect under observation; this often comes with an assumption of performance or behavior. For example, a study of a firewall that aims to understand the performance cost impacts when added to a network would be considered an applied study. Furthermore, the PI would like to test the assumption that the firewall protects better, but with an unknown cost. However, a study seeking to collect data and better understand how human defenders protect a company, which happens to have a firewall, (without any new technology, or change) would fall under the classic foundational observational study paradigm.

In this chapter, we are going to explore how to adapt the techniques and approaches first covered in Chapter 4, Exploratory Studies, and then in Chapter 5, Descriptive Studies, for studying applications of science. While any type of study could be used in an applied context, often case-control

Research Methods for Cyber Security. DOI: http://dx.doi.org/10.1016/B978-0-12-805349-2.00012-1

study, case study, and case reports are most common. The principles covered in this chapter will be applicable to other types of study. Rigorous applied research should come from applying results of basic science. Often those outside of scientific fields assume that research and development follows an orderly process from theory to experiment to applied. In fact, applied study often helps to inform theory and experimentation. And similarly, the results of experimentation and foundational studies help to guide applied research. There is an interrelationship, a back-and-forth exchange that does not often follow a simple linear path to progress. For example, an applied study stress test might inform a future experiment that helps to refine a theory, which in turn leads to more study.

Therefore, the differentiation between applied and nonapplied, or foundational, studies, lies in the motivation and objectives of the study. For foundational studies the objective is understanding the characteristics and behavior of the system. On the other hand, applied studies have the objective of gaining an understanding on performance or function. This requires an expectation of performance and introduction of a specific change or system to be measured.

CHAPTER OBJECTIVES

- Explain the differences between applied and observational studies
- Discuss how to design applied studies
- Walk through example using applied study methods
- Introduce the topic of operational bounds testing
- Provide a template for presenting results

APPLIED STUDY TYPES

The key difference between applied study and observational study is the differing scope. Applied study observes a specific subject for performance, function, security, and so on. Fundamental observational study observes the entire system without presumption of behavior. In the natural sciences this is often described as studying nature "in the wild" or in its "natural habitat." It can be challenging to complete the comparison in cyber space. Yet it does follow, that the subject of fundamental observational study is the entire cyber system without injection or introduction of a change or variable from the observer. On the other hand, applied study introduces a specific change or subject that is to be evaluated.

Much like foundational observational research, there are two categories one can define for applied *observational study, exploratory* and *descriptive*. In the case of *applied study*, exploratory refers to the researcher's quest to determine the consequences or extent of cyber system behavior. For example, classical stress testing of performance, for example read/ write speed, communication latency, or something more germane to cyber security, such as cryptographic performance or password response times are examples of applied exploratory study. Another example is sensitivity analysis. This type of study explores the limit or bounds of system behavior such as how fast, how far, how much, and so on, the solution can operate. Moving on to applied descriptive studies we have a myriad of examples to draw from. The classic "my security widget is 12% faster than last year," is perhaps a monumentally, poor albeit all-too-often encountered example. A better example would be the description of how you applied the results of foundational research. A case study that describes the implementation of a new training program based on the results of a study is an example of an applied descriptive study. As we mentioned at the beginning, there is an interrelationship from foundational research and applied. There is often a false assumption that one starts with foundational research, which then develops, over time, into applied research. Instead there is often an iterative back and forth with descriptive study leading to experimentation or exploratory studies. The research done using this chapter can help inform and improve future foundational and applied research and development.

In this section, we are going to examine how to adapt the techniques and approaches first covered in Chapter 4, Exploratory Studies and then in Chapter 5, Descriptive Studies. Those efforts focused on gaining an understanding about a system's behavior, so-called basic research (foundational). Here, with applied research, we will explain how affective knowledge is applied to solve a problem and explore measuring the performance of some system or event. This is the key focus of applied studies.

Applied Exploratory Studies

Applied exploratory studies observe the behavior or results of a cyber system, when the researcher is attempting to study the performance or effect of a system under specific conditions (as opposed to the general behavior of foundational research). This kind of study can introduce a specific change or subject that is to be evaluated. Example studies include sensitivity analysis and operational bounds testing such as load, performance, and stress testing. We will use an example of a new anomaly-based intrusion detection system to demonstrate the concepts of applied exploratory studies.

Operational Bounds Testing

The area of operational bounds testing is fairly self-explanatory. That is to say, the objective of this type of applied observational study is to explore the boundary conditions, limits, and extremes of an observed cyber system. For example, how accurate is a system or process? How long does it take to conduct a task? What type of performance is possible under different conditions? This is often related to resource utilization. For example, will your solution run in real time, but need a large supercomputer cluster to do so? Or, how much capacity can the system or process handle? Basically, what we are looking at are the dimensions and measures of the system under test.

Operational bounds testing is actually comprised of several different flavors of testing. These types can include stress, performance, and load testing. To conduct an operational bounds testing type of exploratory study, the researcher would collect or generate sufficient data to test the performance boundaries of application. These datasets would be analyzed to determine, stress, performance, or load.

- **Stress testing** evaluates how to what extent a system can perform at extremes.
- **Performance testing** evaluates how well system behavior conforms to expectations.
- **Load testing** evaluates the system or processes as maximum expected load.

Stress testing is conducted to see how fast, or much, or how far a system can perform. This is often done beyond the bounds or expectation of normal or even extreme expected user behavior. This sort of testing is critical in safety or other high reliability applications, and is related to, but distinct from security testing. Both are based upon an expectation of "normal user behavior," but security testing assumes that humans would step out of the boundary. Not all systems have user input or interaction, of course. Someone might want to study the network impact of a new security proxy. This would require an environment without direct human input.

Stress testing a new anomaly-based network IDS would consist of seeing how much data it could process. There are multiple vectors around the amount of data we could test; large amount of the same type of data, wide breadth of data, large number of small connections, and large connections. If we were the developers of this new IDS we should have some intuition if any of these different perspectives on the amount of data would have lesser impact based on the inner workings of the IDS algorithm and could be downprioritized or ignored completely. However, for this example let's assume that we are testing a new IDS developed by someone else. For each test we would increment the amount of data until either a physical limit of our testing capability is reached or the IDS fails. For instance, in stress testing the number of small connections we would start by creating synthetic communication between two network devices. At each step of the test we increase the number of communicating pairs by 1. We would keep increasing the pairs of devices until we either reach the physical bandwidth limitation of the IDS's network interface card or until the IDS algorithm is unable to keep up in processing the data.

Performance analysis requires an expectation of system behavior. While stress testing might push a system to extremes, which are unlikely to occur is "natural" operating conditions, **performance testing** will exercise the system to determine if behavior conforms to expectations. This, of course, requires expectations. For example, if we are studying the example network IDS, and we know that our network can see 100 Mb traffic, then, we might reasonably have a performance expectation of this IDS being able to handle 100 mb of sustained traffic when we test it. Additionally, performance testing can be used to establish baseline behavior on known system for future comparison. Performance testing addresses responsivity, speed, delay, and utilization. The key is establishing an expectation of performance based upon previous study, theory, or experience.

Load testing exercises the system or processes as maximum expected load. This type of analysis that can be thought of as in between stress and performance testing. This too, is based on expectation, but the key is to ensure sufficient utilization to mimic full anticipated load. Often the system can start under light load, and steadily have increasing utilization until maximum anticipated use occurs. This is used to characterize system behavior while in use. Often this is used to understand how it might behave in real-world conditions.

In load testing our example IDS, we would want to define some common communication patterns we would expect to see. These could be learned by observing real systems or by theoretically deriving them. For instance, you could anticipate small bursty traffic for Internet communication to websites. Long steady streams for video, calls, and Internet radio. You would test these realistic loads on the device to see how it will behave under realistic conditions.

Ultimately, this type of research is what is largely considered the validation process. A development team might want to ask themselves "did you build what you thought you built?," "does it meet the requirement?," and "are the requirements known?" This is a good initial step to determine validity and see if future research and investment is worthwhile. Often full-scale experimentation, pilots, or evaluation can be quite resource-intensive, initial evaluations like this can help refine and revise, before major investments.

Sensitivity Analysis

Formally, **sensitivity analysis** is the study of how precisely the outputs of a system are correlated to the inputs of the system. Or mathematically, how the uncertainty in the outputs can be related to the inputs. In the field of cyber security research models, mathematical techniques or algorithms might be devised to detect or analyze cyber system behavior. From something as traditional as a network-based intrusion detection system, to as complicated as an enterprise-wide topological-based graph model analysis for anomaly detection. The objective of sensitivity analysis is to study and understand the scope, variability, and limitations of the system based on changes to the inputs. This is even more important when based on mathematical models. This type of study is truly an exploration of the input space uncertainty, variability, and sensitivity to stimuli. When developing entirely new paradigms or techniques, a researcher might not understand precisely what sort of applications toward which the technique might be predisposed. For example, imagine we took our graph example a bit further. We might have research that has applied a novel technique from graph theory that uses topological features of the logical network structure to detect cyber security phenomenology. The problem is that the researcher might not yet know what sorts of behavior the technique can characterize well, somewhat well, or not at all. This sort of exploration of the problem space will help inform the understanding of the sensitivity, utility, and relevance of the approach. The researchers will want to explore the application of this new detection algorithm to better understand what type of cyber telemetry it best inputs. Example categories of tests for the detection of structures through sensitivity analysis could include: sensitivity to the amount of data seen, sensitivity to the sample size needed, or the sensitivity to the signal-to-noise ratio, (at what level of noise will we still detect an event). The types and number of sensitivities tests can vary broadly depending on what you are testing.

An additional issue for sensitivity analysis is understanding the role of sensitivity analysis in helping nonexperimental-based studies address the challenge of an unobserved, or unobservable confounding inputs of variables.

DIG DEEPER: CONFOUNDING VARIABLES

A confounding variable is an element or variable in the study that can effect the study results. For example, a hypothetical study of cancer rates in the male population might try to correlate smoking with lung cancer. But if the study did not think to look for other factors that might cause cancer, like working in an asbestos factory, then the confounding variable might have substantial effect on the result. An unobservable confounding factor is one that cannot be measured in the current study approach. In the 1950s, pioneering research done by Cornfield in smoking and lung cancer research helped pave the way for observational study from population samples.[1]

Applied Descriptive Study

The second type of applied observational study, is an applied descriptive study. Like in Chapter 5, Descriptive Study, this type of research is more focused on a specific subject under test. The focus is often more on an individual subject or more specialized target subject. Examples of this type of applied study include case studies, elicitation studies, and case reports. **Applied descriptive studies** observes how application of knowledge, process, or a system work in a real setting. These studies can be used to test and evaluate a prototype, study the effects of a new policy or procedure on a population, or evaluate the effectiveness of a new security technology. It is important to point out that in differentiation of applied experimentation, controls are not used, per se. The inclusion of any sort of controls or dependent and independent variables would make this an experiment, quasi-experiment, or applied experiment.

Case Study: Case studies follow a formal process for collection and evaluation. While it is important to realize that a case study is not anecdotal evidence, it is very limited in scope and applicability. An applied case study will focus on the performance or expected outcome of a specific event.

Elicitation Studies: Elicitation is the act of gathering information from human subjects. Examples include surveys and human subject interviews. Surveys are both a method of data collection and a means of observational study. Interviews might elicit a response for a computer system, but the topic of elicitation studies will be limited to human subjects. For an applied elicitation study, the topic of such an interview might be feedback on a new tool, or insights on how well a new cyber security tool was rolled out.

Case Report: While in that field they are used (like case studies) to describe a specific incident of disease or occurrence, in cyber security, case reports are less rigorous than case studies. An applied case report might document the observations of a practitioner or researcher. This might include notes or findings that did not warrant a full case study or more in-depth approach, but are still worth sharing.

The basic tenets of this sort of research is to simply add the subject to the environment, then observe what happens and finally describe it. This can be broadly thought of as performance: Does it solve the problem better than before? and Is it cheaper, faster, 'better?' These sorts of questions can be addressed with an applied descriptive study. This sort of research should also be sure to describe any adverse, negative, or unintended consequences. For example your users in the study quit because the system flooded them with false positives. Ultimately, as this is a descriptive endeavor, effort should be made to document in great detail: the environment (your case will be unique in some aspects), what happened during the case study, and as much as you know as the observer.

APPLIED OBSERVATION METHOD SELECTION

Operational bounds testing and applied descriptive studies have different objectives. Operational bounds testing are techniques that are good for exploring if you have developed or selected the right solution based on your believed requirements. Applied Descriptive studies on the other hand are good for documenting how you operationally integrated a new solution into a real-world environment and to capture.

DATA COLLECTION AND ANALYSIS

Applied Exploratory Studies

Data from operational bounds testing will be either collected or generated around specific test conditions. If it is for stress testing then a large amount of data will be generated or if it is load testing you may collect data from a real environment. However, generation of synthetic is often the used and preferred method for operational bounds testing as it is cost effective and enables you broad flexibility in what is produced. As the objective is investigating the behavior of the solution under a broad range of conditions, not having the complexities of real traffic is okay. For example in sensitivity analysis, the purpose is to evaluate extreme conditions that are rare or unlikely in normal operation. For those types of study, the researcher's goal is to understand under what conditions the application would work or start to fail.

Analysis of operational bounds testing will largely be checking boxes. You will generally establish a predefined set of tests that will explore the functional properties of a solution to provide you with enough knowledge on if it meets your requirements. Each test can be set with a pass or fail criteria so that it is clear from the analysis if the solution is able to meet your minimum thresholds for different performance variables.

Sensitivity analysis on the other hand requires more analysis. For a general analysis of sensitivity analysis, using graphical methods is helpful. Plotting the results generated from sensitivity analysis can help expose trends as you vary the amount of a variable. In addition to visualizing results, the **receiver operator characteristic** (ROC) curve is a sensitivity analysis technique well suited to large categories of cyber security solutions. As many of the problems in cyber security problems are classification problems, such as malware detection, attack detection, and anomalous behavior detection there is the possibility of having a false- and true-positive rate. Most cyber security solutions can have their detectors or sensors vary sensitivity parameters, which affect the true/false-positive ration. The ROC curve shows the true positive versus false positive rate as the sensitivity is varied. This is often called the sensitivity or recall or the model. This approach can be used to explore the results even after the data is collected.

Applied Descriptive Studies

When using, or generating, datasets for applied observational studies, the advice set out in Chapter 5, Descriptive Studies, is still relevant. Issues with bias and sampling can inadvertently influence and even ruin the results of an applied observational study. Data collected from descriptive studies will largely fall into qualitative categories. This includes interviews, surveys, stream of thought journals, and so on. See Chapter 5, Descriptive Studies, for a more in-depth description of some of these data collection methods.

When we are ready to collect data, we should understand the line of inquiry or study it sufficiently well enough to understand what sort of information will be irrelevant to this particular observational study. Undoubtedly, our specific questions or ways of both analyzing the data and coming to conclusions will change, but if we have insufficient clarity to start with, then we run the risk of gathering data that does not end up being relevant to our study. One of the advantages of an applied exploratory study is the relative ease with which a study can be conducted, revised, and conducted again. This can be used as a precursor to more in-depth study or experimentation.

Applied observational research will still use the same statistical techniques to make sense of the data collected. Approaches such as regression testing and statistical tests such as the T-test will be applied. See Observational Study Method Examples.

APPLIED EXPLORATORY STUDY: STRESS TEST

Let's posit that you are a part of a larger research team working on Internet of Things and mobile applications for first responders and emergency response. The team has come up with a new communication application that enables peer-to-peer communication, without hierarchical infrastructure (which would often be down in times of disaster). The team wanted to make sure that the communication is as secure as possible. The problem is that the cryptographic tools used could be power hungry, which might unreasonably drain the battery and burden the end user.

We have been asked to conduct a study on the battery consumption. Since we are evaluating a specific device or system, and not exploring the holistic system, "in the wild," we know we are conducting applied research. We are part of the team that built the application, after all. Given our desire to evaluate performance, we can see that selecting an applied exploratory study evaluating the sensitivity and performance of the battery might be a reasonable approach. More specifically, we will pursue a power consumption stress test.

This study, "Stress test the power consumption impact of a new secure ad-hoc communications protocol for first responders," will need to be just are rigorous and careful as any foundational observational study. After all, we want to have confidence that our results will be accurate and will affect the viability of this technology. We also realize that if we were to collect, so-called "negative results" is this case, such as if the application performed very poorly and was a battery hog, we have an ethical responsibility to report the findings, and make sure our results are accurate. Since applied research is often funded by stakeholders who have a vested interest in the results come out a certain way, conflicts of interest can arise. Indeed the fact that you are a part of the team that is developing the application itself, might be a conflict of interest.

For the purposes of this example, we will identify our own possible conflict of interest. Let's say after consulting with some colleagues about your concerns, they suggest a remediation by having another researcher from the same company but different group peer review the study methodology and results. The scope of this effort is fairly narrow, which allows you to define conditions of the study quite well. We will divide the study design into three categories, the *system*, the *behavior*, and the *testing methodology*.

System

The first part of the study that needed to be defined is the system under test itself. Since we are evaluating the battery consumption of software performance, the choice of hardware will have an incredible impact on battery, computation, and network performance. However, for our test, we are fortunate to have several copies of the exact devices that will be issued to the first responders in the field. This standardized hardware is a crucial component of the stress test. If we were to conduct testing and evaluation on hardware that is too dissimilar to the devices that would be deployed in the field, then we could have little confidence in the performance results. We initially select 10 devices to ensure that we do not have a hardware failure disrupt our results.

Behavior

Next, we will need to define the behavior to be studied. Since the software in question secures communication, and because radio frequency (RF) transmission is typically the greatest consumption of energy, we will scope the focus of this study to evaluate at the extreme level of communication. This is an example where the datasets used for this study need not be "realistic." For example, we do not need to draft up realistic messages or define user behavior that is typical of a back-and-forth dialog. Instead we are simply interested in pushing the system to the limit. We know that these new mobile devices are using the newest communication protocol for neighborhood area networking. We will assume full broadcast at maximum bandwidth for the system behavior. This is an extreme case to stress the battery performance to its maximum possible level. No user should be performing a full broadcast for the entire life of the system, most ad-hoc and even hierarchical applications are primarily receivers, or at best symmetric, for this intended application.

Testing Methodology

Finally, the last piece of the study is the testing methodology itself. We have several host-based testing tools that evaluate system battery consumption of mobile devices, but the problem is that those tools themselves run on the device. There is concern that the collecting of battery consumption telemetry will inadvertently affect the results using a host-based tool. Initial tests were run with this approach, but for this study direct evaluation of battery status will be used (via wired hardware taps). Initially all 10 devices were going to be used in the test, but because stress testing might inadvertently damage the hardware, we will pare this back to 3 baseline and 3 study devices (Note: baseline tests are not needed for stress testing, but the resercher wanted to ensure that no bad lemons (hardware failures) affect the results of the stress testing). The specification of these batteries state 500 cycles before 80% of their original capacity. Open literature seems to indicate numbers ranging from 400 to 1000 cycles. Since these batteries are brand new, and because we want to make sure that inherent battery flaws or behavior does not affect the study, we first will establish baseline behavior on all six batteries. To do this we propose to measure several values from the batteries, discharge them to 75% remeasure, discharge to 50%, remeasure and finally discharge to 25%, and measure once more. Note, this battery manufacturer recommends not dropping to zero if possible, and so we will avoid that for this study. We do not think that the inability to fully discharge will affect the comparative values of consumption. At each test we will measure: the capacity (Ah), state of charge (to get our % battery), depth of discharge (%), open-circuit voltage (V), and time elapsed. We plan to run this test 10 times to evaluate battery consistency, but 10 times is a fraction of the 500 cycles the manufacturer claims. Unfortunately, during the test runs, we found one battery to behave substantially differently from the other nine. This caused us to throw out that battery and select a new one from the remaining four. We were concerned that the new one was fresh, so we cycled it down to 25% 10 times (to make it equivalent to the 5 remaining test batteries), and then we retested all 6 again. This time all six batteries were consistent. Now for our performance and baseline runs we will additionally measure the number of bytes transmitted. We intend to run both the baseline systems (without the secure communication application) and the test systems through 30 cycles. Again this is a double stress test, evaluating the devices without the new secure communication software and with it installed. This is two simultaneous stress tests. We will then collect the data to determine if that is sufficient for analysis, before performing more tests. The first 3 phones were programed to perform full bandwidth transmission until the battery hit 75%, 50%, and 25%, then the capacity (Ah), state of charge (to get our % battery), depth of discharge (%), open-circuit voltage (V), time, and number of bytes transmitted are recorded. Similarly, the test devices were evaluated using the exact same protocol. Thirty cycles later we collected sufficient information to conduct our statistical analysis. We used a T-test to compare the two datasets.

When we reviewed our results with our outside colleague, they pointed out a concern that our current testing paradigm might not be as accurate as we originally thought. The testing for security will assumably be equal to or greater than the power consumption without it. So the race to 75% and so forth should be quicker for those systems. The problem is to determine when to stop and test for the various checkpoints. We discussed this and decided to fix the size of the messages. Therefore, we would transmit sufficient number of packets to equal a 25% drop in battery capacity in the baseline system, and then do the same for the secure communicating systems. This would eliminate the checkpointing at every quarter. After conducting another 30 runs, we got consistent results. Essentially, we are blasting an extreme amount of traffic to both systems to ensure that we push the performance to limit.

The final test was to determine the impact on the entire lifecycle of the device to determine if it held out for large numbers. The test was again conducted, but this time for 100 battery cycles. This was done four times to determine if more than 400 charge and discharge cycles would have an appreciable effect on the consumption and drain of the ad-hoc communication software.

This sort of testing is used to evaluate the speed, consumption, utilization, and general performance of systems. This example illustrates the steps and care needed to conduct a stress test on secure communication software. Additional factors can always be added, but an effective study will try to isolate the conditions and behaviors under test. This is what is largely considered validation process. Did we build what you thought were we doing with regard to communication and battery performance? Did it meet our expectations? This is a good step before diving into real datasets, experimentation, or human subject study.

APPLIED DESCRIPTIVE STUDY: CASE STUDY

Let us explore an example of an applied observational case study. We will continue on with the same example. Imagine we have the same research team that has developed a new secure communication tool for First Responder mobile devices. Stress testing has been conducted to understand how the system performs in laboratory conditions, and extreme use cases. But now we want to study how real users will use the phone. Our plan is to conduct two phases of a study. We will initially conduct "An applied study on the effectiveness of a new secure ad-hoc communications protocol for first responders." First, we will provide the devices to first responders and ask them to use it for their regular work phone. We will work with each subject to ensure that their typical applications and functionality is available. But because this is the standard hardware used in this field, the transition will hopefully be minor. We will then conduct interviews every month to determine how the system performs for four months. We would like to focus on (1) perceived decrease in performance or functionality (2) any increased functionality (when traditional service was unavailable but secure neighborhood area networking was available) and (3) any user feedback to help improve the system.

Since this study obviously deals with human subjects, we first start by reaching out to our company's institutional review board. We get some feedback on what sort of questions to avoid in a questionnaire, that might be irrelevant, but lead to more personally identifiable information than is needed for the purposes of this study. We plan to use our local first responders for this study, to simply access and reduce costs. We will not need to address the generalizability of these first responders to the larger field of first responders, because this is a specific applied study (the limited scope and specificity is inherent in this approach). Since we are working locally, we also involve the chief of police and fire. They have volunteered their staff for this study and we want to make sure that they are aware of, and can inform, the direction of this study to (1) provide their practitioner perspective and (2) ensure that we do not interfere dramatically with the day-to-day mission. Our initial study plan identifies the *purpose*, the *subject*, the *means of intervention*, and the *process*. We get this reviewed by all stakeholders (including the IRB).

The issues of response bias are of direct concern here. Since the subjects are aware of the questions and the fact that they are participating, we might have a variety of factors that can affect the validity of the results. If, for example, the users wanted to please the study researchers they might overinflate the positive aspects or underreport the negative ones. To address this, the researchers will be collecting functional metrics from the phone themselves. How often it is used, how the secure communication app is activated, for how long, and so on. This was not disclosed to the subject beforehand to address concerns about bias, but limited information was collected, the IRB approved this, and the consent was gained after the fact. Second, the subjects are briefed on the context and importance of their reporting. A consent form details the importance and usefulness of this effort. Third, the questions were designed to limit the subjectivity as much as possible. Specific quantitative terms, ordinal values, and short answer questions were designed to eliminate ambiguity and help address subjectiveness in the answerer. And finally, the duration is sufficiently long enough to eliminate any short-term preferential biases. Efforts like this can often go for 6 to 12 months with check in points.

For this study the purpose is as mentioned previously. The goal is to collect information for human users to determine (1) perceived decrease in performance (due to the security application) (2) perceived increase in performance or capability (due to the security application), and (3) any additional user feedback (due to the security application, but this also could include a variety of factors).

In this case the subject under study is the human, in combination with the newly introduced mobile devices (work phones). Since this is a cyber security study, we recall for the introduction that cyber space is the combination of computing devices, networks, information, and users. This study exemplifies how a study of just human behavior, or just mobile phone performance in isolation, would not be as effective in understanding the complete cyber picture.

We first solicit volunteer participants from the fire and police departments. After collecting feedback, we were able to identify 22 police officers and 20 fire and emergency service members who would like to participate. We are concerned that we might not have enough people to be as representative as we like, but we are limited in resources, and we only have 50 devices to loan out, (including a 10% holdback for damage or loss). The first step is to explain the purpose of the study, the operation of the device, the format of the questions, and answer any questions. This study is not meant to be blind, or surreptitious in any way. We want to get feedback on the usability of the new secure communication features. After answering any questions the first month is begun, the staff are asked to use their phones as they would with their normal work phone. Several participants had follow-up questions that were addressed by the study team. After one month, questionnaires with pre-approved questions were distributed to the 42 participants. The questions were largely targeted as specific answers to the first two goals. This was repeated twice more. The final interview was in person again. The users were asked the same battery of questions addressing goals 1 and 2, but they were also given the chance to have open-ended responses. The intervening months, the users has little contact with the study administrators, only for technical problems with the devices or communication software. This was to limit the invasiveness between subject and observer.

Phase two would be an intense case study in mock disaster conditions, coinciding with a regional exercise to test the secure communications in disaster-like environments. The case study like the one just described does not necessarily cover the edge or abnormal conditions. A exercise is the perfect time to study the operations of the system in areas that might not normally be used in day-to-day activities.

This is an example of adding a component to the system to observe what happens. The approach taken makes this a case study, the fact that a specific tool or method was added to the environment makes it applied research. The challenge is to ensure that you document sufficient information about the environment, the system or process being introduced, and the events during the study.

REPORTING YOUR RESULTS

The final important step of an applied observational study is reporting your results. This is, however, another area where the process for applied observational research might differ from foundational observational research. Specifically, contract research is conducted on the behest of the sponsor organization, unlike grant-funded research, which is conducted in the public interest. Not to complicate things, any government might use a contract to fund research in the public interest, but it is important to realize the distinction. Any research should have a broad understanding of how their research is being paid for and what expectations are placed upon the researchers.

DIG DEEPER: RESEARCHER EXPECTATIONS

Legally the responsibility and expectations on the researcher can vary substantially depending on the funding contract. A classic example of this is a government grant versus a government contract agreement. A contract is legally binding agreement to fund a list of promises. A grant is a federal vehicle to create or transfer a thing of value to the public good. http://science.energy.gov/grants/about/grants-contracts-differences/

For example, a commercial grant might specifically exclude publication, or publications or certain types of content. Typically, limitations on research dissemination can become quite contentious in academic or other research institutions. Contracts, can and will, be enforced by law. However, regardless of peer review publication or not, everyone will expect a researcher to document their results thoroughly. It is possible to publish a stress test, applied case report, or study in a conference, or perhaps a journal, but alternatives include: letters, technical reports, public announcements, or other alternatives that can be used to disseminate the information. These methods, while often not be peer-reviewed, are often appropriate for the subject matter and ensure that the community gains access to the material. Technical reports, especially are often used by commercial or nonprofit research institutions that does not have as much of an emphasis on peer-reviewed publications like academia does. It bears repeating that, peer review does provide a validation check against the topic of research, methods of research, and the quality of reporting the research to ensure that a certain level of quality is maintained. In this section, we provide a general template for reporting applied observational studies, and point out where changes might need to be made.

Sample Format

In the following, we will provide you with a general outline for publishing your results. Every publication will provide their own formatting guidelines. Be sure to check your selected venue's submission requirements to make sure you follow any outline and formatting specifications. The outline provided here follows a common flow of information found in published papers and should meet the requirements of a larger number of publisher specifications.

Every paper is unique and requires some different ways of presentation; however, the provided sample flow includes all of the general information that is important to cover in a paper and is a general starting format we take when starting to write a paper and then modify it to support the topic and venue. We understand that every researcher has their own style of presentation, so feel free to use this as a jumping-off point. The discussions of each section are provided to explain what is important to include and why, so you can present the important information in whatever way best suits your style.

Title

This title section should be self-explanatory. Provide sufficient information to help audience determine if they should read more. Some authors enjoy clever or amusing titles, your mileage may vary. You should indicate what type of study you conducted and note that it is applied research. See the examples of, "Stress test the power consumption impact of a new secure ad-hoc communications protocol for first responders," and "An applied study on the effectiveness of a new secure ad-hoc communications protocol for first responders" for unexciting samples. But, note the tile covers the type of research, the purpose, and the subject, briefly.

Abstract

The abstract is a concise and clear summary of the paper. The goal of an abstract is to provide readers with a quick description of what the paper discusses. You should only talk about what is stated in the rest of the paper and nothing additional. Each submission venue will provide guidelines on how to provide an abstract. Generally, this includes the maximum length of the abstract and formatting instructions, but sometimes this will include information on the type and layout of the content to provide.

Introduction

The first section of a paper should always be an introduction for the reader into the rest of the paper. The introduction section provides the motivation and reasoning behind why the research was performed. This should include a statement of the research question and any motivating questions that were used for the research. If any background information is required, such as explaining the domain, environment, or context of the research, you would discuss it here. If the audience is significantly removed from some aspect of this topic, it may be worth it to create an independent background section.

Related Work

The related works section should include a quick summarization of the field's knowledge about this research topic. Are there competing theories? Have other experiments, studies, or theoretical studies been done? If there are a lot of works in this field, cover the most impactful or influential work for you. For applied research, this can be the area where you introduce the system or process under development. This can also fit under previous work, if you have that section. But either way, do not skip covering other similar examples of research.

Study Methods

The study methodology section of your paper should clearly define the process you took to conduct your study. It is crucial that this section is clear and complete, such that a reader would be able to replicate it. In this section, you should detail the specific observational methods (exploratory or descriptive), the setting/environment, and the size of the study. Additionally, the participants/subjects should be detailed. The variables under observation should be described including outcomes, quantitative values, and any confounding factors. Next, the biases should be acknowledged and also address how they were controlled and mitigated. Finally, you should define the statistics you used and the motivation for using them; you can also address if you have any missing data and how you dealt with that. If you conduct an interview, or survey, the means of developing the questions, and sample questions can be included here as well.

In the stress test example, this methods section would include the *system* description, the *behavior* being observed, and the *testing methodology*. And in the applied study example, this methods section would include information about the *purpose*, the *subject*, the *means of intervention*, and the *process* (unless the subject was covered in the related works section).

Study Results

In the results section of your paper, explain what you found after you performed your analysis. Lay out the significance, confidence intervals, and effect sizes for all of the study. Creating tables to show results is usually an efficient and effective method. You should address the participants in the study. Also, you could show pictures of interesting results; that is, if a data anomaly occurred, or to display the distributions of the data samples. This should include descriptive data (the inputs) and outcome data (the outputs), and the analysis. If anything unexpected occurred, and shows up in the data, explain it in this section.

Discussion/Future Work

The discussion/future work section is for highlighting key results and results you found interesting or noteworthy. You should mention any limitations about which the reader should know. You can interpret and discuss any important correlations and discuss generalizability and causal relationships as relevant. Discuss where you think this work should lead next.

Conclusion/Summary

In the final section of the paper, summarize the results and conclusions of the paper. The conclusion section is often a place readers jump to quickly after reading the abstract. Make a clear and concise statement about what the ultimate results of the study were and what you learned from them. Be frank about the success and failures.

Acknowledgments

The acknowledgments section is a place for you to acknowledge anyone who helped you with parts of the research. This is also a good place to acknowledge funding sources that supported your research. As this is applied research, you might have requirements for acknowledgments. Be sure to include those as well.

References

Each publication will provide some guidelines on how to format references. Follow their guidelines and list all your references at the end of your paper. Depending on the length of the paper, you will want to adjust the number of references. Usually, the longer the paper, the more references. A good rule of thumb is 15—20 references for a 6-page paper. Applied research might have less than this, technical reports somes do. However, completeness and thoroughness are always something to strive for, and peer-review quality is fine, even if the document will never be publically released. For peer-reviewed publications, the majority of your references should be other peer-reviewed works. Referencing web pages and Wikipedia doesn't generate confidence in reviewers. Also, make sure you only list references that are relevant to your paper, that is don't inflate your reference count. Good reviewers will check references and this will likely reflect poorly on you and disqualify you.

Endnote

1. Hill, G., Millar, W., and Connelly, J. (2003). "The Great Debate": Smoking, Lung Cancer, and Cancer Epidemiology. *Canadian Bulletin of Medical History*, 20(2), 367–386.

Additional Materials

Science is a way of thinking much more than it is a body of knowledge.

Carl Sagan

## CHAPTER 13

Instrumentation

The ability to measure is the foundation of empirically based science. Observation is the process through which we study and understand phenomena. Measurement is the process of turning observations into comparable quantities. What you measure, how you measure it, and what information can be extracted from those measurements are critical questions that must be answered when executing research.

Data can come from everywhere. From operational environments, data collection efforts, or controlled laboratory environments. Wherever data comes from, it is important to understand with what tools and how the data is collected. The method of data collection can become an extraneous uncontrolled variable that impacts the results if improperly used. Whether your sensors have out-of-sync clocks across a network that impairs the ability to determine the true order of events, or a sampled IP Format Internet Exchange (IPFIX) flow sensor that can't capture the fidelity of a value necessary to determine an effect, the method through which data is collected is often just as important as the research method to ensure that data is appropriate for answering the question at hand.

Cyber security is unique in that most of the sensors available were not developed for scientific exploration. Instead, most sensors in cyber space were developed for operational uses. Whether it is monitoring performance of systems or providing detection of malware, most sensors' goal is not to ensure scientific coverage and fidelity, but instead is designed for usability, efficiency, and cost. The most ubiquitous or easy-to-access sensors are not always sufficient to answer research questions. Understanding how sensors work, their limitations, and how to calibrate them for research is very important.

This chapter will discuss what constitutes scientific instrumentation. This will include a discussion and comparison to operational instrumentation. Topics discussed are: data sampling, instrumentation coverage, and axes of data fidelity. In addition, overviews of common sensors will be provided with use cases provided. Finally, a discussion of testbed environment attributes with existing example capabilities will be provided.

Research Methods for Cyber Security. DOI: http://dx.doi.org/10.1016/B978-0-12-805349-2.00013-3

CHAPTER OBJECTIVES

- Explore how data requirements drive what is needed for instrumentation.
- Discuss difference between instrumentation for operations and for science
- Discuss an overview of current sensor types
- Define controlled environments for cyber security experimentation (testbeds)

UNDERSTANDING YOUR DATA NEEDS

The first and most important step in scientific instrumentation is fully understanding the information needed to answer the research questions posed. As was discussed in previous chapters, when designing a research plan, you must determine what information is needed to answer your questions or invalidate your hypotheses. The required information can then be broken down into raw data feeds from which the information can be extracted. Understanding what information is needed is the first step in defining what instrumentation and data collection is needed for research.

Mapping needed information for research to data types is not always straightforward or easy. A common and often-challenging aspect of cyber security research is that our questions involve understanding concepts that are not easily observable. Cyber space is a metaphysical space that operates independently of physical space. Therefore, all observations of cyber space require mapping metaphysical constructs to a physical medium. For example, a cyber attack. Cyber attacks are, in general, theft or alteration of the information being transmitted through cyber space. A challenge in observing an attack in cyber space is that most of the information needed for the attack is contained in the context, intent, and purpose of capture and alteration of information within cyber space. To observe this, we have to map this to data sources. However, the common data sources, which we will describe in more detail later, such as network and host-based logs are at an atomic action level and lack easy ways of determining things like intent or purpose. Therefore, it is important to understand what your information requirements are and what information can be derived from possible data sources.

There are a few different attributes of data that are relevant to what information they can provide. Understanding the requirements of data sources around these axes is important to ensure that you select the appropriate data sensor type. Incorrect selection of instrumentation for research can lead to inconclusive results or reduced confidence in conclusions. The following sections describe different attributes of data that should be reviewed when developing an instrumentation plan for your research.

Fidelity

Fidelity is how accurate a sensor is at representing the data it is collecting. As cyber space is mostly a discrete space, it is often possible to capture data at the "atomic" or smallest level. However, capturing this much data can become a burden if unnecessary, as there is a resource cost in storing and processing data. Therefore, you should think about the fidelity requirements of your research question to achieve the answer desired to select the appropriate level of data fidelity.

There are multiple axes around which the fidelity of data can be measured. Depending on your research question and the data source, the prioritization of these attributes will change. However, you should still think through all of them for your data collection efforts to ensure that you are getting the appropriate fidelity of data needed.

- *Time fidelity*: **Time fidelity** is the accuracy or precision of the time of a sensor measurement. Time is important to understanding the order of events that helps with determining causality. However, time is a continuous variable and can be measured at increasing levels of precision. Therefore, one sensor could measure at the precision of milliseconds, while another might only measure at the scale of seconds. A measurement from the first that falls within the time window of a measurement from the second leads to uncertainty of which observation occurred first. A good example of this is time synchronization methods for sensors. A computer using the network time protocol (NTP) to achieve time synchronization can only measure time to the accuracy of milliseconds. If the computer used Global Positioning System (GPS) instead for time synchronization, it could measure down to the tens of nanoseconds. Understanding the time fidelity of your data sources is critical to understanding the limitations of the analysis you can perform.
- *Sample rate*: **Sample rate** is the frequency, speed, or ratio of sampling of a data source. Cyber space is discrete, so it is possible to have complete sampling of data sources. However, cyber space can generate data as fast, and sometimes faster, than you can sample. For instance, doing full packet capture on every link of a 10 GbE network requires a very expensive set of equipment, both in processing power and storage. Therefore, it often becomes a cost/benefit ratio discussion. To accommodate situations where it is too expensive to collect everything, instrumentation can be set to collect data that is filtered, truncated, or

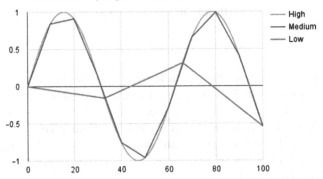

FIGURE 13.1
Instrumentation Sampling Effects.

downsampled. **Filtered data** is when only specific subsets of data are collected such as only collecting errors and not warnings. **Truncated data** is when only a subset of a measurement is kept. For example, when capturing network communication it is common practice to only record the protocol header information and not the data payload to reduce space requirements. **Downsampled data** is when you only record a measurement at a specified interval like when sampling netflow you might only collect 1 out of every 1000 flow record. It is important to understand your data collection requirements to answer your research questions with sufficient confidence when deciding instrumentation sampling, lest you don't collect enough and the effort was wasted.

Physical sources of data can be continuous. For these data streams it is important to understand what characteristics the stream will exhibit and what phenomena you are expecting to see. For instance, if you are sampling data from a wave-based source such as AC power or RF communication, if you sample too slowly you may miss the high speed dynamic oscillations when an event occurs. If you look at Fig. 13.1, you have an example of the effects of sampling on what you see. The blue line shows a high fidelity sampling of a sine wave signal, which shows the perfect smooth wave form. The red line shows slower sample rate. The form of the sine wave is still detectable but the smoothness and the exact amplitude of the wave list lost. The orange line shows an even slower sample rate. With this you can see that you lose a lot of information from the signal and you may not even be able to detect that the signal is following a sine wave.

■ *Summarization/Compression*: The **summarization** or **compression** of data is the level of specificity of the data. There are two perspectives of summarization; truncation and aggregation of data. **Truncation** of data is only capturing information to a set threshold. For instance, with tcpdump it is an oft-use capability to truncate the size of packets recorded to save space. This enables you to get packet-level fidelity without having to manage the burden of storing all of the data. However, before utilizing truncation, it is important to understand what information is needed to answer your research question. If you truncate to only include up to the Transmission Control Protocol (TCP) header, but part of the phenomena is only present within an encapsulated HTTP header, for example, then you will miss important observations.

Aggregation is when you aggregate events to generate summarizes of data. For instance, netflow is a summarization of packet captures by aggregating information from packets by just looking at the flows, or packets, from one IP/port pair to another IP/port pair. Summarizing packets at this level provides information on what IP addresses, which are loosely associated with devices, are communicating and their patterns of communication, that is, time of communication, how often, amount of data, and so on. However, this summarization removes information on what is being communicated. Too many times researchers make strong conclusions from inadequate summarizations of datasets because they are easy to get or it is the information that can be shared from operational environments. Only use summarization and compression techniques when you know that it doesn't remove information needed to answer the questions you have.

- *Proxy*: It is not always possible to directly measure the phenomena you are studying; such as an attackers actions. In these scenarios, you have to find **proxy observations** that indirectly measure a phenomena. When looking for a measurement to capture a phenomena, it is important to be careful of not capturing the right perspective of data from a too high or too low a level. While monitoring every electron as it moves through computational systems is about the lowest level and highest fidelity you can achieve, it may be too low scale and miss the correct context needed to provide the answers to a research question. Looking at data from the right perspective is important, and understanding where phenomena of study would present themselves. In the cyber security field, it is often assumed that technical logs such as network or host captures are sufficient to capture malicious actions; however, it is often the case that actions are considered under specific contexts and completely acceptable otherwise. Mapping behaviors is important to ensure you collect the data that is an appropriate proxy.
- *Scale*: The fidelity of scale is important for understanding how much data to collect. Is collecting from one system sufficient or do you need

to collect across hundreds. Do you expect the phenomena under study to be contained to a small scale or is it much bigger? While we have discussed the statistics of how much data is necessary to ensure significance of results, the scale question is different. **Scale** fidelity refers to the necessary number and placement of sensors across cyber space to capture all aspects of a phenomena. For instance, to study the behavior of a worm, we might place sensors on the hosts that are infected. However, if the worm uses fast flux DNS with servers as a command and control structure, having sensors that can watch the DNS and command and control communication would enable studying the progression of the worm.

Types

What type of data do you need to collect? Are you researching a computer or a system of computers? Are you researching the users or the hardware? Is there direct observables or will you have to measure indirect observables as is often the case when studying threats? The types of data you need to collect are directly tied to what research questions you are asking. As we have discussed in the previous chapters, having tight and focused research questions and hypotheses will help you in determining what data to collect.

There are many different types of data that can be collected, but at the highest levels there are two categories: cyber and physical data. **Cyber data** is data that is collected within cyber space or is data collection that represents logical information within cyber space. **Physical data** is more traditional scientific data collection, which includes everything from the electrical voltage of computational devices to physiological data of users. An overview of common data types and sensors is covered in the next section.

Amount

The amount of data you should collect is driven from a few different places that have been discussed in previous chapters. The first set is based on the statistical power you require. If you are using a frequentist statistic, then the significance level you select will affect the amount of data required. The variability of the data you are using will also impact the amount of data you require. While not part of the scientific process, resources and collectability will also factor into how much data you collect. While the easy answer is to collect everything, it is often the case that you can't collect all the data you can think of because of cost or restrictions. Another input to the amount of data is the time period you collect. If you are performing a longitudinal study over the years, you will be collecting data throughout the study. The fidelity of the data affects the amount. If you collect the data in aggregate it may be a significantly smaller amount than if you collect the raw data. The overarching point is that you need to understand the data amount requirements for your research and that there are multiple parameters for data collection that can affect the resultant amount of data.

Source location

The location of data collection can alter what the data tells you. For instance, an oscilloscope measuring the voltage of an ethernet cable would tell you information about the devices communicating on each side: Do they follow the ethernet specification and stay within acceptable ranges, or how much does their behavior vary? The same oscilloscope measuring the voltage on a motherboard might tell you what type of activity is occurring on the device: Is the processor under a heavy load, is disk input/output (I/O) occurring, and so on? Another example could be where you place a packet capture sensor. If you place it inside a firewall of a department, you will get information on how that department interacts and who they interact with outside the department. However, if you put the packet capture sensor outside the corporate firewall, it will give you information on who is trying to contact the organization and what websites your users visit. The same sensor and same measurement is providing different information based solely on where it is measuring. It is important to understand what information you expect to gain from collecting data and then map it appropriately to where you collect data.

Difference between Operational and Scientific Measurements

While it is natural to use operational sensors for scientific measurements, it is important to know that the objectives of operational and scientific sensing are different. While scientific sensing needs are to collect the appropriate amount of data to ensure a high level of confidence drawing a conclusion about what events happened over a time period, operational sensing is focused on maintaining stable and efficient operation of business processes. It often means that operational sensors are put in place to monitor for operational performance metrics. Whether it is system uptime and status or sampling of network traffic to ensure normal operation, operational sensing is generally designed to collect the lowest amount of data necessary to detect operational problems.

Cyber security is a perspective of operational performance so there are sensors that are very useful in operations, but they are not always sufficiently deployed across an environment. Cyber security sensor deployments are generally designed to enable detection of problems and, when they are found, additional processes are enacted that enable the collection of more data to determine what event happened and how extensive the impact. For instance, sampled netflow at the core of a network may be the normal operational sensing, but when malware is found on a host, full packet capture is enabled on the network segment to discover if and with what the malware is communicating. To ensure the capturing of enough information for causality, scientific sensing on the other hand may require full packet capture throughout the full event. Operational sensing is very useful and helpful, but do not assume that it is sufficient. Always start by defining your requirements and then determine if operational systems are sufficient or require augmentations.

OVERVIEW OF DATA AND SENSOR TYPES

Now that you know what attributes of data to think about, such that you can decide on requirements to meet your research objectives, we can discuss current capabilities of instrumenting cyber space. In cyber space, data sensors are the common means of instrumentation. Most of the sensors we utilize were actually developed more for performance measurements and to monitor systems than for operational effectiveness. For the most part they were not designed as scientific instruments. This leads to some challenges and limitations. While some researchers develop purpose-built scientific instruments, it is often the case that these sensors are used due to expediency and because they are already in place within real systems. The remainder of this section will provide an overview of common sensors within cyber systems.

Host-based Sensors

Host-based sensors are sensors that run on or instrument a cyber device. They focus on the cyber aspect of a device where hardware sensors, discussed below, focus on the physical aspects of a device. Host-based sensors largely consist of software that executes on a device that generates data or logs about other applications or processes. A brief description of common host-based sensors is given below.

- *Event logs*: System logs are logs generated by the operating system or applications of a host. Both messages of operation and errors are logged as events. There are multiple mechanisms by which event logs can be captured. Operating systems provide event log frameworks for applications to also log operational information. Windows provides the Windows Event Log as seen in Fig. 13.2,[1] *nix variants leverage the syslog,[2] and MacOS provides the Unified Logging facility,[3] which is an extension of the syslog framework. However, applications do not always leverage system event log APIs and sometimes log to local files or databases.

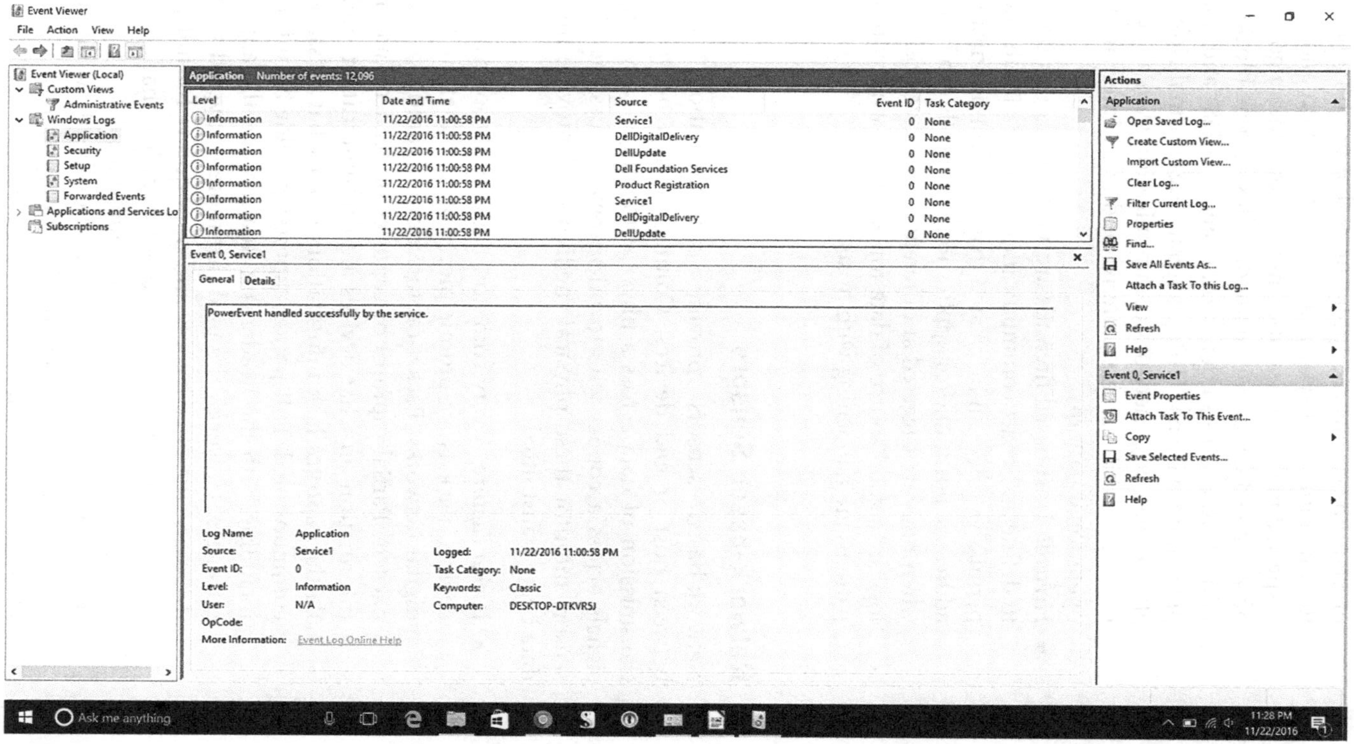

FIGURE 13.2

Windows 10 system event viewer.

- *Antivirus/HIDS/HIPS*: Antivirus, host-based intrusion detection and prevention systems are applications that run on a host and monitor files, memory, and system operations to detect and react to known or suspected malicious events. Antivirus provides a good mechanism for observing when known malicious files or code blocks are found. While host-intrusion detection systems(HIDS) and host-intrusion prevention systems (HIPS) generate logs on malicious files, they can also provide logs network communication with a specific host, memory and file access patterns, and other internal system operational patterns.
- *Firewall*: Host-based firewalls are applications that provide the ability to define and enact communication policies with the host. Therefore, permissive rules can be created that allow communication from specific addresses, ports, and/or applications. Firewalls can be configured to log when rules are triggered at different levels of verbosity. Host firewall logs are a good source of data for observing what communication patterns are happening with hosts.

Network-based Sensors

Network-based sensors provide instrumentation of communication between host or end devices. Communication between devices requires transmission of data across a physical medium: everything from electrical signals across a copper wire to microwaves across the air. Network-based sensors monitor these physical medium and provide information on the data being transmitted.

- *Packet capture*: A very common network sensor type is packet-capture devices. Packets are atomic pieces of data that are transmitted over digital networks. Packet-capture devices capture a portion or full packets. Partial captures or captures of header data provide information on what devices are communicating, and in what ways. Partial captures lack information about what messages are being communicated. Full packet captures provide all information, including both the header information and the application messages. However, the push for more encrypted traffic has decreased the effectiveness and opportunity for full packet capture. There are tools for proxied communication that can decrypt Transport Layer Security (TLS) communication[4] to re-enable full packet capture. However, be aware of its effects on your experiment.[4] See the Sensor Calibration section later in this chapter for more discussion.

DIG DEEPER: TCPDUMP AND WIRESHARK

Two of the most useful and quick-to-use packet capture tools are tcpdump and Wireshark. Tcpdump is a command line tool that allows the capture and display of packets on the network. Wireshark provides a graphical interface for capturing and analyzing packet data. Understanding how to perform full packet captures is a commonly needed ability in cyber security research. Learning to be efficient with one or both of these tools will go a long way in helping you in executing network communication research.

Traditional network communication, that is Internet protocol stack-based communication, are not the only communication media. There are other specialized communication media that also exist such as low power wireless communication and legacy serial communication. They both have software for analysis[5,6] as well as tools for collecting data.[7] Generally, tools exist for all media for sensoring communication.

- *Firewall*: A network firewall is very similar to a host-based firewall; however, it can cover more than one device's communication. Rules for network ingress, coming into the network, and egress, going out of the network, can be set up to block communications between devices, between networks. Network firewalls do not see communication between devices within the same network. As with host firewalls, logged information includes blocked and user configurable amounts of allowed communication.
- *IDS/IPS*: Network intrusion detection systems (IDS) and intrusion prevention systems (IPS) are also similar to host-based IDS/IPS. However, these devices only monitor network communication. There are two different types of these sensors: knowledge- and behavior-based IDS. Knowledge-based include IDS built around the knowledge of both the malicious threat vectors, which are called signature-based IDS, and the specification and configuration of the target, protocol-based IDS. Behavior-based IDS use statistical and other mathematical processes to determine when communication is anomalous in relation to the general communication patterns of devices on the network.[8] Network IDS don't provide the full amount of data that packet-capture facilities provide; however, they can provide statistical analysis of network behavior and signatures can be created when looking for specific phenomena.

Hardware Sensors

Hardware sensors measure the physical behavior of the machines that are executing cyber space. These sensors sample the physical effects of the processes that enable transmission and processing of cyber space information. Hardware sensors can measure everything from the internal I/O channels to the blinking LED status lights. Hardware sensors are useful when cyber space behavior has physical manifestation.

■ *Signal analysis*: Cyber space is built upon analog signals, such as radio waves or electronic voltages, that are measured digitally. Information about how systems are behaving, whether doing unexpected actions or starting to fail, can be gained by monitoring the physical signals of cyber systems. Oscilloscopes can provide a good means of sensoring the I/O signals within a cyber system,[9] between processing components, and between cyber systems transmitted across copper wires, such as CAT5, USB, or DB9 cables. Spectrum analyzers are good tools to sensor wireless communication signals between cyber devices.

DID YOU KNOW?

The well-known actress Hedwig Eva Maria Kiesler or, more commonly known as Hedy Lamarr, well known for her movies in the 1930s to 1940s was one of the inventors of a signal transmission technology that underlies most modern wireless communication. Along with composer George Antheil, Lamarr developed frequency hopping spread spectrum radio transmission to create a hard to jam communication format. Spread spectrum techniques have become a common mechanism in wireless communication such as WiFi, Bluetooth, and cellular technologies to reduce interference of other communicating devices.

■ *Temperature*: Physical temperature of cyber components can provide a proxy of system processing load and operation. As such, temperature patterns may be used to determine what a cyber component is doing and if the system is operating within safe conditions. As most cyber systems are sensitive to high temperatures, they generally have temperature sensors built-in for self-monitoring and protection. There are tools that enable collection of the built-in sensor information.[10]

Physical Sensors

Physical sensors provide means of measuring the physical space around cyber devices. The sensors defined in this section are mostly good for monitoring the human activities and participation within cyber space context. They provide a good way to tie events within cyber space to physical actions by a human user enabling the study of cyber-physical phenomenology.

- *Camera*: Cameras have become a commodity in computer systems, whether it is built-in cameras for laptops and cellular/tablet devices or USB or other common interfaces to connect cameras to cyber devices they are an extensive number of options. Cameras provide a method of capturing the physical activities of human users or cyber systems. The can provide visual proxies of attitude and emotion, a log of what behaviors they were physically doing, that is keystrokes or mouse actions, or they can provide a validation of the presence and authentication of users. (Note: While there is extensive research on using cameras for authentication systems for cyber security operation, that is not the intent of this statement, but instead that cameras can provide the raw data through which you can verify, through whatever means necessary, such as manually, who is performing actions on a cyber device.)
- *Microphones and recorders*: Microphones are a common tool for monitoring communication between users or for providing stream-of-thought collection for monitoring the reasoning of actions by users of cyber systems. Microphones and recorders are also good for interviews. While there are more appropriate sensors, microphones can also provide proxies for logging activities such as keystrokes or mouse clicks. It is also important to point out that microphones and recorders are common tools when doing user studies, especially elicitation studies.
- *Biological*: Biological sensors leverage the other sensors in this category, along with hardware sensors such as vibration and spatial orientation, with purpose-built analytics to sensor processes. Heart rate, eye tracking, and facial expressions, among other biological measurements, can provide information on the state of the user: how they feel, what is drawing their attention, if they are stressed. Even specialized medical equipment, such as functional magnetic resonance imaging (fMRI)[11] or electroencephalography (EEG)[12] can be used to fully explore human behavior in the context of cyber space.

Honeypots

Honeypots are cyber systems and processes set up to appear operational to collect information on threat behavior and vectors. Real or simulated systems and processes are configured to appear as if they are real systems, often with vulnerabilities. Many of the previously described sensors are inserted within and around honeypots to collect data on threat behaviors. Honeypots have been used for everything from single servers to networks of servers, through client processes and files or information. Honeypots are a common technique and tool for sensoring uncontrolled threat sources.[13]

DIG DEEPER: HONEYPOTS

HoneyPot concepts and technology have evolved significantly. Initial honeypots were simple simulations of services to capture threat behavior. Overtime threats have modified their behavior to prevent getting caught by honeypot technologies. Advanced platforms, called distributed deception platforms, are the current wave of honeypot technologies with multiple levels of deception and high interaction honeypots all through centralized control and management services. These systems create real network services along with fictional account credentials and data spread on operational user machines across a network to make it appear as used services to attackers.

Centralized Collectors

Centralized collectors are not sensors but they are common repositories for collecting sensor data that can be a good source of data. These collectors are generally databases that accept data from distributed and, often, heterogenous sensors across a system. All the collectors provide an API or interface to look at the data but most collectors today also provide analytical tools for performing analysis on the data in situ.

- *Log collectors*: Log collectors are tools that enable the centralized collection of logs from a heterogenous set of sensors. Centralized log collection can vary from simple processes like setting up rsyslog[14] collectors with a syslog server, or forwarding event logs[15] up to full feature collection frameworks.[16,17] Centralized log collection can provide a place to look to large amounts of data in operational environments or can provide an efficient means of collecting data from large experiments.
- *Security information and event managers (SIEM)*: SIEM systems provide both sensor collection capabilities and querying and analytical capabilities. They provide a facility to centralize cyber logs and interfaces to enable the collection of the logs from the other sensors discussed in this and the host-based sensor sections. Additionally, capabilities for querying and analyzing the data collected are often provided. SIEMs provide a good mechanism to gather data for studies and experiments and their analytical platforms can be used to set up analysis and generate graphs and plots as data is collected.[18]

Data Formats

For logs to be understandable, they must follow a data format specification. Data formats generally define the syntax, structure, and semantics for storing a specific type of information. Over time, there have been a set of commonly accepted data formats that the cyber security community uses. The following list provides a brief description of the common data formats that you might see or find useful in performing cyber security research.

- *Syslog*[19]: The syslog format is supported broadly across applications and system services. It is a fairly loose standard in that it only requires a log type, severity level, application or process tag, and content. The formatting of the content field is unspecified, which has led to some inconsistency and interoperability issues. There are plenty of tools for capturing syslog messages including built-in services within Unix and Linux kernels.
- *IF-MAP*[20]: The interface for metadata access points is a data format and communication framework developed by the Trusted Computing Group[21] to provide an interoperable and standard for communicating security logs between sensors. A few different use cases of for metadata mappings exist. While IF-MAP doesn't have ubiquitous support, there are a large number of sensors that do have support.[22]
- *CybOX*[23]: The Cyber Observable eXpression is a standardized language for encoding and communicating high-fidelity information about cyber observables, whether dynamic events or stateful measures that are observable in the operational cyber domain. It provides a standard format for documenting observable events that are either empirically found or are theoretical in nature. The goal for the format is to enable the sharing of threat indicators between collaborating entities.
- *SNMP*[24]: The Simple Network Management Protocol (SNMP) provides the ability to collect the status of network infrastructure and to control devices. To enable interoperability, the SNMP protocol defined management information base (MIB). The MIB defines information structures and formats which provides a method of hierarchically storing information about entities in a communication network.
- *Pcap*[25]: Pcap is a binary format that provides a simple structure for recording network packet captures. The structure of the file format includes a global header that provides information on the capture attributes followed by a series of packet headers, which provide capture information such as time and size, and packet data. Pcap next generation (pcapng)[26] is a newer extension of pcap to provide higher precision timing and extensibility. However, the original pcap is still the most supported and used packet-capture format (Fig. 13.3).
- *IPFIX*[27,28]: The IPFIX is a binary format and transportation protocol for recording IP flow summarization information. It is based on the

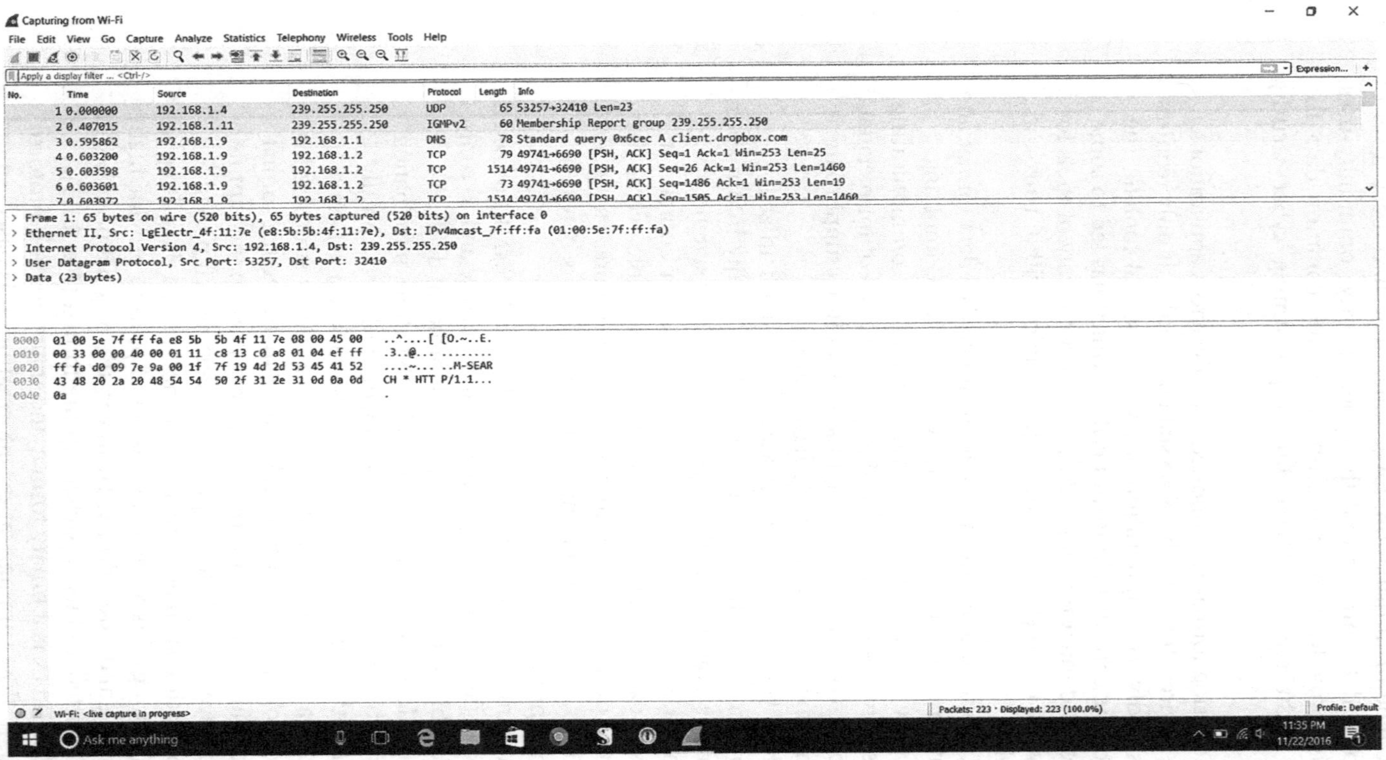

FIGURE 13.3

PCAP frame dissection in the Wireshark tool.

Cisco Netflow protocol. An IP flow consists of a series of packets between two cyber devices on the same transmission ports. IPFIX provides summarization information like which devices are communicating, for how long, how much data is exchanged, and the time of the flow. Most IPFIX is unidirectional, or only includes information on transmission from one device to another. However, most cyber communication is bidirectional and IPFIX does provide the ability to capture bidirectional flow information. IPFIX captures less information than the pcap format, but it is also less resource intensive. IPFIX is deployed more frequently and in more places than pcap because of the resource costs.

- *STIX*[29]: The Structured Threat Information Exchange (STIX) is a data format for storing information about threats. The goal of STIX is to provide a standard mechanism by which information about threats can be encoded and shared. Information on observables, tactics, and known defenses of threat sources is standardized and presented in both machine and human readable formats.

Sensor Calibration

Sensors are important tools in the pursuit of scientific research, but it is crucial to understand that the sensors you use provide a perspective on your problem and can be a source of bias in and of themselves. Understanding the capabilities of your sensors is important when analyzing the data generated by them. It is easy to generate incorrect conclusions if you are unaware of limitations of the sensors that collect and bias data.

There are three general concepts that are important when discussing continuous value sensor measurements: resolution, accuracy, and precision. **Resolution** is the granularity or fineness of a measurement. **Accuracy** is the closeness of a sensor's measurements to the true measure. Finally, **precision** is the reliability and repeatability of a sensor. Together these characteristics define the capabilities of sensor. While cyber space is a discrete space, it does exist upon physical systems that measure analog variables. As such, even digital sensors can miss data if their underlying physical system is insufficient in resolution, accuracy, and precision.

One of the most critical calibration efforts for cyber security sensoring is time synchronization. Often you will be faced with many distributed sensors collecting data across cyber and physical space. In order to determine the order of events to support causal inference and trend analysis, it is crucial that time is appropriately synchronized between sensors. As such, time is a good example to discuss these concepts. Time resolution in the Linux operating system kernel was introduced previously in a "Did you know?" Linux leverages system jiffy, or HZ of the system, to determine time resolution. The jiffy can be altered to increase or decrease time resolution. Since kernel 2.6.13, the HZ value is a kernel configuration parameter and can be 100, 250 (the default) or 1000, yielding a jiffies value or time resolution of, respectively, 0.01, 0.004, or 0.001 seconds.[30] If time synchronization is performed with NTP you can expect time accuracy with Coordinated Universal Time (UTC) to be within 10 s of milliseconds. However, if you were to use a local GPS time clock, you can achieve time accuracy of micro- or nanoseconds. As NTP is based on periodic time checks with distributed clock sources, the precision of the time on a node is based on the hardware and software that is maintaining the time between synchronizations. As such, common computers can be expected to have lower precision because they lack hardware time sources and user operating systems are not real-time, so have no expectations to have consistent executional behavior. Fluctuations in network performance can also affect precision. NTP doesn't have protocol specifications to address router or switch queuing issues. IEEE 1588 Precision Time Protocol (PTP) addressed this by defining transparent switching and routing capabilities to increase precision.

Another common tool used in cyber research is virtualization. Virtualization provides the ability to scale a small number of physical resources into a larger number of virtualized resources. However, this process can impact the performance of cyber systems. There can be many factors that determine the performance impact. Everything from the different chipsets used, type of virtualization,[31] and the type of applications being run. In some situations you might see that performance increases. Another tool calibration that is important to think about is when you are sharing physical resources between virtual cyber components. There is potential for one virtual machine impacting and biasing the performance of other virtual machines.[32] If you use virtualization as part of your experimentation, then it is important to first quantify and understand the effects of the virtualization on the data.

As the tools you use for testing can bias your sensors, it is important to understand the capabilities of your sensors and how your tools can affect the results. Therefore, it is good practice to do an initial study of your tools, if they haven't already done, so that you know what expectations you can have of them. This process strengthens the amount of confidence you instill in the conclusions you make from your research.

CONTROLLED-TESTING ENVIRONMENTS

Instrumentation is important for all empirical research, that is observational studies and experiments. However, experiments often require platforms beyond operational environments to support control and manipulation. We categorize all pseudosynthetic, controllable cyber environments as testbeds. Testbed is an overloaded word with many different meanings by different research subcultures. It can mean everything from a prototyping environment, to a demonstration capability, to a training facility. However, for the purposes of this book and for scientific exploration a **testbed** is defined as a controllable cyber environment that enables experimentation.

Testbeds are an important and necessary component of cyber security research. Just as chemists need chemistry laboratories, so do cyber security researchers need testbeds. It is often the case that experimentation cannot be performed in operational environments. Whether it is due to risk avoidance of unleashing a new worm to study infection patterns, or the inability to alter policies to meet the objectives of the research, operational environments are generally not sufficient for experimentation. As such, it is necessary to have an independent, controllable environment where variables can be controlled and isolated to explore effects and causal relationships.

A testbed's capabilities can greatly vary from some experts with a pile of equipment to a highly dynamic and configurable capability. There are a few attributes around which a testbed can vary its capabilities. The following table provides a brief discussion of each. Here the term is best defined around a set of attributes. For our purposes, a cyber testbed includes the following attributes:

Attribute	Description
Purpose	The purpose is the driving objective or use case for a testbed. Different toolsets and capabilities lend themselves to some purposes better than others. Educational and training testbeds[33] provide the capability to create environments to learn and explore a topic. Exercise testbeds[34] support organized exercises for readiness training. Experimentation testbeds[35,36,37,38] provide sandbox environments for exploring concepts and understanding system interaction. Testing and evaluation testbeds[39,40] provide the ability to test devices or applications in the context of a realistic environment to see how they will behave and react. Finally, demonstration testbeds are designed to showcase a specific capability or application.
Resources	The resources of a testbed determine the domains and types of research to which it is best suited. Resources include what types of hardware and architectures are supported in the testbed, as well as what applications are provided or allowed. Resources also include the people that support the testbed and the experience and expertise they provide users. The assets of a testbed can include networking applications,[35,37,41] cyber-physical hardware,[36,38,39] military architectures,[34] wireless communication,[42,43] cloud architectures,[44] and so on.

Continued

Continued

Attribute	Description
Resource management	Resource management and allocation is the process by which a testbed infrastructure is configured to execute its purpose. The tasks associated with this range from manual configuration to full automation. In the midst of this range are hybrids, where some parts of a testbed are manually configured, while the rest is automated.
Configuration/ Initialization	Configuration and initialization extends beyond the infrastructure that supports the experiment and includes configuring the services, applications, and test equipment that are part of the experiment. This involves defining and configuring the software (operating system, applications, services), firmware (version, capabilities), and accounts (user, service). As with resource management, the spectrum of tasks associated with this can range from manual labor to full automation.
Experimental design	Experiment design is the process by which a user describes their experiment so that the testbed can be configured for its execution. This process could be a proposal that initiates equipment operators to configure the proper environment. It could also include the use of an experimental configuration language that initiates an automated configuration process. The definition may contain the entire infrastructure of the testbed, up to the services and traffic, or any subset. How this attribute is defined in a testbed greatly influences the amount of repeatability to which it is capable.
Experimental control	Experimental control is an attribute that illustrates the functionality of a testbed to control and manipulate components of the experiment once it has begun. This could include capabilities such as access to equipment during an experiment, the ability to manipulate or control configuration of experimental equipment or software, the ability to emulate system characteristics (user behavior, network traffic, threat behavior), or the ability to inject faults or scripted actions.[45,46,47,48]
Instrumentation and data collection	The instrumentation and data collection attribute defines the capabilities of a testbed. This includes network and hardware (virtual machine introspection) sensors, software log collection, and experimental metadata storage (event logs). These capabilities can be automated, user driven, or manually deployed.
Access	The final attribute is the accessibility of the testbed. This can include remote accessibility: portals for viewing, configuring, and executing experiments,[35,36] or having access restrictions and requiring physical presence to access the testbed.[34]

It is important to keep your research requirements in mind, in addition to your resources, when you are selecting a testbed framework or service. There are trade-offs in fidelity, scalability, usability, and so on, based on the attributes of each testbed.

Testbeds can provide additional abilities to sensor an environment more than is possible in operational environments. This could mean installing sensors in more places, which will generate more data and have a higher operational cost, or installing additional sensors. For instance, a lot of testbeds are being developed upon cloud infrastructure. Using virtualization of resources enables the use of hypervisor capabilities to sensor and monitor an experiment. Traditional cloud capabilities allow monitoring of virtualized hardware usage: that is, processor, memory, disk drive loading, and so on. In addition, virtual machine introspection[49] also becomes a possibility. Through virtual machine introspection, the memory of virtual machines can be directly inspected to determine everything that is executed by a machine all while being undetectable.

Testbeds are excellent resources and there are a number of them that are provided as a resource for the research community. When you are developing your research plan, keep testbeds in mind. They may be the perfect tool you need to answer your research question. If you need a controllable environment for experimentation, evaluate the different capabilities of the different community of testbeds. Select one that fits your needs or, if you found a gap, maybe it is worth developing a new capability for the community.

Recently, the United States National Science Foundation sponsored a community survey of requirements and needs to enable and support future cyber security experimentation.[50] This report represents multiple workshops that brought together researchers from across the community to discuss current open research questions that need improved experimentation capabilities and what is necessary to achieve the improved capabilities in the future. In addition, this report provides a good survey of existing testbed capabilities that are operational and potentially available for use by the community.

DIG DEEPER: CYBER SECURITY EXPERIMENTATION OF THE FUTURE

The NSF supported Cyber Security Experimentation of the Future report was developed from three workshops that brought together researchers to discuss open research questions, what tools and instruments were needed to answer them, and a prioritized plan. The final report summarizes the information collected from the workshops. Reading this report can provide a cross-sectional view of cyber security research in 2015.

CONCLUSION

Our understanding of the world is limited by our ability to observe and measure it. The sensors and instruments we use become the monocle through which we can observe cyber space. The limitations and inaccuracies of the sensors used affect what we can learn about cyber space. Owing to this, a major part of research is understanding available sensors and selecting the appropriate set for collecting the data needed to answer a research question. At times, this may mean that you will have to develop a new sensor as currently available tools are insufficient. Either way, as with all the research methods your process for selecting the sensors used should be methodical, rigorous, and deliberate.

Endnotes

1. Windows Event Log Reference. (n.d.). Retrieved November 20, 2016, from https://msdn.microsoft.com/en-us/library/windows/desktop/aa385785(v = vs.85).aspx
2. Syslog.conf(5) - Linux man page. (n.d.). Retrieved November 20, 2016, from https://linux.die.net/man/5/syslog.conf
3. Logging. (n.d.). Retrieved November 20, 2016, from http://developer.apple.com/reference/os/1891852-logging
4. Pirc, J. W., and DeSanto, D. (n.d.). Is the Security Industry Ready for SSL Decryption? Speech presented at RSA Conference 2014, San Francisco. Retrieved November 20, 2016, from https://www.rsaconference.com/writable/presentations/file_upload/tech-r01-ready-for-ssl-decryption-v2.pdf
5. ASE2000 RTU Test Set (Version 2) [Computer software]. (n.d.). Retrieved November 20, 2016, from http://www.ase-systems.com/ase2000-version-2/
6. SerialTest [Computer software]. (n.d.). Retrieved November 20, 2016, from http://www.fte.com/products/SerialAnalyzers.aspx
7. Edgar, T. W., Choi, E. Y., and Zabriskie, S. J. (n.d.). SerialTap [Program documentation]. Retrieved November 20, 2016, from https://www.dhs.gov/sites/default/files/publications/csd-ttp-technology-guide-volume-2.pdf
8. Kabiri, P., and Ghorbani, A. A. (2005). Research on intrusion detection and response: A survey. *IJ Network Security, 1*(2), 84–102.
9. Zhou, Y., and Feng, D. (2005). Side-Channel Attacks: Ten Years After Its Publication and the Impacts on Cryptographic Module Security Testing. *IACR Cryptology ePrint Archive, 2005*, 388.
10. Open Hardware Monitor [Computer software]. (n.d.). Retrieved November 20, 2016, from http://openhardwaremonitor.org/
11. Anderson, B. B., Kirwan, C. B., Jenkins, J. L., Eargle, D., Howard, S., and Vance, A. (2015, April). How polymorphic warnings reduce habituation in the brain: Insights from an fMRI study. In *Proceedings of the 33rd Annual ACM Conference on Human Factors in Computing Systems* (pp. 2883–2892). ACM.
12. Chuang, J., Nguyen, H., Wang, C., and Johnson, B. (2013, April). I think, therefore i am: Usability and security of authentication using brainwaves. In *International Conference on Financial Cryptography and Data Security* (pp. 1–16). Springer Berlin Heidelberg.
13. The Honeynet Project. (n.d.). Retrieved November 20, 2016, from https://honeynet.org/project
14. Rsyslog. (n.d.). Retrieved November 20, 2016, from https://wiki.debian.org/Rsyslog

15. Configure Computers to Forward and Collect Events. (n.d.). Retrieved November 20, 2016, from https://msdn.microsoft.com/en-us/library/cc748890(v = ws.11).aspx

16. Fluentd | Open Source Data Collector. (n.d.). Retrieved November 20, 2016, from http://www.fluentd.org/

17. Logstash [Computer software]. (n.d.). Retrieved November 20, 2016, from https://www.elastic.co/products/logstash

18. Kavnagh, K. M. and Rochford, O. (2015) Magic Quadrant for Security Information and Event Management, Gartner.

19. Gerhards, R., "The Syslog Protocol", RFC 5424, DOI 10.17487/RFC5424, March 2009, <http://www.rfc-editor.org/info/rfc5424>.

20. Trusted Network Connect Working Group. TNC IF-MAP Metadata for Network Security Version 1.1, Revision. May 2012. https://www.trustedcomputinggroup.org/wp-content/uploads/TNC_IFMAP_Metadata_For_Network_Security_v1_1r9.pdf

21. Welcome To Trusted Computing Group | Trusted Computing Group. (n.d.). Retrieved November 20, 2016, from https://www.trustedcomputinggroup.org/

22. TNC IF-MAP 2.1 FAQ. (2012, May 1). Retrieved November 20, 2016, from https://www.trustedcomputinggroup.org/tnc-if-map-2-1-faq/

23. Barnum, S., Martin, R., Worrell, B., & Kirillov, I. (2012). The CybOX Language Specification.

24. W. Stallings. 1998. SNMPv3: A security enhancement for SNMP. Commun. Surveys Tuts. 1, 1 (January 1998), 2-17. DOI = http://dx.doi.org/10.1109/COMST.1998.5340405

25. The Libpcap Format. TCPDump.https://wiki.wireshark.org/Development/LibpcapFileFormat

26. Tuexen, M., Ed., Risso, F., Bongertz, J., Combs, G., and Harris, G. (n.d.). PCAP Next Generation (pcapng) Capture File Format. Retrieved November 20, 2016, from http://xml2rfc.tools.ietf.org/cgi-bin/xml2rfc.cgi?url = https://raw.githubusercontent.com/pcapng/pcapng/master/draft-tuexen-opsawg-pcapng.xml&modeAsFormat = html/ascii&type = ascii

27. Claise, B., Ed., "Specification of the IP Flow Information Export (IPFIX) Protocol for the Exchange of IP Traffic Flow Information", RFC 5101, DOI 10.17487/RFC5101, January 2008, <http://www.rfc-editor.org/info/rfc5101>.

28. Quittek, J., Bryant, S., Claise, B., Aitken, P., and J. Meyer, "Information Model for IP Flow Information Export", RFC 5102, DOI 10.17487/RFC5102, January 2008, <http://www.rfc-editor.org/info/rfc5102>.

29. https://stixproject.github.io/

30. Time(7)—Linux manual page. (n.d.). Retrieved November 20, 2016, from http://man7.org/linux/man-pages/man7/time.7.html

31. Felter, W., Ferreira, A., Rajamony, R., and Rubio, J. (2015, March). *An updated performance comparison of virtual machines and linux containers*. In *Performance Analysis of Systems and Software (ISPASS), 2015 IEEE International Symposium On* (pp. 171-172). IEEE.

32. Matthews, J. N., Hu, W., Hapuarachchi, M., Deshane, T., Dimatos, D., Hamilton, G., ... and Owens, J. (2007, June). *Quantifying the performance isolation properties of virtualization systems*. In *Proceedings of the 2007 workshop on Experimental computer science* (p. 6). ACM.

33. CERT, "StepFWD." [Online]. Available: https://stepfwd.cert.org/vte.lms.web. [Accessed: March 15, 2015].

34. A. Sternstein, "Army Awards No-Bid Cyber Range Deal to Lockheed Martin." [Online]. Available: http://www.nextgov.com/cybersecurity/2014/05/army-awards-no-bid-cyber-range-deal-lockheed-martin/85186/

35. J. Mirkovic, T. V. Benzel, T. Faber, R. Braden, J. T. Wroclawski, and S. Schwab, "The DETER project: Advancing the science of cybersecurity experimentation and test," in Technologies for Homeland Security (HST), 2010 IEEE International Conference on, 2010, pp. 1−7.

36. T. Edgar, D. Manz, and T. Carroll, "Towards an experimental testbed facility for cyber-physical security research," in Proceedings of the Seventh Annual Workshop on Cybersecurity and Information Intelligence Research, Oak Ridge, Tennessee, USA, 2011.

37. J. Lepreau, "Emulab: Recent Work, Ongoing Work," in Talk at DETER Lab Community Meeting, 2006.

38. T. Yardley, "Testbed Cross-Cutting Research." [Online]. Available: https://tcipg.org/research/testbed-cross-cutting-research. [Accessed: March 15, 2015].

39. A. Hahn, A. Ashok, S. Sridhar, and M. Govindarasu, "Cyber-Physical Security Testbeds: Architecture, Application, and Evaluation for Smart Grid," Smart Grid, IEEE Transactions on, Vol. 4, pp. 847–855, 2013.

40. M. Benjamin, "INL's SCADA Test Bed." [Online.] Available: http://www4vip.inl.gov/research/national-supervisory-control-and-data-acquisition-test-bed. [Accessed: March 15, 2015].

41. L. Peterson, A. Bavier, M. E. Fiuczynski, and S. Muir, "Experiences building planetlab," in Proceedings of the 7th symposium on Operating systems design and implementation, 2006, pp. 351–366.

42. D. Raychaudhuri, I. Seskar, M. Ott, S. Ganu, K. Ramachandran, H. Kremo, et al., "Overview of the ORBIT radio grid testbed for evaluation of next-generation wireless network protocols," in Wireless Communications and Networking Conference, 2005 IEEE, 2005, pp. 1664–1669 Vol. 3.

43. D. Raychaudhuri, K. Nagaraja, and A. Venkataramani, "Mobilityfirst: a robust and trustworthy mobility-centric architecture for the future Internet," ACM SIGMOBILE Mobile Computing and Communications Review, vol. 16, pp. 2–13, 2012.

44. A. I. Avetisyan, R. Campbell, I. Gupta, M. T. Heath, S. Y. Ko, G. R. Ganger, et al., "Open Cirrus: A Global Cloud Computing Testbed," Computer, Vol. 43, pp. 35–43, 2010.

45. L. M. Rossey, R. K. Cunningham, D. J. Fried, J. C. Rabek, R. P. Lippmann, J. W. Haines, et al., "LARIAT: Lincoln adaptable real-time information assurance testbed," in Aerospace Conference Proceedings, 2002. IEEE, 2002, pp. 6-2671-2676, 6-2678-6-2682 Vol.6.

46. K. Gold, Z. J. Weber, B. Priest, J. Ziegler, K. Sittig, W. W. Streilein, et al., "Modeling how thinking about the past and future impacts network traffic with the gosmr architecture," in Proceedings of the 2013 international conference on Autonomous agents and multi-agent systems, 2013, pp. 127–134.

47. "Montage: Experiment Lifecycle Management." [Online]. Available: http://montage.deterlab.net/magi/index.html#. [Accessed: March 15, 2015].

48. T. Champion and R. Durst, "Skaion Corporation Capabilities Statement." [Online]. Accessible: http://www.skaion.com/capabilities.pdf. [Accessed: March 15, 2015].

49. Payne, B. D. (n.d.). *An Introduction to Virtual Machine Introspection Using LibVMI*. Speech presented at Annual Computer Security Applications Conference in CA, Los Angeles.

50. Balenson, D., Tinnel, L., & Benzel, T. (2015, July 31). *Cybersecurity Experimentation of the Future (CEF): Catalyzing a New Generation of Experimental Cybersecurity Research* (Rep.). Retrieved November 20, 2016, from National Science Foundation website: http://www.cyberexperimentation.org/files/2114/5027/2222/CEF_Final_Report_Bound_20150922.pdf

## CHAPTER 14

Addressing the Adversary

The fundamental nature of cyber security is predicated on the notion of an adversary. Going back to the introduction of this book, the very nature of security is to keep *something* secure from someone. In this chapter, we will explore that *someone* in more detail. When designing a house, for example, security considerations are often put into place to deal with perceived threats. For example, a door might have a deadbolt added because the concern is that the conventional lock might be susceptible to picking or brute force circumvention. This is a vulnerability-based approach. A perceived weakness in a system (your home) is mitigated by an additional feature (a stronger lock).

All too often, however, decisions about security, like this, are made without a thorough exploration of the so-called threat model. This will be defined in more detail shortly, but without an understanding of *who* you are protecting against, you will be at a disadvantage. This might require you to think like a criminal and realize that a locked door next to a large glass window is hardly a problem for a criminal who doesn't mind breaking and entering. Research is necessary to provide the required data to inform an adversarial approach to security. An adversarial-focused approach to home security might observe that 39.1% of burglaries occurred during the day[1] and that the top three entry points were the front door, a first floor window, and a back door.[2] Furthermore, they might realize that the national average, in 2014, for burglaries was 542.5 per 100,000 people, but the burglary rate in Richland, Wash, was 169 per 100,000 people.[3] Researching adversaries is necessary to enable better security decisions.

Understanding of adversaries is also crucial in enabling theoretical and experimental research. The ability to model and simulate adversaries is a fundamental requirement in performing research to answer questions that involve adversarial actions or effect. The adversarial nature of cyber security is one of the key features that makes it different from most other fields of science and that makes it difficult. Understanding and leveraging knowledge of adversaries is crucial to enabling your research. In this chapter, we will delve into the specifics of the adversary challenge. We will describe the categories and

Research Methods for Cyber Security. DOI: http://dx.doi.org/10.1016/B978-0-12-805349-2.00014-5

characteristics of research that require an adversarial component. We will discuss the challenges and needs for adversaries in research.

CHAPTER OBJECTIVES

- An introduction to this unique aspect of cyber security research
- A historical context of adversarial studies
- Ways to understand and model threat actors (adversaries)
- The interactive and adaptive nature of this topic
- A brief discussion on attribution

DEFINING ADVERSARY

In its most simplistic definition, a cyber **adversary** is someone or a group that intends to perform malicious actions against other cyber resources. However, there is a lot of nuance in defining adversaries, which the simple definition doesn't cover. The US Department of Defense (DoD) Joint publication 3-0 defines it as, "A party acknowledged as potentially hostile to a friendly party and against which the use of force may be envisaged."[4] Subsequently, the Defense Science Board drafted a Task Force Report on "Resilient Military Systems and the Advanced Cyber Threat."[5] This report goes into much more detail about cyber adversaries, and is very well worth a read. Specifically, it defines cyber adversaries into six tiered categories, from I to VI.

> Tier I–II Adversaries: Use off-the-shelf vulnerabilities and tools.
> Tier III–IV Adversaries: Have more resources and capabilities, and will be able to discover new vulnerabilities.
> Tier V–VI Adversaries: Can invest billions of dollars and years to develop vulnerabilities into systems.

Fig. 14.1, from the DoD report, illustrates the incredible resources that top adversaries can bring to bear for an attack. This could include intercepting purchases, tampering with hardware before it is installed, social engineering, on premise attacks, as well as a myriad of other approaches.

Appropriately understanding the nature of the adversary can help (1) defenders craft appropriate protections, and (2) researchers gain a more complete understanding of the contested cyber landscape. There are other taxonomies of adversaries, as well. Some categorize them into groups such as criminal, hacktivist, script kiddy, nation state, insider threats, and so on. The problem with this approach is that it might create a ranking where the nation state is at the top and the script kiddy is at the bottom. This belies the fact that adversaries are often engaged on multiple fronts and might span a variety of

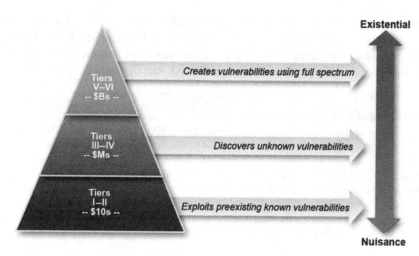

Existential

Creates vulnerabilities using full spectrum

Tiers
V–VI
-- $Bs --

Discovers unknown vulnerabilities

Tiers
III–IV
-- $Ms --

Exploits preexisting known vulnerabilities

Tiers
I–II
-- $10s --

Nuisance

FIGURE 14.1 DoD cyber adversary tiers.[5]

categories. They also often share and use the same toolsets, so a script kiddie can at times wield capabilities that were once only the purview of nation states.[6] Criminal adversaries in particular should not be underestimated because they do not have the resources of a nation state. The understanding of adversarial intent that comes from categories like this, however, can be quite useful as we will discuss later.

Threats are a similar concept to adversaries except they can be considered in a more abstract sense. A **threat** is a source of possible, deliberate harm that might befall a protected entity. The National Information Assurance Training and Education Center defines threat as: "The means through which the ability or intent of a threat agent to adversely affect an automated system, facility, or operation can be manifest." It is important to point out that "threat" is a widely debated term. Many in the field use it to mean all possible sources of harm (accidental, environmental, faults, etc.). We believe, that while it might be poetic, weather, hard-drive failures, and other nonsapient sources of harm should not be characterized as threats. Succinctly, threat is a person with capability and intent to cause harm. Threat is very similar to adversary, but a threat is the specific source of harm, for example a known hacker, a specific employee, whereas the adversary is the collection or group of threat, for example a hacker collective or nation state. Threat is sometimes represented notationally as the Threat Equation, $threat = intent \times capabilities$. This might be useful at an abstract level, but tends to reduce complex issues and challenges to overly simplistic equations. Threat is synonymous with the terms **threat actor**, **attacker**, **competitor**, and **opponent**.

While threat is the broad case there are specific cases of threat that are reoc-curring conceptions in cyber security, one of which is the insider threat. An **insider threat** is a threat that resides within your organization or system and has legitimate access (it need not be privileged, but that makes it worse).

DIG DEEPER: UNDERSTANDING THREATS

An easy way to understand that threats are not attacks (DoS, spoofing, tampering), vulner-abilities, or failures, as some sources claim,[7,8] is to think through the logical implications. If natural failures, tampering attacks, and acts of God within a company, are threats, as men-tioned in literature, then wouldn't those all be classified as insider threats? Yet, it seems that while failures along with attacks are often classified as threats they are never labeled as insider threats when they occur inside an organization (server room flooding, for exam-ple). This is likely because they are not actually threats after all. This is a case of imprecise and evolving terminology in the field.

To clearly delineate our definition of threat it is important to define all-hazards. An **all-hazards** perspective includes all sources of harm that might befall a protected entity. All-hazards include threats that are deliberately mali-cious, and hazards that include accidents, environmental catastrophes, failures, and faults, and so on. All-hazards is typically used in a risk-based approach to security that evaluates the sources of all possible harm and determines the severity and likelihood of events to plan the best course of mitigation. This phrase is often used in emergency management, and national disaster prepara-tion.[9] The challenge to all-hazards approaches is the dilution of effort across all-hazards. Not all-hazards are equal, but if consequence, or moreover likeli-hood, are unknown, an organization might spread its resources too thinly try-ing to address all-hazards instead of mitigating the higher value ones. The second challenge is that the mitigations and defenses for one hazard may have no bearing, or even be counterproductive for another hazard. Expertise and interdependency awareness is critical, as well.

THE CHALLENGE OF ADVERSARIAL RESEARCH

With a clearly defined understanding of adversaries and threats we can now discuss how they fit into research and the requisite challenges they bring. A major portion of cyber security research is the understanding of the interac-tion of humans across cyber space, largely in an adversarial relationship. As such when we study cyber security it often means that we have to study this adversarial relationship and how it plays out in cyber and physical space. This often puts having an adversary to study as a key requirement of answer-ing major cyber security research questions.

However, this presents a challenge. Adversaries generally don't want to be studied and when their strategies and methods are discovered they alter their behavior. The hidden nature of threats lead to challenges for both observational and experimental research. From an observational research perspective, this leads to difficulty in acquiring data on threats. The dearth of quality datasets is a common complaint in the cyber security research community. This issue is multiplied by the resistance of businesses to release data when they are successfully attacked.

From an experiment perspective the challenge of threats is how to include them in controlled environments. This issue comes down to how you want to model and emulate threats as adversaries, in most cases, will not willingly join an experiment. A **threat model** is a formal means to represent a specific adversary (threat). From an operational perspective a threat model is often in the context of your organization, resources, and entities, and their capabilities and intent. However, for research there are various characteristics of threats around which threats can be modeled.

As we mentioned previously, one common way to model threats are by their capabilities. This is often a crucial portion of the so-called threat equation. **Capability** is the resources, means, training, and abilities of the threat to conduct their attack against a vulnerability to achieve their objective (and coincidentally) cause harm. Capabilities can be measured in money and time (seconds, days, months, etc.), but it is important to note that, again, cyber space is a great equalizer. It might cost millions of dollars and years to develop exploit but it might only take weeks for the second threat to adopt and use the exploit for their objectives. Additionally, resources are rarely specialized. That is to say, while expertise is important, the rarity and uniqueness of cyber-attacks are not predicated on a highly controlled material, process, or know-how (as compared to nuclear weapons, or rare chem/bio specimens). Cyber space is all around and so capabilities for cyber-attack (and defense) can be a great equalizer.

Another simple model that is well accepted to categorize threats at a high level is developed around intent. Table 14.1 defines the categories of threats. In the past, these categories more tended to represent capabilities, both expertise and resources. However, with the capitalization of vulnerabilities and exploits, the same advanced tools that state-sponsored threats use can be purchased and utilized by nonexperts or so-called script-kiddies. This categorization now more suitably follows intent or objectives.

In the cyber context, **intent** refers to the motivation, objectives, and mission of the threat. It connotes deliberate forethought, but not all adversarial consequences are deliberate. Differing threats will have drastically varying intent. Nonthinking sources of risk cannot have intent, it is intrinsic to threats. It is

Table 14.1 Categories of Threats by Intent

Category of Threat	Description of Intent
State-sponsored	Economic and military disruption-based attacks. This can include industrial espionage and critical infrastructure damage.
Organized crime	Profit-based attacks. They generally represent the category of tool developers for sale and represent highly skilled capabilities that can be bought through tools or provide bot farms as attack platforms.
Hacktivists	Politically motivated attacks. Their goal is to make a statement of their political views through cyber-attacks.
Hackers/Crackers (aka criminal hackers)	This category represents independently motivated threat actors. Threat actors from this category generate sets of vulnerabilities for the black market. Script kiddies are now included within this category as it is so easy for them to get access to very powerful tools.

worth noting that intent is often a crucial factor for criminal liability. In 1962, the American Law Institute published the Model Penal Code, which aimed to help reduce the ambiguity around culpability, or mens rea, in US courts. They identified degrees of intent: purposely, knowingly, recklessly, negligently.[10]

Threats have motivation and intent but they must use tools to inflict their damage. Another attribute around which threats can be modeled is their TTP. TTP is a tradecraft term that stands for *Tactics, Techniques, and Procedures* for cyber behavior (often criminal, or adversarial in nature). This term came from the US military from conventional conflict. This is sometimes alternatively expanded to Tools, Techniques, and Procedures. TTP is often used to help characterize and describe how adversaries operate. This can be thought of as the modus operandi or calling card in a traditional criminal investigation. But, it is important to understand that TTP, like most anything in cyber space can be faked, so using TTP for validation of identity can be problematic by itself. *Tactics* include how resources and skills are applied to accomplish mission objectives. The term *techniques* describe the processes, methods, and approaches employed to achieve mission objectives (see the similarities in cyber space). *Procedures* are the proscribed sequence of events and actions or the cause and effect. Tools are the equipment and capabilities employed. Given the heavy reliance on technology and tools in cyber space, the TTP discussion should include the technologies and tools leveraged by the adversary, as well. Malware is a common vector threats use through various stages of executing attacks. As with threat actors, there are categories of malware that exist. And similar to threats, we can also categorize malware based on its objective. Table 14.2 provides a description of the different categories of malware.

Table 14.2 Taxonomy of Malware

Type of Malware	Description	Example
Adware	Malware that injects advertisements into the user's experience to entice clicking on links to products.	Bonzi Buddy, Cydoor, Gator
Ransomware	Malware that holds hostage, i.e. prevents access to, cyber resources via encryption or other mechanisms to force users to pay a ransom to get it back.	CryptoLocker, TeslaCrypt
Virus	Malware that alters the operation of a system in an unauthorized way and upon execution infect, or copies itself into other system files or resources.	Anna Kournikova, ILOVEYOU
Worm	Malware similar to viruses, but which has the ability to self-replicate without user interaction.	Blaster, Code Red, Sasser
Trojan	Malware that appears as something innocuous or desirable, but actually executes unauthorized behavior.	Sub7, Koobface
Backdoor/Remote administration tool (RAT)	Malware that, when executed, establishes an unauthorized access to a system.	Sobig, MyDoom, Back Orifice
Bot	Malware that executes an automated agent for a threat actor. A bot executes actions on behalf of the threat actor.	Confiker, Kraken, Zeus
Spyware	Malware that sensors and collects unauthorized information about a user.	Finspy, Zlob
Rootkit	Malware that attempts to hide its existence by integrating with and using operating system kernel resources.	Sony BMG copy protection

Finally, threats can be modeled around the actions they must take to achieve an attack. Lockheed Martin coined the term *Cyber Kill Chain*, which is a model for how threats conduct attacks on target systems.[11] Alternatively, Microsoft has introduced the Stride Threat Model: spoofing, tampering, repudiation, nonrepudiation, denial of service, and elevation of privilege.[12]

A common way to quantify threats is through risk modeling. **Risk** is sometimes represented notationally as an equation, *Risk = threat × vulnerabilities × consequence*. This might be useful at an abstract level, but tends to reduce complex issues and challenges to overly simplistic equations. Many in the field feel that a static algebraic equation does not capture the dynamic and changing nature of cyber conflict, and some suggest a function such as *Risk = f(threat, vulnerabilities, consequence)*, which encapsulate more complex relationships between the variables. Often attempting to reduce an entire organization's risk to a single number or value is misleading, the end result might be less important than the process itself of surveying systemic vulnerabilities, evaluating grave corporate consequences, and understanding the threat landscape. Risks can be addressed in, traditionally, four different ways: *Owned/acknowledged; mitigated/reduced; transferred; or avoided*. A risk that is owned or acknowledged, means that a process and review has been undertaken to understand the nature of the risk, the impacts to the organization, and that the level of risk has been accepted by the appropriate parties in the organization as tolerable. Risks that are mitigated or reduced are sources of harm that have had active or passive controls put in place to lessen or eliminate harmful consequences should that risk materialize. NIST SP 800-30 rev. 1 defines *risk* as, "Risk is a measure of the extent to which an entity is threatened by a potential circumstance or event." ISO Guide 73:2009 Risk management—Vocabulary defines risk as, "effect of uncertainty on objectives."[13] Several risk management terms are defined in that standard as well. While we have already defined threat, there are two additional variables we must define for the risk equation.

Vulnerability can be defined as a weakness or limitation that can be exploited to cause harm. While classically, vulnerabilities are thought to be flaws or bugs in software and hardware, it is important to understand that a vulnerability is anything that can cause harm. This could include assumptions made in supply chain or financial decisions based upon flawed prediction, and so on. The issue to remember is that while bugs (nonvalidated input, unbounded variable) are often the first topic to spring to mind as a type of vulnerability, issues such as supply chain security, staff retention policies, and even denial of service (in several guises) are all vulnerabilities as well. NIST SP 800-30 rev. 1 defines vulnerability as "a weakness in an information system, system security procedures, internal controls, or implementation that could be exploited by a threat source."[14]

DIG DEEPER: CONSEQUENCE BASED RISK ANALYSIS

Let's propose, for the sake of argument, that consequence-informed risk management should be the primary means of evaluating cyber risk. It seems unreasonable for any organization, no matter how many resources they have, to enumerate, identify, and understand all their vulnerabilities. Similarly, while open source intelligence and sources are very useful in providing information on threats, it is also unreasonable to expect organizations (outside of the very large) to staff threat intelligence analysts who can monitor and identify how global trends and actions might translate to specific issues for their employer. This, of course, leaves consequence. And consequences, or impact, is the very topic that anyone should be prepared to evaluate. What is most important to you? To the function of your core business? Your customer's? and so on. This is not to say that consequence analysis is easy, often far from it, (What are the dependences, both hidden and overt, for example?), but any well-run organization, from a family to a multinational corporation, should understand what sort of disruptions and harm can be least tolerated. And from this, plans can be made for household evacuations in case of fire, and prepared press releases in case of PII compromise for a corporation. Finally, consequence or impact costs can be quite well quantified, which will help with identifying appropriate levels of investments for countermeasures and remediation.

The final variable in the risk equation is consequence. **Consequence** is often synonymous with impact. This is traditionally understood to address both the magnitude and type of harm, damage, or loss to a system. This harm is due to a vulnerability that a threat exploited. The threat may not have intended every consequence that occurred, and they may have and affected a consequence that is not currently observed. Impact or consequence is often given in qualitative or downright fuzzy terms, such as low, medium, and high. While this might be useful for ordinal ranking, if it can be relied upon as impartial and accurate, the level of ambiguity for consequence is often too much to enable mathematical or quantitative analysis. This is not to say it cannot be done. Consequence-driven design and other approaches (design-basis threat) can be quite successful and are predicated upon a rigorous analysis of consequence. Consequence can also be measured, like capabilities, in terms of lost revenue, resources, time, and even reputation. While much of this can be reduced to money the intangible consequences such as reputation, opportunity loss, and staff are not to be overlooked. Often the concept of the risk equation includes a concept of likelihood. How likely is this consequence to occur based upon a threat-taking advantage of a vulnerability? History is replete with examples of defenders not understanding the likelihood. This is often the weakness in risk and consequence-based approaches. Suffice to say as little assumptions as possible should be made about the likelihood of cyber events. Consequence should be predicated on annual severity. In time, perhaps frequency and likelihood will be better understood, which would be a boon to the insurance and actuarial fields. NIST SP 800-30 rev. 1 defines *impact* as: "The level of impact from a threat event is the magnitude of harm that can be expected to result from the consequences of unauthorized disclosure of information, unauthorized modification of information, unauthorized destruction of information, or loss of information or information system availability."[15]

ADVERSARIES IN OTHER FIELDS OF STUDY

The notion of adversarial engagement and understanding are hardly new to this field of cyber security. The history of civilization and mankind is replete with conflict. An exploration of other fields of inquiry into conflict and adversarial understanding can be conducted for two reasons. First, is to not repeat the successes or failures of other fields. Science is the culmination of understanding and effort. Building on the shoulders of others is not only expected, it is how the field progresses. Second, other fields can often offer insights or new ways of thinking that might not directly port to cyber space, but can be a starting point or inspiration for further inquiry. Other fields of study can bring useful ways of looking at the problems and tools for understanding and measuring that we can apply, specifically here, to adversarial understanding. This can include military science, criminology, conflict studies, common law, and even scientific collaboration.

Military science is inherently an adversarial field of study. This particular scientific field focuses on observational and theoretical explorations of both conflict (war fighting), and the systems and processes within military organizations. The study of conflict is divided into three categories: strategic war, operational war, and tactical war. Strategy is focused on the top-level context, policy, and security of a nation. The operational level, unsurprisingly couples the tactical to the strategic, by mapping the high-level objectives to the lower level tactics, and informing strategic decisions with tactical results. The tactical level includes the methods and ideas for accomplishing military objectives. Tactical war can be referred to as "the art and science of winning engagements and battles."[16] Sounds familiar, doesn't it? Furthermore, Karl von Clausewitz stated: "Unlike any other science or art, in war the object reacts."[17] This seems so strikingly familiar to the conversations surrounding cyber security and the challenges in dealing with the intelligent adversary. Indeed, the exploration of applying science, or research methods, to the military is often met with exasperation, and that science cannot be applied beyond the material, the technology, and so on.

Conflict studies as a field is an outgrowth of Western thinking about war, conflict, and peace in the 20th and 21st centuries. Sometimes called Peace and Conflict Studies (PACS), it involves aspects of various social sciences, political science, geography, history, economics, and philosophy. Some consider the peace and conflict studies departments as the opposite of military science. That is to say that conflict studies' aim is to study and understand conflict, war, and peace to enable lasting peace, whereas some argue that military science is the study of war, warfighting, and conflict to win. These points of view are simplistic and belie the fact that there is considerable overlap in these topic areas. Often military personnel take peace and conflict studies as part of their coursework. Conflict studies can also cover intranational issues such as civil rights, violent and nonviolent protest, police militarization, privacy, use of force, citizen rights, and so on. When looking for methods to understand and deal with the adversary, quantitative approaches may be limited in conflict studies. While military science produced the Lanchester Doctrine of how much opposing force is needed with a mathematical equation,[18] peace, and conflict studies could provide a cyber security researcher with qualitative means to understand intent and motivation of adversarial action, including context and socioeconomic factors.

During WWI, Frederick W. Lanchester was an automotive researcher. He worked to formulate mathematical equations to represent concentration of force in adversarial combat. He first characterized a linear model for close-based, mêlée combat. Subsequently, he developed a square law formula for ranged combat. He acknowledged that artillery and aerial forces were out of scope. The application of these models are best for tactical, full force engagements. If engagements utilize only partial elements, including weather, cover, terrain asymmetries, suppression, and fire control, then the current relevancy and use of the models are limited. Note, it would be interesting to explore, further, how these models might apply to cyber conflict, if at all.

While stretching far afield, the western legal framework of common law, is itself adversarial in nature. Much like the Devil's Advocate, the common law legal system (as opposed to civil law) is built upon judicial findings. Common law systems were traditionally found in England and its colonial heirs (United Kingdom, Canada, United States, New Zealand, Australia, Malaysia, Hong Kong, Singapore, South Africa, etc.). Alternatively, civil law was spread throughout much of Europe, Middle and South America, Russia, and their colonial heirs. Civil law is also called Roman Law, based upon codified civil, or civilian laws, as determined by the people. A distinction between the systems is the use of judges and judicial findings. To over simplify, judicial findings in civil law are limited to the case as hand, and so no precedent. On the other hand, in common law, the ruling often do set, or contribute to precedent. These common law, judicial findings are typically based upon an adversarial engagement between prosecution and defendant. In civil law an inquisitorial system is used. In an inquisitorial system the court itself, is involved in the investigation and determining of facts.

DID YOU KNOW?

Louisiana's noncriminal law is similar to civil law found elsewhere in the world, and is the only outlier for common law in the United States.

The Devil's Advocate is the colloquial name for Advocatus Diaboli, or the Defender of Faith, Promotor Fidei, which was a position in the Catholic Church that represented the opposing position for any candidate for Sainthood. This position was first established in 1587 by Pope Sixtus V.[19] This position was made optional and greatly lessoned by Pope John Paul II in 1983.[20] Additionally, the term *Adversary* has been used to refer to the Biblical Devil, Satan. Indeed, the Hebrew word, שָׂטָן, Satan, means, among other things, Adversary.

Additionally, in common law, the court sets precedent, that is to say, rulings, findings, and opinions, from courts are often cited in subsequent court cases and law. This is opposed to the civil law approach that does not empower the courts to define the rule of law per se, and only allows for code or civil laws, defined by the legislature to influence subsequent findings. (Note: this is a very high level summary, with many sweeping generalizations.) The intent is not to provide an introduction to Western legal systems but to illustrate, yet another aspect of our lives, that calls upon a formalized understanding of adversarial behavior to, in this case, dispense justice. The role and plaintiff and defendant are very well understood. And the legal system is used to dealing with, understanding, and resolving adversarial contexts. In the application to cyber security, there is first the obvious, cyber security law. Many of the actions that cyber security defenders must deal with, and researchers address, are criminal acts. Understanding the context of legal system, even before jumping to cyber security specific statutes or laws, can be helpful in understanding the larger context. Typically, the law lags technology and in cyber environments and cyber security, this is, definitely, no exception. Cyber security researchers should be familiar with the laws and legal issues that are relevant. This topic will be discussed more fully in Chapter 15, Scientific Ethics. Secondarily, however, is the formalized approach to dealing with conflict. Legal systems are set up to acknowledge and deal with conflict. The language, formalisms of the law profession can be leveraged by researchers to help constrain and formalize the language and representation of information in our own research.

DIFFERENT WAYS TO THINK ABOUT THREATS

In this section, we will introduce various aspects of adversarial behavior, and study that can be a challenge for a researcher. These topics include attribution, the adversaries own perspective, and adversaries versus threats. This will be an exploration of these issues to provide context and background for readers. Not every issue will be confronted by every researcher on every project, but reviewing these topics will help to ensure that appropriate context for adversaries is considered in cyber security research.

Given the discussions in previous sections about adversary, threat, vulnerability, and so on, you can understand that there are different ways to understand, model, qualify, and study threats. Using the industry standard NIST 800-37[21] framework for cyber security risk management, we can divide the conversation of threats and their risks into three layers: Organization (governance), Business/Mission processes (essential functions for information and information flows), and system (IT/OT; environment of operation). This delineation is as useful as any to understand the different types of risks, and therefore different threats that an organization might face.

It is important to point out that all risk are *not* technical in nature. For example, a flaw in a business governance (e.g., not having a CISO or not having sufficient oversight between IT and security, or IT and physical security) could easily lead to exploitation and damage of the business. Similarly, insufficient knowledge of information flow (how do you backup?; how often?; where?; testing?) combined with an out-of-date understanding of how 3rd-party and customers' interface with your information systems could provide yet another avenue. By now readers can imagine any number of system vulnerabilities that would lead to compromise and damage.

Adversary Perspective

It is very important to realize that *adversaries do not look at target systems in isolation*. If they are interested in stealing secrets from a secure server, they might go after offsite tape backups, or through a 3rd party who has a maintenance contract, and so on. The key is to not study systems in isolation. The three tiers from NIST are clearly interdependent. They help to breakout and understand the different types of risks but should not be treated in isolation. What happens in one layer will undoubtedly affect the others. The adversary will study the systems as a whole, from where the VPs send their children to school, to the subcontract details on the food service providers. This can seem like an overwhelming challenge for defenders, and sometimes it is. But the goal is to understand the modalities and the way the adversary operates, thinks, and acts.

Now that we have explored a valid framework for articulating risks to the system, we need to point out that this is not how the adversary thinks, per se. That is not to say that all the previous thinking or material should be thrown away, indeed that is not the case. The critical issue is that often the way the defender conceives of their system, purpose, and objectives, are clearly, quite different from the adversaries' understanding of the system, purpose, and their own objectives. Two examples to help identify this distinction.

First a defender might consider the domain controller the crown jewels to the enterprise, indeed the domain controller and its privileged admin accounts provide "keys to the kingdom" protecting this is vital because as we have learned while this is at the system level, it clearly affects the information, and even organizational level if compromise is grave enough. A defender might focus on the domain controller protection, extensively, which again is good. But realizing that the adversary does not want the domain controller, but, it is, possibly, one avenue to obtain their objectives. If they want specific files, there are several paths to achieve this.

Defining Adversaries as Threats

Several aspects are important when studying and attempting to understand adversarial behavior. First, be careful in assuming you understand their objective. False flag or 5th column activities can muddy what appears to be a straightforward attack. Threat objectives is ultimately one of the hardest topics on which to achieve clarity. Continuing to understand adversaries would include knowledge of their capabilities. I would refer the reader back again to Fig. 14.1: DoD Cyber Adversary Tiers. Understanding that not all threats are equal, not all threat actors have similar skills, resources or abilities, will help enable a more nuanced study and observation of this aspect of cyber security research. Contextualizing adversaries into whatever modalities you prefer (DoD tiers) common label (hacktivist, organized crime, nation state, etc.) will all add more precision and fidelity that the overloaded, often inaccurate "hacker" label.

DIG DEEPER: FALSE FLAGS AND 5TH COLUMNS

False flags is a term from spycraft when one actor will plant or leave, indicators and evidence that they are associated with a different organization or country. This could be as simple as wearing a uniform of another country, or as complex as mimicking TTP, language, and stylistic details of another cyber actor. Similarly, the 5th column is a hidden element within an organization or contrary that covertly works to subvert the objectives of the host. This is akin to an organization or a group of insider threats.

In addition to understanding capabilities, adversary Tactics, Techniques, and Procedures can be studied to better understand how they operate, what their intentions are, and perhaps even attribute them to a specific organization. This line of inquiry requires, often, considerable information to be collected from the various IT systems throughout the adversary campaign. Models such as the Cyber Kill Chain, conceptualized by Lockheed Martin, can be used to collect information (some of which will be outside the victim network, and very hard to get) and the rest (inside) might be tampered on unavailable. Alternative approaches would include lurking on various criminal and semicriminal message boards, website, and darknet forums. Open source information is often provided to the public free of charge from commercial organizations and other researchers. Often the raw information is missing, but the information can be a reasonable starting point. Organizations with an appropriate risk tolerance can actually set up a Honeypot or Honeynet.[22] This can be a very hard system to set up and integrate, but it can be an invaluable source of information. The key challenges are to ensure that the honeypot is of sufficient quality and realism so that sophisticated threats do not realize that they are not on a real system. However, you also do not want to allow any vital resources to be compromised, or worse your systems to be used to compromise some other organization. Similarly, the integration of the honeynet into your operations network can be a technical challenge. For more details on Honeypots refer to Chapter 13, Instrumentation.

Attribution

Attribution is the process of making a determination of what threat actors performed an attack. To understand threat actors it is necessary to attribute actions to them; however, this can be a complex undertaking. Depending on your research context and objective, this could be a major hurdle or a nonissue. The first disclaimer, is that indeed, attribution is hard. Tracing the source of an attack, malware, or event, back to the origin is fraught with technical, political, jurisdictional, cultural, and financial barriers. Attribution is typically only needed in forensic (criminal and civil court proceedings), nation-state actions, and now, more recently, in political discourse. Even if all those various challenges were addressed, the final mapping between cyber space and real space, between the computer and user, is often tenuous at best. Research many not care about attribution, and often it is in the researcher's best interest to ensure anonymity. If you are conducting interviews or surveying cyber active individuals, often anonymity and nonaccountability will be very important. Ensuring that information collected will not be attributed to you might be the only way or securing your collaboration.

Additional issues to touch upon are the legal burdens required in evidence collection, handling, and presentation for cyber-crimes. While conducted today in various courts around the world, there is hardly consensus on the appropriate methods, sufficient due diligence, and so on. As a point of fact, some of the common real-world approaches for collection, examination, and presentation of DNA, fingerprints, and bullet trajectory are being called into question as insufficiently grounded in science.[23,24,25] This does not bode well for cyber security forensics.

Another issue is hack back, sometimes called active defense. If more organizations felt they had solid attribution, they might take overt or covert action to eliminate the threats and deter future action. While often outright illegal, some gray area exists. Collaboration with law enforcement is also an option for companies that are pursuing this course of action. From a research point of view this aspect is not well understood. For obvious reasons, it is very hard to determine how widespread, and perhaps it might even increase as technology continues to permeate our lives. The ethics of attack back are discussed in Chapter 15, Scientific Ethics.

INTEGRATING ADVERSARY MODELS INTO RESEARCH

Adversarial modeling can mean different things to defenders, researchers, theorists, and practitioners. Given the research focus of this text, we will use the phrase to connote a scientifically useful representation of the adversary. (Note: This need not be simulated, or even mathematical, to be an adversary model.)

Approaches

Many different approaches exist in modeling adversaries for use in research. One traditional model of the adversary is the cryptographic Eve. In cryptography researchers, and moreover students, consider the system where Alice and Bob are legitimate communicating parties.[26] Eve is an eavesdropper who would like to surreptitiously interfere with their communication. To enable security proofs Eve is given varying levels of access and capabilities. To determine under what circumstances a cryptographic algorithm is secure, you must consider what information is known to Eve, Alice, and Bob, what methods are there for securing communication (symmetric, and asymmetric cryptography), and what resources are available to Eve. Generally, Eve is not assumed to have infinite resources, but is roughly assumed to have resources equivalent to the computing resources for the entire planet for several years into the future. The determination of how many resources and of what kind (quantum computing for example) is an important and sometimes overlooked aspect of the discussion. Given this context, cryptography attempts to prove that the mathematical encipherment of the plaintext will remain secure given the mathematical foundations, for example substitution—permutation cipher (Rijndael and AES), discrete log (public key), prime factorization (hashes), while cryptanalysis attempts to break them.

Another means of exploring adversarial behavior that is commonly used is game theory. Many books have been written on this topic and many papers on its application to cyber security contests. There are, however, a few key points to consider when using game theory for cyber security; game theory doesn't handle uncertainty well. The incomplete knowledge of game state, incomplete knowledge of moves or actions (both your own and adversary) or even an ability to bound what moves are possible, all make it very difficult to use game theory. For a more in-depth discussion of using game theory for cyber security, read Chapter 7, Formal Theoretical Research.

In experimental research, we have red teaming. Red teaming is also variously called tiger teaming, penetration (pen) testing, security evaluation/testing, and so on. In red teaming, the approach is to identify a core team of staff with a high degree of cyber security training and experience, especially on the offensive side. Teams are used in multiple ways. Traditionally, red teaming consists of searching an environment for vulnerabilities and pathways into a system. This could range from a tabletop plan and critique all the way to a multimonth full scope cyber security, social engineering, campaign to compromise, and gain entry into the operational system under evaluation. Two key skillsets are required, the first is experience and knowledge of how to compromise, attack, exploit, and take advantage of the target system. This skillset will obviously vary depending on the system under test. The second skillset, which is equally important, but constant, is the ability to communicate, document, and recommend. Recommendations are usually context-specific and include the experience from the team on how to address the vulnerabilities and weaknesses that they found.

There are two very important additional takeaways when using red teaming: coverage and validity. Given the highly human expert—centric nature of this sort of model, there is little assurance that all vulnerabilities were addressed and that nothing more is lurking in the shadows. No one would claim that, and no one should expect that. Ideally triage, based on a shared prioritization scheme, was used to ensure high value and high consequence, and adversary relevancy was used to determine what to evaluate. Even a continuous pen test could not ensure complete coverage. Second, is determining the validity, or generalizability, of the red teams you use to the actual adversaries. Pen testers come from all walks of life, but it can be very hard to ensure that multiple adversary TTPs are included without considerable resources.

Finally, a second tool for experimentation is simulating or emulating a threat. Simulation of adversaries can take on many forms. A simple fuzz test on a protocol, or stress test on a device simulate normal (and moreover) abnormal use and behavior. Other tools might include hardware and network simulators. Technology such as SteelCentral from riverbed (formerly OPNET),[27] and NS3[28] are commonly used for network traffic. These technologies understood and used environments to model aspects of cyber systems, but the adversary component, however, continues to be a challenge. At the end of the day, what we are asking for, is a complete, well-informed, dynamic model of human agency—something that currently eludes the best minds in A.I. research. However, pieces of it are available, technology such as Simspace,[29] Deter Agents Simulating Humans,[30] and open solutions such as Python.[31] Alternatives to modeling all human agency, can break the challenge into more tractable problems. For example, modelings of HTTP traffic for entertainment websites, or news, could be used to provide components to develop over time. See Chapter 8, Using Simulation for Research, for more details on how simulation is used in cyber security research.

Challenges

Along with the various approaches to integrate adversarial behavior into research, come challenges and issues. Several of these have been mentioned already, but a few deserve special mention.

Coevolution

One of the fundamental attributes of cyber security is the coevolutionary nature of cyber conflict. First the adversary takes some action, to steal, destroy, or tease. This causes the defender community to circle-up develop protections, build firewalls, and perimeter sensors, develop access controls and policies for behavior. This in turn encourages the adversaries to develop new technologies and new means of achieving their objectives. They move to where the defenders focus is now (hardware, OS, browser, plug in, user, it doesn't ultimately matter to them). Call it a cyber arms race, call it human nature, but this single aspect differentiates cyber security research from most other sciences. In physical and natural sciences, the universe is not actively and intelligently conspiring against us. Even in medicine and criminology, where the subjects do lie, mislead, and have ulterior motives, the resources of the scientist and the defender, usually outstrip any of the subjects. But in cyber space this too is backward. Offensive resources and development far outstrip defensive, and classically, multiple equally useful points of entry exist for an adversary to take advantage of. A key issue that is not always recognized in the discourse about defense and offense is the unintended consequences.

Developers of malware clearly realize that once released into the wild anyone can understand, play with, and use (be it defenders, or other aggressors). The challenge is when targeted or limited impact is desired, targeting some machines but not others is a challenge. But, moreover, understanding the consequences of both the action and the potential for others to replicate the same action can be a challenge to appreciate. For example, a kinetic weapon, a bomb, delivered to a target, will likely have the intended consequence, in a given radius with a known plus or minus of consequence and area.

A cyber weapon given to a target, will have a hopeful consequence known, a initial area known, but all downstream areas are now up for grabs. The nature of this dichotomy is twofold. First determinism of consequence in complex systems such as cyber or cyber-physical are not well understood. Second, unlike kinetic weapons that are destroyed (albeit leaving substantial evidence) cyber weapons are hard to fully destroy. Furthermore, having the cyber weapon is much closer to using the cyber weapon than for kinetic equivalents. This coevolutionary nature, of course, works both ways. Since a new defensive technique is deployed, the impact (both in terms of cost and performance) should be well understood, and the anticipated adversal adaptation should be explored. Perhaps it is better to leave the status quo, so as not to encourage the adversary to evolve, and change, because that might put the defender in a more precarious circumstance. Either way, understanding the impact, the downstream consequence, and the adaptation are vital in and exploration of cyber conflict.

Normalization

Another challenge is the limited ability to measure and quantify cyber security in the absence of an adversary, let alone with an active threat present. Granted there would be no need for security without a threat, but assume for a moment, that is system is not under current attack in any manner, how would you measure security, the status, operations, progress, cost, surplus capacity, deficit, and so on. This is only compounded when an intelligent, motivated, resourced, adversary is added into the mix. Another aspect of this is the normalization of the experience. That is to say, as a researcher we might introduce a silver bullet, in the lab, and under rigorous testing its performance quite well, cost, effectiveness, color, everything. The challenge remaining would be to compare this to any off-the-shelf solution to determine how well it performs in context. This however is not a fair challenge, because the adversary has had time to scrutiny test, evaluate, and break the competition, but has no time, yet with your tool. This issue renders such comparison suspect, but is very hard to address in a research setting. Ultimately, limited testing can be done to evaluate this aspect, but this limitation, like all other limitations should be noted.

A corollary to this normalization challenge is the inclusion of red teams in cyber security research. Ignoring the validity of the red team to an adversary, for the moment, how do you normalize the red team so that you have a consistent equitable evaluation "force" for the duration of the study. For example, if one wanted to red team the commercial solution and the research solution, how many red teams would you need? If you have more than one how do you ensure they are consistently skilled? How do you ensure they have the same operating conditions? Do you give the red team evaluating your technology the source code, design specs, and so on, to level the playing field? Say you run a campaign first against the commercial tool, will they then use that knowledge in the second campaign? If they switch from commercial to research tool, how do they ensure consistency of knowledge and process? It becomes very hard to normalize human beings themselves, which is what an Subject Matter Expert (SME), pen test, or red team, really is. This problem will take acknowledgments of all limitations and concerns, and repeated trials by the community to understand what protocols and methods work best in situations like these.

Modeling the Use of Community Knowledge

Similar to the normalization challenge is the challenge of measuring the impact of community knowledge. As we discussed previously, the current situation is that even inexperienced and unskilled threat actors can get their hands on highly advanced tools that enable them to wield power similar to organized crime or nation states. Through dark net markets and forums, the knowledge and techniques to exploit well-defended systems is easily disseminated. This leads to the challenge of quantifying this effect in applied experiments. Using red teams or existing exploits suites to assess the security performance of new applied solutions is a common approach. However, there is almost never accounting for the confounding variable of community knowledge investment. To improve process, it is important to discuss why this variable is important and we will provide our thoughts on how to address it.

The pen testing tools and exploit kits that are used by red teams and threat sources consists of a suite of capabilities to find and exploit discovered vulnerabilities. Each one of these tools consists of large investment both in the time to research and discover vulnerabilities that are exploitable and effort to develop and weaponize these exploits to be usable in attacker tools. When these tools are used to assess the performance of a new solution against previous solutions, the metric is often the amount of time to successfully break the system if at all. However, this is not a fair comparison. The amount of time invested in the tools in researching current solution weaknesses is significant. Therefore, if tools exist that enable the easy exploitation of current solutions, you can't just measure the time it takes to run the tools; you have to account for the effort to develop them. This unfair comparison often leads to a quick exploitation of current solutions and either much slower or unsuccessful exploitation of the new solution, which makes it appear that the new solution performs better. However, if an investment of 6 months of study and development went into the tool used on the current solution, then a fair comparison would be to give the red team or researchers 6 months to see if they can come up with an equal or faster way to exploit the new solution.

Given this challenge, the question leads to how best to integrate it into our research process. As it is difficult and impossible to quantify how much time was invested in tools, we need a way to capture relative costs. Fortunately, markets have formed around exploits that quantify their value.[32] Some of this value is accounted for by the market size of the target, which is confounding; however, mostly this value is based on demand, which relates to lack of supply and the difficulty of developing them, which is perfect for our needs. Therefore, if we map effort to a dollar amount, such as hour of effort equals $200, then we have our measure of effort. Now if a prepackaged exploit tool is used in an applied experiment, we can quantify how much previous effort was required to give a more fair assessment of the defensive performance of the new solution.

CONCLUSIONS

Dealing with the adversary is one of the most challenging, yet intriguing and important aspects of cyber security research. We would encourage readers not to worry about understanding or designing the perfect representation for the adversary for your research or development. Instead, make sure that consideration for adversal perspective is included in all aspects of your work. Perfection is never required, but diligence is. This would include acknowledgments where your research might deviate from adversarial behavior, or limitations in modeling, or your own understanding. The more information that we can share about our own limitations, assumptions, and conditions, the better for other researchers to pick up the mantle and move the research forward.

This is not a call to give up on adversarial research in and of itself, either. Indeed quite the contrary, far too often, much research is done in the absence of adversarial awareness, modeling, or consideration. Designing more secure computers, or networks, without understanding how the adversary operates (or your own users) is doomed to fail. Cyber security research and development can leverage the body of work that has gone before in other domains that study conflict and human agency. Furthermore, substantial current work is available to characterize adversarial intent, methods, abilities, resources, and so on. Models of various techniques also exist to describe adversarial behavior in context. In the end, this field is fraught with limitations and challenges, but as researchers continue to answer questions about adversary-cyber-defender interactions, the entire field is advanced and development can continue its frenzied pace on a more solid foundation of knowledge.

Endnotes

1. FBI: Uniform Crime Reporting. (June 22, 2015). *Offense Analysis Number and Percent Change, 2013–2014*. Retrieved February 25, 2017, from https://ucr.fbi.gov/crime-in-the-u.s/2014/crime-in-the-u.s.-2014/tables/table-23
2. Gromicko, N. and Shepard, K. *Burglar-Resistant Homes*. Retrieved February 25, 2017, from https://www.nachi.org/burglar-resistant.htm
3. FBI: Uniform Crime Reporting. (August 20, 2015). *Crime in the United States by Metropolitan Statistical Area, 2014*. Retrieved February 25, 2017, from https://ucr.fbi.gov/crime-in-the-u.s/2014/crime-in-the-u.s.-2014/offenses-known-to-law-enforcement/murder.
4. JP 3-0 Joint Operations. (August 11, 2011). Retrieved February 25, 2017, from http://www.dtic.mil/doctrine/new_pubs/jp3_0.pdf.
5. Defense Science Board Department of Defense. (January 2013). *Resilient Military Systems and the Advanced Cyber Threat*. Retrieved February 25, 2017, from www.acq.osd.mil/dsb/reports/ResilientMilitarySystems.CyberThreat.pdf.
6. Nixon, A., Costello, J., and Wikholm, Z. (November 29, 2016). *An After-Action Analysis of the Mirai Botnet Attacks on Dyn*. Retrieved February 26, 2017, from https://www.flashpoint-intel.com/action-analysis-mirai-botnet-attacks-dyn/.

7. Muckin, M., and Finch, S. C. *A Threat-Driven Approach to Cyber Security*. Retrieved February 25, 2017, from http://lockheedmartin.com/content/dam/lockheed/data/isgs/documents/Threat-Driven%20Approach%20whitepaper.pdf.

8. Microsoft. (2005). *The STRIDE Threat Model*. Retrieved February 26, 2017, from https://msdn.microsoft.com/en-us/library/ee823878(v = cs.20).aspx.

9. Blanchard, B. W. (October 27, 2008). *Guide to Emergency Management and Related Terms, Definitions, Concepts, Acronyms, Organizations, Programs, Guidance, Executive Orders & Legislation*. Retrieved February 25, 2017, from https://training.fema.gov/hiedu/docs/terms%20and%20definitions/terms%20and%20definitions.pdf.

10. Model Penal Code and Commentaries (Official Draft and Revised Comments) (1985).

11. Martin, L. (2014). "Cyber Kill Chain®." http://cyber. lockheedmartin. com/hubfs/Gaining_the_Advantage_Cyber_Kill _Chain. pdf.

12. 9. Microsoft. (2005). *The STRIDE Threat Model*. Retrieved February 26, 2017, from https://msdn.microsoft.com/en-us/library/ee823878(v = cs.20).aspx.

13. ISO/Guide 73:2009(en). (2009). Retrieved February 26, 2017, from https://www.iso.org/obp/ui/#iso:std:iso:guide:73:ed-1:v1:en.

14. NIST Special Publication 800-30 Revision 1. (September 2012). Retrieved February 25, 2017, from http://nvlpubs.nist.gov/nistpubs/Legacy/SP/nistspecialpublication800-30r1.pdf.

15. NIST Special Publication 800-30 Revision 1. (September 2012). Retrieved February 25, 2017, from http://nvlpubs.nist.gov/nistpubs/Legacy/SP/nistspecialpublication800-30r1.pdf.

16. US Marine Corps. (June 20, 1997). *Warfighting*. Retrieved February 25, 2017, from http://www.marines.mil/Portals/59/Publications/MCDP%201%20Warfighting.pdf.

17. Gat, A. (1992). The Development of Military Thought: The Nineteenth Century. Oxford University Press.

18. Johnson, R. L. (1989). Lanchester's Square Law in theory and practice. Army Command and General Staff Coll Fort Leavenworth KS School of Advanced Military Studies.

19. Burtsell, R. (April 3, 2015). "Advocatus Diaboli." The Catholic Encyclopedia. Vol. 1. New York: Robert Appleton Company, 1907.

20. John-Paul, I. I. (1983). Divinus Perfectionis Magister.

21. NIST, S. (2010). 800-37, Revision 1. Guide for Applying the Risk Management Framework to Federal Information Systems: A Security Life Cycle Approach, 16.

22. The Honeynet Project. Retrieved February 26, 2017, from https://www.honeynet.org/.

23. Worth, K. (June 26, 2015). *The Surprisingly Imperfect Science of DNA Testing*. Retrieved February 26, 2017, from http://stories.frontline.org/dna.

24. National Research Council. (2009). *Strengthening Forensic Science in the United States: A Path Forward*. National Academies Press.

25. Ferrero, E. (March 11, 2009). *U.S. Department of Justice Failing to Enforce Critical Forensic Oversight, New Innocence Project Report Finds*. Retrieved February 26, 2017, from http://www.innocenceproject.org/u-s-department-of-justice-failing-to-enforce-critical-forensic-oversight-new-innocence-project-report-finds/.

26. Alice, Bob. (February 24, 2017). Retrieved February 26, 2017, from https://en.wikipedia.org/wiki/Alice_and_Bob.

27. Riverbed. *OPNET Technologies—Network Simulator*. Retrieved February 26, 2017, from http://www.riverbed.com/products/steelcentral/opnet.html?redirect = opnet.

28. Nsnam. Ns-3. Retrieved February 26, 2017, from https://www.nsnam.org/.

29. SimSpace. *Cyber Range Capabilities*. Retrieved February 26, 2017, from https://www.simspace.com/products-components/.

30. The DETER Project. *DETERLab Capabilities*. Retrieved February 26, 2017, from http://deter-project.org/deterlab_capabilities#dash.

31. Project Mesa Team. (January 29, 2017). *Mesa (Version 0.8.0)*. Retrieved February 25, 2017, from https://pypi.python.org/pypi/Mesa/.

32. Zerodium. *Exploit Acquisition Program*. Retrieved February 26, 2017, from https://www.zerodium.com/program.html.

## CHAPTER 15

Scientific Ethics

The prototypical academic perspective is that science is a pure form of knowledge generation, unshackled by consequence or cost. Or more plainly stated, that all knowledge gained from science is worth the effort. However, the world quite often isn't that simple. Research always has a cost; whether it is financial, time, or even suffering. Sometimes the cost of gaining some knowledge is too high to be justifiable. Or the cost of the science is greater than the benefit of the knowledge. As human beings it should be our overall objective to limit the pain and suffering of others and this philosophy must be applied to our scientific endeavors. Scientific ethics define the research world norms that direct what is and isn't philosophically acceptable and justifiable science.

Ethics play an important role in all science by ensuring that scientists behave in justifiable ways. As cyber security involves protecting users from attacks, it is critical that researchers do not put users at additional risk in the pursuit of knowledge. Ethics for cyber security research defines what types of researches are risky, and processes to ensure that research is ethically executed. However, the application of ethics is not always clearly distinguishable. In this chapter, we will provide an overview of the current ethics for cyber security research and discuss some common scenarios that fall in a grey area of ethics.

CHAPTER OBJECTIVES

- Defining scientific ethics
- Providing an overview of the history of scientific ethics and why they were formed
- Contextualizing scientific ethics for cyber security research
- Describe ethical guidelines for cyber security research

ETHICS FOR SCIENCE

As cyber security professionals, our objective should be to make the world a better place. Meaning, our research should lead to improvement in the safety and

367

Research Methods for Cyber Security. DOI: http://dx.doi.org/10.1016/B978-0-12-805349-2.00015-7

security for users of cyber space. However, science can be used incorrectly such that it causes more harm than good. It is the duty of all scientists to evaluate the worth of the research, not just from a perspective of novelty and impact, weighing the usefulness of the results with the cost of collecting it. Every research field is guided by a set of ethics on what is and is not acceptable research.

Morality is a set of guiding principles in determining what is right and wrong. Morality is often viewed from the perspective of individuals. However, the study and application of morality at a group or society scale is **ethics**. Ethics, in the general sense, define acceptable behaviors for individuals within a community. Each community defines its own ethics and ethics evolve overtime.

Scientific ethics are a set of accepted guidelines on what constitutes justifiable research actions and those behaviors that are intolerable. While there are some generally held ethics across all research, such as knowingly causing physical harm to people is not acceptable, each field of study develops their own ethics. Professional bodies often codify these ethics and journals and conferences enforce them by preventing the publication of unethical research.

You may ask, why is ethics so important for research? Shouldn't it be obvious when research is going too far? Well it is not always a simple cut-and-dry answer. For instance, researching cures to diseases. It could be very informative to experiment by infecting people with diseases to learn how they behave and respond to different treatments. Cures for some diseases could be found this way. However, this could lead to many test subjects dying. This leads to the moral question, is causing the death of a few worth the potential to save many? Depending on your governing philosophy either answer is justifiable.

While there are many differing philosophies of thought, two philosophies are normally referenced for research. The **common good** philosophy is an ethical structure that views the context of the whole system. Therefore, individual benefit is viewed as less important than the collective benefit. This allows for situations where some individuals may be harmed if the utilitarian benefit is greater for the group. The opposing view is the **individual rights** where the individual's interests outweigh the collective. Under this philosophy it isn't okay to cause detrimental effects of even one research subject even if it would improve the situation for the rest. While the case should be viewed subjectively and there are always caveat cases, current scientific research ethics tend strongly toward personal rights as a guiding philosophy of justifiability. It is important to not connect research ethics with political or societal ethics where other philosophies can come into play.

Discussion and contemplation of ethics in cyber security research is important. As cyber space is a relatively recent and evolving phenomenon, our behavior and understanding of it is still growing. The same differences between cyber and physical space that are open questions for cyber security lead to questions in appropriate application of ethics in cyber security research. What constitutes user damage in cyber space? I think we can all agree opening people up for identity theft is damaging but what about privacy? While the research community has made decisions on some aspects of ethics of cyber security research, there is still a lot of open ethical questions that are in debate.

- *Antiworm use*: Researchers often discover new threat vectors and malware implemented to exploit vulnerabilities. These researchers could create cyber inoculations that could be sent out, much like malware, to patch systems of the discovered weaknesses and prevent further exploitation. The research community has pretty much decided that this is not ethical behavior as most organizations want to control their patch processes to ensure that patches don't cause system stability issues.
- *Attack back*: Much like the previous example, researchers can find themselves on the front lines of a threat campaign. Botnet researchers, for example, are generally the first to find how big a botnet has become and how it is controlled. This enables them to have the ability to attack the botnet and take it over. As botnets are not attacker computers but victim computers, is it ethical to attack victim computers that are being manipulated by threat actors? This is a grey area of ethical behavior. In the general case, ethically researchers should not attack unauthorized systems as defined in the next section. However, with the right legal authorization researchers have been[1] and continue to be[2] integral to shutting down command and control infrastructure of botnets.

DID YOU KNOW?

In the 2001 film Swordfish, John Travolta's character Gabriel, an American CIA operative gone rogue, used the common good philosophy to justify his attack back methodology against terrorists. He kidnapped and murdered people to rob a bank with a large amount of money to fund his war on terror. The following dialog between Travolta's Gabriel and Hugh Jackman's Stanley highlights this philosophy:

Stanley: How can you justify all this?

Gabriel: You're not looking at the big picture Stan. Here's a scenario. You have the power to cure all the world's diseases but the price for this is that you must kill a single innocent child, could you kill that child Stanley?

Stanley: No.

Gabriel: You disappoint me, it's the greatest good.

Stanley: Well how about 10 innocents?

Gabriel: Now you're getting it, how about a hundred; how about a THOUSAND? Not to save the world but to preserve our way of life.

- *Unauthorized access to computer/data*: Researchers could learn a lot about user and system behavior if they were able to access any systems they desire. Using the same techniques as malicious users, researchers could potentially gain access to any system. However, this access would be involuntary and unauthorized. Again the community has decided this is unethical behavior and has been documented in various ethical codes we will discuss later. It is also important to note this behavior is also classified as unlawful by many countries and could have criminal or civil consequences.

- *Research use of ill-gotten goods*: Ill-gotten goods refers items that have been obtained illegally. Datasets that are collected through illegal means are often released. Is it ethical to leverage these datasets in research that would not otherwise be available? Many research papers have been published[3,4] that used illegally published datasets. This is an ethical question that is still being debated[5] but at this point it seems that if the case can be made for a common good benefit the use of data that has already been released is ethical. We will discuss this in more detail later in the data privacy section.

- *Privacy*: Privacy is a major topic in the world due to how cyber space has become integrated into our lives. The definition of privacy is still in debate and what is necessary to ensure privacy in research is still uncertain. There are plenty of research examples where datasets have been released that were thought to be adequately anonymized but were found to expose private information.[6] We will discuss data privacy in more detail later in the chapter.

- *EULA and TOS (reverse engineering and web scraping)*: As the computing world has moved away from an ownership model to a licensing model, the **end user license agreement (EULA)** and **terms of service (TOS)** has become a prominent fixture in cyber space. EULAs often include restrictions on what is allowed with software and services. Restrictions often include items that are relevant to cyber security research, such as restricting reverse engineering or data collection and web scraping. Fair use, which is a concept that determines what is allowed for copyright law for educational purposes, comes into play here but again it isn't a clear-cut ethical situation. Research has been done that breaks TOS[7] but it is still an open debate on when it is ethically acceptable to break a TOS or EULA for research or not.[8]

- *Vulnerability disclosure*: One of the most discussed ethical cyber security research topics is vulnerability disclosure. Cyber security researchers are the core effort in discovering vulnerabilities in cyber space. The process of disclosing vulnerabilities presents an ethical quandary. The personal rights perspective would follow that researchers should not publicly disclose vulnerabilities until there is a fix to prevent exploitation. This leads to researchers notifying software and service vendors of the vulnerabilities. However, while vendors should have ethically fix disclosed vulnerabilities in expedient fashion, there isn't any legal or liability reason to do so. It has been found over time that not all vendors act ethically, which flips the disclosure quandary on its head. When vendors do not fix these vulnerabilities it leaves users open to exploitation.[9] Under this situation, it is more ethical to publicly disclose vulnerabilities, called **full disclosure**, to inform users of vendors who prioritize security. While this ethical situation hasn't been definitively answered, current popular practice is called responsible disclosure.[10] In **responsible disclosure** a vulnerability is first privately disclosed to a vendor. If they haven't provided adequate evidence of addressing the vulnerability within 6 months it is then publically disclosed.

HISTORY OF ETHICS IN CYBER SECURITY

Just like a field of science, ethics for research has grown and evolved over time. As researchers have pushed the bounds of knowledge they also push the bounds of societal acceptability. When questionable research has occurred, it has forced the international scientific community to develop codes of ethics to prevent others from following similar bad paths of research. Over the history of science there have been multiple examples of "bad" research that have led to our current ethical practices. Some of these ethics were so offensive that their results are generalizable to all fields of research, including cyber security research.

During World War 2, the Nazis created concentration camps for prisoners of war. At these concentration camps Nazi doctors performed experiments on the prisoners. Obviously the prisoners did not consent and were not voluntarily part of the experiments. This research was one of the great atrocities that came from World War 2. After the war, the people involved in the research were put on trial, which required the definition of ethical and legitimate research. From this the Nuremberg code[11] was developed. The Nuremberg code set forth doctrine for human subjects research including the requirements of informed participant consent, restriction of use of coercion, and limit risks to participants.

Around the same time and until the 1970s, the Tuskegee Syphilis Experiments were occurring. This research including studying the progression of untreated syphilis in African-American men. The study was established under the premises that the participants would receive free medical treatments while in the program. However, most participants were neither informed that they had syphilis nor were they informed that a treatment was found during the study. Penicillin had become the method of treatment for all syphilis diagnoses in the late 1940s, but the study researchers neither informed the participants of this nor did they provide them any treatment. The study continued until 1972 until whistleblowers leaked information to public media. The ethical problems found in this study led to the Belmont report,[12] which lays out guidelines for ethical treatment of participants in medical and behavioral research. It also led to the creation of IRBs as a check against ethical practices being followed. IRBs have become an important part of human subjects research and will be discussed at more length later in the chapter.

The field of cyber security research started as a grassroots effort through the Phreaker movement. **Phreaking**, also known as phone freaking, was a cultural movement of technologists interested in studying, understanding, and manipulating telephone communication systems. Phreakers would reverse engineer hardware and analog communication protocols to learn how the telephone systems worked and operated. One of the main objectives of this study and experimentation was to develop methods of manipulating and exploiting the systems to gain free services such as long-distance calls. Phreaking culture was the first showcase of the duality and ethical dilemmas of cyber security research. Studying and experimenting with the telephone system was not illegal or unethical. It wasn't until some in the movement used the knowledge gained to enable free phone calls that the legal lines were crossed.

DID YOU KNOW?

One of the first methods used by phreakers to get free long-distance calls was to play a 2600 Hz tone into a phone. John Draper discovered that toy whistles provided in boxes of Cap'n Crunch cereal blew a perfect 2600 Hz tone that worked to indicate an unused (free) long distance line for phreaking. Owing to this discovery, Draper was given the moniker of Captain Crunch.

In the late 1980s, a graduate student researcher at Cornell, Robert Morris, wanted study how big the Internet had become. To execute this study, the first worm was created and transmitted, using multiple exploits of vulnerable services on the unix platforms dominantly deployed across ARPANET. Morris made a mistake in how he developed the propagation of the worm such that it infected machines multiple times and DoS their operation. This was the first highly publicized cyber worm. The actions of forcefully inserting code into other unsuspecting computers was deemed not only unethical but also illegal. Morris was the first to be convicted of a felony under the Computer Fraud and Abuse Act.

The code red worm was a major security event in 2001 causing widespread damage. The code red worm exploited a vulnerability in the Microsoft IIS web server to propagate. After 20 days, an infected system would start to DoS a list of IP addresses. In response to this worm, two vulnerability researchers developed fixes for the code red worm and packaged them into worms.[13] One named code green would monitor for attacks of code red and would prevent the exploitation and then would copy itself to the attacking machine for cleaning. In this way, the code green was a self-propagating benevolent patching worm. However, the community decided that this was not ethical and presented a risk to systems that were being unauthorized patched. Even the researchers agreed with this view point and they only released source code for their patching worms. The code green worm was never released into the wild. This idea resurfaces ever so often and it has again been posited[14] to combat the massive DDoS attacks seen lately.[15]

In 2001, two groups of researchers were impacted by Digital Rights Management (DRM) researcher.[16] Ed Felton and a team of researchers had a paper covering weaknesses in the Secure Digital Media Initiative (SMDI) Digital Rights Management system. Prior to presenting the paper at the Fourth International Information Hiding Workshop, Felton was contacted by an SMDI representative stating he would be sued under the Digital Millennium Copyright Act (DMCA) if any information were publicly released about their DRM software. Felton did not present his results. With the help of the Electronic Frontier Foundation, it was declared by the courts that there was no validity in the suits. Felon finally presented the paper at the Usenix Security Workshop. Also in 2001, Dmitry Skylarov developed an ebook processing software for his employer ElcomSoft, which circumvented the DRM security protections for Adobe's eBook technology. After Skylarov presented how he cracked the ROT-13 DRM protection at DefCon, he was arrested and charged with violation of the Digital Millennium Copyright Act. Ultimately the charges were dropped. Both cases highlighted the tense interplay with cyber security and copyright laws.

In 2005, security researcher Michael Lynn was prepared to present discovered vulnerabilities within the Cisco iOS. Cisco threatened lawsuits against both the conference organizers and Lynn if the presentation was given or distributed.[17] Lynn's employer, Internet Security Systems (ISS), also tried to prevent him from presenting the researcher. Lynn ultimately quit his job and presented the vulnerabilities. Cisco and ISS filed lawsuits that were settled out of court with injunctions barring the further release of the research. This event was one of the most publicized events around public vulnerability disclosures and if it is ethical. While not definitive, the research world has agreed upon responsible disclosure.

In 2011, Aaron Swartz was arrested under the computer fraud and abuse act for connecting a computer to a switch in a network closet on the MIT university campus to automatically download papers from the JSTOR academic repository to be released as part of the open science movement.[18] The government indicted Swartz under 13 different provisions of the Computer Fraud and Abuse Act,[19] which ultimately led to his suicide in 2013. This was a highly publicized case around the new and burgeoning open science movement and its clashing with legal constructs. A group of activists and government officials have since proposed "Aaron's Law" to amend the Computer Abuse and Fraud Act (CFAA) to remove terms of service violations as being a criminal offense.

ETHICAL STANDARDS

There are no specific standards of ethical behavior for cyber security research. However, there are general standards of behavior that can be referenced as guiding behaviors. The ethical standards described in this section are those that are most pertinent to cyber security research. However, these standards do not cover all situations of cyber security research. Therefore, while it is good to follow, these standards do not assume that uncovered scenarios are automatically ethical.

Association for Computing Machinery

The Association for Computing Machinery is one of the major professional organizations for general computing research. The ACM adopted a general set of ethics applicable across all of the research fields it supports. These apply to cyber security but lack a specificity to cyber security use cases. The guidelines outlined by the ACM Code of Ethics and Professional Conduct[20] are expected to be followed and abided by every member. The following is a brief overview of the ethical codes that ACM defines.

1. GENERAL MORAL IMPERATIVES.[a]
   As an ACM member I will . . . .
   1.1 Contribute to society and human well-being.
   1.2 Avoid harm to others.

DIG DEEPER: HARM IN CYBER SPACE

The ACM Code defines "Harm" means injury or negative consequences, such as undesirable loss of information, loss of property, property damage, or unwanted environmental impacts. This principle prohibits use of computing technology in ways that result in harm to any of the following: users, the general public, employees, employers. Harmful actions include intentional destruction or modification of files and programs leading to serious loss of resources or unnecessary expenditure of human resources such as the time and effort required to purge systems of "computer viruses."

"Well-intended actions, including those that accomplish assigned duties, may lead to harm unexpectedly. In such an event the responsible person or persons are obligated to undo or mitigate the negative consequences as much as possible. One way to avoid unintentional harm is to carefully consider potential impacts on all those affected by decisions made during design and implementation." *This seems especially relevant to cyber security issues.*

    1.3 Be honest and trustworthy.

    1.4 Be fair and take action not to discriminate.

    1.5 Honor property rights including copyrights and patent.

    1.6 Give proper credit for intellectual property.

    1.7 Respect the privacy of others.

    1.8 Honor confidentiality.

2. MORE SPECIFIC PROFESSIONAL RESPONSIBILITIES.

    As an ACM computing professional I will . . . .

    2.1 Strive to achieve the highest quality, effectiveness and dignity in both the process and products of professional work.

    2.2 Acquire and maintain professional competence.

    2.3 Know and respect existing laws pertaining to professional work.

    2.4 Accept and provide appropriate professional review.

    2.5 Give comprehensive and thorough evaluations of computer systems and their impacts, including analysis of possible risks.

    2.6 Honor contracts, agreements, and assigned responsibilities.

    2.7 Improve public understanding of computing and its consequences.

    2.8 Access computing and communication resources only when authorized to do so.

3. ORGANIZATIONAL LEADERSHIP IMPERATIVES.

    As an ACM member and an organizational leader, I will . . . .

    3.1 Articulate social responsibilities of members of an organizational unit and encourage full acceptance of those responsibilities.

    3.2 Manage personnel and resources to design and build information systems that acknowledge and support proper and authorized uses of an organization's computing and communication resources.

    3.3 Ensure that users and those who will be affected by a system have their needs clearly articulated during the assessment and design of requirements; later the system must be validated to meet requirements.

    3.4 Articulate and support policies that protect the dignity of users and others affected by a computing system.

    3.5 Create opportunities for members of the organization to learn the principles and limitations of computer systems.

4. COMPLIANCE WITH THE CODE.

    As an ACM member I will . . . .

    4.1 Uphold and promote the principles of this Code.

    4.2 Treat violations of this code as inconsistent with membership in the ACM.

Ask an Ethicist

ACM provides a service where members can posit ethical questions to a board of ACM ethicists. Some of the posed questions are answered in a column. However, as ACM is a research community organization the advice is not legal advice or an endorsement by the ACM organization. However, this can be a helpful avenue for questionable research.

Institute of Electrical and Electronics Engineers

The Institute of Electrical and Electronics Engineers is another large professional society for technical fields of research. IEEE has also defined a broad code of ethics to which all members should comply.

IEEE Code of Ethics[21]

We, the members of the IEEE, in recognition of the importance of our technologies in affecting the quality of life throughout the world, and in accepting a personal obligation to our profession, its members and the communities we serve, do hereby commit ourselves to the highest ethical and professional conduct and agree:

1. to accept responsibility in making decisions consistent with the safety, health, and welfare of the public, and to disclose promptly factors that might endanger the public or the environment;
2. to avoid real or perceived conflicts of interest whenever possible, and to disclose them to affected parties when they do exist;
3. to be honest and realistic in stating claims or estimates based on available data;
4. to reject bribery in all its forms;
5. to improve the understanding of technology, its appropriate application, and potential consequences;

6. to maintain and improve our technical competence and to undertake technological tasks for others only if qualified by training or experience, or after full disclosure of pertinent limitations;

7. to seek, accept, and offer honest criticism of technical work, to acknowledge and correct errors, and to credit properly the contributions of others;

8. to treat fairly all persons and to not engage in acts of discrimination based on race, religion, gender, disability, age, national origin, sexual orientation, gender identity, or gender expression;

9. to avoid injuring others, their property, reputation, or employment by false or malicious action;

10. to assist colleagues and coworkers in their professional development and to support them in following this code of ethics.

Changes to the IEEE Code of Ethics will be made only after the following conditions are met:

- Proposed changes shall have been published in THE INSTITUTE at least three (3) months in advance of final consideration by the Board of Directors, with a request for comment, and
- All IEEE Major Boards shall have the opportunity to discuss proposed changes prior to final action by the Board of Directors, and
- An affirmative vote of two-thirds of the votes of the members of the Board of Directors present at the time of the vote, provided a quorum is present, shall be required for changes to be made.

Ten Commandments of Computer Ethics[22]

The Computer Ethics Institute was developed as a public policy group to help define ethical behavior with the use of technology. The CEI was one of the first organizations to define a set of ethics for the use of computers. The specified 10 commandments of computer ethics.

1. Thou Shalt Not Use A Computer To Harm Other People.
2. Thou Shalt Not Interfere With Other People's Computer Work.
3. Thou Shalt Not Snoop Around In Other People's Computer Files.
4. Thou Shalt Not Use A Computer To Steal.
5. Thou Shalt Not Use A Computer To Bear False Witness.
6. Thou Shalt Not Copy Or Use Proprietary Software For Which You have Not Paid.
7. Thou Shalt Not Use Other People's Computer Resources Without Authorization Or Proper Compensation.
8. Thou Shalt Not Appropriate Other People's Intellectual Output.

9. Thou Shalt Think About The Social Consequences Of The Program You Are Writing Or The System You Are Designing.

10. Thou Shalt Always Use A Computer In Ways That Insure Consideration And Respect For Your Fellow Humans.

Certification Bodies Ethics

There are multiple certification bodies for cyber security, including SANS,[23] (ISC),[2,24] ISACA,[25] and ASIS.[26] As the certifications provided by these organizations are targeted for professional cyber security practitioners and not researchers, their ethics are more guided toward performing cyber security assessments and handling user services. The group of certifications bodies formed a joint ethics board to try to create a merged ethical standard. However, nothing yet has been produced by this group.

CYBER SECURITY EXPERT CLASSIFICATION

The difference between cyber security professionals and malicious hackers can often be just the intent and ethical behavior exhibited. As the tools and techniques used by cyber security professionals can be the same as those used by malicious hackers. In the early days of cyber security becoming a profession, there was a negative perspective due to the shared techniques. In order to handle this, different classifications were defined by cyber security professionals based on their ethical and legal perspectives. These classifications were defined to make clear distinctions between ethical and unethical security professionals and malicious hackers.

Black Hat: A black hat hacker is someone with objectives of studying and using cyber security techniques and tools for personal or private gain through malicious or threat activity.

DID YOU KNOW?

Richard Stallman, the famed software freedom stalwart, coined the terms *black* and *white hat hackers*. As the original term for hacker meant someone with a desire to understand and tinker with technology, it came at odds with the popular meaning of hacker which mean a cyber criminal.

Therefore, Stallman coined the term *black hat* to represent a criminal hacker as opposed to the benevolent hacker termed *white hat*. Stallman based these terms on traditions in old Western films where the good guys wore white hats and the bad guys wore black hats.

White Hat: White hat hackers are security professionals who follow ethical and legal behavior. Their objective is to help improve security.

Grey Hat: A grey hat hacker has the intent of improving security but will do things that are unethical such as unauthorized hacking or doing full disclosure of vulnerabilities without providing lead time to vendors.

CYBER SECURITY AND THE LAW

Ethics and laws are overlapping concepts. Both dictate what is right and wrong for a group of people. However, ethics and laws are generally not aligned. While it is always unethical to break the law, not everything that is legal is ethical. Some ethical choices may not rise to the level of criminality but are still socially unacceptable behavior. These differences come from the fact that different governing bodies define ethics and laws, which may not have the same perspectives.

Cyber space essentially doesn't have any country boundaries. This makes the legal aspects of cyber security very confusing and hard to interpret. Research can sometimes come up against or even cross the lines of legality. While there are some allowances for research in laws, they do not always enable you to; therefore, it is important to be aware of the relevant laws on cyber security when doing research.

Laws are always in flux and they generally lag behind technology. The progress of technology is fast and it takes time for society to decide how technology should be used. In this section, we will define some the biggest international laws on cyber security that might impact research. This list of laws is not comprehensive and is focused on computer misuse and data privacy laws, as those are the laws most influential for data collection and experimentation controls. Therefore, it is important to investigate your local laws pertaining to cyber security before starting to perform research. It is important to understand that these laws are a snapshot in time and what is legal for research today may not be in the future or vice versa.

United States

Digital Millennium Copyright Act[27]
The DMCA pertains to copyright law, which includes computer software and services. The DMCA has provisions for anticircumvention that make it illegal to break access-control and cryptographic mechanisms. Over time, there have been exemptions added for different fair use situations. **Fair use** is a concept in US law that defines under specific conditions someone may legally use copyrighted material without first gaining permission from the copyright holder. The fair use exemptions in the DMCA are largely to enable interoperability and for educational pursuits. However, the DMCA has been used as a

380 CHAPTER 15: Scientific Ethics

tool for legal actions against researchers performing reverse engineering and vulnerability discovery research.

Computer Abuse and Fraud Act[28]

The CFAA defines unlawful access to computers and defines the penalties. This Act has been amended over time and is still being proposed for changes. This law has been used as multiple times against researchers, so it is important to understand the legal status of your researcher in the United States. In the wake of the Aaron Swartz case, a group legislators have proposed an amendment to remove the violation of terms of service as a criminal offense.

Electronic Communications Privacy Act[29]

The Electronic Communications Privacy Act (ECPA) is a law that specifies it is illegal to tap, or capture communication, over wires. In addition to the ECPA there are also state laws that cover wiretapping legality. For researchers the important thing to understand about these laws is consent. To legally capture electronic communication requires consent. Whose consent depends upon which legal jurisdiction under which your research falls. Some states require dual consent, which means that all communicating parties must consent to the data capture, but others only require single consent, where only one of the communicating parties has to consent. As a lot of cyber security research includes electronic communications it is important to be aware of these laws.

Personal Information Laws

Cyber space is now used for all facets of life. This means that personal information is often present in cyber space. There have been a number of laws created in the United States to cover regulations on protecting personal information. The Gramm—Leach—Bliley Act defines that financial institutions must provide information on what personal information is collected on its clients and how that data is shared and used.[30] In addition, it is required that users have the option to opt out of the use and sharing of their data. The Health Insurance Portability and Accountability Act (HIPPA) defines Private Health Information (PHI) and how it may be used by medical organizations.[31]

Canada

Criminal Code[32]

The Canadian Criminal Code includes a section on data privacy that deems unauthorized access to data communication as unlawful. This law is enacted between any communication where one of the subjects is located in Canada and the originator of the data has the expectation that the data will not be intercepted.

Personal Information Protection and Electronics Data Act[33]

Much like the European Union, Canada developed the Personal Information Protection and Electronics Data Act (PIPEDA) to define regulations on how organizations may collect, use, and disclose personal data from the public. It requires companies to get consent to collect and disclose data and requires the option for opting-out. This act is inclusive of multiple industry segments and includes provisions for medical, airlines, and financial institutions.

United Kingdom

Computer Misuse Act[34]

The computer misuse act defines unlawful access, modification, or use of computer systems. It also defines the penalties for different unlawful acts. Included are provisions on the legality of obtaining or selling items for computer misuse. This law has drawn criticisms to its lack of graduation for levels of offenders. Also, its provisions on obtaining and using tools for computer misuse have been criticized because many cyber security professionals and researchers leverage tools that would fit under this definition.

France

Data Protection Act[35]

The French Data Protection Act defines personal data and how it can be used by a data controller. This includes consent and disclosure rules. In addition, this act also defines sensitive personal data that cannot be captured or processed.

European Union

The European Union issued the Data Protection Directive,[36] in 1995, setting forth guidelines of data privacy protections for member nations to follow. This has led to the development of many of the data protection acts created by nations of the European Union. However, a new unifying directive has been passed, the General Data Protection Regulation (GDPR),[37] which will supersede the Data Protection Directive. The GDPR will become the single law for data protection and privacy for all EU members starting in 2018.

Japan

Act on the Prohibition of Unauthorized Access[38]

The Act on the Prohibition of Unauthorized Access is the Japanese law that defines what is considered unauthorized access to computer systems and damage to data.

Act on the Protection of Personal Information[39]

The Act on the Protection of Personal Information is the Japanese law that covers data collection and retention for businesses. It includes data privacy provisions and opt out and data sharing guidelines.

South Korea

Personal Information Protection Act[40]

The Personal Information Protection Act defines data privacy laws. The penalties defined by this law that go along with breaches of privacy are some of the highest and strictest in the world.

DIG DEEPER: WORKSHOP ON CYBER SECURITY RESEARCH AND LAWS

The topic of addressing the challenges of cyber security research under current definitions of law is a pressing matter. As such the National Science Foundation funded a workshop on this topic define the challenges, understand what research is being stymied, and what modifications to law would improve the situation.[41] While this workshop has an US centric view of law, it provides a good overview of the challenges and what standards could be developed to improve the interaction of cyber security research and laws.

HUMAN SUBJECTS RESEARCH

An organization that receives, *any*, federal funding is required to establish an Institutional Research Board. The IRB, which is variously called, Ethics Review Board, Independent Ethics Review, Research Ethics Board, and so on, is officially designated at any institution to review research that might involve human (and other sensitive) subjects in research. This goal is not to meet absolute criteria, but to determine if the benefits of the research outweigh the potential risks. There are various federate statues that will apply such as the Code of Federal Regulations Title 45 Part 56 "PROTECTION OF HUMAN SUBJECTS."[42] Additionally, research that is funded by the Federal Drug Administration has CFR Title 21 part 56 "INSTITUTIONAL REVIEW BOARDS,"[43] which details how to create and use IRB. The analog for animal welfare is the Institutional Animal Care and Use Committee (IACUC). This review is similarly required for federal funding. These, and many other regulations came out of mistakes and horrors from World War 2. While the Nazis and others conducted horrific studies and experiments in the name of science, the US organizations closer to home have prompted these laws. For example, in the 20th century (and for 40 years) the US Public Health Service enrolled, exposed, and failed to treat 600 men who volunteered for a study in exchange for food, medical care, and burial insurance.[44] The study never informed them that they were suffering from any disease. They never treated the patients (their funding ran out), even though common treatments were known about and available. They even prevented patients from seeking treatment elsewhere. The researchers then, through inaction, exposed 40 spouses and 19 children to congenital syphilis.[44] More recently, in the 1970s, Native American women were coerced or tricked into forced sterilization. This is a poorly studied tragedy, so numbers range from 4300 to 70,000 sterilizations out of a total 100,000 to 150,000 childbearing women of that age and time.[45]

In response to these incidents, researchers from the National Commission for the Protection of Human Subjects of Biomedical and Behavioral Research convened and drafted a report on ethical research. The so-called Belmont report, after its location, describes ethical principles and guidelines for research involving human beings. The guiding principles are Respect for Persons, Beneficence, and Justice.[46] More recently, the Department of Homeland Security, convened a group to develop similar guidance for cyber, computer, and network researchers, "The Menlo Report: Ethical Principles Guiding Information and Communication Technology Research."[47] This document also identified guiding principles based upon the Belmont. They took the original three and adapted them for the Information Communication Technology domain. They also added a fourth "Respect for the Law and Public Interest." Subsequently, a companion report for more details, and example cyber security studies was published, "Applying Ethical Principles to Information and Communication Technology Research: A Companion to the Menlo Report."[48]

DIG DEEPER: GUIDANCE ON USING SOCIAL MEDIA IN RESEARCH

Often the federal government lags behind time and does not provide technological or social trend relevant advice. However, the National Institute of Health does provide guidance on using social media in research:

https://www.nih.gov/health-information/nih-clinical-research-trials-you/guidance-regarding-social-media-tools

This guide helps to address potential risks to study participants, data controls, study planning, and other relevant topics.

Institutional Review Board

One of the main outcomes of the Belmont Report were the definition and establishment of IRBs. IRBs were created as an independent review and check on human subjects research. After multiple incidents of unethical research that was harmful to human participants, the US created the concept of IRBs. An IRB is an organization that is built of a diverse set of individuals with varying expertise and experience. Generally, they included scientists and individuals from the community to represent broader interests. The Federal Drug Administration defines the guidelines on how an IRB should be formed.

An IRB review includes a presentation of the research plan and the weighing of the ethical and risk factors versus the benefits of the research. Each institution has their own specific documentation guidelines on how to define your research plan for submittal to the IRB. Please investigate what IRB oversees your research and the documentation requirements they have for review. Filling out documentation for the IRB can be tedious but it also constitutes a well thought-out and organized research plan, so it is work that you should be doing anyway. A full review of a research plan often requires the majority of the IRB members. Generally, IRBs meet once or twice a month so you need to schedule a review.

Protected Groups

Protected groups are categories of people who are protected from becoming test subjects. Protected groups include economically disadvantaged, racial and ethnic minorities, children, the elderly, the homeless, prisoners, and those with mental illness. It is not ethical to target a group of subjects who either do not have the power to say no or may be incapable of understanding the risks and consequences.

ETHICAL USE OF DATA

Data is the cornerstone of research. Data is the portal by which we view and understand the world. Data can contain an immense amount of information. While most of the information data provides is relevant and useful for answering research questions, other information comes along too. Some of the ancillary information, if exposed or delved into can have negative consequences. You need to understand your data and what other information could be present to determine risks to the providers of the data and if you need to have mitigations in place.

As cyber space is largely a projection of behaviors in physical space, information about people and their behaviors will often be present in cyber data. While a lot of this information is innocuous, there can be data that is sensitive to their lives. Privacy is an important topic when it comes to cyber data. As was discussed in the laws section, collection, protection, and use of data can be a sensitive process and can fall into unlawful territory. Even when you are within legal bounds there are a few issues with data that are important to consider when gathering and using data for research.

Consent

Consent is one of the most important aspects of data collection. When collecting data on individuals, it is important to get their consent to stay within legal bounds and to remain ethical. Consent generally consists of users signing a consent form or agreeing to a consent notification. There are also situations where consent is given as part of terms of service or EULAs. Consent is a key factor of passing an IRB review.

There are situations where data is collected for operational purposes. Generally, data that is collected under one pretense is not then acceptable to be used under another pretense. In these situations, it is often the case that data can be anonymized or summarized to remove individual information from the data. Data and privacy will be discussed more in the next section. If researchers are unable to attribute or discover where the data came from, then it is generally accepted practice that they no longer require consent.[49]

There are some scenarios where exemptions for full consent can be given. If a researcher is studying something where the results can be impacted by the knowledge of the participants an IRB can allow deception or incomplete disclosure.[50] After the study, participants are then informed about what the experiment was and consent is given ex post facto.

Consent can also be waived under strict guidelines.[51] These waivers are pertinent to cyber security research. If the consent form is the only document that ties the participant's identity to the study and the loss of confidentiality could cause harm. This is an important privilege as it enables the study of sensitive subjects such as criminal behavior where discovery of participation by subjects could incur repercussions.

IRBs can be a good check on a research plan and can be a requirement for some publication venues. However, as cyber security is often taught as a subfield of computer science, most cyber security researchers are not aware of them nor know when to use them. When research is funded with US federal dollars and includes human subjects an IRB should be contacted. If is often the case that research is exempt from IRB review because it doesn't meet the requirements but it is important to get the exemption from an IRB representative.

Privacy/PII

When collecting cyber data it is easy to capture some PII. Personally Identifiable Information (PII) is information that can uniquely identify or locate an individual. A list of PII examples provided by the NIST is provided in Table 15.1. As you can see some cyber data, such as email addresses or even IP addresses, can be considered PII. Therefore it is important to consider PII when designing data collection, storage and analysis mechanisms.

Table 15.1 PII Examples from NIST SP 800-112

Category	Examples
Name	Full name, maiden name, mother's maiden name, or alias.
Personal identification number	Social security number (SSN), passport number, driver's license number, taxpayer identification number, patient identification number, and financial account or credit card number.
Address information	Street address or email address.
Asset information	Internet Protocol (IP) or Media Access Control (MAC) address or other host-specific persistent static identifier that consistently links to a particular person or small, well-defined group of people.
Telephone numbers	Mobile, business, and personal numbers.
Personal characteristics	Photographic image (especially of face or other distinguishing characteristic), X-rays, fingerprints, or other biometric image or template data (e.g., retina scan, voice signature, facial geometry).
Personally owned property identification	Vehicle registration number or title number and related information.
Information about an individual that is linked or linkable to one of the above	Date of birth, place of birth, race, religion, weight, activities, geographical indicators, employment information, medical information, education information, financial information.

There are multiple levels of impact of release of PII. The low category means the impact of released information would only cause an inconvenience to subjects or would break the agreement that subject data would be kept confidential. The moderate level impact of PII release would result in financial loss, identity theft, or public humiliation. The final level of impact, high, would result in physical harm, loss of livelihood, or incarceration.

When collecting data it is important to understand what is in the data, the risk of exposure of the different information collected to its owners, and what mitigations are necessary to ensure the user's privacy is maintained. Some example security controls could be encrypted storage, anonymization techniques, or access controls for gaining access to the data. For more in-depth discussion on PII, how to properly assess risk, and what security controls to use, see NIST Special publication 800-122.

Criminally Released Data

It is a common occurring in cyber security research to use a dataset released by another organization or researcher. As data for specific types of scenarios, such as attacks, are hard to come by researchers flock to good datasets when they become available. However, not all data is collected and released ethically. Under these situations, the question is, can a researcher use data from a criminal action?

It has become more and more common for Doxing attacks, where attackers break into a system, collect large swaths of data, and sell the data or release it to the public to show their skills and to humiliate the victim. These datasets can include a wealth of information that is normally not available: communication habits of people, password patterns used, login patterns, and so on. Studying these datasets could provide great insights and useful knowledge. However, the users present in this data never consented to their information being used in research.

This is an ethical question that has yet to be answered by the cyber security research community. There have been papers published using stolen data. Yet, this has the potential of becoming a more common scenario as more data is released from attacks. The community needs to discuss the ethics of this situation in more depth and develop guidelines for researchers. Until then we believe that the ethical question you must answer is the utility of the research outcomes. Is the use of data gained through exploitation of others worth the utility of the results?

INDIVIDUAL RESPONSIBILITY

Plagiarism

One of the most common ethical scenarios is plagiarism. Plagiarism is copying other's ideas, images, writing, or content and presenting them as one's own. In scientific literature, plagiarism can easily happen as it is expected and promoted that research build on past results. When referencing previous work by others or yourself it is critical to properly cite the reference. There are multiple citation style guides such as MLA, APA, or CMS. Each publication venue generally provide guidance on citation style.

Some common cases of plagiarism for scientific publication include copying others ideas, copy one's own previous work, or using another's graphics without citation. When referencing other's ideas it is important to understand that plagiarism is not just the direct copying of text but also includes rewritten sentences or passages. If you are using someone else's content you should cite it. Another tripping point is self-plagiarism. Self plagiarism is when you copy your own previously published text. The issue with self-plagiarism arises from the publication process and transfer of copyright. In the general case, you transfer the copyright of a publication to the publisher when you get a paper accepted. What this means is that the publisher now "owns" that work for publication. When you copy that work and attempt to publish it again you are attempting to transfer a copyright you no longer control. One of the biggest issues with self-plagiarism there a not really any general guidelines. Some publishers will provide you with specific guidelines but neither ACM[52] or IEEE[53] provide specific guidance on what is acceptable amount of reuse of material to constitute a new original contribution. There are always grassroots rules of thumb that are passed around between colleagues but these are rarely documented and hard to find for reference.[54] Your best option is to be explicitly clear on what material is reused and to do your homework on your publisher and specific subfield of research for guidelines to follow on how much of a previous work is acceptable to reference. The final common area of trouble for plagiarism is the reuse of pictures. Plagiarism isn't just for text but all creative content generated by someone. Therefore, you must be careful when using pictures from the Internet. You should always assume that you must cite a picture used in papers and presentations you generate. In the open source movement over the past couple of years copyleft rights have been developed like the Creative Commons. Pictures that use some of these copyleft rights allow you to use them uncited but you need to make sure that this is allowed as part of the license.

With the pressure of "publish or perish" being the norm, it can be tempting to plagiarize to produce more publications faster. However, it is the individual responsibility of every researcher to be ethical and to properly cite all references and produce original material. Being found for plagiarization can get you removed from professional organizations and haunt your career.

Authorship

A closely related ethical quandary to plagiarism is authorship credit. Publications have become the sole metric of how successful a researcher is in the academic realm. A consequence of this is every researcher is forced to publish as many papers as possible. This leads to author padding.[55] Author padding is when additional names are added as authors to a publication to give credit to more people. If you ever review papers for a publication, there is always one or two papers that have a long list of authors and you always wonder if they all contributed significantly to the paper. Papers should be original contributions to the scientific community. Only those who have contributed significantly to the creation of the paper should be listed as offer.[56]

While we all like to be kind and generous to one another, this should not lead to adding authors to a paper. In addition, there may be scenarios that people with authority ask to be put on a paper when they should not. Instead there are multiple ways in which you can acknowledge the help of others that are not on the author's list. You can include an acknowledgments section to a paper thanking the help and support of others. The integrity of the publication process depends on credit being given to those who produced the new and original content.

DID YOU KNOW?

Authorship guidelines are different by research field. Fields such as particle physics and astronomy where research has progressed to the point of requiring extremely expensive instruments that require the collaboration of many researchers and institutes over years to generate datasets to answer scientific questions. In these fields, authorship of papers can be in hundreds to account for all the researchers involved over the years necessary to achieve the results. A recent example is the first detection of gravitational waves, which provides evidence for Albert Einstein's theory of general relativity. The effort to detect gravitational waves required hundreds of millions of dollars and two decades of work. Thus the first detection paper[57] included 1011 authors from 133 research institutes.

CONCLUSION

In this chapter, we have discussed various aspects of cyber security ethics. As you have seen, ethics can be based on a standard developed by a professional organization, can come from the law, or even can be a de facto standard that is set by how research has been done by others in the past. When it comes to ethics the responsibility to behave ethically falls on the shoulders of each individual researcher. It is your job to make sure that the research design, methods, and data collection actions you take in your research is ethical. The scientific community has created some mechanisms and processes, such as peer review and IRBs, in place to catch unethical behavior but it is up to you to make the determination on when to use them. Being a researcher can allow you to understand and change the world. But this power comes with the responsibility to ensure that you are not causing damage or harm. Ethics should be an integral part of every research project and program. At every step of research you should ask yourself and your peers if what you are doing is ethical. Only by making ethics a high priority can we as a scientific community ensure that we make the world a better place instead of causing atrocities.

Endnotes

1. BBC. (July 19, 2012). *Huge Spam Botnet Grum Is Taken Out by Security Researchers*. Retrieved February 26, 2017, from http://www.bbc.com/news/technology-18898971.
2. Goodin, D. (April 09, 2016). *Researchers Help Shut Down Spam Botnet That Enslaved 4,000 Linux Machines*. Retrieved February 26, 2017, from http://arstechnica.com/security/2016/04/researchers-help-shut-down-spam-botnet-that-enslaved-4000-linux-machines/.
3. Weir, M., Aggarwal, S., Collins, M., and Stern, H. (2010). "Testing metrics for password creation policies by attacking large sets of revealed passwords," in *Proceedings of the 17th ACM Conference on Computer and Communications Security (CCS'10)*.

4. Dickey, R. (2015). Taking a Closer Look at Cracked Ashley Madison Passwords. Avast, September.

5. Egelman, S., Bonneau, J., Chiasson, S., Dittrich, D., and Schechter, S. (February 2012). "It's not stealing if you need it: A panel on the ethics of performing research using public data of illicit origin," in *International Conference on Financial Cryptography and Data Security* (pp. 124–132). Springer Berlin Heidelberg.

6. Ohm, P. (2010). Broken Promises of Privacy: Responding to the Surprising Failure of Anonymization. *UCLA Law Review*, 57, 1701.

7. Kirkegaard, E. and Bjerrekær, J. D. (2014). *The OKCupid Dataset: A Very Large Public Dataset of Dating Site Users.* Open Differential Psychology.

8. Electronic Frontier Foundation. (January 08, 2016). *Coders' Rights Project Reverse Engineering FAQ.* Retrieved February 26, 2017, from https://www.eff.org/issues/coders/reverse-engineering-faq.

9. Schneier, B. (January 23, 2007). *Debating Full Disclosure.* Retrieved February 26, 2017, from https://www.schneier.com/blog/archives/2007/01/debating_full_d.html.

10. Berinato, S. (January 01, 2007). *Software Vulnerability Disclosure: The Chilling Effect.* Retrieved February 26, 2017, from http://www.csoonline.com/article/2121727/application-security/software-vulnerability-disclosure–the-chilling-effect.html.

11. Code, N. (1949). The Nuremberg Code. Trials of war criminals before the Nuremberg military tribunals Under Control Council Law 10, 181–182.

12. United States. (1978). *The Belmont Report: Ethical Principles and Guidelines for the Protection of Human Subjects of Research.* Bethesda, MD: The Commission.

13. Edwards, M. (September 3, 2001). *Code Red Turns CodeGreen.* Retrieved February 26, 2017, from http://windowsitpro.com/security/code-red-turns-codegreen.

14. Pauli, D. (October 31, 2016). *Boffin's Anti-Worm Bot Could Silence Epic Mirai DDoS Attack Army.* Retrieved February 26, 2017, from http://www.theregister.co.uk/2016/10/31/this_antiworm_-patch_bot_could_silence_epic_mirai_ddos_attack_army/.

15. Arghire, I. (October 28, 2016). *Mirai Botnet Infects Devices in 164 Countries.* Retrieved February 26, 2017, from http://www.securityweek.com/mirai-botnet-infects-devices-164-countries.

16. Electronic Privacy Information Center. (March 29, 2004). *EPIC Digital Rights Management and Privacy Page.* Retrieved February 26, 2017, from https://epic.org/privacy/drm/.

17. Lemos, R. (July 27, 2005). *Cisco, ISS File Suit Against Rogue Researcher.* Retrieved February 26, 2017, from http://www.securityfocus.com/news/11259.

18. Sieradski, D. J. (March 30, 2014). *Aaron Swartz and MIT: The Inside Story—The Boston Globe.* Retrieved February 26, 2017, from https://www.bostonglobe.com/metro/2014/03/29/the-inside-story-mit-and-aaron-swartz/YvJZ5P6VHaPJusReuaN7SI/story.html.

19. United States of America v. Aaron Swartz (United States District Court District of Massachusetts July 14, 2011).

20. Association for Computing Machinery. (July 29, 2016). *Code of Ethics.* Retrieved February 26, 2017, from http://ethics.acm.org/code-of-ethics/.

21. Institute of Electrical and Electronics Engineers. *IEEE Code of Ethics.* Retrieved February 26, 2017, from http://www.ieee.org/about/corporate/governance/p7-8.html.

22. Computer Ethics Institute. *Ten Commandments of Computer Ethics.* Retrieved February 26, 2017, from http://computerethicsinstitute.org/publications/tencommandments.html.

23. SANS. (April 24, 2004). *IT Code of Ethics.* Retrieved February 26, 2017, from https://www.sans.org/security-resources/ethics.

24. (ISC)². (n.d.). *(ISC)² Code of Ethics.* Retrieved February 26, 2017, from https://www.isc2.org/ethics/default.aspx?terms = code of ethics.

25. ISACA. *Code of Professional Ethics and ISACA Harassment Policy.* Retrieved February 26, 2017, from http://www.isaca.org/Certification/Code-of-Professional-Ethics/Pages/default.aspx.

26. ASIS. *Code of Ethics.* Retrieved February 26, 2017, from https://www.asisonline.org/About-ASIS/Pages/Code-of-Ethics.aspx.

27. Digital Millennium Copyright Act, Pub. L. No. 105-304, 112 Stat. 2860 (Oct. 28, 1998), codified at 17 U.S.C. 512, 1201-05, 1301-22; 28 U.S.C. 4001.

28. U.S. Code § 1030—Fraud and Related Activity in Connection With Computers.

29. Justice Information Sharing. (July 30, 2013). *Electronic Communications Privacy Act of 1986*. Retrieved February 26, 2017, from https://it.ojp.gov/privacyliberty/authorities/statutes/1285.

30. Federal Trade Commission. (July 01, 2002). *In Brief: The Financial Privacy Requirements of the Gramm-Leach-Bliley Act*. Retrieved February 26, 2017, from https://www.ftc.gov/tips-advice/business-center/guidance/brief-financial-privacy-requirements-gramm-leach-bliley-act.

31. U.S. Department of Health & Human Services Office for Civil Rights. (April 16, 2015). *The HIPAA Privacy Rule*. Retrieved February 26, 2017, from https://www.hhs.gov/hipaa/for-professionals/privacy/.

32. Government of Canada Justice Laws. (February 09, 2017). *Consolidated Federal Laws of Canada, Criminal Code*. Retrieved February 26, 2017, from http://laws-lois.justice.gc.ca/eng/acts/C-46/page-40.html#h-61.

33. Act, P. I. P. E. D. (2000). Personal Information Protection and Electronic Documents Act. Department of Justice, Canada. Full text available at http://laws.justice.gc.ca/en/P-8.6/text.Html.

34. The National Archives. (June 29, 1990). *Computer Misuse Act 1990*. Retrieved February 26, 2017, from http://www.legislation.gov.uk/ukpga/1990/18/contents.

35. Act N 78-17 of 6 January 1978 On Information Technology, Data Files and Civil Liberties, France

36. Directive, E. U. (1995). Directive 95/46/EC of the European Parliament and of the Council, 24 October.

37. General Data Protection Regulation. (April 27, 2016). Regulation (EU) 2016/679 of the European Parliament and of the Council.

38. Japan. (2013). *Act on Prohibition of Unauthorized Computer Access (Tentative translation)*. Retrieved February 26, 2017, from https://www.npa.go.jp/cyber/english/legislation/uca_Tentative.pdf.

39. Japan. (June 5, 2009). *Act on the Protection of Personal Information Act No. 57 of (Tentative Translation)*. Retrieved February 26, 2017, from http://www.cas.go.jp/jp/seisaku/hourei/data/APPI.pdf.

40. South Korea. (March 29, 2011). *Personal Information Protection Act*. Retrieved February 26, 2017, from http://koreanlii.or.kr/w/images/0/0e/KoreanDPAct2011.pdf.

41. Mulligan, D. and Doty, N. (September 28, 2015). *Cybersecurity Research: Addressing the Legal Barriers and Disincentives. Report of a Workshop convened by the Berkeley Center for Law & Technology, the UC Berkeley School of Information and the International Computer Science Institute under a grant from the National Science Foundation*. Retrieved February 26, 2017, from https://www.ischool.berkeley.edu/sites/default/files/cybersec-research-nsf-workshop.pdf.

42. U.S. Department of Health & Human Services. (February 16, 2016). *45 CFR 46*. Retrieved February 26, 2017, from http://www.hhs.gov/ohrp/regulations-and-policy/regulations/45-cfr-46/index.html.

43. US Food & Drug Administration. (September 21, 2016). *CFR—Code of Federal Regulations Title 21*. Retrieved February 26, 2017, from https://www.accessdata.fda.gov/scripts/cdrh/cfdocs/cfcfr/CFRSearch.cfm?CFRPart = 56.

44. Tuskegee Syphilis Experiment. In Wikipedia. Retrieved February 26, 2017, from https://en.wikipedia.org/wiki/Tuskegee_syphilis_experiment.

45. Ralstin-Lewis, D. M. (2005). The Continuing Struggle against Genocide: Indigenous Women's Reproductive Rights. *Wicazo Sa Review 20*(1), 71-95. University of Minnesota Press. Retrieved February 26, 2017, from Project MUSE database.

46. National Commission for the Protection of Human Subjects of Biome Beha Resea and Ryan, K. J. P. (1978). The Belmont Report: Ethical Principles and Guidelines for the Protection of Human Subjects of Research-the National Commission for the Protection of Human Subjects of Biomedical and Behavioral Research. US Government Printing Office.

47. Kenneally, E. and Dittrich, D. (2012). The Menlo Report: Ethical Principles Guiding Information and Communication Technology Research.

48. Dittrich, D., Kenneally, E., and Bailey, M. (2013). Applying Ethical Principles to Information and Communication Technology Research: A Companion to the Menlo Report.

49. US Department of Health and Human Services. (2014). Guidance Regarding Methods For De-Identification of Protected Health Information In Accordance With the Health Insurance Portability and Accountability Act (HIPAA) Privacy Rule.

50. University of California, Berkeley Committee for Protection of Human Subjects. (July 2015). *Deception and Incomplete Disclosure in Research.* Retrieved February 26, 2017, from http://cphs. berkeley.edu/deception.pdf.

51. US Department of Health and Human Services. (2005). Code of Federal Regulations (45 CFR 46). Section §46.117 Documentation of Informed Consent.

52. Association for Computing Machinery. (June 2010). *Plagiarism Policy.* Retrieved February 26, 2017, from http://www.acm.org/publications/policies/plagiarism.

53. Institute of Electrical and Electronics Engineers. *IEEE Identifying Plagiarism.* Retrieved February 26, 2017, from https://www.ieee.org/publications_standards/publications/rights/ ID_Plagiarism.html.

54. Bretag, T. and Mahmud, S. (2009). "Self-plagiarism or appropriate textual re-use?." *Journal of Academic Ethics, 7*(3). 193–205.

55. Lozano, G. A. (2013). The Elephant in the Room: Multi-Authorship and the Assessment of Individual Researchers. arXiv preprint arXiv:1307.1330.

56. American Psychological Association. (n.d.). *Publication Practices & Responsible Authorship.* Retrieved February 26, 2017, from http://www.apa.org/research/responsible/publication/.

57. Abbott, B. P., Abbott, R., Abbott, T. D., Abernathy, M. R., Acernese, F., Ackley, K., ..., and Adya, V. B. (2016). Observation of Gravitational Waves From a Binary Black Hole Merger. *Physical Review Letters, 116*(6), 061102.

Index

Printed in the United States
By Bookmasters